A History of the
Liberal Party.　.

Author of

JUDGMENT RESERVED
THE LAW (*Heritage Series*)
THE PASTURED SHIRE (*verses*)
THE JUDICIAL OFFICE AND
   OTHER MATTERS

A History of the Liberal Party

The Right Hon. Sir Henry Slesser, P.C.

HUTCHINSON & CO. (*Publishers*) LTD.

LONDON : NEW YORK : MELBOURNE

BOOK
PRODUCTION
WAR ECONOMY
STANDARD

Made and Printed in Great Britain at
Greycaines
(Taylor Garnett Evans & Co. Ltd.)
Watford, Herts

CONTENTS

A*

CHAPTER I

INTRODUCTORY

THE unique pragmatic genius of the English people to contrive working principles out of elements apparently incompatible is nowhere more clearly disclosed than in the history of the Liberal Party. There, gathered into one political unity, have been found great landowners suspicious of the new plutocracy and wealthy capitalists complaining of territorial predominance; working men in revolt against the severity of their masters, erastian defenders of the State Church and those who refused to conform to it; constitutional monarchists and extreme Radicals dabbling with Republicanism; the defenders of oppressed nations, clamouring for British intervention, and the denouncers of armament and war and, lastly, the disciples of *laissez faire*, who deplore the encroachments of the State, acting in common organization with those who see in ever-increasing collective activity the protection of the distressed and the only hope of future social development.

The Liberal, far more than his Tory opponent, is characteristically a product of English ways of thought and action. Conservative ideals of loyalty to tradition and authority, imperial expansion, toleration (where necessary) of coercive law and the maintenance of defined status, are in no sense limited to this country. Such notions are to be found in many countries at all times, and though the Continent has known of Liberal politicians, they have had about them an academic quality which, fortunately, is here wanting—invariably, owing to their divorce from the opinions and habits of their fellow citizens, they have failed; in England alone have the Liberals succeeded in accommodating their advocacy of freedom to the instinctive desires of their compatriots.

Despite all inconsistencies and antagonisms, therefore, it would appear that there has always existed in Liberalism a unanimity as to the value of liberty which made the development of the Party possible. It is not easy to summarize this fundamental libertarian idea, but perhaps it may be expressed in the conception that, to the Liberal, authority is only to be supported as a regrettable necessity; for him, individual freedom is the *summum bonum*; whereas in the Conservative case (possibly also in the Socialist) external discipline and regulation have generally been regarded as inherently unobjectionable.

Throughout the Victorian era, and for a decade after, the diverse Liberal interests were able to co-operate so successfully that during the greater part of the epoch they maintained themselves in power. Then at length the logic of fundamental disparity overtook them; the wealthy, alarmed by the growing Radicalism of their colleagues, drifted over to the Conservatives. The advanced Liberals, infected by Socialist ideas, broke away to help to found the Labour Party; the religious interests declined—in the end, it was not easy to see what would be left. For a time the compelling personality of Gladstone had arrested the coming disruption; it was left to that mysterious statesman, Joseph Chamberlain, to bring about the disintegration. Why he did so is not clear

—it is obvious that, had the Home Rule question never arisen, it was but a matter of time before such Whigs as Hartington and Goschen would have found the new Liberalism intolerable; but Chamberlain was a Radical, the Party was fast moving in his direction, indeed he was in command of that new social insurgence which in all probability, had he wished, would have developed on his original lines. As it is hoped to show later, his differences with the Home Rulers were at the outset negligible; yet he chose the perils of isolation and political impotence rather than attempt to accommodate the comparatively small differences which existed between his Irish self-government scheme and that of Gladstone. On this he broke his party—for no one else could have reconciled the elements which later were to find independence in the Labour Party. In the result his action was more fatal to Liberalism than the Home Rule policy of Gladstone, for in the defection of Chamberlain the fate of the Liberals was irrevocably determined.

Liberalism, whose cause is the defence of personal liberty against the coercions of authority and the State, can only arise where there has come into being a desire for the vindication of the right of personal expression and action, and an attempt to suppress it. Without the possession of an ideal of freedom Liberalism would be purposeless; in the absence of imposed restraint its appeal would be unnecessary.

In seeking therefore for the origins of the Liberal idea, we cannot disregard the time when first it was that the attempt to achieve free self-expression arose, and in this matter it is generally conceded that the Greeks have the supreme honour: it was they who first countenanced *homo sapiens*, the independent thinking man.

Impartially to ask, "What is the supreme Good?" was to enquire to what end a man voluntarily should dedicate his life. The question assumed as possible a conscious choice; a capacity in the individual, irrespective of tradition, uniquely to criticize existent morality and out of individual meditation to develop a personal method of behaviour and responsibility.

From these self-conscious efforts came the Sophists, culminating in the Socratic, Platonic and Aristotelian questionings. At Athens the art and science of Politics arose—in little more than a hundred years, the most momentous period in human history—a new culture, dependent upon free speculation, had come into being.

It was not long, however, before the second necessary condition for Liberalism, that of opposition to these bold speculations, began to develop: the need for an aggressive and protective party had come—Socrates was its first outstanding martyr.

Such freedom, however, as was claimed was admittedly regarded as the privilege of a small class. From Pericles to Cicero, the notion, now obtaining among the Germans, that "civilized" man must be supported economically by slave labour, was almost universal. The early Christians, in the political and economic spheres, also assumed it—only in the world of the Spirit was the Christian to be free; as Whitehead has put it, "For a thousand years, to be civilized was to be a slave owner." (*Adventures of Ideas*, p. 16.) Yet once Christianity had made familiar a belief in the integrity of the human soul, the question was bound to arise, how far slavery could be reconciled with the Faith? Sometimes as a result of these questionings slavery was pronounced a blessing, because, like poverty, it afforded the opportunity of practising the virtues of humility and patience. By St. Augustine slavery was justified as one of the penalties of man, incurred by his original sin in Adam. (*De. Civ. Dei.* XLX. 14.) Finally, St. Thomas, following Aristotle, declared that some men are born to command and others to obey: slavery obtains both through original sin and as a consequence of capture in War, which being necessary, is just: slavery is therefore not contrary to natural law; if used according to Christian methods, like private property, it may be justified. There is, however, both in St. Augustine, and more markedly in St. Thomas, an apologetic note which is entirely absent in Aristotle. In truth, in the Middle Ages, slavery had already given place to serfdom; the right to services had largely taken the place of control of the person and the way to the later wage contract was open.

As to liberty of the mind, it is to be noted how already the right to free opinion had come to be appreciated by the time when Cicero and Seneca wrote. The mind, says the latter, cannot be given into slavery. (*De Beneficiis*, III, 20). The Christian, Lactantius, speaks to the like effect; indeed, from the Christian recognition of personal responsibility and ultimate judgment, no other conclusion could long remain possible.

The early Church itself was constituted upon the most democratic basis. Bishops were elected on a universal suffrage and, says Lecky, "if the principles had been continued, the habits of freedom would have been so diffused among the people, that the changes our age has witnessed might have been anticipated by many centuries and might have been effected under the patronage of Catholicism". (*Rationalism in Europe*, Vol. 2, p. 141.)

The Church, however, became absorbed in theological conflicts and later, in disputes with the secular power of the Emperor, and in these and other disputes the notion of the liberty of the individual was almost ignored. Indeed, it came about that it was in the religious field that liberty was particularly menaced; the belief in the exclusive power of the Church to ensure salvation led to a hatred of the heretic comparable only to the modern nationalist attitude towards treachery in war. The converted Emperor lent his aid; Constantine persecuted pagans and heretics indifferently and he was followed, even more rigorously, by Theodosius. St. Augustine took upon himself to formulate a theology of persecution. He declared heresy to be the worst of crimes though but few were, in fact, persecuted before the days of the Albigensians. The view had come to be taken in the Church that she should never take the responsibility of blood shedding, but Pope Innocent IV enjoined heretical extermination by torture, and even Luther, the reformer, thought that heretics might be properly punished by the civil magistrate. In this country, by the statute of Henry V, "de Heretico Comburendo," the Church could consign heretics to the civil authority for death—a power not revoked until 1677.

Nevertheless, in England, the first liberal advocates of toleration were believers. As Protestants they were bound to uphold the rights of private judgment and on that basis found it increasingly difficult to support the view of exclusive ecclesiastical power compulsorily to enforce credal salvation. Although there were many who still, illogically, com-

bined the right of private opinion with an assertion of the political and
legal coercive supremacy of the Church (even the atheist Hobbes justifies
religious persecution as an attribute of the strong State) yet, the notion
of the fallibility of human reason to decide on ultimate beliefs displayed
by such Anglicans as Hooker, Berkeley, Chillingworth and Taylor; the
freedom of religious opinion accorded by Milton, Cromwell and the
Independents as against the Presbyterians, and the sceptical Deism
which followed the Restoration, all tended in a Liberal direction.

By Milton, the Catholics alone were to be excluded from toleration
on the ground that they were idolatrous! The argument that as
Catholics themselves disbelieved in toleration they would, if tolerated,
work to destroy the liberty of others, is to be detected in the opposition
to their emancipation which was sought to be established by James II.
For a long time after, the exceptional case of the Catholic presented
the Whigs with a problem which many of them answered in a manner
inconsistent with their doctrine of universal religious liberty. Atheism,
also, for many years stood outside the sphere of permitted opinion.

The mediæval Catholic Church had always held a critical attitude
towards the secular power. The Tyrant, a sovereign who does not
govern according to law, in the opinion of most of the mediæval doctors
of the Church could rightly be deposed, if not killed. Revolt against
him, they declare, is not sedition, and the distinction between a lawful
monarch and the despot was long emphasized by the Society of Jesus.
The libertarian theory (government being the result of a social contract),
so important to the history of Liberalism, was supported by the Jesuit
Suarez as early as the beginning of the seventeenth century. The
Sovereign, he asserts, is the servant of the people; by the Pope he could
be properly slain for heresy: even Catholic kings were to be regarded as
subject to law and papal approval. It would have been disconcerting
to the early Protestant democrats to realize that, in the age of unfettered sovereign power, the Jesuits were actively on the side of the
people.

The French Gallicans, on the other hand, like the Anglicans in
England, exalted the Sovereign at the expense of papal and ecclesiastical authority. Among the first reformers Luther supported the State
erastian, Calvin the republican position. In Scotland the views of the
Calvinist Knox also resembled in their attitude towards Kings the most
extreme of the Jesuits. His follower, Buchanan, openly relied upon the
principle of social contract. Regal power, he says, springs from the
nation, kings otherwise have no right. The deposition of Mary of
Scotland was defended upon such grounds, and the decision to execute
Charles I may well have been influenced by similar considerations.

In Charles II's time, in the year of the beheading of the Whig Russell,
the University of Oxford, in terms, condemned the views of Buchanan
and Milton, and the Church of England broke so completely with
mediæval tradition as to lead a movement in favour of absolute obedience.
It was from such post-mediæval sources therefore that the Tory party
was derived.

Thus, when History is dispassionately read, it will be realized that
the Tories, from Wentworth and Filmer to Bolingbroke, were the party
of innovation in proclaiming personal absolute sovereignty; the Whigs

the party of tradition and common law—though by most people they have, uncritically, been thought to have been the Radicals of their day.

So we come to the testing time of James II, for it was in his reign that the Tory doctrine of divine right inconsistently foundered upon the rock of Roman Catholic assertion. Thereafter, for many years, the Tories were a dismembered opposition; some remaining true to their formularies (the Jacobites and non-jurors), some reluctantly supporting the Revolution Settlement—the selection of kingship by Act of Parliament and Law—essentially a mediæval and Whig conception—and some, at length, in desperation, transferring their exaltation of monarchy to the new parliamentary Hanoverian kings. It was during this period that the Whigs so triumphed that, even after their fall, their political assumptions of the rule of law and popular consent were scarcely challenged. In no other country had the same dilemma appeared—in no other did there develop anything comparable to the English Whig party.

The first attempt to use Parliament for ends which did not accord with the Sovereign will is to be detected in the petitions organized by the Puritans in the later days of Queen Elizabeth. During the Parliament of 1584, conferences of those discontented with Church government, and with the bishops in particular, were convened in London and other towns; in the session of 1586, after provincial criticism of the Church had been voiced, a synod was held in the metropolis. Supplications to the Houses were made, and outside agitation undertaken to purify the Church of the last vestiges of Catholicism was entered upon; even election campaigns were inaugurated. The Queen was driven, in terms, to forbid the discussion of religious matters in the Commons, but the complainants were not to be deterred. Bills were introduced by the bolder Puritans to substitute government by Presbyteries for that of Bishops. The Speaker vainly attempted to intervene, until the Sovereign, enraged, sequestered the Bills, and five of the party who were promoting them—including Peter Wentworth, their leader—were imprisoned in the Tower. In 1591 the Star Chamber took a hand in the attempted suppression. Again, on his release, Wentworth strove to inaugurate a Puritan movement in politics; again he was imprisoned. Though having little toleration about him, yet he may fairly be claimed as a pioneer in the assertion of parliamentary right as against the Executive —in this sense he may be called the first Liberal.

It is common knowledge how the Commons, originally summoned only to grant extraordinary sums to the Crown, had made a premature attempt to control government in the time of the later Plantagenet kings; how Parliament had been regarded by Wolsey, on the other hand, as a mere instrument of the King's will. The failure of the Cardinal in 1523 and 1525 to obtain loans from the Commons induced his successor, Cromwell, to ensure their subservience by creating new boroughs of royal influence by bribery and by direct interference with the elections. Thereafter, until the later days of Elizabeth, Parliament for the most part remained the creature of the Crown. It was the Puritans who first challenged that long royal supremacy.

In the active social legislation of Elizabeth we detect a further change. A committee of the House in November, 1597, was asked to consider "the sundry great and horrid abuses of idle and vagrant persons, and the miserable state of the godly and honest sort of the poor subjects of the realm". The Bills ensuing received such examination and criticism and were so often amended as to display the increasingly active part which the Houses were now prepared to take in domestic legislation.

Once the legislature was active, tension between the Houses grew, the Commons being affronted at their frequent discourteous reception by the Lords—their spirit was rapidly rising.

On his way from Scotland to take the Crown, James had received a petition, said to have been signed by a thousand of the Puritan clergy, that they might be excused from using the sign of the Cross in Baptism, that Saints' days be no longer observed and so forth, and in January 1604 a conference met at Hampton Court to consider the whole matter, the King, like Constantine on a former occasion, presiding. Dr. Reynolds, on behalf of the petitioners, asked that the clergy might meet in Synod— a word of hateful recollection to the King. Enraged, James dissolved the meeting with angry threats, but the majority in his first Parliament supported the Puritans; nevertheless Order was made that the clergy obey the rubric, and three hundred, being recalcitrant, were ejected from their livings. The House of Commons protested—in direct opposition to the King's will, they manifested their anger by refusing to agree to the Union of England and Scotland. In consequence of their obduracy they were dissolved.

Three years later an even more recalcitrant Commons met. It sat a month only, but during that period fearlessly had attacked the foreign policy of the King, his extravagance and favouritism, and the granting of privileges and monopolies by his ministers. There was a breakdown of responsible government; after the death of Robert Cecil, Lord Salisbury, the Privy Council almost ceased to function—the elder statesmen and peers were affronted by the ennobling of the favourites, Carr and Villiers, and refused to act, but an unpopular peace was still kept with foreign nations. Raleigh was sacrificed and, as part of the plan for the propitiation of Spain, the project of marrying Charles to the Infanta was supported in official circles. The substitution of another Catholic princess, a French one, did little to ease the growing Puritan indignation.

Under the leadership of Coke, the Judiciary also began to take an attitude less subservient than heretofore to Monarchy. Coke himself refused to advise the King in private as to the extent of his prerogative powers—these were matters, he said, to be laid down in open court. He was dismissed from the Bench and Council, to become one of the leaders of the anti-authoritarian party in Parliament, which the King, to obtain money, was at length forced to summon in 1621.

Here, in Coke's assertion of the rights of the Law and the subject, we find the juridical foundation of Liberalism. He directed the impeachment of Bacon, the supporter of prerogative, and won for Parliament the right to rid the country of unpopular ministers; a power which the Tudors had exercised through that assembly for their own ends. A fierce anti-Spaniard, Coke next led the House to demand a share in the control of foreign affairs. Following the precedent of Elizabeth, the King sought to forbid the House discussing matters relating to continental policy. They replied by entering in the Journals a protest against the royal claim. The King in his turn sent for their book and, childishly, tore out the offending resolution; in 1622 he again dissolved Parliament.

Thus, by the end of his reign, the coalition of Puritans, common lawyers and patriots had established a claim for the independence of Parliament which a quarter of a century before would have been considered highly seditious. The war which the Commons desired had started, with results so far unsatisfactory. Incited in particular by Sir Robert Phelips, the House of Commons, to manifest their want of confidence in the War Minister, the Duke of Buckingham, refused to grant supplies; this was a grievous blow to authority, for while the King had a private (and diminishing) revenue apart from Parliamentary grant, it was altogether insufficient to maintain costly hostilities. Nevertheless the Crown still thought dissolution to be the only remedy to curb the Commons' arrogance, but next year even greater financial necessity compelled the King again to summon his unruly subjects. In the words of a member, Sir Benjamin Redyard, it was "the crisis of Parliament; by this one we shall know whether Parliaments live or die". This was said in 1628, by which time the King had been told bluntly by Sir John Eliot that if he wished for supply he must first remedy grievances.

The beginning of a Conservative monarchical party is to be detected when Wentworth, who had agreed in attacking the ministers, refused to blame the King. He sought a compromise, and at last half prevailed on the new King, Charles, to consider whether the much-needed subsidies might not be receivable after the Commons had detailed their complaints in a Petition of Right. The Secretary of State, however, was more obdurate than, perhaps, was the King himself, and finally the King was made to say that the Subsidies must come first—then it was that Phelips spoke of the 'crisis'. Eliot persuaded the House to remain firm; the petition in the form of a Bill was sent up first and Wentworth now had to abandon all hope of accommodation. When the Bill was read it openly accused the King of breaches of the Law, and the King, yielding at the last, the royal assent was given to the Petition of Right. Wentworth soon went to the Lords, but his followers remained to defend the King's challenged prerogative powers; the issue between Whig and Tory had arisen.

It is now generally admitted that the dispute as to finance which now began to occupy so much of public attention—whether the King could raise moneys without the consent of Parliament—was the result not so much of royal greed as of necessity. The old feudal idea of the Crown as Supreme Estate had carried with it the royal obligation to provide for the monetary obligations of the realm out of the Sovereign's treasury. The fall in value of money had sadly reduced the regal wealth —the failure of Henry VIII to retain the fruits of the spoliation of the Church in his own hands had thrown away the last chance of monarchical solvency. Increasing expenditure and extravagance and a diminishing revenue precipitated the crisis; the King and his advisers saw that he must, at all cost, find new sources of financial supply.

B

From the earliest times it has been recognized that only grants for extraordinary necessities justified the calling of Parliaments. It was the duty of the Commons, at first their sole function, to authorize the Sheriffs of the counties to raise such abnormal revenue by taxation to supplement the King's own resources; but inevitably there was a border land where free gifts and forced loans might be attempted. The latter had been relied on in 1626; after the parliamentary refusal of a Subsidy. Commissioners for each county were appointed to collect it. Eighty men, more or less wealthy, who would not comply had been imprisoned by the Privy Council or Star Chamber for their recalcitrance. Others, less opulent, were impressed for military service. But the result was a failure, and another Parliament became necessary. Many of the gentry in opposition to these irregular proceedings were returned, to form a Liberal nucleus. That they were for the most part rich will be admitted; richer in many cases than the conservative Lords. That fact has been used in the anti-Whig reaction of recent years by such writers as Belloc, Chesterton, Taylor, and others to support the view that the revolution was but a plutocratic revolt against a benevolent monarchy.

Tonnage and Poundage, originally customs of wine and merchandise imported (save wool, ships and leather which were the King's right)— being taxation which Edward I's Parliament had declared to be illegal to be levied without their consent—were now restricted to one year instead of being granted for life as heretofore; the Customs were to come under the direct annual control of the House of Commons.

"If any merchant," they declared, "shall voluntarily pay subsidies of tonnage and poundage not being granted by Parliament, he shall be reputed a betrayer of the Liberty of England and an enemy of the same." (*Resolution*, March, 1629.)

Buckingham was now dead and the financial government was in the hands of Weston, the Lord Treasurer. Weston it was who, in this dilemma, found the devices for supplementing the exhausted revenue by endeavouring to resuscitate obsolete legal expedients. With the King's decision to dispense with Parliaments altogether—there was none from 1629 to 1640—other methods of finding money had become essential.

Ship money, which had been levied on seaports only, was now sought to be extended to the whole Kingdom. When the matter was ultimately litigated, on the concerted refusal of Hampden and his friends to pay, only seven judges to five supported the Crown. But one, Finch, went so far as to declare that Acts of Parliament to take away the royal power to defend the Kingdom were void, and, apparently, extended the dictum to cover the case of moneys to be raised by extra parliamentary means for that purpose.

On the ecclesiastical side also, bitterness had increased. While it is true that the great majority of the Parliamentarians were of the landed and mercantile classes, this fact—so relied upon by the modern cavalier apologists—cannot be extended to cover the religious controversy, for the most zealous of the Puritan dissenters were to be found among the humbler people.

For all his Catholicism, Laud, in the post-mediæval tradition, admitted and supported the royal supremacy. All power, spiritual as well as temporal, he said, was derived from the Crown. All important acts of

Church government were submitted by him to the King for approval. In the Star Chamber he associated himself in judgment with the secular judges and administrators. If it be not a paradox to say so, his Anglo-Catholicism was thoroughly Erastian.

It was this order of regal-ecclesiastical discipline which Laud sought to enforce upon the Scots, with results which are common history. His control of the Press by Bishop's licence was vainly used to stem the flow of Puritan pamphlets, many of them scurrilous, which nevertheless testified to the democratic nature of that rising movement. The dissenting conventicles were suppressed, but rarely were the parliamentary gentry to be found therein—to assert that the anti-Caroline agitation was composed solely of the comfortable and wealthy is to ignore that whole side of it which was based upon religion—then (unlike now) the chief common interest.

In 1637, Prynne, Bastwick, Burton and Lilburne were all sentenced to mutilation or flogging for their attack upon the Episcopacy. They were of the gentry, more or less, but the crowds which angrily gathered around the pillory and cart-wheel disclosed an increasing revolutionary and menacing aspect—it needed no financial intriguers to make them support these martyrs, as they saw them—in the cause of liberty. The religious rebellion in Scotland accentuated the trouble; finally, in despair, the King recalled Wentworth from Ireland to save the monarchical and conservative interests. The Bishop's War, as it was called, had united the democratic forces in England and Scotland and, for want of an adequate army, Charles was driven temporarily to abandon his military designs.

In September, 1639, Wentworth finally became chief adviser to the King, an office which he retained for over a year. He it was who advised the calling of a Parliament in April 1640. It sat but a month, for, on Pym proposing a resolution to oppose the Scottish War, it was dissolved, but not before he had declared that "the powers of Parliament are to the body politic as the rational faculty to the soul of man".

Thereafter the Conservatives temporarily triumphed: members of the Short Parliament were imprisoned; illegal taxation again revived and Church power was exalted in new canons. The Scottish War, against the will of all—except the courtiers—was renewed. The Train Bands, largely Puritan, would not fight. Pressing and compulsion but led to rioting and further discontent. When the Scots advanced to Ripon practically all their claims had to be conceded and the indemnity which he was forced to give them compelled the King, after long consideration, to call yet another Parliament (for he was bankrupt, both of money and of policy)—it was his last.

The position of those conservatively minded members of Parliament who advised the King, such as Portland, Colepepper and Hyde, was not made the easier by reason of the fact that the King in some of his most momentous decisions, such as the attempted arrest of the Five Members, had never consulted them. Nightly, wrote Clarendon, in his *Life*, these three met. The future Lord Chancellor was by no means an uncritical royalist—he had procured the suppression of the Earl Marshal's court, one of the many which exalted prerogative. He had been offered and declined the office of Solicitor-General—by his own account he was much distrusted by both sides—each thinking him a supporter of the other.

At length two most drastic Bills, for the removal of the Bishops from the House of Lords and the popular control of the Militia, were sent by Parliament to the King. Colepepper advised the Sovereign to agree to the former and, in the end, Charles was prevailed upon to sanction it.

Revolution was now not far off—the Parliamentary leaders, Pym, Hampden, Lord Bedford and others were determined that the Sovereign, in the coming struggle, should no longer have the monopoly of force. The abandonment of Strafford by the King, ending in his attainder and execution, was the result of the clamour of the Long Parliament. Popular agitation was deliberately fomented. The arrest of Laud deprived the Government of yet another of its chiefs. After the failure of the impeachment of Strafford and the passage of the attainder in the Commons, tumults and riots were deliberately organized and rumours of plots and revolution spread. The Lords were mobbed, they faltered, and passed the Attainder Bill. The agitation was, in part, genuine; probably no unrest can be organized without some foundation; and there is little doubt that, in London at any rate, the destruction of Strafford and Laud was exceedingly popular.

Finch and Windebank, the other principal ministers, had fled abroad. The invasion of the House by Charles in his pursuit of the Five Members followed; an act, as has been said, decided on the King's personal initiative. This was in January, 1642. On the tenth of that month the King left London and the raising of the King's forces by Commissioners of Array and the Parliament's by military ordinances proceeded, until the clash of actual war came in August.

It was during this time that the opposition of the parties became apparent. Indeed the Civil War may be said to have created the Party System. The royalist members gradually withdrew from both Houses; they constituted the majority of the Lords and a considerable number of the Commons. There remained at the seat of the legislature three hundred of the Commons and some thirty peers, for the moment all more or less of the same mind. The Conservative organization, we may say, was at Oxford; the Radical in London.

Even now the breach was not complete; Hyde, now of the Privy Council and Chancellor of the Exchequer, relates how, early in 1643, Commissioners of Parliament came to Oxford to treat with the King. Their powers were strictly limited, so much so that Charles told them that they might as well have brought the proposals as common carriers. Even Hyde, a moderate and would-be conciliator, thought the terms so unreasonable as to be impossible of acceptance. In the field the Cavalier forces were temporarily victorious, and people, even in London, were clamouring for peace. The relief of Gloucester and the Battle of Newbury, where the monarchists suffered grievously, stabilized the position; there followed a fresh invasion from Scotland and the battle of Marston Moor; thereafter compromise was impossible. In 1645 came the royal defeat at Naseby and the royal power was over.

In Parliament, after the death of Pym and Hampden, there was sad lack of leadership. No attempt at a settlement was made; instead came the intolerant exclusion of two thousand Anglican priests and the prohibition of the use of the book of Common Prayer. The estates of the Cavaliers were confiscated or compounded for at grievous rates and, even in the forces, sectaries, who did not accept the Presbyterian form of Church government, zealots, anabaptists and the like were persecuted. Laymen were forbidden to preach, and Unitarians and Atheists made liable to death penalties. In the result, the Army under Cromwell took possession. They were far more democratic and tolerant than the Presbyterians. They demanded equality of opportunity, and some, such as the Levellers, an economic equality as well.

Meanwhile, the generals, Cromwell and Ireton, were endeavouring to come to terms with Charles. From Carisbrooke he began to attempt a counter-revolution with the aid of the Royalists and even the Presbyterians, the "Grandees" as Lilburne called them. There is no doubt that by 1648 many of the Presbyterians had repented of their breach with the King. Some already were neutral—it was the Independent Army which carried on the war. The Scots were fast going over to the Crown and, had they not been defeated at Preston, it is probable that they and the wealthier classes in England would have effected a restoration. All this it is which explains that purge of Parliament, which excluded so many members that less than one hundred were left, and abolished the House of Lords. The trial and execution of Charles were now inevitable. Like Louis XVI after him, he was killed by the misdirected policies of his friends.

The most momentous constitutional decisions of the Restoration, the recognition of the validity of all Acts of the Long Parliament to which Charles I had consented, and the fictional dating of the new reign from the time of his death, undoubtedly owe their origins to the juridical genius of Clarendon. To him is due the fact that the special prerogative tribunals, the Star Chamber and the provincial royal councils and prerogative courts, were not restored. Clarendon's attitude to the religious claims of the Nonconformists has given to his memory a reputation for arbitrary government which otherwise he does not deserve. The Parliament elected in 1661 was overwhelmingly Anglican. They forced the King to repudiate his promise to the Puritans of religious toleration, but it is only fair to recognize that freedom in religion was an ideal entirely foreign to the minds of Presbyterians when they held power. The penal laws of 1661–1665 excluded from nearly every public function those who would not give "unfeigned assent" to everything in the Book of Common Prayer. The Chancellor relates in his *Life* how the Presbyterians, who were still numerous in the restored Convention Parliament, ineptly sought to prevent the Book of Common Prayer from being reintroduced and how they formed organizations to exclude the Bishops. Such conduct naturally infuriated the Royalists and Cavaliers. The King was forced to notice that the Puritans "had offered him no advice towards the composing of differences in religion—therefore he would try what he could do towards it himself".

A conference had been convoked between the ministers who were the heads of the Presbyterian party and an equal number of the orthodox Clergy—it was held at the Chancellor's lodgings, and in all probability the idea originated with him. Meanwhile, by royal command, no one was to be punished for failing to use the Book of Common Prayer, though orthodox Anglican practice was also expressly permitted.   The Puritans were certainly unpopular; their discouragement of gaiety of all kinds had been resented long after the autocratic meddling with the private morals of the rich by Laud in Church courts and the Star Chamber had been forgotten.   The parliamentary election of 1661 had largely been fought on the religious issue, whether Presbyterianism or Episcopacy should be the creed of the national Church; the attempt at a concord had failed completely and nothing was left but to give effect to the will of Parliament, which, far less tolerant than the King, insisted on the full enforcement of what, somewhat unfairly, has been called the "Clarendon Code".

Here, then, is to be seen the origin of the Tory Party, though the name was not generally used until 1680.   It was theologically undemocratic in the sense that it wished to see Church government taken out of the hands of the congregation.   On the other hand, the influence of Clarendon, trained in the Common Law, prevented the growth, at any rate while he held power, of any movement to diminish parliamentary authority. Standing armies, such as those which had ruled England under Cromwell, were abhorred; thus, unlike the later Conservatives, the first Tories were at once anti-militarist and aristocratic—the squires, the country clergy, and the Universities became their main support.   The Church in particular, writes Woods (*History of the Tory Party*, p. 17) had now become a very definite vested interest within the fabric of Toryism—conversely, in the small minority in the Cavalier Parliament, the remnants of the Presbyterian and other sectarian parties came to form the rudiments of the Opposition.   In their relations to the Crown, the maintenance of the supremacy of Parliament, in legislation and in the granting of supplies, in the preserving of the Common Law and in regard for the sanctity of property, they were scarcely divided from their religious opponents.

The failure of the Dutch War, following four years of peace, and the disasters of the Plague and the great Fire, strengthened the Opposition, until then concerned only for Puritan Protestantism—but the whole Parliament now united to attack Clarendon.   But Clarendon, though the Cavaliers knew it not, was in essence a constitutional Tory, and his defeat proved, ultimately, to be a defeat for the Cavaliers.   Thereafter, the King chose his own ministers.   A close Cabinet arose, the "Cabal," of much diversity of opinion: Clifford, a Roman Catholic; Ashley, a tolerant sceptic, with whom Buckingham may be associated—there was scarce a convinced Anglican among them.   Their secret relations with Louis XIV were looked upon with distrust by the Anglican patriots, and the new-formed country party of Roundheads, Presbyterians and Nonconformists was ready to support a Protestant alliance against the Catholic French despot and his English friends.   It was not long before the King and his ministers found themselves in the sinister position of Charles I, opposing a united Parliament—the dismissal of Clarendon and the French intrigue had shattered the loyalty of that Cavalier Parliament which, originally, had combined to support the Crown.

Thus it came about that the underlying purpose of the King was to free himself from that very Parliament which had been elected to support him.   To the Tory politician such a cleavage was fatal—the Whig "country" party alone could hope to benefit by the estrangement.

To make himself an absolute King, which was now his objective, Charles, in the Treaty of Dover, had sold himself as vassal to the King of France. He had received secret subsidies and even his religion was to be determined by that great tyrant. Despite the pleading of Bryant, in plain fact Charles II was a traitor, and had he been a subject would have been guilty of High Treason.

By the secret Treaty of Dover he was to be freed from Parliament by receiving bribes from Louis—no such device had been considered by Charles I or his father—such a policy was not Toryism but treachery. The Secretary of State, Arlington, and the Catholic, Clifford, alone were fully in the secret, for Charles descended not only to cheat his Parliament and his People, but even the majority of his own chosen ministers.

The obligation to help Louis demanded a declaration of war on the democratic Dutch. In 1673 the expenses of that contest compelled the summoning of Parliament—it had not met for two years. The recognition of Dutch gallantry could not be suppressed in England, for Holland had been saved by a fearless voluntary inundation of her borders. Before the days of the psychological treatment of the masses by a controlled Press, broadcasting or cinema, the people, it would seem, were more swift and independent in judgment than they are to-day and often expressed themselves by open violence. The Commons swung with opinion—again the country party raised its head. Shaftesbury, on the issue of religious indulgence and dispensation of penal laws (primarily designed as part of the French concordat, to help the Catholics), deserted the Cabal. The Opposition demanded the dismissal of Lauderdale, the supporter of Scottish Episcopacy, and the impeachment of Arlington. Buckingham, whose resignation was also asked, joined Shaftesbury in opposition to the King, and the exasperated Monarch, in breach of his French undertaking, was compelled to make peace with Holland and dismiss his remaining ministers. Once more Parliament had triumphed over irresponsible monarchy.

The exhibition of hatred against Catholicism (which had become so strong that even Nonconformists denounced the General Declaration of Indulgence and supported the Test Act which excluded them from office) at length persuaded Charles that, although he might still hope for a subservient Tory Parliament or, better still, by living on Louis, do without one at all, he must abandon the hope of converting England by bribery or muskets to the Roman faith. His choice of First Minister, Danby, an Anglican Tory, shows clearly the drift of his policy at the time. During the four years of Danby's rule, the reconciliation of King and Parliament was zealously attempted. The hostility of Danby to Louis disarmed suspicion. According to Burnet, Danby publicly drank "confusion to all who were not for a war with France", and the Tories, once more united, turned to attack the Whig country party again.

A Tory non-resisting Bill would have made it illegal for anyone to hold public office who did not declare that the King should never be opposed. Seeing that Danby himself had come into power by resisting and destroying the King's French alliance, the proposal had its cynical side—still, it was good enough to harass the Whigs. The only hope for them now lay in a dissolution. Shaftesbury, for impugning the legality of that Parliament which had now sat for over fifteen years, was imprisoned by the Peers, but both Houses and all parties were unanimous against the Papists. They carried with enthusiasm a resolution that there "was, and still is, a damnable and hellish plot to murder the King, subvert the Government and destroy the Protestant Religion". It was now universally believed (particularly as the result of the discovery of the letters of Coleman, once secretary to the Duke of York) that there was being concocted a design to enable James, now an avowed Roman Catholic, to introduce, sooner or later, his detested religion—the King, curiously, was still regarded as potential victim rather than as fellow-conspirator.

On November 2nd, 1678, it was moved in both Houses that James should be ejected from the King's Councils. Sacheverell, the leader of the "Exclusionists", boldly raised the question whether the King and Parliament might not control the succession to the Throne. On this issue as to the defeasible right of James, a new cleavage arose between the Royalists and Whigs; it was in this anti-papal turmoil, fed by Titus Oates, with every degree of misrepresentation (based largely on unknown but exaggerated fact), that Danby, very unwisely for his cause, to avoid impeachment advised the King to dissolve Parliament. At the ensuing elections, in February, 1679, the Protestant anti-Catholic party won a great victory. The Whigs, as they were now commonly called, compounded of malcontent nobility, small Protestant yeomen, Republicans, Dissenters and city merchants smarting from aristocratic hauteur, together with many disinterested patriots, were now organized under the skilful direction of Shaftesbury. Pageants and music, colours, pamphlets and speeches, together with the requisite financial inducements, all were employed in this, perhaps the first, electoral contest to be conducted by direct appeal to the people. Small as was the franchise the Court was greatly alarmed. Louis, secretly, to defeat Danby, exposed the solicitations of Charles for money, for which Danby, probably without justification, was held responsible. If it was thought that the election would stop the impeachment of Danby, never was there a greater miscalculation. Despite the King's pardon, the trial went on and he was imprisoned. The Tories found themselves in a dilemma. The Exclusion Bill to keep James from the Throne had passed the Commons, but in the Upper House, Halifax and Rochester, with the support of the Bishops, ensured its rejection. In March, 1681, the Parliament was dissolved. The new one had a smaller Whig majority. They were summoned to meet at Oxford and, on the Commons once more introducing the Exclusion Bill, were again dissolved. But by this time the Catholics had been excluded from all offices, save that of the Throne itself.

The cautious and wise Halifax, who had originally supported Shaftesbury, still wished to keep James as King, but under parliamentary control. Many Whigs supported him and opposed total exclusion, for as a party, on this question, they were by no means united. From Temple arose the idea of a mixed government by a reconstituted council, some Tory, some Whig, thirty in all, which proved quite unworkable. But not until the reign of George I was the idea of a government entirely of one party again acceptable to the Crown. The notion long lingered, particularly in the Lords, that each minister is entitled to advise the Sovereign according to his individual opinion. The disappearance of the principle was only possible when the King was no longer held responsible for the Crown's governmental acts.

Charles now recognized that, in ordinary circumstances, Whig majorities were almost unavoidable; the middle classes, who were mainly on that side, controlled the boroughs, and to some extent the same tendency was shown by the small landowner in the country. The King and the Tories alike realized that their only hope was to dispense, as far as possible, with Parliaments altogether. The Catholicism of James was overlooked and absolute submission to the Crown extolled, the city loans to the Crown were repudiated and local government overturned by the confiscation of charters in Whig boroughs. In the words of Trevelyan, "The second Stuart despotism had come into being. It was based, as Charles had designed in 1670, on a standing army and financial help from France." (*England under the Stuarts*, p. 425.) It remained for James, in raising universal opposition to himself, to restore the temporarily routed Whigs.

The notion of toleration of opinion, if not of complete freedom in the expression of it, which later became the basis of Liberalism, found little support among the early Whigs. It has been remarked how even their dissenting supporters refused a toleration which would have had the effect of benefiting the Roman Catholics. The release of thousands of Catholics and Nonconformists by James, one of the first acts of his reign, was more unpopular with the latitudinarian Whigs, in so far as it freed the Catholics to practise their religion, than with the orthodox Anglicans who were mostly Tory. His later attempts to suspend the penal laws against all religions met with the fiercest objection from the same quarter. Not until James directly attacked the Church in the promotion of a Papist to be President of Magdalen College, Oxford, and in the prosecution of the Bishops for refusing to read the King's toleration declarations, did the Tories join the Whigs in inviting William over. Even then, it must have been a most unpalatable decision for the advocates of non-resistance—Danby, the anti-Gallican; Trelawney, Bishop of Bristol; Shrewsbury (who had actually crossed the seas to visit William), Sunderland and others.

Though the Tories had thus reluctantly been driven to deny their own precept of the Divine Right, yet, on William's arrival, they were naturally unwilling to do more than confer on him a Regency or make him consort to Mary as reigning Queen.

William, as was expected, refused any such offers, and in the proposal of joint Sovereignty (William as elective, Mary as hereditary) the prejudices of both parties, it was hoped, would be satisfied. But the current of affairs had changed. In the past, even when the Whigs had a majority in Parliament, the Stuart Kings had never given them their confidence. With William it was otherwise—by the nature of their profession the Whigs from the first supported him *ex animo*. Himself a Calvinist, he readily obtained Puritan support and his anti-French sentiment had been expressed upon the battlefield. Though his first government was a coalition, he came inevitably in the end to repose more and more upon the Whigs, who were the first to welcome him and who, from the outset, had displayed a genuine anti-Jacobite enthusiasm. From now onwards the Whigs were no longer a semi-seditious opposition—they represented, far more completely than the hesitant and semi-

B*

treasonable Tories, the royal as well as the popular policy. Disguise it as the Tories would, the Glorious Revolution was a Whig triumph—the Toleration Act proved it. After a temporary recovery in the reign of the High Church Queen Anne, the Tories sank for many generations into supine, and sometimes disloyal, opposition.

The acerbities, which, since the failure of Tudor paternal government, had so distracted the Nation, both in religion and politics, were only in part healed by the triumph of an essentially liberal constitution in the acceptance by the Convention Parliament of the limited monarchy of William and Mary. The Tories (divided between the Jacobites, now outside the State pale, and those who reluctantly recognized the abdication of James as a final end to absolutism), though unable to enforce their reactionary principles, were sufficiently powerful to cause a breach in that unity which was so essential if the country was to cope with the aggressive and, as we should now say, totalitarian ambitions of the French King.

There can be no doubt that at this time the Tories were fundamentally unpatriotic; they grudged the King supplies to fight his enemies, and a new issue developed, not so much between the Sovereign and the Parliament (for that matter had been decided by the Bill of Rights and other legislation in favour of the Houses), but on the question which leaders in Parliament should exercise power. In the first government of William, Tories were to be found in the Ministry, for both parties had in the end combined to bring him over. Foreign matters were directed by the King himself; but at home, the Tory, Danby, became President of the Council and Nottingham, with Shrewsbury, Secretaries of State (there were then but two), while the equivocal Halifax was made Privy Seal. The Treasury, however, was in Whig hands, though the inescapable Godolphin did the business, and the Council, generally, had a Whig majority. In the Commons the Whigs were also supreme, for the Convention Parliament, elected without the menace of soldiery or threats, was composed for the most part of enthusiastic adherents of the new régime. In the Lords, the Tories were more powerful.

Notwithstanding that the Convention had not been summoned by royal writ, it declared itself, with royal approval, to be a Parliament, though already the Tories, who wished for another election, pedantically argued that it was not one. With these increasing contentions, coalition government became almost unworkable. The Whigs insisted that no one should sit without taking oaths of allegiance to the new monarchs —it was a very essential requirement—and nearly all the members of both Houses, save a few Bishops and Peers, Clarendon among them, complied. It was the first great Whig triumph. Meanwhile the Tories in the government were becoming recalcitrant, Halifax and Danby renewed their old quarrel and the two Secretaries of State were at serious odds. In ecclesiastical politics feuds soon broke out as to the toleration of Dissenters. The low Churchmen, who, with the Nonconformists, formed the backbone of the Whig party, had as their chief the King himself. Burnet, the Whig, was made a Bishop and Nottingham, a zealous High Churchman, reluctantly had to concede a Toleration Act. On the other hand the blasphemous obligation to take the Sacrament as a condition of municipal office, on the motion of the Tories, remained untouched. The Test Act was not repealed, toleration was denied to believers in Transubstantiation and disbelievers in the Trinity, and a general attempt at religious comprehension failed. These disputes and the failure of Parliament to concede the customs for more than a year or give the King more revenue than the amount levied in December, 1690, induced him to dissolve Parliament. The Whigs, to his personal chagrin, had refused to pass that General Act of Indemnity which the King thought would unify the Nation in their great struggle with France, and they had also sought, vindictively, to exclude from municipal rights those who had surrendered the Charters in Charles's time. The party value of this move was manifest. The freemen who possessed votes in many towns had been admitted by the City oligarchy, and to drive the Tories therefrom was to guarantee a permanent Whig domination. Doubtless the King became enraged at these petty factional manœuvres; for the time he gave his support to the constitutional Tories, though many of them were in correspondence with James; and in the result, in the spring of 1690 there was returned a Tory majority. Gratefully, a Tory House voted William moneys for the Irish campaign, then beginning. Nevertheless, as Woods thinks, by reason of incompetence in the Commons (*History of the Tory Party*, p. 63), in their jealousy of William's Dutch advisers and, still more, because of their refusal, whole-heartedly, to co-operate with his foreign policy of military opposition to Louis (which was the purpose of the King's coming to England), notwithstanding the apparent Tory success at the polls, the Government gradually became more Whig. The Whig leaders, the Junto, as it was called, were anti-French and patriotically Protestant; to them William became reconciled and, with patronage in their hands, enough Tories seceded once more to give the Whigs a working majority.

At first, after the election, Danby, now Carmarthen, had become in effect Prime Minister and First Lord of the Treasury. Shrewsbury resigned, but there remained as Danby's colleagues Nottingham, the other Secretary and Lowther—for the time it looked as if a Tory government might be formed. In any event, in the Council of Nine they formed a majority. On his return from Ireland William was entertained almost entirely by them—but soon, as has been said, it began to be impressed upon the King, more particularly after his discovery of the many affiliations of the Tories with the Jacobites, that the Whigs who were willing to push matters to extremes against France (though some of their supporters might seek to reduce the King to a cipher) were yet, in principle, pledged to his own purposes and that their allegiance was less qualified than that of their opponents. It is said that Sunderland, in particular, urged upon the King that a strong united government, which would support him faithfully, could only be found on the Whig side—certainly the Tories had openly said that England should leave the defence of the Netherlands to the Empire and other German powers. By 1690, the King having fully accepted this view, the Whigs again are to be found in control, and power passed to Somers, the Lord Keeper, and Montague, the financial expert, while the manipulation of the electorate was left to be controlled by the unscrupulous Wharton.

It was under Montague that the most far-reaching of financial expedients to support the War was arranged, the supplementing of tax revenue by loans provided on the security of the State itself. In return for an accommodation of over a million pounds at 8 per cent interest, a new corporation, the Bank of England, received a chartered privileged position. The East India Company granted a loan of two million pounds to the country and, in their turn, obtained substantial monopolies in the East India trade. The days of Charles's repudiation of debt were over and the Government and King eventually were driven to depend upon the wealthy lending classes for their solvency and credit. The interests of the City thus came to be closely associated with that party by whom their rights and monopolies had been secured. For many years, whatever else failed, the Whigs could always count upon the support of the moneyed classes.

War continuing, with estimates constantly growing, the dependence upon the lenders of money increased yearly. Land taxes and customs proved utterly insufficient; borrowing became a necessity. A million was raised by a lottery loan, in addition to that already mentioned. The Tories, much perturbed, in order to counteract the influence of the financiers, suggested the alternative of a bank consisting of capital raised on the security of land—the contest was passing from that of King and Parliament to a fight between Land and City. The latter, however, were victorious. Montague became Chancellor of the Exchequer, Shrewsbury returned, and all the other great offices were filled by Whigs; Carmarthen only remaining of the old Tories, together with Godolphin, who was regarded rather as an essential administrator than a politician.

It happened that in 1695 there was much concern in the public mind regarding allegations of corruption, more particularly in relation to army contracts. The three principal names mentioned were Carmarthen (now Duke of Leeds), Trevor, who was Speaker, and Seymour—all three were Tories. Seymour was said to have trafficked in saltpetre with the East India Company, and Trevor was censored for receiving money from the City in relation to the passage of one of their Bills. Leeds, for the second time, was impeached, but the accusation was put an end to by prorogation. Thereafter, though nominally President, he was not summoned to the Council, and the entire Government, save for the accommodating Godolphin, was at last Whig.

In these latter days, when Liberals have so often been taunted with lack of patriotic fervour, it is interesting to observe how entirely loyal they were to the King at a time when their opponents grudged him support in a contest as far-reaching in its consequences as the twentieth-century German wars. The consuming Whig desire for victory over the tyranny of Louis made them markedly less vindictive and petty than in the earlier years of the reign and William, in consequence, now gave them his support without reservation. Even Marlborough, the Tory, as a soldier was reconciled to Whig government. The Assassination Plot, in which no reputable member of opposition was associated, nevertheless still further strengthened the patriotic ideals of the Whigs. They seized the opportunity to inaugurate a great declaration to safeguard the Protestant Succession. Over four hundred members of the Commons subscribed, though, in the Lords, a few Peers, led by Rochester (while agreeing that William had a right to the Crown), refused to sign.

This hesitation did the Tories much injury; the concurrent failure of their Land Bank accentuated their plight.

On the other hand (though in 1696 it had suspended payment of its notes), new moneys poured into the Bank of England, and the only rival to Montague, Godolphin, on an allegation that he had knowledge of the designs of the suspected plotter, Fenwick, resigned. The Bill of Attainder directed against Fenwick was a serious error and found many opponents, but it is interesting to the historian of politics as disclosing a new method by which the Whig leaders sought to enforce discipline —the dissentient members of their party were summoned to a meeting where their duty as loyal Whigs was expounded to them; it was the beginning of the coercive Whip system.

The Treaty of Ryswick (wherein Louis acknowledged William to be King of England) was a great Whig achievement, for though the King admitted no interference in foreign matters, yet the concession was effected under Whig administration. Like all triumphs it demanded its price; the urgent need for patriotism was over, and now that the perils of war were past, the burden of taxation was not so readily acceptable and the Tories were less liable to be suspected of treachery. Moreover, the feeling of emergency dispelled, the cohesion of the Whigs was shaken and their majority began to fall away.

The King and the more far-sighted of the Whigs had no illusions— they knew that, dealing with Louis, nothing more than an armistice could be expected, but this opinion was not shared by a peace-loving people. Agitation for the reduction of the army and the taxes grew; particularly did the nation wish to see the foreign troops leave the realm. Harley, in origin a Whig, now joined the peace party. In an angry House he carried a motion with the support of many dissident Whigs, by 185 to 148 votes, that the armed forces should be reduced to the number obtaining in 1680.

The operation of the Triennial Act necessitated a general election in 1698, and it was soon evident that the new majority was critical of the policy of the King and his Government. The army was to be reduced to 7,000 men, all of whom were to be natural-born subjects; the Dutch Guards were to go. Government was changed. Montague left the Exchequer and Lowther, now Lord Lonsdale, returned. Soon Somers and Russell were succeeded by Godolphin and Rochester—the Tories were again in the saddle. At this juncture, James II dying, Louis, in breach of his word, recognized the Pretender. Back swung opinion to Whiggery; the King and his advisers had been right when they refused to trust the perfidious Frenchman! War was again declared, and when William died in 1702 the Whigs were unmistakably in possession—the more trusted because of their foresight. The settlement of 1701 accepted the House of Hanover as heirs presumptive on conditions as to Protestantism and other matters which marked the achievement of future Whig domination. They it was who had insisted on the rights of the Electress Sophia and, in the end, they were to benefit from a line of grateful dependent foreign monarchs. Meanwhile, the High Church Anne, though battling with Louis, lent a fitful support to the distracted and semi-seditious Tories.

Their difficulties were great; the war with France was at its height, and to the waging of that war the Whigs alone had ever given enthusiastic countenance: Louis in his desire to control Europe by placing the Crowns of France and Spain under the Bourbon had made all reconciliation impossible. Although in 1702 the Tories had won a majority, they were forced to continue the strife. Marlborough in the field was disgusted with their equivocation and almost was persuaded by his wife to join the Whigs. Godolphin, another Whiggish Tory, agreed with the great general. Against them stood Nottingham, the Secretary of State, Dartmouth and the quasi-Jacobite Rochester. The Government, on the most serious question of the day, resistance to Gallic aggression, was thus divided and by a cunning expedient sought to placate their differences and please the Queen by harassing Nonconformity, a policy which the Whig House of Lords deplored in its tendency to divide the Nation in the face of the enemy. Again the Tories showed themselves to be both illiberal and unpatriotic.

At length the exigencies of war compelled the expulsion of the reluctant Tories from Government—in 1702 Rochester resigned and Nottingham in 1704. It was now sought to form a war party by the introduction of Harley and St. John, both of whom at the time affected a support of Marlborough and Godolphin. The victory of Blenheim, in 1704, greatly strengthened the Whigs; even such a writer as Woods, in his *History of the Tory Party*, concedes that the Tories were thought to be tepid to the national cause. (p. 105.) In 1708 Harley and St. John, being suspected of intrigues against Godolphin, who was in effect Premier, were dismissed. The Government was now indubitably belligerent and Harley took upon himself the leadership of the opposition.

His skill in organization and the very completeness of victory operated to develop the feeling that the war had gone on long enough. The army was, at this time, mostly recruited as to its officers from the landed gentry and in the ranks from proletarians. In either case the great Whig financiers and merchants had nothing to fear; either in person or in loss of their sons or in money. As the war proceeded more loans were raised and a greater supply of commodities demanded, and the City bankers and contractors grew increasingly rich; but to others the hostilities, like all wars, brought little but hardship and sorrow. As early as 1711, St. John was in secret communication with the French, through Torcy, their Foreign Minister. The terms included the abandonment by England of the objection to a Bourbon Spanish King. The Tories, who had been in office since the summer of 1710, had not yet broken openly with Marlborough, but Godolphin, who had never been one of the Whig Junto, was forced out and the attack on the absent general began to mature—without Godolphin to protect him at home, his position was becoming precarious. His wife had lost all influence with the Queen, and the foolish prosecution of the High Churchman, Dr. Sacheverell, had already thrown his royal supporter into an ungrudging reliance upon Harley and St. John, soon to become respectively Lords Oxford and Bolingbroke.

On the last day of December, 1711, twelve new Tory peers were created to support a final peace and Marlborough's dismissal followed. There resulted the Treaty of Utrecht. On the whole, it was a good settlement for the allies—France was exhausted, Holland safe, and

Austria remained in possession of her part of the Netherlands, retaining a hegemony in Italy: the balance of power was restored and Louis frustrated. It was little recognized at that time that it was due to Whig pertinacity that he was reduced to such a condition.

So great was the desire for peace that the achievements of Marlborough were forgotten; like another great national saviour, Wellington, he was abused in the streets, and with less justification, for he had never opposed popular demands.

But soon stalked the bogey of the Succession: undoubtedly, an active minority of the Tories would have welcomed the Queen's brother. At any rate, they were sufficiently strong to prevent their party establishing contacts with Hanover; the Queen's own attitude was ambiguous and, to make matters worse, a blazing quarrel broke out between Oxford and Bolingbroke. The latter, although he afterwards denied it, was far more zealous for the succession of James than was the cautious Oxford. In December, 1713, Bolingbroke had told Gaultier, a French Jacobite priest and envoy, that he could not tolerate a German King in England and assured him that Parliament could be persuaded to repeal the Act of Settlement if James would but follow Charles II's example and dissemble his religion. On being solicited, however, the Pretender would do no more than undertake that he would not disturb Protestantism.

Meanwhile the Whigs, who were in close touch with Hanover, were vainly urging the Queen to receive the Electoral Prince. Oxford was dismissed and Bolingbroke, after vainly seeking an understanding with the Whigs, was about to fill the Government with men of marked Jacobite sympathies. On July 28th, 1714, the Treasury, now vacant, was temporarily put into commission and next day Anne was taken with a fatal seizure. The proposal that Shrewsbury, the semi-Whig, should be nominated Treasurer, was inexplicable save in Petrie's view that Bolingbroke was "at any rate temporarily off his balance". (*Bolingbroke*, p. 250.) Next day, August 1st, Anne died and the foreigner, George, who could not speak English, was declared King without overt opposition. Immediately, abroad, he nominated a council of Regency (it had long been in preparation), from which Bolingbroke and all his fellow ministers, except Shrewsbury, were omitted. The long period of Whig power, to last nearly fifty years, had begun.

CHAPTER II

OLD WHIGGERY

IN so far as the Whigs can be said to have had any formulated political principles, they are to be found principally in the works of John Locke and, particularly, in his *Essay on Civil Government*. At the outset of that treatise Locke, following Sidney, launches an attack upon the doctrine of the Divine Right of Kings, more especially as expounded by Filmer. In its place, like Hobbes, he reverted to the notion, which, as has been said, was supported by the Jesuits, of a social contract between men whereby they have mutually agreed to put themselves under government, but his reason for this surrender of individual freedom is directly opposed to that of Hobbes; the absolutist philosopher believed men to have come together because of their individual savagery, whereas Locke, following Aristotle and St. Thomas Aquinas, conceives them under the law of Nature to have possessed social qualities and thereby, from the beginning to have had a capacity for co-operation.

Thus assembled, it was through human conscious choice that government arose, and if it departs through tyranny from the assumptions of that universal concordat which gave it power it can rightly be overthrown. Although few of Locke's followers realized it, to proclaim this doctrine was to revert to the mediæval view that Princes are under the Law, in any case it was the direct contradiction of the doctrine of unlimited power and, therefore, very congenial to the Whig mind.

In pursuance of this idea of conditional obedience, Locke formulated four conditions of just government—it must be according to established laws of universal application, it must legislate for the good of the people as a whole, the legislature must not part with its power save to the electors or the people who bestowed it and, finally—and most significant for the future of Liberalism—interference with private property is only justifiable when occasioned by taxation or otherwise by the express consent of Parliament; it would seem that Locke, like the French and American revolutionaries after him, regarded private ownership as a primary condition of Liberty, not merely as the mediæval sociologists conceived in user, but also as conferring a right of almost absolute possession.

It has been remarked that Walpole, the greatest of the old leaders, rarely quoted and probably had never read Locke, yet, nevertheless, that writer's direct influence upon the more intellectual of the Whigs was considerable; indeed, it was not until the days of Bentham and the Utilitarians that any Liberal political philosopher arose to supplement him.

The rule of law and the legal limitations of kingship having been accepted in the Revolution, the original purpose of the Whigs may seem to have been achieved. The oligarchy of great landed nobility, supported by merchants and Dissenters, held an impregnable position in politics. Yet, though by the accident of Stuart folly they had come into power, it would be erroneous to think that at any time they commanded the respect or adherence of more than a moiety of the nation. Against them, unflinchingly, were set the smaller landowners (often of longer pedigree than the new peers), the bulk of the clergy other than Whig Bishops, the Universities and a large number of the agricultural poor who were still deferential tenants and devout Anglicans. The Catholics, though few in number and still in subjection, were not without reactionary influence. Among those normally Whig, many Dissenters were disappointed at the very limited amount of toleration which had been conceded to them, and the Quakers, who would not accept sacramentalism or the doctrine of the Trinity, were discontented at their ostracism.

But the official Whigs, though antagonizing the more radical elements in State and Church, had set their faces against any further electoral or religious reform: they did nothing to alleviate the conditions of the poor in town or country; they had no conception of the possibility of social legislation to improve the cities, roads or harbours of the realm, and readily left the maintenance of local amenities to the fox-hunting Justices of the Peace or to corrupt oligarchic municipal corporations. Their control of the new trading monopolies overseas was negligible, nor did they display any interest in the development of the plantations and colonies—they failed to improve the savage criminal law or to clarify the growing confusion attendant upon civil litigation—indeed, for a hundred years and more, whether the Government were Tory or Whig, it might fairly be said that, save in the conduct of foreign affairs and war, it was negative and impotent. The Kings had ceased to rule and Parliament had copied their example. Sinecures abounded and an increasing number of "Place-men", as they were called, supported indifferently any government which would guarantee them pensions, annuities and honours. Administration was in the hands of a small class in whom, it must be admitted, taste and discrimination in the Arts were most noticeable, but orthodox religion was moribund and good manners had come to be substituted for piety as the essential requirement of behaviour. It was by these aristocrats—so typified in the writings of Chesterfield, Hervey, Selwyn and Horace Walpole—that the "cits" and drinking squires, not to speak of the "mobile" in the towns, for the most part were content to be governed. The majority of the Commons were related to the Lords—indeed, it may be said that nearly all the governing families, in whichever House they sat, and on whichever side, were kinsmen.

Meanwhile, confining their civic energies to the municipalities, business men were increasing their riches. At the time of the South Sea scandal no less than a seventh of the total wealth of the country was already invested in Joint-Stock undertakings; money was clamouring for investment and the speculator had become a fashionable figure. The collapse of the South Sea Company gave to Walpole his unique opportunity, for the Chancellor of the Exchequer had himself been involved and other ministers were ruined in that adventure. This, however, did not have the effect of discouraging activity in finance; on the contrary, once Walpole had adroitly liquidated the trouble, the search for markets and commercial exploitation in India and elsewhere increased in vigour. The steadfast refusal of that Premier to involve England in continental wars nourished the rising wealth of the country. War eventually came again; but, for the most of Walpole's time, the commercial class, other than army contractors, had reason to bless that pacific Whig country gentleman who so sedulously protected their interests.

Prosperity enabled Walpole to placate even the squires by lowering the land tax. The factious opposition to Excise compelled him to modify his financial policy but did nothing to shake essential Whig power. Not only the rich but the Dissenters, who were still in a position of social and constitutional sufferance (though Walpole did next to nothing to help them) gave him their support in lack of any better hope.

"As a minister," writes Lecky (*England in the Eighteenth Century*, Vol. I, p. 400), "Walpole combined an extreme and exaggerated severity of party discipline within Parliament with the utmost deference for public opinion beyond its walls." His insistence on peace, it must not be forgotten, was alien to Whig tradition—their policy and success had long been based upon a challenge to French power.

It was in this connection that they had wished to restrict trade with

that country, and argued against free trade that "mercantilism", as
it was called, demanded the restriction of imports. The Tories on
the other hand advocated free commerce; they saw no harm in the
importation of French commodities, said by the Whigs to be "exhausting
the wealth of the nation". The leading trade writer on the Tory side
had been Dudley North. In his *Discourses upon Trade*, published in
1691, he states that money is a merchandise "whereof there may be a glut
as well as a scarcity". The world traders should "accommodate one
another". The Tory Davenant similarly declared that "Trade is by
nature free, finds its own channel, and best directeth its own course".
The great bankers took the same objection to the Mercantile theory.
As against these advanced thinkers, Locke the Whig was an orthodox
supporter of protection, yet one cannot but suspect that a political
suspicion of France, rather than the logic of his individualism, went to
produce his economic outlook.

However this may be, Walpole succeeded for a time in wooing the
Whigs away from their belligerent past. His task was not an easy one,
the dynastic disputes in Spain, involving France and Austria, had nearly
caused a British intervention at the time of the Succession of George II,
for Austria and Spain had entered into an understanding and the former's
encouragement of their Ostend Company alarmed both English and
Dutch competitors. The alliance of England, Prussia and the French,
in 1725, was most unpopular—it was regarded as a device to save Hanover
from the Austrians and thus angered both political parties; the Whigs
because of the contact with France, their opponents on account of the
succour given to the detested Hanoverians. Yet the power of Walpole,
the architect of the plan, was not seriously affected. As a counterpoise,
in 1731, by the Treaty of Vienna, he conciliated the Austrians and left
the French to fight them, but the success of France in this contest
rekindled the lurking fear of that nation in Whig hearts and the opposition
within the Party to Walpole increased. The King also, who was by nature
martial, added to the Premier's difficulties.

Walpole, however, had one invaluable instrument to achieve his
pacific end—political corruption. George II was promised one hundred
thousand pounds a year more than his father had been voted, the Queen
was to have a similar jointure. Bribery, direct or concealed, was not
a new thing, either of members of Parliament or other electors. In
theory it was condemned; Trevor, Ranelagh, Aislabie and the Craggs
were all persons of high office who had recently been politically destroyed
by the exposure of their direct receipt of moneys from interested persons,
but there were other methods, less blatant, to achieve the same ends,
and it must be conceded that Walpole's use of public moneys was to
obtain votes to maintain his policy and not for his personal enrichment.
As to the elections, the Whigs did nothing as a constitutional party to
purify the methods of filling Parliament, save sporadically to unseat
their opponents, nor did they complain when the Prime Minister gained
support by offering lucrative sinecures to the dependable—a method
later improved by Bute when he granted to his friends the promotion of
loans on advantageous terms. Systematic corruption, in one form or
another, now that the power of monarchy was spent, was the recognized
method by which both parties for many years ensured their power.

There can be no doubt that it was the un-Whiggish desire of Walpole to come to terms with France and Spain which ultimately undermined him. If the Tories had hoped to gain by his removal they were disappointed. Though Bolingbroke, their only leader of intelligence, had returned to England, he was still excluded from the Lords—Walpole had seen to that. The dissident Whigs, who complained of Walpole's want of martial patriotism, were even further removed from Tory and Jacobite French sympathy than was the Prime Minister; for with Walpole an understanding with France was sought only to preserve the peace. In Tory policy such amity was necessarily inherent.

That unimpressive nonentity, the Prince of Wales, was chosen by the "Boy Patriots", as Walpole scornfully mocked them, to be a rallying centre, and for a time it looked as if a union of the young Whigs and Tories against the Premier was possible. The restraining hand of Wyndham, the Tory leader, being removed by his death in 1740, his party again became intransigeant, and when Walpole finally resigned, in 1742, the power was still with the Whigs Pulteney and Carteret; Walpole himself, now Lord Orford, helping them to construct the new Government—the Tories had again been outwitted.

But the future lay with Pitt, the young dissentient Whig—for the moment he was refused office—he had been used by Pulteney and Carteret to exclude Walpole, but there was to be no reward. For a time he dabbled with Toryism, denouncing the Hanoverian connection as fiercely as any Jacobite—for this the Court never forgave him. At length, in 1744, Pelham succeeded Carteret, the Hanoverian, and Pitt, once more turning patriot, in 1746 became Paymaster-General.

The incapacity of the Government, displayed during the Scottish invasion of 1745, was, of course, of no assistance to embarrassed Tories suspected of Jacobitism; Carteret's ideal of a "broad-bottomed Ministry", to include the Opposition, became impossible. During the Pelham administration France was victorious in Europe. Tournay and Ostend, Mons and Namur, were theirs, and the invasion of this country was considered probable—it was under the pressure of such events that the King had been forced to accept Pitt. In April, 1748, came the Peace of Aix; it was to the disadvantage of England. "We are too weak to fight", said the Prime Minister—through necessity he was inclining to the pacific principles of Walpole.

Government proposals to naturalize foreign Protestants and the Jews were attacked both by the Anglican Tories and the Whig city magnates, who feared alien competition. In March, 1754, Pelham died and there followed a general election. Not more than one hundred and fifty were returned in Opposition; but these, significantly, were mostly from the counties where a wider franchise of small freeholders existed than in the close, doctored electoral rolls of the towns. A new war was brewing; already hostilities with the French had broken out in America. Pitt, now become an extreme Whig and patriot—he was a close student of Locke—to unify the nation began to support the long-postponed civic emancipation of Dissenters. For this and other reasons, after much intrigue, he was dismissed and the avaricious Fox became leader of the House of Commons. At length, after an alliance between Austria and France had put the country into dire jeopardy, Fox resigned, and a genuinely popular patriotic movement arose which could not be confined within official Whig fences. America, to be saved; a militia on a national scale to be raised; the foreign troops to be sent home, and the seas to be secured by a strong navy—such was the policy which Pitt, with magnificent eloquence, advocated. The French had already invaded Germany and the services of Pitt were demanded by the country. He became a hero, but on a national stage, not merely in the opinion of a few excited young men at Westminster.

Under his direction there followed the great years of victory, Pitt being now Secretary of State, and in effect Prime Minister, though the ubiquitous Newcastle controlled the votes. On the Continent, Frederick, the Prussian, was perhaps really the victor; but in Canada and in India the modern British Empire arose on the ruins of French power. Party politics were forgotten in a universal congratulation and relief and, whether he deserved it or not, Pitt emerged as undisputed national leader.

But again the very completeness of victory produced a general desire for peace, and the administration of Pitt, like that of Marlborough, fell in a vain endeavour to prolong the war. By this time the young George III was reigning, and a new Government, favouring his personal rule, had been formed—until October, 1761, Pitt and his brother-in-law, Temple, remained the only members of it who supported the pursuance of the war.

Unfortunately for the administration, a Scotsman, Lord Bute, had been chosen by the Sovereign to preside, and the feeling against that country, inflamed by the recent invasion, was so strong that his presence was enough to imperil the whole administration. "No Scotch, no foreigners", was a cry which appealed to all the people. In any case, as Fielding rightly points out (*The Second Tory Party*, p. 72), "it is a mistake to regard the new Government as a Tory one". Actually, the Tory Party "in the Parliament of 1761 was not much stronger than it had been for many years".

On October 5th, 1761, Pitt and Temple resigned on the question of extending the war to Spain, a country which had recently concluded an alliance with France. The former's acceptance of a pension temporarily lessened his popularity but soon it revived.

For the moment the war with France continued. The West Indies fell to England and Frederick regained Silesia—Bute and his friends were confronted with a nation-wide enthusiasm for Pitt; for him it "rained gold boxes" containing the freedom of cities, but the day of pacification was near—Grenville, a peace-maker, led the Commons, and Bedford in the Lords, another pacificator, became Privy Seal. On a refusal to continue further assistance to Prussia, Newcastle at length resigned—in November preliminaries for peace were signed in Paris.

The underlying purpose of the young King, however, was not so much to promote a peace policy as to encourage the ideal of the restoration of active Kingship as a factor in government. That he and his mother had absolutist ambitions cannot be doubted, but the framework of the constitution had been so established during the long Whig domination that an attack upon it could only be made by concealed and devious methods. As has been said, the foolish selection of an incompetent Scotsman as figurehead had enabled the opposition to the new régime to marshal more support than would otherwise have been possible, and the popularity of Pitt was another factor in their favour—though it can hardly be thought that the long corrupt ascendancy of Whiggery itself could appeal strongly to people other than those who had directly benefited from it. Those benefits were now to be conferred upon the King's friends and the temptation to change sides proved overpowering.

In 1763 there was launched from the Palace a general proscription of the Whigs. Not only Lords-Lieutenant but humble Customs officers were dismissed. Newcastle, Grafton and Rockingham were relieved of the headship of their counties, followers of Fox and Bute being installed in their place. Fox pressed for a general extirpation of the Whig interest, but soon he resigned with a peerage, and in the new, more tolerant, ministry of Grenville, appeared several names afterwards to become notorious: North, Sandwich and Egremont.

These in name were mostly Whig, yet they it was who broke up the Whig party and hazarded constitutional government. Grenville was a strong supporter of authority. He was a haughty, aloof man, but the King saw in him a useful instrument—he forgot that the power which Grenville sought was for himself alone; to that extent he was no Tory; the Church and King received his respect but his own office of Prime Minister was his chief concern. It was not long before the Monarch wearied of his hauteur. He had taken office to prevent "unwarrantable force being put upon the Crown", but he—and not George—was to be master. Grenville's least fortunate actions were his programme for taking the colonies and regulating their trade, a plan which included the unfortunate Stamp Act, and the prosecution of John Wilkes.

This latter disastrous act was apparently suggested by the King himself. Wilkes had committed the unpardonable offence (with intention rather to inculpate the Ministers than to belittle the King) of regarding the royal speech at the opening of Parliament as the words of the Government, George being treated as a mere mouthpiece. This, perhaps, was not unpleasing to Grenville but to the Court it was blasphemy. In his polemic journal, the *North Briton*, Wilkes had gone so far as to refer to the Sovereign as "Chief Magistrate". He had already insulted the King's mother, elliptically comparing her and Bute to Edward II's mother and her paramour Mortimer—he was a fervid patriot and supporter of Pitt. To George and his friends, this somewhat absurd demagogue soon came to be regarded as chief enemy.

There is reason to believe that the Premier was still sufficiently Whig to dislike the raising of the delicate legal and constitutional questions which an attack upon the fearless Wilkes would certainly precipitate, but he was dependent upon the Court and Tory votes; his own family, Temple, his brother and Pitt regarding him as a family traitor, were his most insatiable opponents. His position was precarious; he decided to yield to the King's insistent demands and to arrest Wilkes.

The historic importance of the imbroglio which followed cannot be over-estimated. Wilkes himself was a curious mixture of patriot, radical, adventurer and rake. From the standpoint of literature his writings are cumbrous and involved; he was a poor speaker, yet he had the fortune to be the man on whom the principles of the common law were to be tested. The Whigs were ashamed of their champion—Pitt's personal dissociation from him was accompanied by an acknowledgment of the justice of his cause—but while the opposition could have wished for a more reputable protagonist, they could not ignore his usefulness to them in their cry that the Constitution was in danger—they regarded Wilkes, more particularly after his expulsion from Parliament, as the best means of vexing and criticizing the administration and the King. The proud Temple did not hesitate openly to support the Wilkeites and their leader.

The judicial condemnation of the intrusion into Wilkes' house of the servants of the Government and his own seizure were taken by the masses, ignorant of the niceties of law—(in reality he was released by Chief Justice Pratt on the very technical ground that he had not committed a breach of the peace and so fell within the privilege of a Member of Parliament)—as a vindication of Pitt and belligerent patriotism. Riots and demonstrations broke out all over London. Wilkes was expelled the House of Commons, and in the Lords his erstwhile companion in salicity, Sandwich, further enraged the public by inaugurating an attack upon him for privately printing an indecent poem. On a vote declaring General Warrants to be illegal (it was under such a one that Wilkes had been imprisoned), the Government majority fell to fourteen; it looked as if the radical agitator had rallied the Whigs against the Court. Even now the King failed to realize the seriousness of the issue; "the impudence of Wilkes is amazing", he wrote to Grenville; "his ruin is so near".

The growing opposition in Parliament, however, made the King doubt whether Grenville was not a failure. His personal distaste for the Court circle made accommodation to the King's will the more difficult. Reading George's letters it is not difficult to detect that he soon came to think that the Premier had mismanaged the Wilkes affair. Vindictively he writes to that harassed statesman: "The defection (on the General Warrant question) is undoubtedly very great. I hope those who have deserted may feel that I am not to be neglected unpunished".

The King was as good as his threat—in April, 1764, Conway, Lord Hertford's brother, was deprived of his regiment and a similar course was taken with many other independent Members of Parliament. The device to coerce the House had been used by Governments before, but the personal intervention of the Sovereign without the approval of his Government was now carried to lengths which made things unbearable even for such a mild Whig as Grenville.

The final breach came over the first Regency Bill, necessitated by the King's mental derangement. Grenville and his friends decided that the King's mother was not eligible to be appointed to the Council of Regency, as "not being of the Royal family". On his recovery, the King took this as a personal insult. Temple and Grenville, now in their common opposition to the new personal rule, were reconciled. They demanded the dismissal of Bute's brother and wished the Duke of Cumberland to be made to yield up his office of Commander-in-Chief; some even of the more independent Tories supported the Prime Minister. In the end, the King, saying that "necessity not choice" compelled him, with grief entrusted the Government to the orthodox Whig, Lord Rockingham.

Pitt had attempted to form a Ministry, but the obduracy of Temple made it impossible; the Tories were still too weak in the House to take office, and in the end the Duke of Newcastle agreed to help Rockingham. The King was compelled to take back Conway, whom he had recently dismissed from the army, as Secretary of State; as a solatium, Mackenzie, the brother of Bute, was restored to the insignificant office of Lord Privy Seal for Scotland.

The Rockingham administration succeeded in repealing the Stamp Act which had caused such friction in America, but it was really to conciliate Pitt that the Stamp Act was repealed: an accompanying measure was passed declaring that Parliament had the right to enact laws binding the colonies "in all cases whatsoever". This was a compromise, but, even so, most of the Scots, the Tories, and the Bishops voted against it. In the Government were now nearly all the leading Whigs except Pitt and Shelburne, but all the praise from the merchants who had lost so heavily by the interference of trade caused by the Act went to Pitt. The demand to bring back Pitt into the Government grew, and his refusal to co-operate with Rockingham ultimately brought down the Government. In July, 1766, Pitt, as Lord Chatham, accepted the Privy Seal, Rockingham was dismissed and a new Ministry formed by the new Earl and Grafton, the erratic young Townshend being Chancellor of the Exchequer. From the outset, however, the warring Whig groups, the Bedford, Rockingham and Grenville factions, all made difficulties. Meanwhile, Chatham being ill, the irrepressible Wilkes, who had received a temporary pension from the Rockingham Whigs, returned to London. "Wilkes and Liberty are everything", wrote a contemporary diarist. To shout and riot for him and to chalk up the figures "45" everywhere was the means whereby the disfranchised masses began to show their restlessness at all these aristocratic intrigues and governmental indifference to their lot.

The usual aftermath of long war had come; wages were falling, and the obsolescence of the old statute powers of the Justices to fix minimum wages had deprived the operatives, in the absence of effective powers of combination, of their last protection. A few favoured older trades—curriers, hatters, wool-staplers and calico printers—still limited their numbers by apprenticeship systems and occasionally succeeded in getting through Parliament some special Act to protect their remuneration; but prices were rising and in the new industries developing under primitive machinery, in the spinning and weaving trades, in the expanding coal and iron industries, and in the pottery trades, the operatives for the most part were without any means, industrial or political, to improve their condition. As Adam Smith pointed out, the masters had all the advantage; there were Statutes against combining to raise wages, none against combining to lower them. The masters could generally starve the men into submission, the men's agitations "generally end in nothing but the punishment or ruin of the ring-leaders".

It is not suggested that the agitation which centred round Wilkes was directly connected with this economic servitude; on the contrary, nothing is more noticeable than the absence of all reference to social amelioration in Wilkes' speeches, but the terrible conditions of the poor in London and other growing towns may well have furnished the ground-swell of that discontent which so rapidly developed. After scenes of great disorder, on March 29th, 1768, Wilkes was returned with popular acclamation as Member for Middlesex.

The burden of coping with this democratic agitation fell upon the new leader of the House of Commons, North, rather than on the indolent Grafton. North had obtained the ear of the House and was himself conspicuously free from that corrupt ambition which had disfigured the careers of so many of his contemporaries. He was a good and skilful debater and of placid temperament—no better man could be found to ride out a storm, and storm there certainly was.

The election of Wilkes had taken place amid riots and confusion in London, exceptional even in the days when the police did not function, and the intervention of the military was entirely casual and ill-directed. The houses of the wealthy were attacked and the great assaulted. Meanwhile, the sailors in the docks had struck for higher wages and were marching on the King's palace, and other working men were following their example. Horne Tooke, a radical clergyman, and the Dissenters saw a means to raise their grievances and, more alarming to the Government, the City of London magnates proved to be largely on Wilkes' side. In the Lords, Chatham and Shelburne supported the constitutional protest; nor did the condemnation of Wilkes, after his outlawry had been reversed, help his opponents. On the contrary, his prison became a centre of political agitation. Outside, the great journalist known as Junius, fed the fire. Law suits against Ministers for illegal practices were started or re-opened by Wilkes, no longer an outlaw; in some cases, such as that of Halifax, resulting in large damages for the aggrieved Radical. After the domestic contentions of the Whig oligarchy, which had for so long filled the political stage, it was obvious that something bigger and more sinister was afoot. The troops in quelling one of the riots unfortunately had killed some people, and Lord Barrington, the Secretary for War, had the folly to congratulate them just at the time when those responsible were being charged by a Middlesex grand jury with murder.

The King was now determined that Wilkes should be expelled the House. On February 4th, 1769, this was accomplished, but only by a majority of eighty-two. A new by-election was held on February 16th and Wilkes was again returned, almost unanimously. Again, on March 16th, after a further expulsion, the same result occurred. The position was becoming serious: cries of "Wilkes and no King" were heard. Merchants pledging support to the King were rabbled, and London, at any rate, was in a revolutionary condition. On the fourth occasion of Wilkes election, the House declared the minority candidate, Luttrell, elected though he had received under three hundred votes. Petitions for the dissolution of Parliament flowed in. In the Lords, Chatham moved for enquiry into the Middlesex election, and the Chancellor, Camden for supporting him, was dismissed. Thereupon Grafton resigned on January 27th: Wilkes and Junius had overthrown the Government!

The new Prime Minister, North, was not officially a Tory. He himself would never use the word. He had served under the Whigs, Newcastle and Chatham, and had few affiliations with Bute and the Palace party He favoured further relief to Dissenters, which was emphatically not Tory position, and during the whole of his administration displayed no sign of High Churchmanship. On the other hand, undoubtedly, he was supporter of the King.

Most of the old Whig leaders had died or were aged. Until Fox passed over to the Opposition, Burke was nearly the only strong man left among the official Whigs. Grenville, Bedford, Egremont and Beckford, one of the few sitting Wilkeites, who never numbered half a dozen in the House, were all gone, and North proceeded to try to eliminate what hostile influence was left by dealing with specific grievances in a manner novel to the legislature. Thus, in 1770, the wages of coal-hewers were stabilized by Statute and, later, journeymen and weavers had their wages similarly improved.

Parish reform was undertaken, naval pensioners helped—for the first time since Elizabeth's day Parliament was used, though sparingly, for the conscious betterment of social conditions.

In Canada, the Catholic priesthood was recognized, together with the maintenance of French Civil Law. The old Corn Law was repealed and importation allowed when wheat was forty-eight shillings, and in India the East India Company was put under some governmental control, Warren Hastings being nominated Governor-General.

The Royal Marriage Act, passed on the personal insistence of the King, lost the Government the powerful support of Charles Fox. As a poor exchange, George Germaine and the Tory, Meredith, joined the Government ranks. A general election in 1774 gave North a majority of nearly three-to-one; exceptionally, the City of London went Radical and Wilkes, unmolested and unopposed, sat for Middlesex. Fortunately for the administration, he had now turned his attention almost exclusively to municipal affairs, seeking to be Lord Mayor of London.

The American problem now emerged, rapidly passing into a warlike stage, and in that contention new issues arose and new reputations were to be made. Broadly speaking, three solutions had been advocated; the first, the King's, which North reluctantly supported, was to treat the Americans as rebels outside the law—the men who took this view, the King above all, regretted the repeal of the Stamp Act, declaring that the token exception of tea as an affirmation of principle had but been used to cause the Boston demonstration in 1774 or had, at least, been an excuse for it. In 1775, North had proposed that each colony might be exempted from Imperial taxation as regards the cost of its own defence, but such a remedy was then too late.

The second suggestion, that of Chatham, was to allow the Americans, through Congress, generally to tax themselves, a plan which Franklin had for a time supported—the third view was that taken by the advanced Whigs in England—that the Americans were entitled to a Bill of Rights which would give to their Congress complete self-government.

Largely through the influence of Chatham, support of the colonists became an essential part of the Whig programme; one result was to produce a new body of Court Whigs who, once war had started, agreed with the Government that before any further discussion could be considered, the war must be won. The fact that Wilkes and his friends protested against the treatment of the Americans did not ease the fears of the more timorous of the Opposition. On the Government side, the leader was probably the most eager of his party for reconciliation, but the King and his friends were of a different opinion and every failure in the field made them the more stubborn. Although Fox and Burke were vehement in opposition, the support they obtained was poor, nor is there any reason to suppose that the country was substantially behind them—on the American matter there is no sign of any public animation comparable to the excitement roused by Wilkes. In the House, Burke's plea for conciliation had been dismissed by a majority of nearly two hundred votes, and although Grafton resigned—he had taken office under North—Burke and Fox were systematically voted down, while promises of royal victory receded and ultimate defeat became the more certain.

The dilemma which inexorably pursues statesmen who continue to oppose a war after it has started confronted Fox on two occasions in his life. In the midst of hostilities, more particularly if unsuccessful, antagonism is not only unpopular but distasteful to a patriotic opponent. In these circumstances, two courses are open to the subject who wishes to remain loyal: the one is to withdraw from public life altogether; the other, to criticize the conduct of the war itself: in 1776 Rockingham and Burke chose the method of secession—Fox determined to remain and fight.

In December, 1777, came the news of the surrender of Burgoyne at Saratoga. Fox concentrated his fury upon Germaine, the Secretary for War, and found ample material for his attack. Back came the Whigs, some to suggest a settlement, others to urge further and more efficient warfare; for the time being, the pertinacity of Fox had saved the party.

All his hesitations, however, were ended when France joined the Americans in 1778. Fox had early private news of the fact and exposed the weakness and folly of the Government. Again a cry arose for the old veteran, Chatham—North would have been only too willing to hand over the direction of so terrible a situation to him; Fox would have served— the Rockingham group, alone, raised difficulties. But Chatham soon died and the last possibility of accommodation with the States, now "United", was gone. Richmond, who led the Opposition in the Lords, had been half-hearted, but the fight against France had resolved his doubts also—of that war he was without hesitation a keen supporter. The Whig anti-Gallican past sustained the Party—France was ever the foe, cried Fox; "the war against America is against your own countrymen, France is an inveterate enemy". He demanded that the navy, the militia and the army should all be strengthened. From 1778, the Whigs became critical but enthusiastic patriots—many of them, Grafton, Richmond and Devonshire, left London to command the militia in their respective counties.

In June, 1779, Spain joined the enemy, but George, against the private protests of North, still clamoured to destroy the Americans. The recognition that the King's infatuation was ruining the country was fast spreading. In the Commons in April, 1780, a motion by Dunning, the Whig, that "the influence of the Crown has increased, is increasing and ought to be diminished", to the horror of the Monarch and the Court, was carried against the Government by eighteen votes. An attack on the Civil List revenues, the principal source of royal patronage, followed, and without a division an enquiry was ordered. The utter incapacity of the Government to cope with the riots organized by Lord George Gordon as a protest against the relief of Catholic disabilities—a measure promoted not only by the Whigs but by North himself—showed the administration to be as feeble in domestic as in foreign affairs. In October, 1781, Cornwallis surrendered at Yorktown: as North truly said:

"It is all over". In December he had to tell the House that it "is not the intention of the Government to reduce America by force". This admission was followed by a motion of Conway in February, 1782, to abandon the American War, to be lost by only one vote. On March 20th, North, braving the King's anger, found courage sufficient to resign.

The unscrupulous Chancellor, Thurlow, was employed by the King to find him a new government and Rockingham entered on his second administration, the terms being the Independence of America and the abolition of those sinecure offices by which, in the past, George had systematically corrupted Parliament—together with the retention upon the Woolsack of Thurlow himself.

The new Cabinet, with the exception of the inescapable Chancellor, was Whig, though from the outset there was friction between the Rockingham and Shelburne groups. The latter supported electoral reform; Burke, the mentor of Rockingham, relied upon the exclusion from Parliament of royal influence. The two ideals were not inconsistent, but Burke had an irrational objection to tampering with the existing franchise in any way. It is interesting to note that the young Pitt, though he would not join the Government, favoured franchise reform, as did the Duke of Richmond in the Lords.

In 1782 Rockingham publicly declared that there were 11,500 revenue officers and that 70 elections were decided by their votes. Borough jobbers assessed the average value of seats at, at least, £3,000. Some contests had risen in cost to over £30,000 (according to Horace Walpole). In 1761, Sudbury advertised itself for sale, he writes, and at length a few brokers in borough seats actually had to stand their trial (*Memoirs of Geo. III.* pp. 129–135). As to the House itself, in 1774, 254 members in England and Wales represented 11,500 voters and 56 had constituencies of 38 electors, while six members had only three electors each. In Scotland the matter was even worse. Political reform societies were fast rising, but all they could do was to make speeches and petition. Pitt had inherited his early desire for reform from his father. Chatham's chief interest had been in cautious redistribution—he would have increased the county representation (he was hesitant about destroying the rotten boroughs), and so by increasing the shire's vote would have diminished the influence of the "mercenary borough".

It was not so much Pitt's particular proposals, however, but the fact that so important a statesman thought franchise reform necessary at all which makes his opinion significant. He by no means accepted the new fashionable view of Horne and his supporters that a member of Parliament should be but a delegate, but Chatham was of opinion that "there should be a permanent relation between the constituent and representative body of the people." (*Chatham Correspondence*, III, 457.) In the words of Johnson, "Chatham was a Minister given to the King by the people"—he had the support of the unenfranchised, and once a minister got into such a position, it was natural that he should wish his followers to be able to give legal expression to their enthusiasm.

The objection of Burke to parliamentary reform is not easy to understand. Personally he disliked Chatham. He thought he was an "ambitious man of light and no principles". (*Correspondence*, II, 276.) Burke had a far greater fear of the public than had the Great Commoner;

the Legislature was a trustee for the people, he wrote. He went as far with the reformers as to approve the reporting of debates and divisions, but of the new idea that members were mere delegates, as he told his Bristol electors in 1774, he would have nothing; "your representative owes you his judgment and he betrays you if he sacrifices it to your opinion—Parliament is a deliberative assembly of one nation with one interest, that of the whole—not local prejudice ought to guide but the general good". That was very noble and very wise, but its connection with the perpetuation of the right of very rich men to buy parliamentary seats is not very easy to discover. He thought that "the machine itself is well enough to answer any good purpose provided the materials were sound". (*Correspondence*, II, 383.) On this basis he and his friends opposed all attempts to redistribute seats or enlarge the franchise; he denounced the societies who urged these reforms and objected to any attack upon "the tried usages of the Constitution", even going so far as to say that "our representation is as nearly perfect as the necessary imperfection of human affairs will suffer it to be". (*Works*, x, 92–108.)

Thus, through Burke's efforts, the young Pitt's motion in 1782 for enquiry into parliamentary representation was defeated by twenty votes, for while Fox and Sheridan supported his demand, not only did Burke denounce the very moderate request for investigation as "revolutionary", but many less important Whigs and Tories also, fearful of losing both their seats and financial electoral assets, were unsympathetic to any change. Ten days later, Pitt asked for shorter Parliaments. Here, it is true, he was seeking to amend the Whig expedient of William III's time when the Septennial Act was passed, but in truth he was a better Liberal than those who opposed him. Not until 1910 was the period of Parliament lowered from the undemocratic length of seven years— but in 1782 it was Burke, the real Tory, who led the Opposition. In the Lords, on the other hand, that early noble Radical, the Duke of Richmond, moved for manhood suffrage. The difference of opinion on this matter provided the comic spectacle of Pitt and Wilkes serving on the same reform committee.

Although Fox was now joint Foreign Secretary, America, still in law a colony, fell under the jurisdiction of Shelburne. It was that states-man's object to promote a peace simultaneously with France and the United States, while Fox wished without any delay to acknowledge the independence of the American colonies. Shelburne began negotiations with Franklin, who asked for the yielding of Canada—this was refused, and the Cabinet was inclining to Fox's view of a separate peace, apart from France, when, on July 1, 1782, Rockingham died.

The King sent for Shelburne, but Fox, Burke and others, to avoid serving under him, demanded that a comparative nonentity, the Duke of Portland, should become titular head. The King, as he was entitled constitutionally to do, declined the dictation, and thereupon Fox resigned, Burke with him. The Duke of Richmond, however, disapproved the secession and remained in the Cabinet.

In the Cabinet, Lord John Cavendish alone had followed Fox, and Pitt, at the age of twenty-three, became Chancellor of the Exchequer. It was in December that Shelburne had to announce that in the end he had been compelled to sign preliminary articles of peace with America before all the outstanding French problems had been solved. Feeling his weakness, he desired to strengthen his position by bringing in North, but Pitt refused to agree.

It was clear that Fox's desire for peace with America first had been satisfied, and he generously admitted it in a speech in the House. He wished, however, to be further assured. Was the treaty with America dependent upon an agreement with France? Pitt said it was irrevocable, but the foolish King thought otherwise. He would not, he said, recognize American independence unless the French pacification went through; Pitt had spoken without authority. In January of 1783, however, the preliminary treaty with France and Spain was signed. By nineteen votes it was carried in the Commons that the concessions to France were unjustified and Shelburne was thereupon compelled to resign. At last Pitt was given permission to endeavour to bring Fox into the Government, but that fiery politician refused to come unless Shelburne went out and the negotiations broke down on the personal hatred of Fox and Burke to the Prime Minister, who certainly had treated Fox with great equivocation over the American negotiations when they were both Secretaries of State.

The King long struggled to keep Fox out of the Government. It was suggested that Pitt should be Premier, but he refused. North, being asked to come in without Fox, declined, and, in the end, on April 2nd, the Duke of Portland, Fox's former nominee, became First Lord of the Treasury; North and Fox to be Secretaries of State.

Much criticism had been directed against Fox because in this ministry Lord North found a place. It cannot be suggested that Fox was not entitled to join his own nominee, Portland, and therefore the condemnation of the coalition must rest primarily upon North. Yet North had never been a Tory, his own inclinations, as has been shown, on the whole were Liberal—now that the American war was over there was little to divide him from the Whigs if but he would abandon his subservience to the royal will. By this time the King had come to regard his erstwhile servant as a deserter—he was almost as uncongenial to George as was the detested Fox. North now declared to Fox that he had come to believe in united Cabinet control; he abandoned the Tory doctrine that each minister was responsible only to the King. As Fox said: "The American war was the cause of enmity between myself and the noble Lord. The American war and the American question is at an end".

Socially, Fox and North were in the same jovial circle. Shelburne was a frigid and exclusive man who stood aloof, a fact which counted for much in the days of select aristocratic government. Horace Walpole, usually so censorious a critic of Fox and his friends, to judge from his contemporary letters was not much shocked at the alliance. Perhaps the best test of opinion is afforded by the re-election of Fox without opposition for that democratic and intractable constituency, Westminster.

A much more serious difficulty was the difference among ministers on such fundamental matters as that shown by the rejection of Pitt's renewed demand for electoral reform. The endorsement by the Government of that treaty of peace with France which they had condemned when Shelburne introduced it was probably inescapable and wise, but their tolerance of Burke's retrograde refusal to consider the franchise

question—an inaction which postponed all adjustment of an indefensible
mode of representation for fifty years—shows how far they were from
achieving any higher notion of Government than the maintenance of a
perpetual freehold for the Whig oligarchy.

The major problem which concerned the Government was the future
of India. Wealth from that country was now affecting public life, as
did the incursion of moneyed interests from South Africa at the end of the
Victorian era. The new Governor-General, Hastings, was at odds with
the Directors; the majority of the Court of Proprietors were on his side.
Fox and North determined to overthrow the vested interests which had
collected round the Nabobs and adventurers who were now living on
India and buying influence at home. Here Burke was whole-heartedly
with them; he had, he believed, discovered grave injustices, if not cruelties
perpetrated in the administration of that great country. The Government, for once united, suggested that the sovereign control should be
taken from the Company and vested in Commissioners to be nominated
by the Government and subsequently appointed by the Crown, while
an executive in India should work under them. This scheme was necessarily regarded as an invasion of their chartered monopoly rights by the
proprietors and it is not difficult to foresee that from the outset interested
persons would seek to wreck it. All other holders of charters were
alarmed; for the first time the City turned against the Whigs, even
Wilkes supported the Opposition; Plutocracy was showing its teeth. By
a great folly, Lord North's son appeared among the proposed commissioners—it was one of those acts which make the historian doubt the
political intelligence of public men. The capitalists organized a campaign
directed against Fox in particular. The King, who had no love for City
opinion, saw in this agitation a means of overthrowing the Ministry.
He declared in his old style that "whoever voted for the India Bill would
be considered by him as an enemy". The Lords, persuaded both by Court
and City, deserted, and on March 17th, 1783, the Bill was rejected there
by nineteeen votes. Next day the King took the seals from his Whig
opponents and Pitt became Prime Minister.

Apart from the India matter, the record of the Coalition was a poor
one. They had refused, as has been said, to help Pitt to eradicate corrupt
boroughs or lessen election expenses; they declined to introduce much-
needed parliamentary reforms in Ireland; they had proposed to grant
the Prince of Wales, their friend, £100,000 a year. A Bill to prevent
waste in Government offices, another scheme of Pitt's, was rejected
and they continued the bad old system of giving preferences in the
floating of national loans to their supporters. Until the split on the
India question, the City had given the Government their support—their
chief claim to honour is that they had not feared to make the moneyed
interests break with them by their advocacy of a progressive Indian
policy.

The new Premier at first sought another Coalition—North to retire
and a compromise on the Indian question to be attempted. This failed
and soon, of the great Whigs, only the Radical Richmond supported Pitt.
Temple, his relation, left him at an early stage and Shelburne was not
invited to join. Against the young Prime Minister stood the great
Coalition majority; what the Foxites chiefly feared was a dissolution—

their leaders went so far as publicly to deny to the Crown the right to call a new Parliament during a session. Fox did not hesitate to hold up the Mutiny Bill, which annually legalized the Army, and in other ways encouraged his followers to practise every possible obstruction.

Pitt, on the other hand, demanded an election—let the country (or such small part of it as had votes) decide. For four years Fox had supported motions for annual Parliaments. Why, asked Pitt, this cynical change of front? At this time, undoubtedly, Fox had lost much of his popularity—whatever may have been the excuses for the alliance with North, though the governing class took it calmly—the unfranchised people as a whole were astonished that the leader should so soon join hands with the man whom he had so vilified for so long a period. In the House the usual Government inducements and threats were brought to bear upon the members and the Whig majorities steadily fell until, finally, in a division against the Government, they had a majority of but one. Then Pitt struck; he dissolved, went to the country, and was returned with a two-hundred majority—the rule of the Whigs was over.

One effect of Pitt's triumph was to kill reform. Though he still appealed for it (he would have enfranchised London and County areas by destroying thirty-six small borough franchises, a turn-over of seventy-two seats), North and Burke both opposed him, though Fox was on his side. It speaks for the utter confusion of party labels at this time that even on so vital a matter as fair representation there was no clear cleavage. Pitt was defeated by seventy-four votes and Reform ceased to be a live issue. The reason is obvious. It was the Tories who in early days had pressed for a more equitable distribution of seats, for most of the small boroughs were then Whig. No member with vested personal interests of great social and financial value was readily going to throw away his status and property. The holders of the impeached seats, whether Tory or Whig, would naturally vote for their retention, but such an attitude deprived such of them as were Whigs of their last justification to be a progressive party.

Another cleavage to be deplored arose over the fiscal treatment of Ireland. Pitt was for low mutual tariffs—a proposal most unpopular with the English manufacturers. Indeed Fox, by taking a strong protectionist line, almost won back the industrialists of the north. Finance and Commerce were becoming very powerful in politics and Pitt was forced by his own Cabinet to withdraw. His attempt at Irish conciliation failed; the menace of disharmony within the United Kingdom remained undispelled.

Money had also influenced the making of the French commercial treaty of 1787. Fox, as usual, opposed all contacts with France—it was the old Whig tradition, but the business interests of Manchester merchants, ironmasters, manufacturers generally, and bankers in search of new markets were vocal in the House and out of it—they insisted on trade arrangements and obtained what they desired. No longer were financiers exclusively Whig; a vast creation of new peers, some forty-eight in all during Pitt's administrations before 1790, included many representatives of finance and commerce (among them the first of Jewish descent, Gideon, Lord Eardly), Robert Smith, banker, and others.

But the support of Pitt was not limited to the City. Men of all kinds of belief, tired of Whig faction fights, acknowledged his leadership. The representation of Middlesex—now shared by Wilkes, the erstwhile Radical, and Mainwaring, a King's friend—was typical. Those who wished to see the Court restored to power and those who favoured parliamentary reform alike trusted Pitt; nevertheless, he himself was an isolated and often thwarted statesman—the very multitude and incompatibility of his supporters was a weakness, for there was scarcely anything that some of them wanted which another group would not oppose. In the field of finance alone, the City insisted that he be given a free hand. He abolished many futile and vexatious duties, instituted the Sinking Fund and laid the foundations for the great Victorian budgets. In this department he was well served by Jenkinson at the restored Board of Trade and by Grenville, Pitt's cousin, who, with Eden, piloted through the difficult Anglo-French commercial treaty.

In all this Pitt was in constant consultation with the moneyed interests —they it was who constituted his chief support, but like many another minister who depends upon commercial men, he had to pay for their concurrence.

Despite Pitt's associations, he himself—at any rate in his early days— was a reformer, indeed a more consistent one than Fox; but, as he used sadly to say, "Fox and Coalition had destroyed the Whig Party for ever". In the absence of any strong party organization Pitt, in his dependence on King and City, was never a free agent.

His advocacy of the reform of the Slave Trade, then a test question for religious and progressive minds, exhibited the weakness of his position. Only by two votes and a threat of resignation could he get a very mild measure curtailing the worst excesses of slave dealers through the Lords. It was a Bill, he said, which he wondered that "any human being could resist". In 1791 the House of Commons rejected a motion for the total abolition of the slave trade by nearly a hundred votes, though the promoter was Wilberforce, Pitt's especial friend, and Pitt had supported him. All the Cabinet would do was to say that the slave trade must remain an open question.

When, therefore, the matter is carefully examined it appears that Pitt's very success and general support, while keeping him in office, by no means gave him complete personal power. He was continually beset by obstruction from his own side. On the prosecution of Hastings the Cabinet was divided, though he, the Prime Minister himself, supported the impeachment; only in the regularization of finance, in simplifying the tariff, instituting assessed taxes and inaugurating the office of Comptroller and Auditor-General and in making loans a matter of public tender, was he allowed a free hand.

As to the Indian question, in 1784 a compromise was reached by setting up a Board of Control ruling through the Company, but in 1786 the Governor-General was given civil and military sovereignty. In effect, therefore, Pitt had followed Fox and defeated the East India Company —as Erskine May writes, "the Company were now accountable to Ministers, in their rule . . . the administration of Indian affairs came . . . under the review of Parliament". (*Constitutional History of England* p. 381.)

But soon followed one of those domestic crises which are so much more interesting to the political world than social amelioration—in the autumn of 1788 it was evident that the King's reason was once again deranged and a Regency of some sort had become necessary.

To the Whigs, this was expected to result in the bestowal of power on their patron, the Prince of Wales. Pitt and his friends were not willing to admit that the King's illness was permanent, they wished for delay. It was moved by Pitt to appoint a committee to seek for precedents. Fox, unwisely, opposed this, uttering the most unwhiggish doctrine that the Prince was in law already Regent and that no parliamentary authority was required. The proclamation of this extreme Tory view alarmed the Whigs, and Pitt was quick to satirize them, saying that he would "unwhig Fox"; he certainly did so. He pointed out that the Bill of Rights, the Revolution, the Balance of Power and all the Whig armoury were against Fox's contention. Needless to say the Committee was appointed; it recommended the Regency of the Prince and gave him the power to choose ministers, though not to make life appointments or create peers. Here, it might be thought, the Whigs had gained their point; but Fox elected to fight again, declaring for the Prince's unrestricted power. All this was to deny the rights of Parliament; if Fox were reinstated it would only be as the Prince's nominee—once more circumstances had tempted him to advocate high Tory doctrine. The conduct of Burke was even worse—he mocked at the King and cried that God had hurled him from his throne. Thurlow, as usual, played a double part. On February 19th the King, by recovering, confounded the whole intrigue.

Never had Whig opportunism sunk so low, never had Pitt been so respected; the antics of Burke and the inconsistencies of Fox had raised general disgust. The Prince of Wales, at best, was not a figure likely to command public approval and some of Pitt's supporters, to show the liberality of their minds, were willing to concede a measure of relief to the Dissenters who were now, particularly when wealthy, drifting away from Whiggery.

In 1787 a proposal to repeal the Test and Corporation Acts, surprisingly, came from the Government side of the House to be defeated by eighty votes, and in 1789 the Bill only failed by twenty. Next year, however, it would appear that the French Revolution had inflamed feeling against the Nonconformists, who were still regarded in many quarters as Radical. This time the proposal was attacked not only by nervous Tories but also by Burke. At the General Election in 1790 there was little change in the distribution of parties, but Burke had already begun to disagree with the Foxite opposition on the question of the French Revolution. Hearing of the fall of the Bastille, Burke denounced France as a nation who had "thrown off the yoke of laws and morals". To contrast this with Fox's famous "how much the greatest event which has happened in the world and how much the best", discloses the fissure which was developing in the Opposition.

In February, 1790, Burke, while agreeing with Fox that France was no longer to be feared, deplored his exaltation of the Revolution. Burke's critical *Reflections* on the Revolution sold to the extent of thirty-two thousand copies in a year—it was violently hostile to the new ideas. Fox, on the other hand, still maintained that the French had erected "a glorious edifice of Liberty". Finally, on the Quebec Bill, Burke took

C

occasion to speak disparagingly of "French Principles"—he was attacked rudely by the Foxites and Fox himself accused Burke of "drawing up an indictment against a whole people". On Burke's side there followed total rupture. Even had the Napoleonic Wars not accentuated Whig differences, the dismemberment of the old Party had become inevitable.

CHAPTER III

DEFECTION AND REVIVAL

EVEN if the views about revolutionary France, which Burke expressed with such vehemence, were shared by the great majority of the small class responsible for Government, how far they extended it is not easy to say. In a House of Commons of which it had been said in 1793 that the majority was elected by less than fifteen thousand electors, it was not easy to collect the national opinion. One hundred and seventy-two members were directly and one hundred and thirty-seven indirectly returned by the Government or by private patrons; in Scotland forty-five members were elected at the will of even less voters; and in Ireland, after 1801, when one hundred members were added to the Imperial Parliament, fifty-one were returned by thirty-six peers and twenty members by as many commoners. When war came, of course, other considerations arose, but it would be an error to suppose that, before that time, Pitt or the gentry in general accepted without qualification the alarms and diatribes of Burke; indeed, if anything, it would appear that at first the Prime Minister was relieved by the outbreak of the French Revolution as tending to weaken England's hereditary enemy, and such a view was by no means confined to him.

The refusal of the new French Government to honour the Bourbon pact with Spain compelled that country to abandon her claims on Canada and thus perhaps prevented war. It was overlooked by Burke that the King of France was in secret covenant with foreign princes to overthrow the Government, and that the Prussian commander had gone so far as to threaten the Parisians on behalf of Louis. How far the Revolution might have been limited to the institution of constitutional government if the foreign Kings had not threatened to intervene it is difficult to decide. At any rate, England cannot be held responsible for the ensuing war. So confident indeed was Pitt of peace that, as late as 1792, the national defences were being reduced. Not until the French broke into the Netherlands did England become involved.

Thereafter, the country being committed to war, different considerations arose. Speculations as to forms of government which had formerly been discussed with tranquillity now assumed a treasonable complexion, but it was not the Conservative theory of Burke, but the menace of Napoleon which had moved public opinion. To emphasize the outrages committed in France now became good propaganda. The very proletarians turned against their radical champions; so discreet and learned a Liberal as Priestly, the scientist, suffered the destruction of his library at the hands of the mob at Birmingham. Lord Stanhope, a sympathizer with the French revolutionaries, had his London house wrecked by the patriotic rabble. Never has a pacifist, however much he may formerly have served the people, been popular during a war. The rejection of Bright by Manchester during the Crimean hostilities is not unique. The contrast in treatment accorded to the bellicose Wilkes and the peaceful Priestly is but an example of almost universal experience.

The Tories, who by this time had united in an opposition to all new ideas and many old ones, found their completest expression in the "anti-Jacobin". All the recent romantic sensibility, for the poor, for slaves, and for animals was lampooned; like the fascists of our time, the Tory journal derided Reason and Philosophy, Peace and Fraternity, as dangerous nonsense.

Now that Napoleon was overrunning Europe, even libertarians such as Coleridge relented of their earlier enthusiasm for the Revolutionaries; Wordsworth followed a similar course. The effect in politics of this division among leaders of artistic and philosophic thought who were formerly of one mind was to cause the old Whigs, as Burke called them, to look wistfully to Pitt and his friends as the real defenders of freedom against the Corsican Tyrant.

Eventually Portland, who for so long had followed Fox, took fright, and after much indecision sought a coalition with the Government. In 1794 he became Home Secretary; the Whig Windham, Secretary for War, while Spencer went to the Admiralty. Another seceder, Loughborough, had led the way by becoming Chancellor under Pitt in 1793.

As so often happens when men leave one party to join another, the coalition Whigs become the most vehement supporters of that which formerly they had opposed. They were as ready as any Tory to suppress meetings, to persecute opinion and to fight against Catholic emancipation —the religion of most of the French refugees. Lord Malmesbury, in his memoirs, tells how he worked to strengthen the anti-Foxites. By their very zeal for reaction the governmental Whigs strengthened Fox among his friends and paved the way for an aggressive Radicalism.

Meanwhile the position of Fox became ever more critical and difficult. Apart from his few loyal friends, such as the Duke of Bedford, the Whigs on the whole disliked the Radical associations which, now that war was raging, trod the narrow path between opposition and treason. The leaders, seeing the position to be impossible, recommended that the remaining opposition Whigs should retire from Parliament. This time Fox agreed, as also did Erskine, their principal lawyer. Lord Holland as a young man was present at the first meeting to decide the best method of secession. (*Memoire*, I, p. 86.) The whole policy of abstention was opposed by Lord Guildford and General Fitzpatrick and finally it was agreed that Grey should move for parliamentary reform as a last venture. When the debate came on Pitt declared that he was still in favour, but thought the times unpropitious as it was "pressed by those who would overthrow all". Such insults were then common form; Burke implored the House to reject the motion—he had always been against Reform, but now he added an appeal to "fly from the French Constitution". Windham, the governmental Whig, joined Burke in the Opposition. On a subsequent vote against the Aliens Bill the minority was fifty strong—this was the full extent of effective Whig opposition at the time. Nevertheless, Sheridan and Tierney, with Lord Lansdowne, wished to continue the fight, but Fox adhered to his resolution to withdraw; after a momentary return in December, 1797, he did not come back to Parliament until the new century.

The occasion for this one appearance arose out of a suggestion of peace from Bonaparte. Pitt himself appears to have favoured negotiations. Life was disturbed; as early as 1795 the mob, pelting the King on his way to open Parliament, had cried: "Peace! Bread! No famine!" In 1797 the fear of invasion and the failure of many provincial banks had compelled the Government to prohibit the directors of the Bank of England from paying their notes in cash, and for more than twenty years a paper currency was in circulation—it fell in value and the labourers, by the subsequent inflation, were the poorer. But rents and profits rose quickly—apart from the workers, only the annuitants suffered —the manufacturers, as a whole, still supported the war, and the mercantile interest (the chief asset of the Whigs) was henceforth undependable.

Outside the parliamentary circle, however, a new Radicalism was asserting itself. Immense open-air meetings were organized by the Corresponding Society and other associations; mutiny broke out in the Navy, and the Government, who had compelled Pitt to continue the war, persuaded him that the only method of suppressing agitation was to render it illegal. To excite hatred of the King or Constitution was made punishable by transportation. To hold meetings of more than fifty persons without a licence from a magistrate, and to make speeches or give lectures without authority was declared to be unlawful sedition. Against these repressive measures and a further Act which suppressed the Corresponding Societies, by name, and declared all unlicensed clubs for debating to be disorderly houses, the small Whig remnant struggled in vain. It would appear that, by the end of the century, nearly all liberty of expression had been lost.

Pitt, liberal when not alarmed by fear of the French, had long favoured religious toleration. In pressing for a Union with Ireland he had gone far to promise his Catholic supporters in that country a measure of concession. The unreliable Loughborough, who had learnt that the King was violently hostile to the abolition of sacramental tests, now veered round and although heretofore an advocate of religious liberty became a supporter of the royal prejudice. The question of the Coronation Oath, which the half-mad King thought must prevent him from ever granting any relief, was skilfully used by the Archbishop of Canterbury to inflame his mind. The Chief Justice, Kenyon, and Scott, the Attorney-General, had, very honestly, told George that the admission of Catholics to Parliament would not contradict his oath; but George preferred to accept the opinion of Loughborough that "the Coronation Oath was understood, at the Revolution, to bind the Crown not to assent to a repeal of any of the existing laws for the maintenance of the Protestant Religion as by law established". (*Thoughts on the Emancipation of Roman Catholics of Ireland and dangers arising therefrom, March 4th*, 1795.) The King passed this opinion on to Pitt; and Lord Fitzwilliam, who was then negotiating for Union on the basis of emancipation, was recalled.

There followed the Irish insurrection of 1798, and the need for Parlia-

mentary Union, in Pitt's view, became insistent, though Fox was still
opposed to it. The Prime Minister, it appears, had given assurances to
the Catholics of which the King was ignorant—the Cabinet were divided,
the ex-Whig, Portland, opposed, while Windham, Grenville, Dundas,
Camden and Spencer supported the Premier. Loughborough, being in
attendance on the King at Weymouth at the end of September, 1800,
had learned what was proposed. With the help of the Archbishop of
Canterbury he worked upon the King, sending George his objections,
so that when Pitt proposed to the Monarch his project for Irish Catholic
Emancipation the mind of the King was already made up. In January,
1801, Pitt refused to agree that he should abstain "from ever speaking
on the subject"; instead, he offered to resign and did so on February 5th
—George, in his old manner, declaring that "he should consider any
person who voted for the measure as personally indisposed to himself"
—a pitiful roar from the fast-decaying old lion.

For the moment, however, the King had his way—High Anglican
Toryism was now triumphant and the insignificant Addington became
Prime Minister; notwithstanding the treachery of Loughborough, an
ultra-Tory, Eldon, received the Great Seal. . . . As on Reform, Pitt
had been defeated by his friends, so now he was forced to abandon the
project of religious toleration. Yet though there were many misgivings
at the change, when the new Prime Minister negotiated a peace with
Napoleon in March, 1802, Pitt discussed with Addington every article of
it; in reality he still controlled foreign policy, though at home he had
refused to support the religious bigotry of the King.

This generous support of the Prime Minister by Pitt was unpopular,
it was felt that in so critical a time the change of ministers was unjustified.
In the principal business of the Government, however, the negotiation of
peace with Napoleon, Pitt took an active part, being, as has been said,
consulted as to every stage. In October, 1802, the discussions which had
been going on since March were concluded and the peace was signed.
"Experimental but unavoidable" was the description of it given by the
King. The Grenville Whigs, as they were now called, objected; Fox and
Sheridan of course welcomed the end of the hostilities which they had
throughout opposed.

In the House a resolution was passed thanking Pitt for his "great
and important services to his country". Canning pressed Addington,
the Prime Minister, to resign in his favour, but Pitt himself, who was ill,
objected to such intervention on his behalf—indeed the only effect of it
was to cause Pitt to refuse any longer to advise the Government.

At the end of 1802, Grenville in Parliament directly called for Pitt's
return and Canning declared him to be the only "commanding spirit"
who could deal with the French. The renewal of war in May, 1803,
increased the universal demand for Pitt; even Fox joined in the attack
upon Addington. The former admiration of Fox for Napoleon (he had
visited him in Paris during the short peace) was dissipated when that
perfidious schemer, contrary to his word, refused to evacuate Malta or
Holland. The Whig leader now went so far as to declare that the French
had acted infamously—as a consequence, when Pitt resumed office, he
felt able to ask Fox to help him in the prosecution of the War.

The King, however, was obdurate. He declared that if Pitt thought of it, he would not employ him. Fox's past visit to Napoleon, "a damned imprudent act" as Creevy commented, had also annoyed many of his former supporters, now enemies of French aggression, such as Coleridge. "Mr. Fox is excluded by the express command of the King", wrote the Sovereign to Addington. Pitt, promising to drop Catholic relief, became Prime Minister again in May, 1804, but as the military situation deteriorated Pitt again asked for a coalition; again the King refused, when Trafalgar saved the Government. At last, after Austerlitz, Pitt died, and the King sent for Portland, who was still sufficiently a Whig to say that he would not serve without Fox. This time the King yielded; the Ministry of all the Talents, as it was called, was formed with Fox as *de facto* leader—his office being that of Foreign Secretary. Immediately his Liberal influence was felt and he was pressing for Catholic emancipation and the abolition of the slave trade when he died. "At this time", writes Lord Holland (*Memoirs*, II, p. 75), "we might have had a separate peace, but it would have been of short duration"; in the event negotiations failed and the Government were censured by Whitebread, a brother-in-law of Grey, for their failure.

Whitebread was one of the first Radicals to censure his more conservative colleagues, but Holland, Fox's devoted nephew, and many other of the young men were also out of sympathy with the elder Whigs; to strengthen himself, Grenville approached Canning, a "left wing Tory". The Catholic question was again insistent, and the young reformers wished to give to the Papists who had the right in Ireland, a power to hold the King's commission everywhere. Howick introduced a Bill to this effect, the King saying "not one step further". On the other side Addington, now Lord Sidmouth, opposed all Catholic liberation—he was also against the emancipation of the slaves and had the support generally of the more obdurate Tories. Lord Eldon, a close friend of the King, was also of this way of thinking—indeed at all times he was against all change whatever. These reactionaries and their associates forced the Cabinet to withdraw the measure enabling Catholics generally to hold commissions, but the younger men, led by Canning, were becoming restless. His rival, Castlereagh, had taken office under Addington, but both were now back in Portland's government, the former being Treasurer of the Navy, Castlereagh President of the Board of Control. As their policies diverged, their personal relations became more strained, and when Canning sought to have Castlereagh removed from the War Office his action resulted in a duel. Before this, in March, 1809, Canning had tendered his resignation, and now it was found that the whole Ministry had been jeopardized by the scandal; Portland, who was infirm, retired, and a dispute arose between Perceval—who led the Commons—and Canning who should be the chief. Canning, disappointed at not receiving first place, withdrew from the Government, to be out of office for seven years; not until 1816 did he accept the comparatively lowly position of President of the Board of Trade. Meanwhile Perceval, after suggesting that he was willing to serve under a peer, Grenville or Grey, was appointed Premier. Canning was altogether excluded and Wellesley followed him at the Foreign Office. Canning was suspected of favouring Catholic emancipation, and although he had proved of great value by discovering the designs of Napoleon on Denmark and perhaps first saw the advantage of attacking the French in the Peninsula, he had aimed too high. When Perceval was assassinated in 1812, Liverpool became Premier, Castlereagh being willing to yield it to him, Canning being again offered the Foreign Office. Once more he refused unless he might lead the House as well—a proposal which was not entertained. His extreme ambition seemed for the time to have destroyed his chances.

Whatever may be thought of the character of Canning, there can be no doubt that his retirement from Government on the death of Portland removed from the administration its last liberalizing element. The general situation was deplorable. Napoleon was still master of Europe. At home, after debate on the Walcheron disaster, Gale Jones of the Corresponding Society, against the will of Canning, had been imprisoned for placarding London in protest against the exclusion of Press and Public; and Burdett followed this up by an attack on the House —he called it a "Whited wall"—to his electors in Westminster. The Government decided to send him to the Tower, but he entrenched himself in his house and was ultimately seized, to the great advertisement of Radicalism. Many towns petitioned for his release; another Wilkes' movement seemed on its way, and this time in the midst of a great war in which the country was in extreme peril. In these circumstances, Canning again was offered employment; again he declined anything but the Foreign Office, together with the restoration of his friend, Huskisson, also an "advanced" Tory.

The Combination Acts of 1800 had made it criminal for working people to combine in Unions—at the same time the old Elizabethan method of fixing minimum wages by the Justices had become obsolete and attempts in Parliament generally to restore statutory wages had been defeated. Despite the efforts of Brougham, in the 1807 election, to fill "every bookseller's shop with pamphlets and provide copy for all the newspapers to enforce the measures of or expose the adversaries of the Whigs" (Holland, *Memoirs*, II, p. 227), the active opposition returned numbered only some twenty, over whom the very timorous "Grenvillite", Ponsonby, had no control at all. Brougham and his friends (he had been returned in 1810) argued for an early peace, universal education, reform of law and of prisons, and for the abolition of the Slave Trade and flogging in the Army. They had abandoned the old protectionist "Mercantile System" and, under the influence of Adam Smith and Bentham, were now rapidly passing to a belief in Individualism. Burdett and Cochrane had been returned for Westminster and were ready for any innovation. Wardle, who had made it his particular business to attack the Duke of York as Commander-in-Chief, especially for granting army commissions on the solicitation of his mistress, succeeded in forcing the Duke to resign his office. The "Mountain", as the advanced Whigs were called, included Whitebread, Mackintosh, Weston and Creevy—they were the only Whigs who received any support from the Radicals outside the House. Despite the paucity of their numbers, Brougham and his colleagues managed to get a Bill through making Slave Trading criminal. Moreover, by his eloquence that fiery lawyer had forced the Government to withdraw the "Orders in Council" which provided, in his words, "that no vessel should enter a French port without having touched at one in Great Britain". By this achievement he pleased the merchants and hoped as a consequence to be returned for Liverpool. Other influences there, however, were too strong and from 1812 to 1815 he was without a seat in Parliament.

In 1811 the King had become permanently insane and the Prince of Wales, by statute, was appointed Regent. Perceval had wished to impose the restrictions on him which had been suggested in 1788. Sheridan, the only Whig with whom the Prince had remained in contact, was for taking the same attitude as Fox had formerly held and, in the end, as the Whig Lords would not give him that support which he expected, the Regent decided to make no change in Government. He would have welcomed a coalition, but the Whigs would not join the Administration unless Ireland were granted Catholic relief. Castlereagh became Foreign Secretary, and the reactionary Sidmouth was soon made Secretary of Home Affairs. On the death of Perceval, Lord Liverpool— the negotiator of the Treaty of Amiens—was appointed Prime Minister, an office he held for fifteen years.

During the earlier part of this period the industries of the country were at a standstill. America had declared war and there was practically no international trade. Riots of unemployed and starving people were endemic. Wellesley, before resigning, had complained that his brother was insufficiently supported in Spain, and the Whigs and Radicals, in despair of any constructive betterment, came to concentrate on the alleged grievances of the Princess Caroline as a means to attack the Regent and discredit the Government. A scandal with regard to the custody of the Princess Charlotte added to the excitement. Even the abdication of Napoleon did nothing to restore the popularity of George, who was hooted in the streets, and the Administration was nearly as distracted as the Opposition.

From the end of the war, for some eight years the country was in a state of unprecedented distress for which the reactionary Government of Lord Liverpool had no remedy except to attempt to allay discontent by suppression. The middle classes took alarm at the destruction of machinery and the burning of ricks by the under-paid and unemployed labourers. Those who supported any claim for social improvement were stigmatized as Radicals—their position was possibly worse in the estimation of the respectable than that of the Communists between the two Great Wars. "It was an awful period", says Sidney Smith, "for those who ventured to maintain Liberal opinions." The reformers, in their defence, formed societies and clubs, lawful and illicit, under the leadership of Owen, Spence, Cobbett, Hunt, Thistlewood and others.

Notwithstanding the fact that the country was at peace, the Government sought in their notorious "Six Mile Acts" to crush all reformative movements. The time was "like a history of civil war". (*The Skilled Labourer*, Hammond, Introduction.) The garden, ale and Sunday leisure which the workman had formerly enjoyed were threatened by the new factory system. His wife now had to work in the mills, his children also. Long working days and night toil were becoming general. Industries which had been artificially stimulated during the long hostilities were collapsing and few new ones were to be found. For all this the Government had no remedy but further prosecution and repressive law. Grenville and the old Whigs on the whole supported the Prime Minister;

even Tierney and Brougham had to walk with care, for, as Sidney Smith wrote, "it was safer to be a felon than a reformer". Nevertheless, though he might deny that he was one, Brougham, on his return to Parliament, of necessity became the real leader of the Parliamentary Radicals. He protested against the passage of the Act preventing public meetings not controlled by magistrates or Lords-Lieutenant. This measure was calculated to deprive the people of their last redress, as Lord Holland vainly protested in the Lords; in the result came the crowd of fifty thousand demonstrators at Manchester with its Yeomanry charges and Thistlewood's plot to assassinate the Cabinet. Brougham saw clearly that the only hope to avoid general violence lay in the revival of a Whig party with a progressive programme.

The times were not propitious; in the absence of franchise reform it was scarcely possible to bring new blood into the House. An attempt to establish connection between the discordant Whig elements was made through Lambton (later Lord Durham), who shared Brougham's opinions, and had married Lord Grey's daughter. To placate the centre Whigs, Brougham now very definitely dissociated himself from the intransigents of the left. It is curious to note that the first Whig victory, in 1816, was to throw out an income tax as "inquisitorial".

Next year the fight against the Government prosecutions of reformers brought Grey, Tierney, Lambton and Holland to Brougham's side, and the secession of so many of the Whig magnates under Grenville to the Government helped Brougham to form—out of the remainder—the elements of a Liberal Party. On the death of the ineffectual Ponsonby, Tierney, with the support of Romilly and Brougham, had been chosen to be Leader, but he proved useless as a means to co-ordinate the remaining Whigs and the "Mountain". The more conservative Whigs hoped, without further reform, for office through Tory divisions, while the Radicals, now fully persuaded of the need for a progressive programme, pressed for the abolition of trade restrictions and thus had succeeded in enlisting the sympathy of the manufacturers and merchants, who, now that agitation was dying down, were beginning once more to take a liberal view of affairs. The Radical policy of reduction of expenditure was another "plank" which appealed to the City; but, above all things, their scheme for providing the middle classes with votes, and so of control of Parliament, had the most unifying effect. It would curb aristocratic privilege while giving no power to the labouring classes; it was inexpensive, and gratifying in its promise of increased power to the growing great "respectable" bourgeois class which for a century was to determine public opinion.

But politics are ever the sport of the unexpected. In January, 1820, the old King died, and almost at once, on the insistence of George IV, came the Bill, introduced in the Lords, to deprive the Queen of her position as Consort. Canning, one of the most potent of the progressive Tories, resigned in order to dissociate himself from the Divorce Bill. Again the people, excited by the Radicals and the speeches of Brougham before the Lords, rallied round the somewhat sordid figure of the Queen, as their only means of expressing discontent. This uninteresting, foolish woman had proved the means which brought Whigs, Liberals and Radicals into one fold. In the Lords, a third reading only obtaining a very small

C*

majority, the Government, not unwillingly, abandoned the Bill and the King was reduced to the petty expedient of refusing his spouse admission to his Coronation. But the work had been done; an unfortunate foreign woman's matrimonial troubles had united those political elements which the skill and intelligence of Brougham had for so long vainly been seeking to reconcile.

In August, 1822, Castlereagh, one of the most hated of the Government, killed himself. The King was angry with Liverpool for his failure in the Divorce matter and the Administration was visibly weakening. Again the obliging Grenville was called in for consultation and talk of Canning being used to renew a coalition was bruited.

But the Catholic question, which had upset so many plans, was at length arising in inescapable form. In 1821, Plunket had moved for Emancipation, Canning supporting him, though Peel, who had moved into Canning's place, opposed. Nevertheless, the third reading was carried. In the Lords the Bill was only rejected by thirty-one votes. Clearly the question demanded solution.

By this time trade was recovering and a general easing of tension was evident in which a mild Liberalism might hope to thrive. The return of Canning to the leadership of the House after the death of Castlereagh inaugurated a new policy. Huskisson at the Board of Trade, and Robinson at the Exchequer, provided the Government with great financial ability of that new mentality which accepted the principles of Adam Smith. Ricardo, the economist, who had entered Parliament in 1819, had now great influence. He had even suggested, capitalist as he was, the paying off of the war debt by a Property Tax and had formulated a law of rent, critical of land holding, which had the result of drawing attention to the enrichment of the great estate owners caused by heavy corn duties. Rent, he declared, was only the surplus profit which any given land, either from the convenience of situation or from the fertility of the soil, yields over the worst land in cultivation. The landlords, in other words, appropriated the surplus profits—a very congenial doctrine for tenant manufacturers and shop people. It is not suggested that the full import of these ideas was understood, even by advanced Radicals, but their very appearance in print pointed to a new outlook in economic affairs. A middle class policy, hostile to the pretensions of the old landlords, concerned for the removal of restrictions in trade, tolerant of variety of religious belief, and, to a point, desirous even of smoother relations with labour, is discernible. In 1824 and 1825 the Combination Laws were amended and workmen's associations became lawful. In 1824 there arose disputes whether the statutory wage-fixing powers for the Spitalfield weavers and other craftsmen should be repealed. It is to be noted that the Radical individualists, such as Ricardo and Hume, were for depriving the workmen of statutory protection, and the whole question of the legality of Trade and Labour combinations came up for review. Huskisson, for the Government, supported Hume's proposal for a general enquiry. Chiefly as the result of the labour of Place, the Commission recommended the repeal of the Combination Laws; only where threats of violence existed should either employer or workman be deprived of the right to "employ his labour or capital as he may deem most advantageous". After the passing of the Bill there were many strikes and the total repeal was modified the next year. Threats to induce a workman to leave his employment were now made specifically illegal and the Courts and lawyers, not for the last time, settled down to a long argument as to the extent of the legalizations and prohibitions; still, the old general veto against workmen's combinations was gone and Trade Unions rapidly increased in numbers and membership. Under the influence of the new philosophy, voluntary association came to be preferred to State activity.

Meetings in general were once more made lawful, and restriction in trade discouraged; duties on importation were reduced in number, and raw material allowed in many cases to enter free of tax. The Corn Law of 1815 had, in effect, prohibited all importation and a new duty decreasing as the price rose was recommended—a sliding scale. This method was carried, despite the insistence of Ricardo on a fixed small duty; if the price rose to eighty-five shillings a quarter the duty was only to be a shilling.

Next was undertaken the question of retrenchment. In this, the Radical Hume was the pioneer: he obtained a reduction of the number of receivers of land tax and their remuneration by fixed salary and not by poundage; he pressed successfully for the reduction of the service and other votes. The malt and agricultural horse tax were repealed on the motion of Western, in both cases against the wish of the Government; the Ministry was again in difficulties and was subject to constant reverses.

One cause of their difficulties was that both Canning and Peel were now outside the Government. On the retirement of Sidmouth, Peel went to the Home Office and a small group of the old Whigs came in with Lord Buckingham, created a Duke for his services in the matter. When Parliament met in 1822, the Opposition still clamoured for economies and in several cases defeated the Government. Both in the demand for reduction of taxation and for economy the Ministry had to yield to public opinion. Yet one thing was needed, the presence in Government of the brilliant Canning. The King, who had before refused him office, was reconciled—to Canning's annoyance he said that he would forgive him for his sympathy for the Queen. Canning at length consented to become Foreign Secretary and brought Huskisson to the Board of Trade and Robinson to the Exchequer—the Government had been greatly strengthened; the days of Eldonian Toryism were over.

Reforms followed fast; capital punishment was abolished save for murder and a few treasonable offences. Romilly's long advocacy had been rewarded though he did not look to see its consummation; but Mackintosh, an old law reformer, with the support of Peel in 1823 carried through both Houses four statutes "exempting from capital punishment about an hundred felonies". Eldon, though still on the Woolsack, was ignored. Other legislation of 1823 included the reform of the marriage law, the substitution of Reciprocity for Protection in Navigation, and the reorganization of the Sinking Fund—all these reforms being due to the activity of Canning, Peel and Huskisson in Government and to the disinterested support of the progressive Whigs; it was the old Tories who had most reason to complain.

The year 1824 was one of trade revival; cash payments were resumed and, as is so often the case, an era of reckless speculation followed. The Bank of England was reduced to very small reserves of bullion and asked to be allowed again to suspend cash payments; all the relief they could obtain was leave to issue £1 notes—in all, seventy-four banks failed and thousands of gamblers were ruined. Yet, under the new libertarian economic theory, the Government, influenced by Huskisson, refused to take any active part in the salvage.

By now, only one-third of the population were working on the land and the commercial influence was ever strengthening. The manufacturers persuaded Huskisson and Canning again to attempt to lower the corn law duties, but in the midst of this dispute with the landed interest the Prime Minister was incapacitated by a stroke—for a time the Government went on without him, and on Canning's suggestion corn was to be imported free when it was at seventy shillings. Tory and Radical proposals respectively to raise and lower this standard were both defeated; all this time the country was without a Prime Minister.

The delay was due to the fact that the King wanted Canning, but did not want to emancipate the Catholics—it was a dilemma; during the interregnum Burdett had only failed by four votes in the Commons to carry a Catholic resolution—on Parliamentary reform, on the other hand, Canning was an irreconcilable opponent and this prevented him from obtaining the support of Grey and the Whigs. There was talk of some alternative Tory government which alarmed both Whigs and Radicals; they saw a return of the old gang—Eldon, Wellington and their school.

At length, on April 10, 1827, Canning was appointed to be Premier; at once Peel resigned, together with Eldon, both ostensibly on the Catholic question. There followed Wellington, Bathurst, Melville, Westmoreland and Bexley—almost the whole Government. Harrowby, Wynn and the two financial experts, Huskisson and Robinson, remained loyal to Canning.

Many of the Whigs, on the other hand, were willing to give him support. They agreed with him on Catholic relief, they approved his general attitude at home and abroad; only on electoral reform were they seriously divided—indeed, even then Grey alone was seriously opposed to an alliance; Lansdowne, Tierney, Holland and last, but most important, Brougham, supported some understanding. Robinson went to the Lords as Gooderich and became leader, Sturges Bourne was appointed Home Secretary, Canning himself taking the Exchequer, while Palmerston went to the War, Lord Dudley to the Foreign Office. Copley was made Lord Chancellor—taking the title of Lyndhurst.

A fierce Tory attack when Parliament met induced some Whigs to go to Canning's assistance; Lansdowne and Tierney both joined him, but Grey was still obdurate—a crisis soon came over the Corn Bill. This measure passed the Commons, but Wellington in the Lords had carried an amendment raising the minimum price for free foreign importation. On this Canning withdrew the whole Bill and shortly afterwards, on August 8th, died. What was feared by the Progressives had come about; after Gooderich had vainly sought to form a Government, the Duke of Wellington succeeded as Prime Minister.

It was the expressed desire of the Duke, who was wholly unacquainted with all the literary and speculative ferment which divided the times from those of his youth, that "Liberalism should be got rid of forever"; unfortunately for his desire, Peel told him at their first interview that the Canningites at least must be invited to come in if a stable government was to be formed. The key man was Huskisson; the Whigs implored him to go into Opposition, but he was induced to take the Colonial Office. The other leading friends of Canning, Palmerston, Dudley and Lamb, also came into Government; Peel returned to the Home Office and Aberdeen appears as Chancellor of the Duchy of Lancaster. Some old Tories complained, the Duke of Newcastle objected to the omission of Eldon, but for the most part they were jubilant. Huskisson's statement that Wellington would tread in the "footsteps of Canning" was interpreted as a pledge that free trade should be continued, but Wellington denied any such undertaking. The position from the outset was unstable. In the Commons a motion to emancipate Dissenters by repealing the now obsolete Test and Corporation Acts was carried against the Government by 237 to 193, and a compromise amendment, asking that a declaration should be made not to subvert the Protestant Established Church, was added to the Bill. In the Lords the words "on the faith of a Christian" were added to the declaration. The effect was to exclude the Jews and atheists, though it is doubtful if such a consequence was thought of at that time.

Ten days after, Burdett again brought the Catholic relief question before the Commons; this time he had a majority in his favour of six. After a conference between the Houses, in the Lords the hostile majority fell to forty-four, but what was more significant, instead of vehement opposition, both the Prime Minister and the Chancellor spoke in compromising terms. On the disfranchisement of East Retford for bribery, disputes broke out in the Cabinet as to what should be done with the seat. The old Tories were for throwing the electors into the adjacent county, the Canningites wished to give the constituency to a large town. On this, in the Commons Huskisson and Palmerston voted with the Liberals and Peel was defeated.

Thereafter Huskisson offered his resignation; to his surprise it was promptly accepted. The effect was momentous for later political history in that Palmerston, Lamb (afterwards Lord Melbourne) and the other Canningites followed him into Opposition. Aberdeen became Foreign Secretary in place of Dudley.

But the Catholic question would not rest; in Ireland after great disorders the Catholic Association had practically taken control of the country. The Duke's scheme was to suppress it and to enfranchise the Catholics simultaneously. He prevailed on Peel to support emancipation and in the end even persuaded the King. In February 1828 it was known that emancipation was in the Government programme. The Tories were disheartened and inclined to be mutinous, but after threats of abdication by the King and resignation by the Duke, the Bill came before the Lords, where the Prime Minister commended it as a means of staving off civil war. This was after a committee had recommended that only the offices of Lord Chancellor and Lord Lieutenant of Ireland should still be withheld. The former great office, despite recent protests in Parliament, is still denied to those who will not take oaths against Transubstantiation, the Invocation of Saints and the sacrifice of the Mass. (*Judgment Reserved*, Slesser, p. 194.)

The change-over was very sudden. On December 11th the Duke, addressing the Catholic Archbishop of Armagh as "Dear Sir", had said that he "saw no prospect of a settlement—Party had been so mixed up with it". A month later Peel told Croker, a subordinate member of the Government, that he was converted.

The majority in favour in the Commons on third reading was one hundred and seventy-eight; in the Lords, the Anglican Eldon, already infuriated by the Repeal of the Test and Corporation Acts, indicated his intention of undertaking even more vehement opposition to the Catholic Bill; he was as good as his word—he presented many hostile petitions; on every line he fought Lyndhurst and Wellington. Nevertheless, on April 2nd, on second reading, he was defeated by one hundred and five; on the third reading the voting was two hundred and thirteen to one hundred. Next day Eldon wrote to his daughter: "The fatal Bills received the Royal Assent yesterday afternoon. God Bless us and His Church!" So ended an age-long dispute. The Irish had saved their co-religionists from further unjust discrimination, but the general growing approval of toleration had done its part. The only criticism was, as Lord Shaftesbury said of the Ministry, "We are not the men to do it".

The real victory lay with the Radicals, who were now a force to be reckoned with, more particularly in the bad times which were approaching. Both manufacture and agriculture were again smitten. Great talk of Unions for labourers alarmed the middle classes, who, none the less, were pressing to take part in government. The death of Canning had made the position of his followers very unsatisfactory; like the Whigs, they had seen their policy of Catholic Emancipation carried by one whom everybody had regarded as a reactionary—Wellington—but until the King died in June no one seemed very anxious to displace him. Meanwhile, under Brougham's direction, the Whigs and Radicals were busy organizing themselves for battle. On the death of Tierney, forty of them had asked the moderate Althorp to be their leader in the Commons and Brougham and Lord John Russell had agreed.

In the absence of any other immediate policy, it became the desire of the Opposition to seek to introduce Canningites and Whigs into Government. Catholic Emancipation had lost the Prime Minister the support of the old Tories and it was thought that he might look with more favour on a centre party. The excitement caused by the attack of the King of France and Polignac on the constitution in France had helped the Whigs. Brougham himself, at the General Election, was returned as a Knight of the Shire for the county of York—a great victory, and, in the Lords, the French King's plot having been defeated, Grey spoke of "our duty to secure our institutions by introducing a temperate Parliamentary Reform". To the general surprise the Duke was obdurate, saying that "the representation of the people at present contains a large body of the property of the country in which the landed interests have a preponderating influence. Under the circumstances, I am not prepared to bring forward a measure of this nature, but will at once declare that, so far as I am concerned, I shall feel it my duty to resist such measures when proposed by others".

This unqualified refusal made all further co-operation between Tory and Whig impossible, and the Opposition in the Commons from this time onwards set out to remove the Prime Minister. On November 15th, a motion for a committee on the Civil List was carried against the Government by twenty-nine votes—next day they resigned and the new King sent for Grey, who took office on condition only that Electoral Reform should be a Cabinet question. The Sovereign agreed, and a new era in politics began.

It is essential, if subsequent developments are to be understood, that it should be realized that, at this time, outside the circle of Radicalism, the idea of general democracy formed no part of prevailing progressive opinion. What rather was sought was an harmonious balance of conflicting interests—a notion which early instruction in the *Politics* of Aristotle would make very familiar to the educated, who alone had charge of affairs. To accomplish this end, both Whigs and Tories bent their minds for many years. To enfranchise the illiterate masses, it was generally thought, would be to overthrow the political equilibrium and give to the class least fit to exercise it a preponderating power. It is not necessary, here, to quote the many opinions from all quarters which gave expression to this idea. Not until the later Liberal days of Gladstone was any other outlook accepted, even by many who called themselves advanced. The long opposition by some Liberals to the enfranchisement of women show how late they were to accept the prevailing modern idea of equal electoral rights.

The view, however, that Parliament should be controlled in one form or another by external opinion was, perhaps, the strongest feature of eighteenth-century Radicalism; a name, according to Harriet Martineau, first definitely assumed in 1819. In 1830 there had been constituted in Birmingham, one of the large cities which had no representation, a Political Union, in the words of Huskisson, "with subscriptions, funds, meetings, discussions and its great agitator". The agitator he mentioned was Attwood, who subsequently became the City's first member. Their proceedings were imitated in other large towns, and in October, 1831, in the middle of the fight in Parliament, there was formed a National Political Union with its headquarters in London. The Union passed into the hands of extremists who demanded universal suffrage, but this was what the respectable classes would never concede. In the end, when the fight was won, the 1832 Act had only added about half a million electors in a population of over sixteen millions. As Sir John Marriott has said, "the Reform Act broke the principle of aristocracy without admitting that of democracy". (*England since Waterloo*, p. 101.) "The general result was to place the borough representation in the hands of shopkeepers, and the county representation into those of landlords and farmers." (*Political History of England*, Brodrick, 1801–1837, p. 306.) Even such Radicals as James Mill would have limited the franchise to men with £100 a year. He argued that working men (who rarely then earned that sum) would follow "the intelligence of that virtuous rank with which they come most immediately in contact". (*Essay on Government*, p. 32.)

What really was affected was the character of the representative the new electorate favoured. Brilliant clubmen, young aristocrats and, above all, ambitious statesmen found it more difficult to be returned. Members were now required, to quote Spender, "to be of character and solid worth, sober, judging, sound men, trained in Quarter Sessions, men who knew all about money and credit, who were sufficiently well endowed to be removed from temptation, and had enough other employments to render them free from all suspicion of being professional politicians". (*The Public Life*, I, p. 27.) As Bagehot declared, "The object of the 1832 Bill was to transfer the predominant influence in the State from special classes to the general aggregate of fairly instructed men" (*Parliamentary Reform*); even as late as 1859 Bagehot wrote that Liberals "would have been shocked to hear themselves called democrats"—in 1832 the objection would have been even greater.

To pass to the actual reform proceedings, it has been shown how, both before and after the long Tory reaction, proposals had been brought before Parliament for the redistribution of constituencies and enlargement of the franchise. Lord John Russell, who subsequently piloted the Reform Act through the Commons, had raised the matter in 1820, moderately asking that towns found guilty of corruption should have their seats transferred to larger cities, and in 1821 he renewed the motion. Next year he suggested the addition of a hundred members for the counties and big towns, each of a hundred small boroughs to lose one member. He was defeated by one hundred and five votes, but nevertheless received the largest support which Reformers had obtained for a long time.

In 1826, Russell, who had now made the subject his own, again pressed for Reform, and in 1830 a direct proposal to enfranchise Leeds, Manchester and Birmingham was only lost by forty-eight votes. At the same time the limit of his ambition was shown when he and Brougham alike opposed a motion of O'Connell for Universal Male Suffrage and the Ballot, in which that Radical could only get thirteen members to support him.

So stood the matter at the time of the dissolution. Lord John was now in office and, as the Cabinet were in disagreement as to details, a small committee of Graham, Durham, Duncannon and himself was appointed to report upon the whole matter.

This Committee proposed the disfranchisement of all boroughs with less than two thousand inhabitants and some disenfranchisement for those with less than four thousand. They suggested members for towns with ten thousand and additional members for counties with one hundred and fifty thousand population. One of their proposals, the adoption of the Ballot, was objected to by Grey and dropped—why it should have been so treated is not clear. The Cabinet reduced the proposed qualification in boroughs to a ten-pound rating and agreed to the Committee's report for the enfranchisement of fifty-pound leaseholders and ten-pound copyholders in the counties.

In this form the Bill was approved by the King—the effect was to eliminate sixty boroughs and halve the membership in forty-six, giving a hundred and sixty-seven seats (including Weymouth, which had previously returned four!) for redistribution. Of these forty-four were to go to the big unrepresented towns, fifty-five to the English counties and the remaining eleven to Scotland, Ireland and Wales. On March 1st, 1831, the first reading took place without a division and on the 22nd the second reading was carried by one vote. A resolution that the number of representatives in England and Wales should not be diminished was conceded, but certain members now deserting, the Government were defeated by seven votes and dissolution resolved upon.

The excitement was now very great; all the streets were illuminated, and the windows of the Tories broken. On June 24th, Russell introduced the second Bill into the new Parliament; he made practically no concessions, and after many debates and divisions, on September 21st the measure was passed by three hundred and forty-five votes to two hundred and thirty-six. In the Lords, on October 8th, the second reading was rejected by forty-one votes.

The news of this defeat was followed by general rioting. Nottingham Castle, the property of Newcastle, was burned; and at Bristol, where a leading opponent, Wetherell, was Recorder, the town was set on fire.

On December 12th Russell introduced a third Reform Bill. In this proposal fifty-six boroughs were to be wholly disfranchised and another thirty deprived of half their members. The total number of members in the House was maintained at the old level. The amendment enabled more boroughs to be saved and also a greater number to be enfranchised. On March 23rd the Bill passed the Commons. It was now that the King consented to the creation of new peerages to carry the Bill and, largely through the mediation of the diarist, Greville, a second reading was carried in the Lords. In committee, however, difficulties were raised, but a change had come over the Court. The King now declined to create sufficient peers to "ensure the success of the Bill in all its essential principles". He was told that at least fifty would be required. On his refusal, the Government resigned.

Lyndhurst now suggested to the King an administration to carry a moderate Reform Bill and Wellington, ever the servant of the Crown, was not unwilling to serve. Peel, however, vehemently refused. Meanwhile, on May 9th, Grey and Althorp publicly announced their resignation, which so far was known to few people. The House of Commons thereupon by a majority of eighty expressed their confidence in the Government. It was suggested that all supplies should be refused until the Reform Bill became law. Another device advocated by the less responsible was to organize a run upon the Bank of England. By Monday, May 14th, Wellington saw that his position had become impossible, and advised the King to recall Grey. Thereafter the Tories in the Lords gradually withdrew their opposition. The King at last gave his authority that peers to an unlimited number should be created to carry the Bill. This decided the matter, and on June 4th, 1842, the Bill was read in the Lords a third time, to receive the Royal Assent on the 7th.

An important consequence followed; in the heat of the contest, Whigs, Canningites and Radicals had been fused into that great Liberal Party which was to dominate English politics for three-quarters of a century.

CHAPTER IV

'LAISSEZ-FAIRE'

IF the proletarian enthusiasts for electoral reform thought to receive some immediate result from the victory, they must soon have become disappointed. The Government remained practically unchanged in composition, it was "perhaps the most aristocratic of the century— only four of its members sat in the House of Commons", comments Spencer Walpole (*History of England*, v. III, p. 195). It had already shown, in dealing with industrial disturbances, that it had no more sympathy with the malcontents than had its predecessors; new proclamations against disturbances and special commissions to try rioters had been issued in 1830. At Winchester alone over one thousand people were prosecuted, Carlile and Cobbett were tried for incitement: the latter called as witnesses Brougham (Chancellor) and Melbourne (Home Secretary), and in the result the jury failed to agree. Though the total wealth of the country as measured by money was rapidly increasing, the condition of the labouring people, now promiscuously collected in insanitary towns, over-worked or unemployed, was becoming intolerable. Forty-one thousand people in Lancashire, it was said in Parliament, in one small district were each subsisting on two pence a day. A penny an hour was normal remuneration. The position in rural areas was little better; the threshing-machine had deprived the labourers of their winter work, the commons on which they had grazed their cattle were being enclosed, arable land was becoming pasture and many demobilized sailors and soldiers competed for what little employment existed. For long it had been necessary to supplement wages out of the rates in many parishes. Emigration alone seemed likely to ease the problem; in 1832 over one hundred thousand people left their native land, driven out by necessity. In Ireland, if anything, conditions were even worse. On January 18th, 1832, O'Connell, the leader of the agitation, was arrested. At the trial he allowed judgment to be entered against him by default, but it was rumoured that a compromise had been reached between him and the Government; O'Connell had supported the Reform Bill and was useful to them. At the general election, in the midst of the Reform excitement, no further proceedings were taken; the whole matter did nothing to strengthen authority, rather the reverse.

By the peasants, the Protestant Church was sought to be made responsible for all the misfortune of the Irish people. An agitation about tithe resulted in refusals to pay; in the end, after many disorderly districts had been proclaimed, £60,000 was advanced to distressed incumbents, and eventually the whole tithe was put under a scheme, to be redeemed for some £10,000,000.

Many Liberals objected; they declared that the established Irish Church was indefensible in a Catholic country and objected to its rehabilitation. The Bill for tithe composition, however, passed, and dissolution followed on December 3rd, 1832, the last day of the unreformed Parliament.

Though the new House was composed primarily of two parties, the presence of such men as Attwood, Pease the Quaker, Jeffrey and Cobbett brought a type into the House which was formerly absent. The Radicals, however, did not number in all more than fifty. They wished to amend or abolish Tithe, the Corn Laws, the Game Laws; sought Church disestablishment, and the reform of municipal corporations and the poor law. In economic matters, under the influence of their individualistic theories, they favoured free labour; all Governmental interference even to protect the labourer they suspected as interfering with that beneficent struggle of "enlightened self interests" out of which, they believed, the finest results would come.

Had they been moved merely by economic abstractions, it is doubtful whether they would not have realized the more obvious ill-effects of unfettered industrialism—unfortunately, their material interests coincided with their opinions. Most of them were more or less wealthy, for until 1858 men who could not show that they had an established income were excluded from the House of Commons. Moreover, since the early eighteenth century, custom had gradually placed the expenses of election upon the candidate. After 1832 this was fully recognized by statute; the present expectation that a member should subscribe to charity then extended to a demand that the municipality should receive assistance from him. They sought to have their roads repaired and other public services paid out of the successful candidate's purse, nor did this expectation die out directly Parliament was reformed.

After 1832, the prescribed qualification remained as it had been since 1760—members must either own land or have it transferred to them by their supporters. In either case, the requirement closed the doors of the House to poor men. Not until 1858 were the property qualification Acts finally repealed, though they had long been an obstacle to free selection. Even in that year there was opposition, among the objectors being the son of that Lord Grey who had carried the Reform Act. It was the borough members who experienced most difficulty, for those who sought election in the counties were normally landed people. The boroughs, in any case, demanded more money from their members than the shires, and so came even more largely to be the seats of very rich men. The patronage system was encouraged, for a wealthy supporter could always finance his nominee—it was the independent man of small means and no influence who tended to be excluded.

All these factors continued to operate after 1832, and they may explain in part the small change of personnel which was brought about at that election.

Such Radicals as there were, immediately on Parliament meeting fell foul of the Whigs. The Government favoured the continuation of the Tory, Manners Sutton, as Speaker; in disgust the Radicals nominated a Whig. The votes in support of their candidate, Littleton, only thirty-one in all, disclosed their numerical weakness. Yet on the other side, the Conservatives, as they were now beginning to be called, were also divided. Peel, their leader, had broken with the old Tory tradition—in 1834 he was to declare that he accepted the Reform Bill "as a final and irrevocable settlement" and to go on to say that he would not oppose "the correction of proved abuses and the redress of real grievances". This was all in the famous Tamworth Manifesto; it disclosed the working of his mind at a later date.

Already in Ireland demands for repeal of the Union were heard, and Stanley, the Irish Secretary, said he would resist them to the death. Repealers and reformers combined to denounce him. He was accused of refusing to hold out an olive branch. An investigation into the affairs of Ireland was refused by 393 votes to 60, the Tories under Peel supporting the Government. It was the first clear Liberal cleavage.

On Irish Church reform also, Peel, in supporting the Government, by no means took the position of the old Tory high Anglicans—the abolition of Church rates followed. Nevertheless, although O'Connell supported the Irish Church Bill, he had nothing but scorn for the Coercion measure which accompanied it. That measure, provoked by the impossibility to get a conviction from an Irish Jury in the midst of severe disorder, partially suspended the Habeas Corpus Acts, and introduced a kind of martial law into the country by providing for offenders in proclaimed districts being tried by Court Martial. Such legislation was undoubtedly a great departure from the existing Common Law. In the Lords it met with no opposition, but in the lower House, on its being admitted that the existing special commissions had been completely successful, it was argued by the Radicals that it had not been proved that the ordinary law was insufficient. Nevertheless, the Bill passed, to be the ancestor of much similar legislation affecting that disturbed island. Thus both the Church Bill and the Coercion Bill, the one antagonizing Tories, the other Radicals, became law. Durham, the only Radical in the Government except Brougham, in disgust resigned, and the hated Stanley took the occasion to leave the troublesome Irish Office and became Colonial Secretary. It was in that capacity that he was called upon to deal with the Slavery question. As has been said, the Slave Trade had already been made illegal, but it was now urged by the Abolitionists, who were very influential in religious circles, that the time had come when the existing three-quarter million slaves in the West Indies, Mauritius and the Cape should be given their complete freedom.

The Abolitionists, such as Buxton, Granville Sharp, Zachary Macaulay and Clarkson were mostly low Churchmen or Dissenters, and thus, unlike Wilberforce, supported the Whig interest. In 1823 Buxton had first moved the House on the slavery question—he had suggested that thereafter all children should be declared born free. The alarmed Jamaican planters talked indignantly of separation and in Demerara there was an insurrection. As a result, regulations as to the treatment of slaves were issued from the Colonial Office to ensure their more humane treatment. In 1830 Brougham moved for abolition, but without success; there followed a revolt of negroes in Jamaica, and, in 1833, the Whig Government was at last persuaded to sponsor abolition. £20,000,000 was offered to the owners as compensation and accepted, and on August 1st, 1834, Slavery ceased; it was the first great measure of the new Parliament.

The treatment of the helpless at home, in factory, field or unemployed, was far less sympathetic. Though the new Parliament was Liberal, with a majority over the Tories of over four hundred, the reformer Lord John Russell in particular, Poulett Thompson, the Vice-President of the Board of Trade, and the majority of the manufacturers (who were mostly on the Government side) were all opposed in principle to factory legislation. In the last Parliament, Sadler, a Tory, had sought to enlarge to all children the little protection obtained by Peel in 1818, which was limited to a maximum of eleven hours a day for apprentices. In 1831 a further limitation, applying to persons under eighteen in cotton mills, had been accorded on the motion of a Radical, Hobhouse. Now, however, a general demand for a ten-hour day for all factory workers had arisen and Sadler sponsored a Bill to effect it. The measure was referred to a committee which heard evidence from many industrial districts—it revealed the most severe hardships.

Despite the appeal of forty thousand factory workers on his behalf, at the General Election Sadler was defeated by Macaulay at Leeds, and in consequence Lord Ashley was chosen by the Unions to continue the fight.

He introduced Sadler's Bill in February, 1832, but the feeling against such a general measure was so strong that he decided to concentrate for the time being on the protection of children. Under his scheme, no child under nine was to be employed at all, those under eighteen not more than ten hours a day. The employers for the most part were hostile. The Government declared that further information was needed and proposed a Royal Commission to collect more information. Chadwick, the Poor Law Commissioner, served upon it, but it was soon evident that the workers as a whole regarded the whole enquiry as a means of shelving the reforms they demanded.

Meanwhile, the Bill of Ashley had been read a second time and the Government now suggested sending it to a Select Committee. The leader of the House, Althorp, said the Bill should provide for an eight-hour day for children under thirteen with facilities for education, but on a division the Government were defeated and the Bill went to a committee of the whole House. At this stage the Commission reported. After attacking the trade unions and "hired agitators" they went on to suggest a total prohibition against working in mills for children up to nine years of age, with permission of eight hours, but not at night, for children up to thirteen. In the House, Althorp asked for eighteen hours as the limit. On a division, 238 members voted for this protection against 93. Inspection also was provided, and with amendments the Bill became law.

The new Act applied to all textile mills—in its final form no child under eight might be employed at all; up to thirteen they were not to work more than forty-eight hours a week or nine a day; up to eighteen the limit was sixty-nine a week or twelve hours a day. There followed an employers' conspiracy to destroy the Act before it came into full operation. On their insistence, in 1836, Poulett Thompson for the Government proposed that, after all, children over eleven should be deprived of their recently-won eight-hour day. He was supported by many Radicals—Hume, Hobhouse, O'Connell and Villiers among others. Russell and Peel were of the same mind. Nevertheless, so active had been the propaganda of Ashley and his friends that the reactionaries only obtained a majority of two. The Bill was dropped—it is here mentioned as an instance of the retrograde commercial Radical opinion of the time.

Though most of the attacks on the mill system of labour came from the Tories, when the poor law came up for consideration they showed themselves as enthusiastic to abolish outdoor relief and to force destitute families inside workhouses as were their political opponents; nor had they displayed any sympathy for the agriculture poor when they pressed for the Enclosure Acts which, in the alleged interest of scientific farming, deprived the labourer of his pasturage or garden without compensation. Only on the Slavery question had either party shown any sign of humanitarian feeling. Indeed it is remarkable, having regard to the plutocratic outlook which prevailed almost universally at the time, that the emancipation measure ever passed.

No interest, territorial or monetary, was benefited by the emancipation. The compensation, considering all the interests at stake, was not unreasonable, and the Government had every reason to fear disturbances by the Colonial owners. The Abolition Act stands out in the legislation of the time as an example of disinterested philanthropy—not particularly popular with the mass of people, themselves in a state of semi-servitude for whom next to nothing had been done, and certainly not popular with the landed gentry.

In 1834, the Poor Law Commission, which had been sitting for two years, reported. It had been concerned chiefly with the able-bodied poor who, particularly in rural areas, had for some time been relieved out of the rates by additions to their miserable wages. The core of the report, which was accepted by the Government with enthusiasm, was the recommendation of the almost complete abolition of outdoor relief. In future the paupers and their families were to be relieved only in the Workhouse, in which already were crowded promiscuously the aged, the sick, the mentally infirm, old and young women and children. Now it was suggested that the able-bodied and their families were to join them.

That the policy might be consistently severe, a strong central authority (itself a novelty in constitutional structure) was to be set up with almost mandatory powers over the new local Boards of Guardians. By 1862, Nassau Senior, was a Commissioner of the 1834 enquiry, was condemning the general mixed workhouse. "We never contemplated having children under the same roof with the adults", he protested. "We recommended that in every Union there should be a building for the able-bodied males, one for the able-bodied females and another for the sick." For nearly a century nothing effectual was done to alter this disgraceful condition—"unique", wrote the authors of the Minority Poor Law Report in 1909, "in Europe". For the continuance of the protracted iniquity no party can take exclusive blame, for all were equally responsible.

The opposition was vehement but helpless. In Parliament, only twenty votes in the Commons were cast against the Bill, among them the young Disraeli and his "Young England" group. The Radicals, led by Grote, supported the measure, Peel and Wellington agreed with it. Cobbett, it is true, denounced the "Bastille"; Disraeli at Maidstone condemned the "flagitious statute" and declared that "poverty was now treated as a crime"; and Dickens and *The Times* added their protest. In five years £3,000,000 was saved to the rates. An Act which enshrined the principle that no one was eligible for relief who was not actually in a state of destitution effectually prevented recourse to the Guardians except in the most desperate cases. It was designed to relieve the rates of the cost of pauperism and in this sense was most successful. Spencer Walpole, a writer typical of mid-Victorian times, says complacently, "A reform of so vast a character, suddenly introduced into every parish in England, could not but be attended with some inconvenience". (*History of England*, Vol. 3, p. 448.) Yet it must be admitted that the poor law reformers thought that they were acting according to the best principles of economics; it was essential that those who for one reason or another did not earn wages should be more uncomfortable than those who worked—the difficulty was to find means to make them so.

Out of the rage of the working people against the "Workhouse test" came the more militant Chartist movement. The class without votes came slowly to realize that they had been abandoned by the Whigs, and, for the matter of that, by the Radicals. Riots broke out, to be suppressed by Melbourne, the Home Secretary. Some labourers who had bound themselves by oath not to work for less than six shillings a week were prosecuted under an old Act because of their swearing; had they merely combined, they would now be acting lawfully! They were transported to Australia. Though the trade unions were impotent in the face of capital, a charter of their new grievances was drafted, and there was talk of a National Convention. In 1839 a monster petition was presented, but the Chartists were not in agreement; some were for seeking electoral enfranchisement; others advocated physical force—in either case nothing came of it. The demand for Free Trade and cheap bread took the place of the far more fundamental social and political criticisms of the Chartists. The riots at Birmingham and Newport alienated the more moderate reformers and greatly injured the whole movement. Though later there was a revival, from now onwards the Government treated the whole agitation with contempt.

In truth the Government were more concerned with O'Connell and his demand for an independent Irish Parliament than they were for the condition of the poor. The King's speech in 1834 had declared that he would maintain the Union. O'Connell's resolution to appoint a Committee to investigate the working of the Union was rejected by 523 to 38 votes after a six days' debate, 57 Irish members voting against him. The Government made itself responsible for the collection of tithes in Ireland under the recent legislation, and out of this obligation arose the refusal of Russell to maintain the Irish Church funds undiminished; he said, supported by the Radicals and repealers, "they were larger than was necessary". In the end, Stanley, Graham and Richmond resigned on a subject which it would seem was very capable of adjustment, the efforts of Brougham for a *modus vivendi* having failed. A misunderstanding about the dropping of the Coercion Act made the position worse, and on an intimation from Althorp that he would resign over this matter the Prime Minister himself, wearied by these foolish factional disputes, retired.

The King sent for Melbourne, and Althorp was persuaded to return. Radicals such as Grote and Hume and even O'Connell himself were conciliated. A Coercion Bill, but without the court-martial clauses, was introduced and passed; it was only to last till August, 1835.

The Tithe Bill, which left the Church four-fifths of its revenues, on the suggestion of O'Connell was amended and had been rejected in the Lords, when, in November, 1834, Althorp, the Leader in the Commons, through the death of his father, was called up to the Lords. Thereupon the King intimated that he thought he would have to dismiss the Government, saying that they had no one fit to lead in the Commons. Brougham apparently told the Press of this communication, and the enraged King demanded the prompt resignation of the whole Government.

For the time, Wellington agreed solely to constitute the Government. Peel was in Italy, but, on returning, became Prime Minister and Chancellor of the Exchequer—it was now that the Tamworth manifesto, to which reference has been made, was issued. Directly Parliament met after a general election he was defeated, both on the election of the Speaker and on the Address. Again the temporalities of the Church of Ireland came under consideration, when Peel was in a minority. Eventually, on April 7th, he resigned. The King had lost, his chosen ministry had only been able to hold office for four months.

If the consequences of the dismissal of the Duke of Portland by George III be compared with that of Melbourne, it will be realized how great, during the half-century, had been the decline in the power of the Crown. In the former case, the King was able, by the lavish bestowal of places and money and the use of threats, to support Pitt until such time as he could win for himself a majority in the Commons; Peel, on the other hand, after vainly struggling against a hostile Parliament, had to submit to its wishes. In both cases the Government which had been superseded was comparatively progressive, but had outstayed its popularity. In the earlier instance, the Fox–North coalition was broken for ever, Peel's failure gave to the Whigs another seven years of power.

The re-installation of Melbourne, however, on Grey's refusal to return, very definitely weakened the Radical element. The new Prime Minister was an erudite student of theology, though himself by no means what can be called a religious man. He was of serene temperament and much disliked any disturbance of his peace. As David Cecil writes, "He was terrified of revolution". Reading *Oliver Twist*, he once remarked: "It is all among workhouses and pickpockets—I don't like these things; I wish to avoid them". (*The Young Melbourne*, p. 266.) It is not surprising that such a man did not object to the new poor law, nor to the prosecution of the Dorchester labourers—certainly he was no Radical.

The jettison of Brougham removed the last forcible protagonist of progress in the Cabinet. During his tenure of the office of Chancellor that erratic genius had done much to reform the law. He had succeeded in establishing a unity of process in the Common Law courts and in setting up a new court of Bankruptcy. Other measures he proposed, to institute local county courts and improve Chancery procedure were temporarily lost, but he managed nevertheless to lay down new rules which much expedited and improved the Chancery practice. He abolished many sinecure offices there, the conveyance of land was simplified and, most important of all, he was able to institute a Judicial Committee of the Privy Council. According to Greville, "he smuggled the Privy

Council Bill through the Lords without the slightest notice or remark". (*Journal*, II, pp. 365, 370.) At first used primarily for ecclesiastical appeals, it gradually developed into a great Imperial Court of Appeal. Brougham's scheme for County Courts became law in 1846.

From now onwards, all legislative change, save in one important instance, was discounted by the Government—the exception was the drastic reorganization of the municipalities, the condition of which was certainly confused, corrupt and deplorable.

The municipal corporation had been the subject of study by a Royal Commission appointed in 1833. They had returned that there were no less than three hundred and two cities, boroughs and bodies corporate, of which a third had no governing bodies; it was not possible adequately to classify them, so various were their constitutions. Most relied upon Charters, real or spurious; some existed by prescription (such as London and Oxford), claiming to have had mayors, aldermen and burgesses before they had received any charter. The possession of its own Hundred Court was not a conclusive test of origin. As Maitland said, "Some had received a few chartered privileges from a mediæval baron" (*Township and Borough*, p. 17), some had received direct grants from the King.

Many charters had been surrendered; some boroughs held contradictory titles—the whole disclosed an inextricable medley of anomalous constitutions. There were those who held considerable real estate, others had only market rights. The majority, but not all, returned burgesses, elected on differing franchises, to represent the borough in Parliament. Many had their own Justices of the Peace, sometimes with separate commissions, but frequently their right to quarter sessions had not been exercised. In thirty-five cases the Borough Justices exercised a concurrent jurisdiction with the county; there was not infrequently a power to hold quarter sessions for misdemeanours and even for felonies. There were instances, such as Exeter and Bristol, of boroughs with their own sessions of Oyer and Gaol Delivery. (*Webb, the Manor and the Borough*, v. 2, p. 282.)

The powers which were possessed showed great variations. There were boroughs possessed of considerable rights to regulate trade, prices, wages and tolls. Others had built and maintained bridges, roads and hospitals —in yet others these functions were performed by special *ad hoc* bodies, or not attended to at all. Again, in the matter of selection of government, some mayors and councillors were elected by freemen; in other cases the mayor was chosen by a very limited group of aldermen; sometimes he was elected by the burgesses at large. He also had differing duties; sometimes he was not only Chief Magistrate, but also Coroner, and the Recorder was often, though not always, subordinate to him. The Mayor was often controller of all civic activities and frequently appointed the town's officers. In forty boroughs, bailiffs exercised all or some of the powers of mayors; in some towns they were under the direction of the mayor himself. The principal officers, Chamberlain, Town Clerk and Coroner, had varying powers and duties, as also did the humbler officers, the Serjeant, overseers and constables.

In the absence of effective control, the funds were often spent on entertainment or the remuneration of sinecure offices—the public had little control. In Liverpool, out of 165,000 inhabitants in 1834, but 5,000

were freemen—in Portsmouth there were only 102. Even then, although
the freemen enjoyed privileges such as a right of free pasturage or
exemption from borough tolls, in many cases they had no share in local
government.

The unreformed Parliament had, of course, a vested interest in
maintaining unreformed boroughs, but once the one had been
reorganized it was impossible long to deny popular election to the
other. In the case of Scotland, in 1833, Jeffreys, the Lord Advocate,
carried a Bill to ensure a general electorate of £10 householders without
much opposition. The English Bill, owing to the greater labours of the
Commissioners, was not introduced until 1835. This time the enthusiasm
for reform was spent and the objectors were more vocal.

Under Russell's Municipal Bill, based on the commission's report, all
governing bodies were uniformly to consist of mayor and council, the
councillors to be elected by resident ratepayers. In the larger boroughs
they were to be elected by wards. The quarter sessions, if continued,
were to be presided over by a barrister Recorder. If the Tories thought
to make much out of their obstruction they were disappointed; to their
chagrin, Peel, their Leader, declared that he was in favour of the reform.
An attempt to save the franchise for freemen was defeated in committee,
and Stanley failed to carry an amendment that a third of the council
should retire biennially, the Government majorities, in most cases,
being over fifty. The Lords, however, under Lyndhurst's influence,
threw over Peel. They decided to preserve the freeman's rights, and to
have the Council elected only by the wealthier ratepayers. They provided for Aldermen to be elected for life. The Bill thus amended, said
Ellenborough, was now "a full, consistent and constitutional reform".
(*Hansard*, xxx, p. 1034.)

When it returned to the Commons, Peel found himself in a dilemma—
it was known that Lyndhurst had ignored him—"What is Peel to me?"
he had said, and used other wounding expressions. For once the Whigs
were resolute, a great Liberal meeting was held and Russell explained to
the House that they would only agree to a few minor modifications.
Aldermen were conceded, to be elected for six years, but any modification
of the electoral rights of the £10 ratepayers was rejected. Peel, who
followed, in substance agreed with Russell—an open division between
the "old" and "new" Tories had been displayed—later to come to a head
in the Free Trade debates. As usual, Wellington, the peace-maker,
advised the Lords to yield, and the Bill, with a few amendments, became
law.

The Municipal Reform Act, to those whose minds are not entirely
centred on electoral machinery, was indeed a far more important measure
than the Reform Bill, though that Act had made the local government
measure possible. Then, as now, the greater part of such social legislation
as existed was carried out by the local authorities. In the boroughs as
now constituted they were ready to receive such powers as formerly had
been given to special *ad hoc* authorities—Turn-Pike Trusts, Highway
Boards, Burial Boards, Town Improvement Commissioners and, eventually, were to become the sole authority for education, public health
and the poor law. Indeed the history of local Government, after the
1835 Act, displays an increasing tendency to transfer all hitherto isolated

powers and duties from special bodies to the municipal authority or to the other general administrative bodies subsequently created, such as the County and District Councils, which were modelled in substance upon the pattern of the reformed municipalities.

In 1835 there was no conception of any national control over the local authorities: as has been said, only in the recent case of the Poor Law had such means of enforcing national requirements been attempted. Gradually, by giving grants in aid and subventions to the financially embarrassed local bodies, the national Government acquired a degree of supervision, but general concern at local incompetence was of slow growth; as against it, the characteristic English tradition of local privilege, nurtured in the common law, regarded with healthy suspicion all encroachments from Whitehall.

As regards Ireland, the Lords were more successful—a fear of giving to Catholics a majority enabled them there to retard municipal reorganization; so also they rejected the attempt to settle the Tithe question, the Government feebly acquiescing in its defeat. Indeed, now that the municipal fight was over, Melbourne in effect refused to legislate any further. The Whigs under his direction now set out to defeat nearly all further Radical measures, and when they failed the Lords could be relied upon to destroy them. Motions for a ballot at elections, shortening of the life of Parliaments, and household suffrage were all successfully opposed by the Government, Whigs and the Tory Opposition. A Radical motion on the state of the Nation, in effect one of censure, disclosed how Melbourne had broken up the Liberal Party. Roebuck, in moving, declared that the Government was as bad as Peel—indeed, now that Melbourne had shown himself as good as a Conservative, many Tories were asking themselves what justification there was for his remaining in office. The Radicals would probably have revolted and formed a separate party, with consequences difficult to foretell, had it not been that at this juncture the King died, and at the consequent dissolution several of the leading Radicals—Roebuck, Thompson and Ewart—lost their seats. The total number was not materially lessened, but the movement towards independence experienced a set-back; the new men were nervous of destroying the Government and, fearful of losing their newly won seats, they sought to use persuasion rather than menace.

Their decision to remain within the Liberal Party was of supreme importance. Until the formation of the Labour Party in the last years of the nineteenth century there was no force, save Tory democracy (an uncertain and weak movement), to compete with Liberalism for the suffrages of Progressives. However cautious might be the Whigs, however truculent the Radicals, never again were they openly to menace one another—the gradations of opinion between the two extremes was calculated to obscure their differences. Whether the right or left on balance had its way it is difficult to determine, and in matters affecting business interests, as has already been indicated, the Radicals and Whigs were of one mind—neither cared to interfere with the free competition of capital or of labour.

As has been said, the Government had anticipated trouble in Jamaica, and they were right. The local legislature refused to assist the emancipation of the negroes or to give any protection to the freed apprentices. Indeed, they used apprenticeship as a means of continuing the young blacks in servitude. Sir George Strickland, in the place of Buxton, moved to abolish the system, and Government tried to placate all parties by introducing a Bill merely to improve conditions. Later, however, though the betterment Bill was given a second reading, a further motion was carried in favour of total emancipation. Nevertheless, the earlier measure was carried, the result of which was that apprenticeship would continue until August, 1840.

In many islands the apprentices were at once freed, but in Jamaica, though the House of Assembly had agreed to the Government Bill, they only represented a minority of the planters, and matters became so troubled there that the Government finally had to ask Parliament to suspend the Jamaican constitution for five years. This was more than the Radicals could stand, and the second reading for suspension was carried by only five votes.

The Government resigned but, on a disagreement between Peel and the Queen with regard to the appointment of her Ladies of the Bed-chamber, Melbourne returned, and a second Jamaica Bill was introduced, which owing to its drastic amendment in the Lords, also failed to pass.

In 1839, Russell made his famous declaration as to the finality of the Reform Act. This was in answer to the Radicals and Chartists who were showing great discontent at the inadequacy of past electoral reform. In 1839, a national convention of Chartists' delegates, the "People's Parliament", as it was called, met in London, and an immense petition, said to have been signed by a million and a half people, was carried down to the House. It was evident that the Chartists' leaders had discovered how great had become the power of the middle classes. The petition was of course rejected, but the social conditions were becoming so serious that economic solutions were beginning to interest the people more than political ones. It was not fully understood that the miserable conditions of the poor might as readily be ascribed to low wages as to dear food, and the Chartists openly declared that the demand for cheap bread was a manufacturers' device to keep down wages. Nevertheless, the Anti-Corn Law League, which had been founded in 1838, through the skilful and tireless propaganda of Cobden and Bright, soon took the place of the Chartists in popular estimation. From now onward the repeal of the Corn Laws was the cry which united all save the most suspicious or extreme of the progressives.

In the Government, Melbourne was a pronounced protectionist. Indeed, in 1837, only three ministers had supported Villiers in his annual motion to repeal the Corn Duties; in 1839, however, their number rose to ten—it was clear by now that the Anti-Corn Law League had become the rallying-point of Radicalism.

Attacked on two fronts, the Whigs could not hope long to survive. To please the Radicals, in 1841 the Government proposed to substitute a duty of one shilling a bushel on corn for the sliding scale and to reduce the duties on foreign sugar. This latter proposal was thought by Radicals to help the slave owners, and a consequent combination of the Protectionists and the Abolitionists against the proposal resulted in a defeat of the Government by thirty-six votes.

Soon afterwards the Government was again defeated on a direct vote of censure. This was the end. In June, 1841, there was a General Election which gave the Conservatives a majority of over seventy, and on August 30th, Peel became Prime Minister. Next year, there being a large deficit, he suggested a revival of the Income Tax, together with a reduction of the Corn Duties. On the latter proposal, Villiers' amendment for repeal was rejected by four to one, and Russell's Whig alternative of a fixed duty of eight shillings was also rejected by one hundred and twenty votes—in Gladstone's phrase, "it was a table-land ending in a precipice". But though the Government carried their sliding scale, the removal of 750 out of 1,200 articles in the tariff, including a reduction of duties on imported cattle, meat and vegetables, already alarmed the Tory Protectionists, who later were to become so obstreperous.

The principal opposition to Income Tax arose, as usual, from the Liberal side. They regarded it as an impost upon commerce rather than upon land—Cobden, in particular, led the attack, but the Income Tax had come to stay. From the beginning it was a success; in the first year it yielded over a million pounds more than had been anticipated.

In 1844 came the famous Bank Charter Act, which had for its purpose the control of paper currency. In effect the Bank was authorized to issue paper to the extent of fourteen million pounds on the security of Government debt, but all issues above that required the holding of an equal amount of bullion, three-quarters of which must be gold—it was a first effort to restrain inflation.

In 1840, Ashley, who, as has been shown, was far more concerned with social improvement than were most of the Radicals, had introduced a Bill to exclude women from mines and to prevent children under thirteen being employed there. The Radicals, who had already fought for the factory owners, now tried to defend the owners of collieries—so great was their prejudice that all Ashley could obtain was a law that children of ten should not be employed more than three days a week. But his protest, as usual, was fruitful. In 1844, the Home Secretary, Graham, introduced a Bill to raise the minimum age from eight to nine in factories, but even now Ashley's desire for a general ten-hour day for women and young persons was defeated. The Prime Minister and Graham joined hands with the Liberal manufacturers to prevent any further protection of labour, though Russell and Palmerston and the Young England Tories—the "Socialist fools", as Cobden called them—supported Ashley's general Bill. So great was the power of the moneyed interest by this time that even Graham's compromise of a twelve-hour limit of labour was not allowed to pass.

A new measure was now introduced and Ashley again attempted to limit the hours of labour for women and young persons to ten. Macaulay declared himself converted but, on Peel's personal intervention that he would resign if the clause were carried, Ashley was again defeated. Not until 1847, when the Whigs were back in power, was the ten-hour limitation made law. Even then, Brougham attacked it on the ground that it must lower wages. In 1845, however, Ashley succeeded in reforming the lunacy laws. He was chairman of the Lunacy Commission from 1834 to the time of his death in 1885.

Meanwhile, the Anti-Corn Law League was growing in strength.

In the House, in 1841, Villiers had received ninety votes for abolition; in 1843 the number had risen to one hundred and thirty-five—many of the Whigs had come over; and at length, in 1844, Russell abstained from voting against total repeal. Next year he declared Protection to be the bane of Agriculture and moved against protective duties generally, in particular against the Corn Law. In the next critical year he openly supported Villiers' motion for repeal; from now onward it may be said that the whole Liberal Party was for Free Trade.

It has been stated that the potato famine in Ireland finally drove Peel to advocate abolition of the duties—however that may be, Russell was first in the field. On November 22nd, 1845, he told his electors in the City of London that he favoured immediate repeal. But before this, unknown to the public, many Cabinets had considered the matter: Peel had expressed his sympathy and Stanley, in protest, had resigned, whereupon Peel resigned also. Russell was asked to form a government, but on Grey refusing to help him, Peel resumed and, with Gladstone in the place of Stanley, on January 27th, 1846, he announced a total repeal of the Corn Laws to be completed within three years.

As is well known, the majority of the Tories, led by Stanley and Bentinck, broke with him, but with Liberal support he was, for the time being, invincible. Majorities of about a hundred carried the Bill through the Commons and in the Lords the decision of the lower House was accepted.

But the position of Peel, without an organized party, was too unstable to last. On a refusal to postpone Free Trade until another Irish Coercion Bill was passed, he was defeated. The way was now open for united Liberalism—for a time, the followers of Peel, though they gave a general support to Russell, who had become Prime Minister, remained a separate party (the Peelites), and Russell constructed his ministry on a strictly Whig basis. But although the Free Traders had been victorious, the Chartists were not reconciled. Under the leadership of O'Connor another convention was collected in London, a fresh petition organized, and an attempt made to assemble a great crowd on Kennington Common. One thousand seven hundred special constables were sworn in, secret military preparation was made, and, in the end, instead of a great procession, O'Connor and his executive committee had to carry the petition in three cabs to Westminster—the agitation had ended in general derision.

Apart from the Chartist disturbance, the year 1848 is remarkable for the passage of the first Public Health Act. This measure, from which London was excluded to receive special treatment, set up a central authority, the General Board of Health, consisting of the Commissioner of Woods and Forests and two other members; in boroughs the Town Council became the Health authority; in other places needing sanitary provision, special boards were set up. The boards were made responsible for drainage, water, streets and burial grounds, and gradually acquired many other powers. They had authority to levy rates. The Bill was opposed by many individualistic Radicals, by romantic individualists who objected to centralization—such as Toulmin Smith (though there was hardly any in the Bill)—and by most of the protectionist leaders, other than Disraeli. Bright boasted that he would always oppose such Smoke

Abatement Acts as interfered with trade. Ashley, who was made a Commissioner with Chadwick, was an enthusiastic supporter; he had long advocated sanitary reform. In 1851 he introduced and carried Bills which made the inspection of common lodging-houses compulsory and gave powers to local authorities to build them. Schemes for a water supply for London and for drainage were also devised by him and the Board.

In 1858 the Board was dissolved, but by then two hundred local boards had been set up outside the boroughs. Palmerston's scheme to place the Central Board under the Home Office was temporarily defeated, and an opportunity to enforce a coherent standard of sanitation lost. Finally, in 1875, the Public Health Act of that year consolidated over a hundred measures which had been passed as occasion arose without any relation to one another.

In 1858 also the functions of the General Board of Health as central authority were transferred, notwithstanding earlier opposition, in part to the Home Office, in part to the Privy Council, and in 1871 the central powers both as to Health and Poor Law were assigned to a new authority —the Local Government Board. Next year the country was divided into rural and urban sanitary districts—the latter being the old Borough Improvement Act and local government districts; they are now known generally as Urban Districts. In London, outside the city, the vestries became the sanitary authorities. Nearly all this legislation, it must be conceded, was carried by Conservatives.

The era in which the Liberal Pary was in process of formation is remarkable for the unusual absence of political interest in foreign affairs. From the end of the Walpole period until the Treaty of Vienna, Europe had been constantly in a state of belligerence; a condition from which this country could not escape. The effect in politics was both to stimulate patriotic enthusiasm and to strengthen the power of whatever Government was responsible for the defence of the realm.

Since Waterloo, such an attitude was less necessary. The growth of the peace movement, fostered by the advocates of Free Trade, at first met with little opposition. It followed upon the triumph of the Corn Law repeal, but the fact of the need for its existence showed how the times were again becoming disturbed.

Those very dynamic elements in Europe which created Western civilization have stimulated also a constant belligerency in conflicting national ideals. Never since the failure of the Roman Empire, save perhaps in the short-lived experiment of Charlemagne, not even when the Catholic Church had universal influence, have European Christians for long abstained from killing one another, or from glorifying war and its practitioners. Regarding the history of Europe for the last fifteen hundred years, it would be fair to say that, throughout that period, war has been endemic, cessation from hostilities occasional and precarious.

It was but natural, therefore, once the exhaustion caused by the Napoleonic struggle was over and a new generation had arisen, that the countries of Europe should again become aggressive and restless. After 1840, a renewal of Chauvinism and unrest are again to be detected in France. Nevertheless, Guizot, to arrest the tendency to new conflagration, succeeded in establishing an *entente* with England, notwithstanding the temporary disturbance caused by Palmerston's suggestion of a Coburg candidate to be Prince Consort in Spain. A treaty between England and France in 1845 had abolished the unlimited right to search each other's vessels, but in 1846 the Spanish marriages of Isabella to the French nominee and of the Infanta to the Duc de Montpensier were regarded in England as a breach of mutual understanding. To Palmerston's satisfaction, the precarious *entente* broke down. He had never accepted Aberdeen's policy of *rapprochement*, and even the Court supported the Foreign Secretary in his indignation at being tricked. To the Prime Minister's more pacific temperament Palmerston's plain speaking to France was disquieting, nor did the trouble end there. Since 1845, Italy had been in a revolutionary condition. In Naples the Austrians still held a police control, but France had warned Metternich that any further intervention would be opposed. Popular excitement was rising in all the Italian States—even the Papal See was affected, where it was believed that the new Pope, Pius IX, was a Liberal. The King of Naples, in particular, was assailed for his cruelties, and when the Crown of France fell, in 1848, the Radical movement in Italy was greatly heartened. A revolution broke out in Milan in March, and at the same time Venice proclaimed a Republic; a revolution in Vienna caused the flight of Metternich, and the whole system which had existed since the great Treaty of Vienna was in ruins. In the German States also revolutions took place. Hungary was in ferment—such was the state of Europe which confronted England in that most significant of years, 1848.

The failure of the Chartists in England, as we have seen, showed more clearly than anything else could how this country, with a very moderate Liberal administration, was determined to give no support to extreme actions. The middle classes, which abroad so often formed the nucleus of revolution, had here acquired political and economic rights. In Parliament, apart from Palmerston, the Prime Minister had the support of few men of ability in the Cabinet—Morpeth, Hobhouse and Labouchere rarely spoke and in 1847 Macaulay lost his seat—the burden of the day fell on Russell himself. Outside his own department, Palmerston rarely intervened, and even then he was more of an embarrassment than an assistance to the peace-loving Russell.

Although Palmerston was inclined to follow his master, Canning, in helping "small nations struggling to be free" and encouraging the development of Liberal institutions abroad, the fear of foreign complication and war compelled the Manchester men to condemn him and to oppose his policy—what Cobden called the "Palmerston system". In Parliament Cobden wrote, in 1848, "three Coercion Bills for Ireland, and the rest talk!"; he complains that all the debates are on the subject of Protection, for which the Tories continued, intermittently, to fight until 1852. Little direct criticism of foreign policy can be detected.

Nevertheless, the Foreign Minister, Palmerston, however little appreciated by the Court or Russell, had become the leading national figure. "There was a comfortable impression in the public mind", writes Guedalla, "that Palmerston was generally inclined to put down the Mighty from their seats". (*Palmerston*, p. 253.) Cobden had suggested a general recourse to international arbitration but had received little popular support—the possibility of England being summoned before a foreign tribunal was generally distasteful. The new Prince-President of France had suggested a mutual reduction of naval armament, but Palmerston would have none of it, nor would he even agree to an international congress. "Sovereigns nowadays count for little", exclaimed this militarist democrat—with psychological insight he saw that the new nations "will submit to no external dictation". He was the first English statesman to realize that popular government does not necessarily involve pacific sentiment. Moreover, he believed in the rising nationalism in Europe. He helped the Sicilians, defied the rulers of Austria and Russia —only in the matter of adequate armament to support his policy was he inconsistent. It must be admitted, apart from naval preparation, that the truculence of the Foreign Minister was largely bluff. In any event, he was too impatient to await that sanction for his activities which could only be achieved by converting the Prime Minister and the Treasury to an expenditure compatible with his demands on foreign nations.

The effect of this ultra patriotic policy on the Radicals was disastrous. Bright, Cobden and their school would have none of it. They instituted Peace Societies, which had none of the success of their Corn Law League. Though Cobden and Bright had joined in the reception of Kossuth, they were both opposed to military intervention on behalf of continental Liberalism. The Conservatives of that time also supported a peaceful foreign policy—the Peelites in particular; Graham, Aberdeen and Gladstone were against increased armaments and international provocation, and neither Stanley nor Disraeli seriously differed from them.

On the other hand, there was a large, perhaps the greater, section of the Radicals and the great unfranchised public who, notwithstanding that Palmerston obstructed further electoral reform, enthusiastically welcomed his foreign policy. They refused to support the Peace Society, which at that time was trying to lessen the growth of anti-French policy. They regarded Napoleon as a dictator, the Tsar as a tyrant and, paradoxically, the despotic Turkish Sultan as an oppressed victim of Russia.

In 1850, in answer to an attack for threatening the Greeks over the treatment of a British subject, Palmerston defended his whole policy. He declared that all British subjects of whatever origin had the like right to be protected; he asserted that every nation should be free; in Belgium, Spain, Italy and Hungary; he defended the assistance he had given to freedom against tyranny. On a division many Radicals supported him, and, later, gave him a congratulatory dinner, at which he repeated his sentiments in fiery language; he proclaimed that he believed it to be the mission of this country, not only to secure Liberty at home, but throughout the world. When it is considered how nearly all the Governing Class, from the Queen downwards, were opposed to him, it is seen how dependent he was upon that Radicalism which, for the first time since the days of Wilkes, had become aggressively patriotic.

Cobden's method to help the foreign Liberal, with whom he had great sympathy, would have been to prevent the granting of loans to reactionary countries. This departure from the commercial ethics of *laissez-faire*—to lend money in the dearest market and borrow in the cheapest—illustrates how even the most obdurate of theories will break against elementary humanity, but to him and his pacific party war was an unthinkable remedy.

He and his friends were probably unaware that ever since 1845 the Duke of Wellington had been urging an extension of the Forces—at the time there were only five thousand regular soldiers in England and a hundred and fifty thousand militia. The Duke wished the latter to be a "trained and disciplined force", seventy-two thousand to be raised by "beat of drum" or from the Poor Law Unions. When Russell came into office, Palmerston demanded one hundred and forty thousand men to be enrolled, if necessary by ballot. Russell wrote confidentially to the Cabinet that "we are in considerable danger of sudden hostilities"; he suggested one hundred and fifty thousand men, but when he spoke in the House it became evident that the prospect of an additional fivepenny Income Tax was more alarming to the commercially-minded Commons that the fear of invasion. While the whole matter was under debate, the French Government collapsed and the scheme was abandoned; but to the historian the incident is interesting as illustrating the reviving interest in, and apprehension of, continental military activities.

Ever since Peel had resigned, the Government had been dependent upon the support of his hundred-odd followers. Both before and after his death, this, for the most part, was ungrudgingly given. There was, however, as yet no coalition, and many of the Peelite Tories were still opposed to much Liberal legislation.

The active part taken by Russell in the protest against what he called "Papal Aggression" (the Pope had created thirteen bishoprics in England with Wiseman as Archbishop of Westminster), calculated to foment a new anti-Catholic agitation, was condemned, not only by Radicals such as Roebuck, as contrary to religious toleration, but also gave offence to Anglo-Catholics who were strong among the Peelites. On the resignation of Russell, Aberdeen and Graham both refused to enter a coalition with him because of his promotion of the Ecclesiastical Titles Bill, which (although the Law Officers had already said that such a course was not illegal) sought to prohibit the assumption of hierarchic styles in the Roman Catholic Church in England. Russell offered to amend the Bill, but he had raised such an agitation that complete withdrawal was impossible, and less Aberdeen would not accept. It is curious to observe that the Pope unwittingly had made possible the return of the Conservatives in England by producing an insuperable disagreement between their common opponents.

In any case the whole position of Russell was unstable—for the need to placate the Peelites had made it most difficult for him to satisfy his own advanced supporters. On a division on further Franchise Reform the Prime Minister had said that he was prepared to lay proposals before Parliament in the next session; but the Radicals pressed for an immediate Bill, and the Government, who had internal budgetary difficulties on the Income Tax question, were defeated by four votes.

On February 21st, 1851, Russell resigned, and Lord Derby declining to form a government, advised the Queen to attempt a coalition between the Whigs and the Peelites. As has been said, the behaviour of Russell on the Ecclesiastical Titles Bill for the moment made coalition impossible, and in the end he returned again, still Prime Minister of a purely Liberal Government.

But soon Palmerston was once more in trouble; by the Court he had for a long time been regarded with aversion; it was said that he acted without consulting either his leader or the Queen. In 1849 and 1850 the Court had complained to Russell about this, and in 1851 the relations were strained to breaking-point by the reception accorded to Kossuth, the Hungarian patriot, by the Foreign Minister. He had received a deputation from Finsbury Radicals in which the Emperors of Russia and Austria were described as "despots, traitors and assassins," and Palmerston, instead of rebuking their enthusiasm, declared that he was gratified at the demonstration. In January, 1852, there followed the *coup d'état* in Paris. The President arrested many of the leading statesmen, and great excitement prevailed. Palmerston, while the Queen was urging neutrality, had told the French Ambassador, Walewski, in London, that he thought that what had been done by the President was to the "advantage of France and Europe". Normanby, the British Ambassador in Paris, complained of his inconsistent instructions, and, the whole Cabinet supporting Russell in the policy of neutrality, she wrote to Palmerston that "no other course is left than to ask the Queen to appoint a successor to you in the Foreign Office".

In less than three weeks Palmerston had his revenge. Russell had at last introduced his Militia Bill, now made necessary by the deterioration in the foreign situation. The Bill would only have reorganized the local forces, but Palmerston suggested that the whole regular militia should be reconstituted. By a majority of Peelites, Conservatives and others opposed to the Government, Palmerston's amendment to leave out "local" in Russell's resolution was carried by five votes and, again, Russell resigned.

During the period of his ministry, although the Radicals disagreed fundamentally on foreign affairs, they had all united to press for an enlarged electorate, and, just before he fell, the Prime Minister had introduced a Bill to lower the borough franchise to a £5-rating qualification and in the counties to £10-rated occupiers; he also proposed to complete the Toleration Acts by allowing Jews to omit the words "on the true Faith of a Christian", which then debarred them from sitting in Parliament, though not from being elected. This measure, however, got no further than its introduction.

There is little doubt that the victory of Free Trade, by bringing many Conservatives over to the Government, had temporarily weakened the Radical element. The division to which we have referred between Bright, Cobden, Gibson and the militants was another source of weakness. In any case, from the point of view of the condition of the great number of the workers, it mattered not whether the Radicals were powerful or weak; their best friends in practical affairs had been Tories such as Ashley, Sadler and Disraeli. By now, the old Chartist enthusiasm itself, principally political, was spent. It has been said how Ashley, in 1847, at last was able to limit the labour of women and young persons in textile factories to ten hours a day, and the comments on his Radical opponents of the time are revealing. "Bright", he wrote, "was ever my most malignant opponent, Cobden bitterly hostile"; so also the old Brougham in the Lords was among his "most heated opponents". Gladstone voted to rescind the division in favour of the Ten Hours Bill, as did Peel— both were of commercial ancestry and outlook. The revolutionary O'Connell was "a bitter opponent". Perhaps the most telling revelation of the mind of Victorian Radical Commercialism is to be found in Bright's speech on the Ten Hours Bill: "If this machinery Bill passes", he said, "I have advised my partners to set the example of turning the keys on our mills and to throw upon the legislators the responsibility of feeding the millions whom they will not allow us to employ at a profit". This was declared as late as September, 1865.

Miss Martineau, the Radical historian, according to Ashley, also gave "her voice and strength in opposition to the factory measures". As Disraeli said: "If a rapacious covetousness desecrating all the sanctities of human life has been the besetting sin of the last generation, in our time the altar of Mammon has flamed with a triple flare". His small band of young Tory democrats and philanthropists, whenever any social issue came before Parliament, were to be found in opposition to the official Whigs, manufacturers and official Tories; a few socialistic Liberals supporting them. Only in a demand for educational provision did the Radicals as a whole show any enthusiasm for social improvement, and in that subject, curiously, Ashley was not very interested.

As an old man he was by no means enthusiastic about the 1870 measure; indeed he said, "I do not expect much from it". He wished to reduce the age limit for compulsory education to ten, so fearful was he of what he called "idleness".

In 1850 the Amalgamated Society of Engineers had been founded and other unions were active, but none of them looked to Parliament for assistance in their work of raising the level of wages and conditions; yet in 1848, unknown to most of them, had been published the famous *Communist Manifesto* of Marx and Engels, in which the whole individualistic theory of betterment, which for the most part the Trade Unionists accepted, was denounced as a bourgeois mystification, and the inevitability of a class struggle was envisaged. But even when the new outlook had been transplanted to England, the "Working Men's International Association", which was addressed by Marx in 1864, was more concerned with revolutionary possibilities and the trade unions with immediate disputes about wages than were either with parliamentary action.

Apart, however, from the avowed Socialists, the departure from the tenets of economic individualism in the middle of the nineteenth century is well illustrated in the later works of John Stuart Mill, once an individualist, the political philosopher of the mid-Victorian Radical Movement.

The ideal improvement of mankind took the place in his mind of that merely negative conception of happiness which had possessed Bentham and Mill's father. Though most concerned to defend the liberty of minorities (which he saw might be challenged as well by a democracy as by a king), in his later books he became increasingly socialistic. In his autobiography he declares that he looks forward to "a time when the rule that they who do not work shall not eat, will be applied not to paupers only, but impartially to all". In earlier years he had been content to found himself upon Ricardo and Malthus, the latter of whom was even against all assistance to the poor in whatever form; now, however, writing in the 'sixties, he welcomes "socialistic experiments". "Before 1860," says Dicey, "in general, political economy was little more than a branch of utilitarianism." (*Law and Opinion in England*, p. 411.)

Thus, in the absence of all considered protest, if we except the writings of Carlisle, Ruskin, Dickens and Disraeli, it is not surprising that the mass of the people should have accepted the arid notion of a universal competitive struggle. The clergy, save in exceptional instances such as Maurice and Kingsley, did little to correct this impression, and concentrated on voluntary charity or personal salvation. The doctrines contained in such works as *Social Statics* of Herbert Spencer (an author who doubted whether even the police had not been given too much power) even in advanced circles remained almost unchallenged.

In all these circumstances, with philosophers, politicians, churchmen and men of literature all of one mind that capitalist competition was not only inevitable but desirable, it is not surprising to find the illiterate labourers for a long time hesitated to accept the alluring temptations of the new socialistic ideas.

CHAPTER V

FOREIGN AFFAIRS

From time to time the English people, who as a rule are concerned only with their own affairs, become conscious of the Continent. Sometimes this notice has been forced upon them by the jealousy or aggression of other nations—instances of such enforced interest may be found in the periods when Louis XIV or Napoleon I, the Emperor William II or Hitler were dominant, but there have been other occasions when it is less easy to account for that sudden popular regard for foreign affairs which has often proved so disconcerting to English statesmen.

As in the days of Walpole, the gentry at the time of Russell's Government were entirely pacific in intention and had been so ever since the fall of Napoleon. The most disingenuous democrat must admit, if he is honest, that the war fever which seized the nation in the fifties, with its accompaniment of alternate truculence and panic, was the direct fruit of popular emancipation. What is peculiar in the years preceding the Crimean War is the sudden change in the personality of the public enemy. When Russell fell, on the plea that he had not provided sufficiently for national defence, the person most feared in England was Napoleon III. The Press was full of alarming matter about him—a French fleet was being built in secret at Cherbourg. Now that steamships existed, the Emperor "could easily land 50,000 or 60,000 troops on the south coast in a single night". In reality, steam having rendered the Navy far more mobile, had made the prospects of invasion much less favourable than they were in the uncertain sailing days of George III.

The Peace Societies and "false economy" were denounced in *The Times*, other less responsible journals were more violent; the attitude of young Beauchamp, as portrayed by Meredith, is typical of the new patriotic Radicalism. The death of the Duke of Wellington, in November, reminded thousands of people of the hated Napoleon, and there were not wanting many to recall the fact that the present Emperor was his nephew.

Meanwhile, Cobden laboured to improve Anglo-French relations. At his side stood Bright, and, less publicly, the new Conservative Government and the Sovereign herself. But a new spirit was abroad, incited by Palmerston. Such Chartists, as still remained, and the patriotic Radicals interpreted their Liberalism as a crusade—if their duty to free the oppressed involved war, that circumstance must be faced; in the exigencies of the time their interest in domestic reform seemed to take a second place.

The first session of Derby's administration was occupied by the majority Opposition in making Disraeli forswear Protection, and this he did, adroitly, with the aid of Palmerston, though old Tories murmured. As regards positive legislation, a strong Militia Bill was passed and a new force of eighty thousand men, to receive at least three weeks' training, constituted. The nationalist Radicals and Liberals, supported by Palmerston, helped to carry the measure, Russell and the pacifists alone objecting. The social interest of Disraeli produced a new Public Health measure, and the Empire was strengthened by the granting of a constitution to New Zealand. These and some legal reforms had all been achieved by the minority Conservative Government when Parliament was dissolved in July, 1852.

Protection found no place in the electoral appeal of the Government. To the dismay of some Protectionists, Disraeli admitted the success of Free Trade—he conciliated his followers by promising some alternative benefit to Agriculture. In the event the Tories were found to be the largest party in the new House, some three hundred strong. The Peelites had fallen to forty; and several important Liberals, such as Sir George Grey and Cornwall Lewis, were defeated; nevertheless the mixed opposition of Liberals, Radicals of every kind, Peelites and the Irish, had a majority over the Government of about forty.

When Parliament met it was made clear that the official policy was to abandon Protection. Again it was sought to embarrass the Government by the passing of academic resolutions on Free Trade. Far more important was the Administration's success in abating the friction with France. Malmesbury, the Foreign Minister, had for long been of opinion that a *rapprochement* was possible. He was a friend of Louis Napoleon, and the Government started to negotiate a commercial treaty. There was no time to complete the matter, but despite the belligerent tone of the newspapers, the work continued and, officially at any rate, good relations were restored before the Tories were defeated on their second Budget in December.

In this final division Palmerston abstained, but Whigs, Radicals, Peelites and Irish, all combined to defeat by nineteen votes the Derby administration. In reality many of the financial proposals of the Tories were of a surprisingly advanced nature; the Conservatives were defeated on the very principles which later Liberal and Labour were to make their own—the increase of direct taxation, and, even more remarkable, discrimination between earned and unearned income. Never did a government fall more gallantly fighting its opponents' cause!

There followed the usual manœuvres incident to a period when there exists no strong party government. For some time the Peelites had been divided as to whether they should support Derby or the Liberals—Graham favoured the latter, but Aberdeen, Herbert and Gladstone, now that the Tories had dropped Protection, were inclined to join the Conservatives. Most improperly, Prince Albert had secretly written to Derby encouraging a coalition and suggesting that Gladstone should take the place of Disraeli in the Commons—how far Gladstone knew of this is not clear. Some decision had become essential—first it was hoped that Lord Lansdowne, a veteran Whig, would form a government. The refusal of Palmerston to serve made Russell's resumption as Prime Minister impossible, and finally Lord Aberdeen, the leader of the Peelites, consented to preside over a coalition of his own party and the Whigs.

Russell, from the outset, made difficulties. The proposal to give seven seats in the Cabinet and the Leadership to a party some forty strong as against the Liberal two hundred and seventy, seemed to him unfair, and so it was, if mere numbers and not capacity were to be considered. Moreover, to assimilate the discordant Whigs and Radicals was artificial. Many of the former were much nearer the Peelites than they were to their own advanced party colleagues; the followers of Palmerston were alienated from those of Russell—the Radicals were deeply divided. Once the Peelites had decided to join their fellow Free-Traders, of all the Coalition their small group was probably the most homogeneous, and certainly contained, in proportion to its numbers, the greatest talent.

Another difficulty was that Palmerston had at first refused to join on the ground that he and Aberdeen had always fundamentally disagreed on foreign affairs. At length, however, though he would much rather have supported Derby, he was persuaded to come in. He took the office of Home Secretary, thus saving his political consistency and gratifying the Court by his necessary abstention from a direct control of foreign matters. One Radical, Molesworth, was included in the Cabinet in the subordinate Office of Works and another, Villiers, was in the Ministry. Of the Peelites there were included Aberdeen, Herbert, Graham, Cranworth, Newcastle and Argyle, with Gladstone as Chancellor of the Exchequer.

Russell, temporarily, went to the Foreign Office, and the other Whigs in addition to Palmerston were Granville, Wood and Lansdowne. It was a coalition of all the talents; but, like most gifted Cabinets, its strength was impaired by the vigorous personalities of its opinionated members. From the beginning there was trouble. Russell wished to combine the offices of Leader of the House and Foreign Secretary. This failing, he would continue to lead, but without office, and Clarendon should become Foreign Secretary. Next, he insisted that the Government should introduce a reform of the Franchise to which both Whigs and Peelites in the Government had pledged themselves. Most surprising of all, he insisted that he should have the *spes successionis* of the office of Prime Minister.

At the Home Office, Palmerston, in the words of the critical Shaftesbury, was ready "to undertake any good work of kindness for humanity and the social good, especially to the child and the working class". In 1853 Palmerston introduced and got passed a measure to include all children in the limitation of twelve hours' factory labour. For men and women, however, he would do nothing; he declared in the House that "it was a matter of considerable delicacy to interfere by legislation with the employment of those who, being of age, were to be considered as free agents, and therefore, ought to be at liberty to work as long or as little as they should think fit to do".

In 1853 he also was responsible foi an Act dealing with youthful offenders and at the Home Office instituted a ticket-of-leave system for convicts. His views on public health were in advance of his times and against Bright he supported proposals for smoke abatement.

The Government decided, principally owing to the opposition of Palmerston, to delay their Reform Bill until the next session. There were now over a hundred and fifty advanced Liberals and Radicals in the House and their desires could no longer be ignored; the most they would concede was a postponement. Had it not been for the outbreak of war, there is little doubt that the Government would have been persuaded to inaugurate considerable reforms, both political and economic.

It was not to be; already the foreign situation, which had been eased by the *rapprochement* with France, was worsening in another quarter. Although Napoleon was denounced by Cabinet Ministers as a despot as late as 1853, the Tsar it was who now came to be substituted by almost the whole Press, save *The Times*, for Napoleon as the great menace to England and Liberty. The real question which perplexed all Europe arose out of the future of Turkey. In 1844 the Tsar had been in England and had discussed with Aberdeen and Peel what was to happen when, as everybody anticipated, the Turkish state "must crumble to pieces". In 1853 the Ambassador in St. Petersburgh, Sir George Seymour, renewed the conversation on the basis of a secret memorandum as to the partition of Turkey which had been drawn up during the Tsar's visit in 1844. A dispute had arisen about the respective rights of Greek and Roman Catholics to the Holy Places in Jerusalem, and it was said that the Sultan had favoured the Roman Catholics, who were normally protected by France. Lord Stratford de Redcliffe, the Ambassador to the Porte, was able to persuade the Turk to give the Greek Christians equal rights, but he dissented from the Russian view that they should have protective powers over Greek Christians such, as it was said, the French had over Roman Catholics. The Turks, thus encouraged, refused the Russian demand and received an ultimatum; the Tsar marched into Waldachia and Moldavia, threatening to hold them as hostages; already as a gesture the French had sent their fleet to Salamis, but England for the time refused to co-operate with them.

Nevertheless, while the Russians were crossing the Pruth to occupy the provinces by way of protest, the English Navy had proceeded to the Dardanelles. Austria and Prussia became concerned, and in July all Four Powers sent a joint Note to Russia to provide for the integrity of the Sultan, while conceding some of the Russian claims. In September the basis of the Note was abandoned, the Turks being dissatisfied, as the

Tsar would concede no more than an admission that he would not interfere at large with Turkey.

Disturbances broke out at Constantinople. The British Navy, to protect British subjects violated the neutrality of the Dardanelles as provided by treaty. Next, the Turks sent an ultimatum to the Russians demanding the evacuation of the occupied provinces and, on a refusal, declared war. Even now, though the English newspapers raved against him, the Tsar strove for peace; after long negotiation he agreed that if England and France would withdraw their navies, he would call back his troops; meanwhile there should be an armistice. Only two matters remained for settlement—whether the Tsar should withdraw before he negotiated, and whether he would abstain from dealing with Turkey direct—to neither of these requirements would he agree.

In reply, England and France in their turn sent an ultimatum demanding that the Russians should evacuate the provinces at once; Austria and Prussia associated themselves in an evasive manner, but on war being declared by England and France, neither of the German countries would take an action.

These facts, and the further one that the Russians had already succeeded in November, 1853, in destroying the Turkish fleet at Sinope, following a consistent agitation by the public journals which had excited even the Queen and her Consort, were the actual reasons for the war which broke out at the end of March, 1854—it remains to examine its reaction on English politics.

Whatever may have been the deficiencies of Cobden and Bright in domestic politics, there is no doubt that they raised an issue of supreme importance to England and the world when they declared that it was impossible, without imposing conscription and accepting the sacrifice of all hope of plenty at home, for Britain to go crusading abroad against every Government or Monarch whom the Liberal-minded thought to be reactionary. Their opposition to Palmerstonian Liberalism, which had first engendered this chivalrous if impracticable desire, was maintained boldly when the country was at peace, and even more courageously when at last it was at war. They were without a Press, they fought against every natural prejudice arising from pride, fear or honest indignation; they braved extreme unpopularity and political annihilation. They were prepared to be burned in effigy or to be howled down at meetings, they faced every kind of misrepresentation and obloquy for what they thought to be right and, hardest of all, had to bear the taunt that they were deserting their fellow Radicals abroad. In the case of the Crimean War that particular consideration scarcely existed. The most ardent Radical had difficulty in representing the Turkish Sultan as a Liberal ruler; from a Christian point of view, it was the enemy Russia which was within the fold. Yet all this did nothing to abate the insane war fever which Radicals like Layard, Roebuck and Lindsay, together with anti-Russians, such as Urquhart, encouraged—for the moment all these vigorous protesters could do was furiously to assert their opinions.

Some weeks before the actual declaration of war, a banquet had been given by the Liberals to the Commander of the Baltic fleet, Sir Charles Napier. Graham, the First Lord, who was present, said that he would

D*

give the Admiral free consent to "declare war" when he went into the Baltic. Palmerston, who was in the chair, declared the Sultan to be "a great reformer" and said that Napoleon (who later tried to make a secret peace with Russia) was a man of "the most perfect good faith"—a few days after Bright rebuked him in the House. That pacifist denounced the "reckless levity manifested by the ministers of a civilized and Christian nation". After war had been declared he spoke again, attacking the loss of freedom of action produced by foreign alliances, more particularly when the ally was the Turk. In his own constituency Cobden had to face hostile resolutions from his erstwhile supporters. There is little doubt that the harassed Prime Minister secretly agreed with them. A month before the war he had asked Gladstone, who was much of his frame of mind, "How could he bring himself to fight for the Turks?" "We stand," answered the compromising Gladstone, "upon the ground that the Emperor has invaded countries not his own." Yet he said privately in November, 1854, that he thought one of Bright's letters of protest to be "an able and a manly one, and though I cannot go all his lengths, I respect him". To the serious and religious Gladstone, the bantering of Bright by Palmerston as the "reverend gentleman" must have been most distasteful.

In the end it was the incapacity of the Government to produce speedy military results and not any disinclination for war which brought them down. When the censure came, it was moved by a Radical, Roebuck, who, after the failure of transport and the terrible diseases of the troops had become known in England, called for a committee to enquire into the condition of the Army and of the departments responsible.

This was on January 23, 1855. Russell, who had wished to go in 1854 and had sought the reorganization of the War Office and the removal of Newcastle, the War Minister, now said that he for one could not resist the motion, and immediately resigned. The refusal of the Government under the persuasion of Palmerston to allow Russell's Reform Bill to proceed, though he supported Palmerston in war policy, had in any event made his position for some time a most uncertain one. Two days after, the Government was defeated by over one hundred and fifty votes, and Aberdeen surrendered his office on the 31st.

To those, like Bright, who were now seeking to bring this "just but unnecessary war", as Disraeli had called it, to an early end, the failure of Derby to form a government must have caused great disappointment. At first that easily desponding statesman had sought the support of Palmerston, who, as Home Secretary, had not been involved in the general condemnation of the Government. It was assumed that there would be no difficulty in forming an administration led by these two, but Palmerston refused to join unless Gladstone came with him. This was probably an excuse, for very soon it became clear that, in any event, the late Home Secretary himself wished to be Prime Minister.

Despite the growth of the doctrine that the Crown acts always on the advice of ministers, there is one occasion when it is comparatively free, namely, when there is no Government to tender counsel. In such cases it had always been the constitutional rule that, subject to support being forthcoming in the Commons, the Monarch can send for whom he will, though of late it had come to be expected that the leader of the Opposition would be summoned. Threatened with Palmerston, on the failure of Derby, the Queen sent for Russell. Prince Albert sought to find whether the Peelites and Palmerston would come in, for Lord Lansdowne reported that in any event Russell would refuse to serve under Palmerston, and Herbert "expressed apprehension at the effect upon the prospects of peace which would be produced by Lord Palmerston's being at the head of the Government". (*Letters of Queen Victoria*, 1851–1861, p. 110.)

On February 2nd the Queen saw Russell. He suggested a government led by Lansdowne or Clarendon, but declared that he thought that he could form one himself, if Palmerston and the Peelites would agree; Lord Aberdeen, however, had already made it clear that such a course was impossible, for it was the desertion of Russell on Roebuck's censure which primarily had brought down the administration. Finally, on February 5th, recourse had to be made to the only man the public wanted, Palmerston. The Peelites retained their offices; though Aberdeen and Russell refused to serve, otherwise there was little change in personnel.

The first trouble which arose was with regard to the appointment of Roebuck's committee of investigation. The late Government having been defeated on this very matter, Palmerston thought that he could not well refuse it; the concession drove Graham, Gladstone and Herbert to resign—they felt that they, among others, would be the subject of enquiry and that such a position was incompatible with office. Their withdrawal gave the Prime Minister a complete supremacy. Russell went off to Vienna to attend a preliminary peace conference and Palmerston immediately proceeded to send Commissions to the Crimea to consider the reform of transport services and supply, and amalgamated the two Secretariats of the War Office into one department.

By now, however, it was apparent that, at the best, no more could be hoped from the War than the capture of Sebastopol. The fact that Russell had been sent to Vienna was hoped by Bright to afford an opportunity for compromise. Indeed, Russell had already agreed to three or four points—a European guarantee of the autonomy of the Danube States, the free navigation of the Danube, and the relinquishment by Russia of her claim to protect Greek Christians in Turkey. Only on the means of regulating Russian naval power in the Black Sea was there any outstanding difference. Russell thought the matter could be settled on the basis of the Austrian compromise, but the Prime Minister had made up his mind that the conference should fail—the public insisted that peace should not be made until Sebastopol had fallen. Nevertheless, when that event happened, the Press still continued to clamour for war, but by this time the French were sated. Napoleon was suspected of desiring immediate peace and, at the conference which met at Paris, the French were often seen to side with the Russians. In these circumstances, Palmerston could not alone continue hostilities, and a final peace was signed on March 30th.

Before the conference adjourned, the parties had agreed to important provisions with regard to marine warfare, which later became the subject of much contention. By the Declaration of Paris, as it was called, enemy merchandise, other than contraband of war, if carried under neutral flags, was not liable to capture, and blockades to be binding were required to be effective. By this treaty the ancient right of search was abandoned, but it was not to be expected that in the increasing tension of later years maritime Powers, such as England, would allow her power to be thus restricted.

At home, the advanced Liberals were still divided, for Bright was prepared to support Palmerston if he would but obtain an early peace, while Layard still wished the war not only to continue but to be extended to cover all oppressed peoples. Soon another cause for hostilities arose— in the autumn of 1856 England went to war with Persia, and a combined naval and military force defeating that country, peace was signed in March, 1857, the Persians agreeing not to interfere with Afghanistan, which had been the principal subject of dispute.

The Income Tax had now reached 1s. 4d. in the pound and it became necessary to reduce the army estimates; but once more Palmerston could not keep out of war. His new quarrel was with the Chinese over a vessel flying the British flag which had been boarded by a mandarin. The admiral seized the ports at Canton and bombarded the city, the Chinese in their turn murdered several Europeans, and on the matter being raised in the House, Derby in the Lords and Cobden in the Commons —an unusual combination—censured the Government. In the Lower House, Palmerston was defeated by sixteen votes and promptly appealed to the nation.

It was a typical "Jingo" election. He claimed the right to oppose the "insolent barbarian at Canton, who had violated the British flag, broken the engagements of treaties, offered rewards for the heads of British subjects in China, and planned their destruction by murder, assassinations and poisons". The sole question for the country was whether they approved of Palmerston and his policy, and the answer admitted of no doubt. The Radicals suffered grievously; Cobden, Bright, Gibson, Fox and Miall all lost their seats; the Peelites also fared very badly, and Palmerston was returned with a majority, pledged personally to him, of over seventy.

In the new House, although the Manchester school Radicals had been defeated, yet there were many advanced Liberals pledged to Electoral Reform and the Ballot. Palmerston, however, was not interested—the most he would concede, to the great indignation of Gladstone, was the secularization of Divorce procedure, which he described as "practical reform". A Royal Commission had suggested Radical changes in the marriage laws. The theological Gladstone wearied a sceptical House with Canon Law and long quotations from the Council of Trent, but the Archbishop of Canterbury and nine of his suffragans supported the measure, and this ecclesiastical dispute and problems arising from the mutiny in India entirely absorbed the time of Parliament. The suppression of the Mutiny by such drastic measures as the blowing of sepoys from guns and the denunciations of Indians as "semi-maniac human beings" and similar cries for "blood, fire, fury and destruction" (*Scottish Review*, April, 1858, p. 125) showed that the long epoch of militant vainglory was even yet not spent. When, unexpectedly, Palmerston fell, it was upon just one of those nationalistic appeals to what Mussolini has called "Sacred Egoism".

Although the actual defeat of Palmerston arose upon a subordinate matter—the desire of the Prime Minister that conspiracies in England to commit murder abroad should be made a felony—there is little doubt that several other factors had contributed to swell the Opposition vote. At the close of 1857 there had been a serious financial crisis which, like later ones, had its origin in America, where there had been a great over-issue of paper. In the autumn the banks of Liverpool, Glasgow, and the Western Bank of Scotland had all suspended payment. The Bank of England was compelled to raise its rate to ten per cent and, owing to the general position, had to issue two million pounds' worth of notes; to do this involved the suspension of the Bank Charter Act of 1844. At the same time fighting continued in India, and it was generally felt that both the Government and the East India Company had shown themselves incompetent.

To meet general criticism, the Government, in February, 1858, had introduced a Bill to abolish that system of dual government Pitt had framed in 1784, which had so lamentably failed. They proposed to abolish the old Board of Control and transfer all the powers of the Company to a new Council for India, the President to be a member of the Government. This measure might have placated Parliament, but Palmerston failed to realize the disquiet which, caused by his levity and insolence in the face of the terrible news through from India. Moreover, according to Greville, nothing had damaged him more than the appointment at the end of 1857 of Clanricarde, who was generally reputed to be a roué, to the Privy Seal.

It was in these circumstances that England was truculently asked by Count Walewski, the French Foreign Minister, to refuse asylum to criminal refugees. The Orsini conspiracy to murder the French Emperor had undoubtedly been arranged in London and bombs had been made here at the request of the plotters. It appears that Palmerston for once failed to satisfy English patriotic sentiment in not answering the insulting letter of the French minister. His Bill was thought to be a servile compliance with French dictation and, as in the case of the Crimean enquiry, again it was a bellicose Radical, this time Milner Gibson, who moved the rejection.

In the debate on the first reading most of the Conservatives voted with the Government, and they obtained a majority of two hundred. But in the ten days which elapsed before the second reading on February 19th, the Press and the Radicals had been at work: the question was now not so much whether the Bill was right as whether the country should remain silent when the French had affronted her. Gibson's amendment was, in effect, a vote of censure, and this time Disraeli persuaded the Conservatives to vote for it. With them were combined eighty-four Liberals, including Russell, and the Peelites, Gladstone, Graham and the malcontent Radicals. By 234 votes to 215 they decided that the Government had lost their confidence and thereupon Palmerston resigned.

This time Derby did not hesitate to take office. He tried to include Gladstone and Grey, but they both declined, and a wholly Conservative Ministry was formed.

Derby soon announced that an India Bill would be proceeded with at once, that Walewski's despatch should be answered, and also promised a Reform Bill for the next session. The relations with France were again very strained, but Walewski replied temperately to Malmesbury, saying that the French government would "place its reliance on the loyalty of the English people", and Disraeli was able to announce to the House that the "painful misconceptions had entirely terminated".

As to the India Bill, that country being yet in disorder, the Government frankly invited the co-operation of the whole House to devise a way out. Both Palmerston's proposed measure and that of the Government were dropped and a basis for a new Act found in a series of non-party resolutions. Russell, Roebuck, Graham and Bright (who had been chosen for Birmingham, after his defeat at Manchester) assisted, and a new agreed Government of India Act was passed with a responsible Secretary of State for India to be advised by an expert Council, another council to be appointed to assist the Viceroy in India: the long rule of the East India Company was over, it had been killed by the Mutiny. The hitherto divided authority of the Board of Control and the Company had been transferred to the new Secretary of State in Council. In India the Viceroy continued to represent the Crown. A settlement had been reached which lasted for over half a century.

This solution was not one peculiarly raising Liberal principles, for few, even of the Radicals, ever thought that the natives, who were still largely in revolt, were entitled to any degree of self-government. But at home the failure to make any advance for a quarter of a century on the electoral settlement of 1832 in certain quarters was once more causing some discontent. It has been recorded how Russell, in 1854, had been compelled to withdraw his Reform Bill. He had then proposed to transfer sixty-six seats from the small boroughs to the large towns. He would have given votes to lodgers and have enfranchised occupiers of £6 rateable value in the Boroughs and £10 in the Counties.

The Radicals had decided to support the second reading, though the Chartists still maintained that the Bill would leave the "aristocracy of labour" without votes. On the whole, however, Labour was more concerned to secure a ten-hour day in factories and an inspection of coal-mines, than to agitate for votes. Russell, as is known, in April withdrew his Bill, and thereafter most Radicals, in the comparative failure of the Crimean operations, concentrated on what was called "administrative reform"—it was, in the words of an association established for that object, to "destroy the aristocratical monopoly of Power and Place". Not only the democratic *Morning Advertiser* but even *The Times* attacked the "incompetency, aristocratic hauteur and official indifference, favour and routine" of the administrative departments. A great meeting was held in Drury Lane in June, 1855, with Charles Dickens as principal speaker, and a strong demand for the complete reform of the Civil Service arose which ultimately induced Palmerston to set up a Civil Service Commission. At the time open competitive examination was not conceded, but the more glaring effects of patronage were restrained by an examination of nominated candidates.

John Stuart Mill had already advocated throwing open the Civil Service to competition, and in 1853 a report by Northcote and Trevelyan had urged this reform. Russell disliked the idea. He did not see how it could be effected without "at last the aristocracy being altogether dissociated from the permanent Civil Service". But in January, 1854, the Cabinet was converted to Gladstone's view of open opportunity— even then the progress to open competition was slow. Not until 1860 was a system inaugurated for a limited competition among nominated candidates, and in 1870 it was agreed that a minister might, if he wished, throw open his department to general competition.

Having disposed of India, the next work of the Government was to inaugurate a general scheme of drainage for London, and, for the first time, a general authority, the Metropolitan Board of Works, was constituted for the whole Metropolis which so far had been administered, apart from the City, by vestries (of which there were no less than twenty-three) and district boards. The Metropolis Local Management Act of 1855, it was later said, had "put a virtual monopoly into the hands of the corruptest shop-keeping class in the world". The powers of the Metropolitan Board of Works were limited, and Government by Vestry was increasingly attacked until the Acts setting up the London County Council and Metropolitan Boroughs were passed in the later years of the nineteenth century.

As to Reform, Disraeli, unlike Russell (who for so long had taken 1832 as a final concession), as early as 1848 had spoken of "a larger representation of the industrial class". His organ *The Press*, had made franchise reform a part of the Conservative policy, and the carrying of a Radical motion to assimilate the County and Borough franchise, in 1851, had actually brought about the defeat of the Whig Government. The Bill of 1852 had perished with the administration, and that of 1854, as has been said, was withdrawn. Palmerston's reluctant proposals had never been introduced, and now it remained for the Conservatives to deal with the matter. Their Bill was introduced in February, 1859—it would have reduced the occupation franchise in Counties from £50 to £10, the Borough one at £10 remaining untouched; what came to be called "fancy franchise votes" to owners of £60 in the savings bank, lodgers in part of a £20 house, and graduates, lawyers, doctors and schoolmasters, were suggested. Disraeli also asked that seats taken from fifteen small boroughs should be given to industrial counties and towns.

His insistence that representation should be given to interest and not to numbers was emphatic. Whigs and Radicals pointed out that the new proposals would do nothing to bring in the working people, and Russell, Roebuck and Bright made mock of the "fancy franchises". In the opinion of the Queen, the Whigs as a whole, however, did not take this view. In writing to King Leopold she said that Russell had allied himself with Bright and Roebuck and had no other followers. She was mistaken, as a motion of Russell that "no readjustment of the franchise will satisfy the country which does not provide for a greater extension of the suffrage than is contemplated in the present measure" was carried by 330 against 291. There followed a General Election, and on June 7th, in the new Parliament, the Government were defeated by a majority of thirteen and resigned.

Lord Palmerston again became Prime Minister, an office which he continued to hold until his death. Again the Queen tried avoiding the necessity of his employment; she sent for Granville without result, but after Russell had agreed to become Foreign Secretary and work under his old rival—Gladstone also consenting to take office—there was nothing left but to entrust the premiership to Palmerston.

Once more the country was excited by foreign events—the French Empire was now at the height of its power and was beginning, at the price of obtaining Savoy and Nice, to support Cavour in an effort to throw off the Austrian yoke. In March, 1860, Victor Emmanuel annexed central Italy to Piedmont and Lombardy, which he already had won, and in April he entered Florence. Garibaldi sailed to Sicily and thence triumphantly marched north. The effect of his entry into Naples and the support which England gave to the Italians indirectly made Louis Napoleon, the friend of Italy, less unpopular in England. On October 27th, 1860, Russell declared the Government were bound to admit that the Italians were the best judges of their own interests, and that the Pope and the king of the two Sicilies had provided so ill for the welfare of their people that their subjects looked to their overthrow as a necessary preliminary to any improvement. In February, 1861, amidst universal enthusiasm in England, particularly of the Radicals, the first Parliament of United Italy was convoked. The excitement, more particularly on behalf of Garibaldi, had much weakened what small interest still existed outside political circles in the Reform Bills. In March, Russell had introduced such Bills for England, Scotland and Ireland, suggesting a £6 householder franchise, twenty-five seats to be taken from boroughs and given to large towns and provincial universal representation, only to withdraw the proposals on Whig and Tory objection in June. In 1861 Radical motions for a £10 householder franchise in the counties and £6 in the boroughs were both defeated, and it seemed for the time as if all enthusiasm had disappeared—the zeal for Garibaldi was more evident than concern for domestic political improvement. As Cobden sadly wrote, "When will the masses of this country begin to think of home politics"; and Bright lamented, when he saw so many working men cheering Garibaldi, "If the people would only make a few such demonstrations for themselves, we could do something for them".

By far the most important circumstance connected with the last government of Palmerston as it affected the Liberal Party was the remarkable rise during this period of Gladstone to celebrity. He had taken office as Chancellor of the Exchequer for the second time with much misgiving. His relations with Palmerston had always been difficult; but the old statesman at least agreed with Gladstone about the emancipation of Italy—there he discovered "real and close harmony". "The overwhelming interest and weight of the Italian question" reconciled him to differences upon electoral reform, expenditure upon fortifications and armaments and many other matters.

The Prime Minister in 1859 was again possessed by his recurrent fear of the French. He pressed for further increases in the armed services and for elaborate strengthening of the coast defences. Volunteers, as an auxiliary force, were encouraged, and Gladstone ruefully saw a constantly increasing expenditure for which he, as Chancellor, would be responsible. The settlement between the Austrian and French Emperors in July, 1859, had ended the Italian war, but the incorporation of Savoy and Nice in

March, 1860, by the French, was intensely unpopular in England, and there is no doubt that, generally, the behaviour of Napoleon did little to ease the position.

In the midst of these alarms, Gladstone conceived the idea of using his office to dissipate suspicion. He persuaded the Government to allow Cobden to interview the Emperor in December, 1859, and ask him whether the French would agree to a commercial treaty. Negotiations followed, and finally Lord Russell was persuaded to give to Cobden an official position. The protectionists in France had made every difficulty, but Cobden persisted and, in the end, an agreement was reached, to be signed in January, 1860. It was a triumph for Gladstone and the pacific school over the Jingoes, who had for so long inflamed public opinion, and it was achieved not by any emotional appeal, but by the more subtle argument of commercial advantage.

From now onwards it was recognized that the future of Liberalism lay with Gladstone. His reputation, already considerable, both with moderate business men, with the middle classes, and the manual operatives, was enhanced by his financial success as Chancellor of the Exchequer. As Morley writes, "Out of the commercial treaty with France grew the whole of the great financial scheme of 1860". (*Gladstone*, Vol. I, p. 657.) The engagement of France to reduce many duties, such as that on iron, enabled the Chancellor to withdraw from customs duty, reciprocally, over three hundred and fifty articles—as the Chancellor said, "Free Trade has reached its zenith". A great dispute arose out of the abolition of excise on paper, which was rejected in the Lords. This raised that long contention with the Upper House which continued for the rest of Gladstone's political life.

He persuaded the aged Palmerston, unwillingly, to attack the Lords, and the House of Commons by a majority of over thirty supported him. For the moment the Government accepted the position; but in 1861, Gladstone, with that ingenuity of mind which his opponents called "jesuitical", tacked the repeal of the Paper Duty to the general Finance Act, and so threw upon the Lords the responsibility of rejecting the whole Budget. For this device, in the Commons he obtained a majority of fifteen—the whole question of cheap newspapers was at stake, and for many years afterwards the Press acclaimed him as their liberator. The Lords surrendered, and, until the Budget of 1910, abstained from interference in matters of finance.

Gladstone, was still, however, in combat with many of the Cabinet on the question of the expense and expedience of great military and naval estimates—he endeavoured to show, on information received from Cobden in Paris, that the fears of French aggression were exaggerated. It is from this time that the growth of friendship between him and John Bright became very noticeable. Bright realized that, at last, his views had obtained a powerful influence in the Cabinet. Russell, despite his earlier promises, had thrown over Reform. Palmerston had tried to betray Gladstone in the earlier stages of the dispute with the Lords— it was evident that the future of progressive Liberalism must depend upon the union of Gladstone and Bright.

At this stage a new conflict, the American Civil War, temporarily disturbed the new nascent Liberalism. There was undoubtedly a Liberal feeling for the South, based upon the ground that the secessionists should be entitled to become free if they do so desire. This was the opinion both of Gladstone and his friend Acton—the Southern states to them were a nation; like the Italians, the Hungarians or the Poles, they were conceived as "rightly struggling to be free". The Conservatives (who were of opinion that the only gentlemen in America were to be found in the South) had the same sympathies. They were alarmed to think that the North, who represented the new democracy, might be victorious. On the other hand, the old dislike of slave owners was still strong in Radical and Evangelical circles, and after Lincoln had declared freedom for the slaves, the Evangelicals, Friends and many Radicals had no doubt which side was right. Bright, addressing the Trade Unions in March, 1863, eloquently pleaded for the abolition of servitude. The Government, on the other hand, by proclaiming British neutrality, had gone far to recognize the Southern States as a separate entity, and Gladstone, who in his early days had defended his father in the House as a slave owner, did not take an active position against slavery, a failure which, at a later date, he frankly regretted. Palmerston and most of his class secretly welcomed any division which would weaken the growing power of the Americans, and for the time a complete accord between Bright and Gladstone was delayed.

By February, 1863, Bright was able to write to an American friend that opinion had greatly changed and that in almost every town great meetings were held to pass resolutions in favour of the North. Nevertheless in June, Roebuck proposed in the House an alliance with Napoleon to aid the Southern States; the Emperor had already suggested mediation. In 1864 the North took the offensive and in the spring of the next year the war was at an end. It was soon after this that Bright was able to declare to his constituents that his preaching "on Foreign Policy and non-intervention had not been without effect"; and although excitement had been aroused by the cruel suppression by the Russians of the Polish rising in 1863, Palmerston no longer actively sought to intervene. Russell was zealous for Poland, it was an old Whiggish cause; he it was, the Queen thought, who now needed restraint, rather than Palmerston. A general Congress, suggested by the French, was not encouraged; the Queen was alarmed that the matter might end with a war between England and France against Germany. In the end the Poles were deserted —it was not the first time.

A far more serious matter for future generations arose when it appeared that the Prussians were threatening to seize Schleswig, which belonged to Denmark. In 1864 the Germans attacked. The French, sore at the failure of England to assist them in Poland, were supine. Russell wished for a naval demonstration to impress the Germans, but Bismarck and his Austrian allies were not to be intimidated. The Danes, unsupported, were defeated; the Germans had tasted the first fruit of that success in the Bismarckian policy of force which was to culminate in the great German wars of the twentieth century.

At the time, however, the British people as a whole were indifferent. They had begun to realize that England had not the power to do more on the Continent than protest. The period of Palmerstonian bluff was over. The Prussians were beginning to organize themselves into a great military machine. Not Goethe and Kant, but Moltke and Bismarck became their exemplars.

The behaviour of the Germans at this period was prophetical. They had been a party to the possession of the Duchies of Schleswig and Holstein by Denmark in 1852. They now alleged the insufferable wrongs of Germans in those provinces! The Liberals in Germany supported Bismarck. They with the Austrians, soon themselves to be routed, decided to crush the Danes while the rest of Europe stood by. In the end Prussia obtained the deep-water port of Kiel which, in truth, had always been the purpose of the whole campaign. Next year it was the turn of Austria to be defeated at Sadowa; and Hanover, helpless, was incorporated into Prussia—the beginning of the era of conscious German chicanery and aggression may confidently be dated from this time. Never till now were politics to be free from a perpetual Teutonic menace to the peace of Europe and the World.

The War Party, according to Gladstone, were Palmerston, Russell, Lord Stanley of Alderney and the Lord Chancellor, but the majority were against intervention. In the House, Disraeli taunted the Government with failure to uphold the independence and integrity of Denmark; Cobden asserted that England had encouraged the Danes to fight and then had deserted them. Gladstone was put up to reply. The reality was that England had not 20,000 men to put in the field against the Germanic hordes and there was little opportunity of naval demonstration. The refusal of the French to move made intervention impracticable, and the Government accepted an amendment which was carried by eighteen votes in favour of inaction; it was a great decline from the earlier days of Palmerston.

In July, 1865, there was a General Election; resulting in a gain of some twenty seats for the Government, and thus encouraged, with a majority of about sixty, on the death of Palmerston in October, a new era of Liberalism, specifically "Gladstonian", started with "Peace, Retrenchment and Reform" for its watchwords. Until the close of his life Palmerston had continued to demand more defences and national expenditure, though, curiously, the rapidly mounting power of Germany did not seem to trouble him.

"Gladstone will soon have it all his own way", he remarked; "whenever he gets my place, we shall have some strange doings"—as clearly as any one, he saw that the day of chauvinistic Whiggery was over.

And now to speak of the new man whose actual leadership might be delayed, but whose coming power was inevitable. What manner of person was he? It is remarkable that no biographer has ever succeeded in making the character of the founder of Liberalism really intelligible. G. W. E. Russell is probably the nearest the mark when he wrote that "Gladstone was essentially and above all, a Christian—it was this religiousness of character which won him the affectionate reverence of great masses of his countrymen, who had never seen his face". (*Gladstone*, Russell, p. 8.) He goes on: "This keen sense of the religious bearing of political questions determined Gladstone's action in not a few of the crises of his parliamentary life. It was the exacting vigour of a religious theory that drove him out of the Cabinet in 1845. It was his belief that marriage is a sacred and indissoluble union which dictated his pertinacious opposition to the Divorce Bill in 1857. Ten years later he felt that the Irish Establishment could no longer be maintained, because it could plead neither practical utility nor 'the seal of and signature of ecclesiastical descent' ". He gives many other instances and concludes, "the administration of Government was in Gladstone's hands a religious act".

But unlike the Saints, Gladstone loved power. Though polite in manner, he was imperious and would not readily listen to criticism. With all his reformative zeal, he was at heart an institutionalist and was ever moved by precedent. He had, even in his later Radical years, though much obstructed by the Queen, a great respect for the Crown. He revered the Constitution almost in the manner of Burke, but also to the profit-making economic system which current finance and business supported he gave unquestioning allegiance. His method of helping the labouring classes was to remove restrictions and exchange commodities —"remove the obstacles of taxation and regulation", he wrote (*Musings for the good of Man*)—in all this he was an uncritical disciple of the old Utilitarians. In theology he admired St. Thomas Aquinas, but that Doctor's attitude towards usury and stewardship would have found little appeal in Gladstone's commercial mind. In his later years he detected a desire among the younger Liberals "To take into the hands of the State the business of the individual man—this idea", he said, "estranged him and had done so for many, many years". (*Letter to Lord Acton*, Feb. 2, 1885.) Morley points out his tendency to over-refine language, which won for him the reputation of being sophistical, yet, at the same time, abstract metaphysical discussion did not attract him; he escaped the reproaches levelled at Balfour and Haldane that they were in some way unfit for public confidence because they were philosophers. He had an overwhelming power of persuasive eloquence; even when his hearers could not understand half his argument, they came away with the feeling that they had heard something very great. His fury at cruelty and oppression, particularly where the victim was a foreigner and a Christian was unappeasable and gave an unquenchable fire to his denunciations. More than once in his life he would retire from public life only to return to expose some atrocity and ruffle the complacency of the comfortable and the opportunist.

"His essence", says Strachey, "eludes the hand which seems to grasp it—one is baffled as his opponents were baffled fifty years ago. Compared with Disraeli, his attitude towards life strikes one as that of an ingenuous child." (*Eminent Victorians*, p. 273.) Yet in this paradoxical compound of Evangelicism and ritual, authority and freedom, national emancipation and industrial servitude, ambiguity and lucid logic, the recipient of consuming hatreds and unexampled political adoration, the Liberal Party found its basic inspiration.

CHAPTER VI

THE ADVENT OF DEMOCRACY

ON the death of Palmerston the Queen sent for Lord Russell, who resigned the Foreign Office to Clarendon, Gladstone continuing to be Chancellor of the Exchequer. A new appointment, that of Goschen, who was connected with a wealthy financial firm in the City, aroused some feeling, more particularly when he was admitted to the Cabinet in January, 1866. His presence there proved useful; in the late spring there had developed one of many periodical financial crises which seemed inescapable in those days of hectic speculative commercial exploitation. For the first time an important railway, the London Chatham and Dover line, failed, and in May came the collapse of the great banking firm of Overend Gurney with £19,000,000 liabilities. As in 1848 and 1857 the Bank Charter Act had to be suspended—the whole crisis was due to faulty finance, for the trade of the country generally remained good.

It is curious that the obvious incapacity of the controllers of money operations to prevent these recurrent disasters did not shake the almost universal acceptance of the prevailing banking system, but little or no criticism is to be detected, even in socialist circles which at that time were more concerned to attack the landlord and the manufacturer than the men of high finance.

The way was now clearer than it had been for a long time for reform of the franchise. With the passing of Palmerston, the chief opponent of electoral advance had gone. Gladstone, by his defeat at Oxford and acceptance by an urban constituency, had now a free hand. Russell having been in the Lords since 1861, he was now leader of the House of Commons and had acquired strong Radical support in such talented members as Professor Fawcett, Hughes and J. S. Mill.

On March 12th, 1866, the Government Bill was introduced; it purported to give a borough qualification of £7 occupation and a county one of £14; this was higher than the £6 and £10 of the earlier Russell proposals and was designed to appease the Whigs; the accompanying lodger franchise had already been contemplated in a Tory Bill.

Nevertheless, despite the propaganda of the National Reform Union and League there was great opposition even from some Liberals. Lowe, himself representing the very small borough of Calne, led from the Government side a general attack upon democracy. The result was rather to stir the working classes to demand their rights than to help the obstruction of Reform. Lowe spoke of the manual workers as being guilty of "venality, ignorance, drunkenness and intimidation", and contrasted them unfavourably with the middle class £10 householder who had hitherto constituted the majority of the electors.

Encouraged by this Governmental division, the Tories took heart. Lord Grosvenor, a Whig, was supported by Stanley in a motion to postpone franchise reform until a scheme for redistribution was announced, an old device which had often before served as a dilatory tactic. This

time it was defeated by only five votes, and a promise was given directly
the Bill had a second reading to bring forward the redistribution scheme.
In committee, however, after a motion from a malcontent Liberal to
substitute rating for rental in the borough qualification was carried by
eleven votes, the Government gave up the struggle and Russell resigned
—for the third time Lord Derby became Prime Minister.

In order that the contentions on parliamentary franchise which
occupied the years 1866 and 1867 may adequately be understood, it is
necessary to realize that, apart from the Radicals, no responsible statesman yet accepted the view that the existence of a Government should
depend upon the decision of a numerical majority of the whole people.
Whig reformers, equally with Tories, were insistent that all that was
required was an adequate representation of the third estate of the realm
in Parliament, where, as Disraeli said, "they sat by proxies".

That the other estates, the Lords Spiritual and Temporal, should
lose their right to legislate—a privilege far more ancient than the
right of the Commons to agree to taxation—despite Parliament Acts,
has not been conceded to this day. In mid-Victorian times the notion
would have been considered revolutionary.

The issue which had formerly divided Tories from Whigs had relation
to the powers of the Crown; that matter had at last been settled in
favour of the Constitutionalists, but the position of the Commons
House was not yet clearly determined. The threat to create peers to
carry out their will had been used so sparingly as to show the exceptional
nature of the power—once only, at the time of the treaty of Utrecht, had
the Queen actually been persuaded to use her prerogative in this way. The
Peerage, probably appointed for life in very early times, had long been
hereditary. Since the Reformation the estate of the Church, represented
by the Bishops, had been in effect absorbed into the lay House of Lords;
indeed, being appointed as individuals, the Bishops were often more pledged
to a political view, at any rate in the eighteenth century, than were the
lay peers.

The concern of Parliament, both in 1832 and again in 1866, was to
give the Commonalty proper representation, and that, emphatically, all
save Radicals agreed was not to be achieved by counting heads of the
male adult population, but by giving to each social class its due weight
and proportion. So, also, in the distribution of seats, the old mediæval
idea of representation of areas according to their significance rather than
their population still lingered. The University representation is the
last surviving example of such representation by "Liberties" or
"Peculiars".

The matter is well illustrated by the speeches of leading men made
about this time. Said a great lawyer, Cairns, "Parliament must be a
mirror—a representation of every class—not according to numbers, but
according to everything which gives weight and importance in the world
without". "The object we have in view is to represent all classes
and give no class a preponderating influence." (Gathorne-Hardy.)

"It is important that the working class should not have a preponderating influence", declared Spencer Walpole; in the words of Lord
Stanley, "no class should be excluded and no one should overbear the
rest".

The first of the Liberals openly to criticize this view was Gladstone. In his debate with Lowe, the anti-reformer, who had said: "If you want impulsive, unreflecting violent people—where do you look for them? Do you go to the bottom or the top?" the Chancellor of the Exchequer had replied: "The persons to whom the remarks apply are our fellow-Christians, our own flesh and blood". The denunciation of these words as "sentimental rant" by Lord Cranborne was applauded by many; it indicated the great distaste for what is now called democracy existent at the time.

The real issue before the House in 1866 and 1867 was thus simply, how to readjust representation so as not to exclude any class entitled to be represented without conceding the full claims of democracy. The whole dispute was as to extent and method.

In these circumstances, the history of what happened is the more amazing. In the face of growing Continental anxieties and perils caused by the new intransigence of Prussia led by Bismarck (conditions which after the war with Austria culminated in the defeat of France in 1870), the Russell Government was forced to resign on a clause in the Franchise Bill which the Conservatives subsequently introduced and passed almost in the same form. The facts were these: on March 12th, 1866, Gladstone introduced the Liberal Reform Bill—for the moment he did not raise distribution questions. Reform Bills had been introduced by five Governments since 1849. Bright had produced one in 1858, and the Tory Government in 1859—this was the one which did not really extend the franchise at all, but Gladstone had voted for it. In 1860 Russell had suggested a £6 occupation limit for boroughs, £10 for counties; now what was proposed was a £7 town and a £14 county on rental, together with a lodger franchise (which was in the defeated Tory Bill), and the addition of copy and leaseholders in the counties. This was denounced by Cranborne the Tory and Lowe the Whig as Democracy. On this issue a fortnight was spent in debate. Thirty Liberals voted against the second reading; the majority was only five. A redistribution Bill followed and the measures were joined.

At length a proposal to substitute rating for rental as the test of eligibility was carried against the Government, who then resigned. It is well to remember that—apart from this trivial matter—all the Bill did was to reduce the county franchise from £50 qualification to £14 and add people not freeholders; and, in the towns, to lower the franchise from £10 to £7; this was the abhorred democracy!

Since the achievement of Free Trade and the failure of Chartism, there had been little public organization of opinion in the country, but Bright and his friends had come to see that it was only possible to create a demand for reform by such means. The times were propitious; the avoidance of all domestic questions had died with Palmerston—instead, under the earnest influence of John Stuart Mill and the new humanistic movement—Carlyle also had his influence from quite a different angle—people had become discontented with the old order. Notions of a society based upon reason and forethought, such as had possessed Bentham and Mills' father, were again in the ascendant, and, as a product of this, there rose a claim that all citizens should, directly or indirectly, participate in Government.

One of the first to be moved was Gladstone. As early as 1863—to the alarm of the Court and gentry—he had declared that "every person, not presumably incapacitated by some consideration of personal unfitness or political danger, is morally entitled to come within the pale of the constitution". The context shows that he was not speaking of that equality before the law for which Wilkes had contended, but of the right to vote at an election.

Reform, it was said, "was in the air". Popular demonstrations, organized openly or in secret by the Reform Associations, were taken up by the trade unions. The National Reform League and the National Reform Union (the latter Bright's especial care) were increasingly active throughout the country. The Secretary of the League, Howell, succeeded in interesting many working-class organizations to demand the suffrage, as did others later when permeating them with Socialism. At this time individualistic notions were still strong; the International Working Men's Association, formed to support the recent pronouncements of Karl Marx made as yet but a small appeal, yet the Socialists supported the Radical and Liberal demand for electoral rights. A ferment such as had not been known since 1832 was developing.

A great conference and public demonstration and a deputation to the Prime Minister, Russell, heralded the opening of Parliament in 1866. In 1865, at the General Election, as has been said, John Stuart Mill, Tom Hughes and Professor Fawcett, all advanced Radicals, had been returned to Parliament, and Gladstone, defeated at Oxford, had thereby increased his popularity, for he had found a more democratic seat in Lancashire. On the defeat of the Russell Government he became a national hero. The crowd surged round his house shouting for "Gladstone and Liberty".

By the upper classes he was rapidly being ostracized. He was a revolutionary—another Wilkes or perhaps even a ritualistic Lord George Gordon: his hegira from the old system had begun.

In these circumstances it was necessary for the new Tory Government to act, but what were they to do? They had defeated the very moderate proposals of Russell and Gladstone, there was no new road down which they could travel; they must either stand still or go the same way as their predecessors.

In April an attempt had been made to ban Reform meetings in Hyde Park; nevertheless, under the plea of the doubtful legality of the prohibition, on May 6th a huge mass meeting was held there. Meanwhile the middle-class Reform Union, having its headquarters in Manchester, stood behind Gladstone. On June 1st it organized processions to London from all the greater towns, fifty-eight deputations in all, which were joined by the Trade Unions and the Reform League. In July the crowd broke down the railings of Hyde Park, a meeting having again been prohibited, and further agitation went on in Birmingham, Manchester, Leeds, Glasgow, and Dublin. In the result, Derby—writing to Disraeli—in September had said: "I am coming to the conclusion, reluctantly, that we shall have to deal with the question of Reform". For the moment Disraeli disagreed, but the Queen took a part in the matter, insisting that the question should be put at rest. She was prepared to work to obtain a measure by general consent.

Remembering the success of the settlement by resolution of the Indian Government problem, the Tories thought the same device might be utilized again. Instead of a limitation by rating or rental, Derby in December, 1866, had suggested Household Suffrage—a Radical proposal emanating from Hume and supported by Bright. By this time Disraeli had been converted to the idea that the public demand for immediate action was real, and declared that Household Suffrage on a rating principle could be supported on Tory principles.

There are two matters difficult to explain in relation to the introduction, after some false starts, of a Bill which, in substance, differed not at all from that for which Russell's Government had been defeated—the attitude of the dissentient Tories and that of Gladstone himself.

As to this policy, the objections were twofold; first, that the Tory measure was in fact a democratic Radical one; and, secondly, that it was not honourable to commend a measure which the promoters had just defeated when introduced by their opponents. Both these considerations moved Lord Cranborne (soon to pass to the Lords as Lord Salisbury), to resign in angry protest. He was remote in responsibility, for he had taken the office of India Secretary, but in the Cabinet, on studying the implications of Household Suffrage, he had come to the conclusion that the safeguards were useless and that in fact if he consented to the scheme he "could not look in the face those whom I urged last year to oppose Mr. Gladstone". At first, many other Conservatives were critical—it looked as if about fifty would desert. An assurance by Disraeli that "the Government would never introduce Household Suffrage pure and simple" soothed many, but Lord Cranborne remained obdurate—it was "a simple proposition of political morality", he said; "the party which behaved in opposition as ours did last year is not the party to propose Household Suffrage".

The position of Gladstone was more invidious. If it were true that the new Bill in principle was not different from his, it would appear to have been his duty to support it; but the indignation which he felt at the trickery which had been practised on him got the better of his judgment. His objections were petty and unconvincing; his party as a whole refused to follow him in an opposition such as the Tories had organized the year before. When he sought to remove the payment of rates as a qualification for voting he was taking a Radical position; at other times he said the Bill was too wide. The Radicals and many Conservative doubters very sensibly declared that the Bill should go to Committee. There many amendments were made, nearly all in a Radical direction. Residence was reduced to one year, and the Bill finally adopted in Bright's words was "the precise franchise I recommended in 1858–59". On July 15th he was able to note, "Bill passed with cheers from our side". A proposal to include women, moved by Mill, was defeated by 196 to 73. The troublesome case of the compounder for rates was met, temporarily, by the abolition of compounding.

Despite all apologies, when the matter is considered in that state of unprejudice which three-quarters of a century may bring, it cannot be denied that the attitude of Derby and Disraeli was morally indefensible. Either they should have allowed the Liberals to take responsibility for their own proposals, or they should have resigned rather than place themselves in so ambiguous a position. The criticisms of Lord Cranborne are just: "If," he declared, "no matter what a man has supported in opposition, the moment he gets into office it shall be open to him to reverse and repudiate it all, you practically destroy the whole basis on which our form of government rests, and you make the House of Commons a mere scrambling place for office." Moneypenny and Buckle (the biographers of Disraeli) have called the passage of the Reform Act "Disraeli's Parliamentary Triumph", but the ironic words of Lord Salisbury have gone unanswered.

On March 5th, 1868, Gladstone, who had succeeded Russell as leader of the Liberal Party, started his campaign in Parliament for the disestablishment of the Irish Church. It was already under examination by Royal Commission, but Gladstone would not await the report.

Already in May, 1867, he had said that the position of that body would have to be fairly and fully looked in the face. As Manning had declared: "The Irish establishment is a great wrong", and there were many grounds on which he could support his utterance. Three-quarters of the people were Roman Catholics, and of the remaining quarter at least a half were Presbyterian. Indeed, broadly, it was only the governing class who could be called Anglican. Liberals, Radicals and Irish, all agreed to support the Leader's resolutions. The first, that the Church in Ireland should cease to be established, was promptly carried by a majority of sixty-five, the others were not challenged. There was little serious opposition, as Manning did not hesitate to point out. Lowe, so long a dissentient, was reconciled; Bright supported with enthusiasm. To all other Irish proposals, Gladstone insisted on the priority of the Church question. The Queen was perturbed, Cranborne suggested that Disraeli would again betray the Tory Party by surrender, for Lord Stanley, showing considerable sympathy with disestablishment, was suspected of being the Tory leader's mouthpiece.

High Churchmen, who were fearful of State interference with religion, trusted Gladstone (himself of their opinion in ecclesiastical matters) more on this subject than on many others. The Coronation Oath, which had perturbed at least two of the Georges, weighed upon the mind of the Queen. Disraeli formulated the objections of the Government under three heads: "It would destroy conciliation, shake property to the centre, and dissolve for the first time the connection between Government and Religion". He suggested a Dissolution to test public opinion or, alternatively, advised resignation. It was suggested that the Prime Minister had unfairly enlisted the Sovereign on his side and the resulting acrimony was great. Gladstone carried a Bill through the Commons to suspend the creation of new interests in the Irish Church, but it was rejected in the Lords. So matters stood until the General Election on the new reformed register.

Before the Conservative Government resigned, as the result of a heavy defeat at the hands of the new electorate, they had taken their first step in Collectivism by acquiring the new electric telegraph, though the purchase was at an outrageous price. Election petitions had been transferred to the Judges; a new registration law and a measure against Corruption passed, but all these counted for nothing in withstanding the new Radical enthusiasm. In Birmingham, in particular, a local party organization had taken much influence out of the hands of the Reform Club in selecting candidates and promoting their return. Gladstone, it is true, lost his seat in Lancashire owing to Church opposition, to be returned for Greenwich. In all, over two million people voted. The Liberal majority was over five hundred thousand, and Gladstone became the first real Liberal Prime Minister.

He had been warned by Dean Wellesley that the Queen "differs from you on the question of disestablishment and will tell you so frankly", otherwise she had no objection even to "advanced Liberals". This, doubtless, was a reference to Bright, who had become President of the Board of Trade. In the Cabinet, however, there were still many peers: Argyll, Clarendon, Granville, Kimberley and De Grey; Hartington, afterwards Duke of Devonshire, was also included. The Radicals in the Government were Bright, Ayrton, Stansfeld, Trevelyan and Otway. It was a compound, but the advanced members were far greater in proportion than ever before.

The Irish Disestablishment Bill was introduced on March 1st, 1869—the incumbents were to be compensated and all churches and cathedrals retained—£1,000,000 was to be taken to cancel Maynooth liabilities to Catholics and certain obligations to Presbyterians. The rest Gladstone proposed to use for general pious uses "in Ireland and for charities". The Tories decided to oppose. The Lords asked for further concessions in money to the episcopalians, but, in the end, after many differences between the Houses, mostly about finance, the Bill became law.

Whatever merits from a Liberal point of view the disestablishment had, it did little to placate Irish discontent. Agrarian crime increased notably in 1869. Landlords were attacked and shot, farmers, bailiffs and the police constantly in danger of sudden assassination, and houses were destroyed. Gladstone's reply was to endeavour to give some security to the tenant. He was to receive a limited estate in the land, so that if he improved it he would have compensation. Disraeli relied upon the old principle of freedom of contract—he prophesied that the tenant would now refuse to pay rent and, on consequent eviction, more disorder would break out. Unfortunately his forecast proved later to be correct. Bright alone saw that the remedy lay in abolishing tenancy altogether and giving the Irish a peasantry owning their own land. To this solution Parliament was later to come.

The introduction of an Education Act by Forster in February, 1869, disclosed that less than half the children of England went to school—of those who went, half were at schools which were uninspected. Of the non-attending half it was said that forty per cent were not at work and were "running wild".

A national Education League was pressing these matters on Parliament and the public when Forster produced his measure. It did not in any way provide for universal education, but only enacted that School Boards might take power to compel attendance if the denominational bodies did not deal adequately with deficiencies in accommodation. As to religious education, where there were School Boards they could provide it if they pleased, with a right of individual exemption at a parent's request.

Joseph Chamberlain was now first heard of outside Birmingham as leading the opposition to the Bill. He and his fellow Dissenters objected to the opportunities it gave to Churchmen to fill up their schools in areas where there was no nonconformist place of education. He thought the optional powers of the School Boards would make the measure useless, but neither Lord de Grey (Lord Ripon), who subsequently became a Roman Catholic, nor the Prime Minister had any sympathy with non-sectarian schools—they adhered to their own plan.

But Chamberlain and his friends were not to be over-awed; the young "screw-maker", as he was derisively called, was fearless. On March 9th for the first time he met Mr. Gladstone face to face. He admitted that the proposal was in many respects "a noble measure", but urged that it would have the effect of handing over the education of the country to the Church of England—especially in agricultural districts—and that a mere conscience clause would not meet the matter.

The Conservatives not unnaturally supported the Bill, and the famous clause of Cowper-Temple, excluding from all rate-built schools "every catechism and formulary distinctive of denomination or creed" was accepted; the denominational schools were deprived of aid from the rate and the Government were driven to augment the State grants in order to help them. In the result Liberalism, to quote Garvin, "was split to pieces". (*Life of Chamberlain*, I, p. 115.) Sixty Liberals voted against the Government. On June 30th, the feeling among Dissenters had so increased that a majority of Liberals voted against their leaders, who were only saved by Conservative support.

It was in this debate that Harcourt first opposed his chief. He was a member of the Birmingham League and stood for national, free, compulsory education with the sectarian influence eliminated. Dilke also opposed the Bill, but he desired an entirely secular solution. It was in part because of Harcourt's thesis that the State "is absolutely indifferent to all forms of religious teaching" and "as regards any funds raised by the State, one form of religious opinion has as full a right to share in the appropriation of such funds as another", that the Cowper-Temple clause was accepted; Harcourt's proposal had been that in rate-aided schools the instruction should only be in the Bible and undenominational.

Subject to this amendment, the Bill went through substantially as it had been introduced. The principle of supplementing, rather than superseding, the voluntary schools had won acceptance. Compulsion was only to be applied in Board Schools, and they were only to come into being where the voluntary schools could not be adequately maintained —even then the School Boards need not enforce the clause for compulsion unless they wished.

In the opinion of Morley, "from the point of view of party strategy the policy of this great statute was fatal. The Church of England was quickened into active antagonism by Irish disestablishment and the nonconformists were estranged by the treatment of endowed schools" (*Gladstone*, I, p. 941.)

The quarrel continued. In 1872 a conference of eight hundred non-conformist churches met in protest at Manchester; of four hundred and twenty-five Liberal candidates, three hundred were pledged to the repeal of that section of the 1870 Act which enabled School Boards to pay fees in certain cases for denominational schools, meanwhile, all consideration of the real purpose and method of education generally was forgotten in a sectarian struggle.

The decision in 1870 to enforce the obligation on parents, to a very limited extent, to provide their children with elementary education was a repudiation of Benthamite individualistic principles, though not so recognized at the time. The then existing law did no more than authorize State grants, not more than £20,000 in all, to be administered by a committee of the Privy Council. The possibility of a strong central authority, a Board of Education, was not considered until 1899—it was never before the minds of Forster or Gladstone. The power to control not only the service but the nature of juvenile instruction, enabling the State in effect to decide what ideas should, or should not, be presented to the young in their most formative period, had never been envisaged. In 1876 the duty of parents to cause their children to receive efficient elementary instruction in reading, writing and arithmetic was enforced by Statute, and, if we may anticipate, in 1880 the compulsory attendance of children at school was made universal. Finally, in 1891, the obligation to pay fees was abolished.

Thereafter, the overriding control of a Central Authority became inevitable; the use to which this may be put has been exemplified in authoritarian States. In England the power is exercised chiefly through the seductive agency of grants paid conditionally upon the local authority, *inter alia*, complying with the requirements of the Board relating to education. Higher education grants and State scholarships are also the subject of central regulation.

The grant regulations in elementary schools must be in accordance with a suitable curriculum. The non-provided schools are also in receipt of grants, except for religious education, and they also in effect are under the ultimate control of the Minister. His inspectors (called in courtesy "His Majesty's") are the means by which he can inform himself how far his principles and the statutory duties are carried out.

It is thus not too much to say that, by degrees, the State has acquired an immense control over the education of its young citizens, nor have the Liberal Party since 1870 ever objected. The matter is cited as an early example of the decay of the old principles and practices of individualism in the matter of parental right.

Soon the attention of all parties was distracted from domestic affairs by the war which France declared on Germany on July 15th. On the 19th France refused the good offices of England to preserve the peace; though it has been said that in fact Bismarck had tempted the French into war. These are questions which do not call for elucidation in this political history. In twenty-eight days ten battles were fought, the Emperor of the French was made prisoner and deposed. In February, 1871, Great Britain recognized the French Republic. In all this affray Gladstone and Granville stood aloof. The neutrality of Belgium, which had been guaranteed in 1839, in fact was not menaced; if it had been, it was apparent that this country was seriously deficient in armament to enforce it. No military preparations were made after the outbreak— apparently neither Gladstone nor Granville, the Foreign Secretary, at first realized their obligations to Belgium; Parliament was equally supine.

In the event practically nothing was done. Disraeli pointed out that we had only "skeleton battalions, attenuated squadrons, batteries without sufficient guns and yet more guns than gunners; a nation without a military reserve; a nation, moreover, which had left off shipbuilding, reduced its crews and its stores, and failed to furnish artillery for its men-of-war". "The balance of power has been completely destroyed," that far-seeing statesman declared. "You have a new world, new influences at work, new and unknown dangers with which to cope."

As if to illustrate his contention, Russia proceeded to denounce the treaty of 1856, which had neutralized the Black Sea, and the Italian Government occupied Rome, restricting the Pope to the Vatican. In all these matters, after protests and discussion, the Liberal Government stood aside and let matters take their course; the days of Palmerston were truly over.

Other matters to be noted at home in 1870 were the granting by the Universities to degrees without religious tests, a serious sacrifice of Gladstone's own prejudice to the public good; the full opening of the civil service to public competition; the reform of the Army by abolishing the dual control of Commander-in-Chief and War Office, and the ending of the purchase of commissions—this latter by royal warrant.

At last, also, the long fight for a secret ballot was won. Why this elementary necessity for the proper recording of opinion should so long have been opposed it is difficult to understand. It had been advocated by the Westminster Committee as early as 1783. Over twenty-five resolutions had been moved by Radicals in its favour before it received a majority of Liberal votes in 1838 on Grote's annual motion. It had formed an important item in the Charter; yet nothing was done. Fawcett complained of the want of enthusiasm of the Government, Gladstone confessed a "lingering reluctance", but helped to carry it with a majority of over ninety. In the Lords it was rejected, but being reintroduced in 1872 the Lords yielded. Voting was at last made secret.

The machinery of registration which accompanied the secret ballot did much to encourage the growth of party organization, in which political activity the Liberals were first in the field. So far such bodies had been for the most part, as it has been said, constituted *ad hoc* to obtain particular measures such as the repeal of the Corn Law or National Education. Now, however, they were coming to be attached permanently to political parties, and their work, therefore, was no longer limited to the achievement of a specific object.

Party associations had started with the Reform Act, primarily to maintain adequate registration of particular supporters. "The battle of the constitution," Sir Robert Peel had said, "will be fought out in the registration courts." On the Liberal side they were called Liberal Registration Societies or, more shortly, Liberal Associations. A Central Office in London took to sending them down names of suitable candidates. The Committees of the Associations varied in power, but as a rule they represented the most powerful influences on their side. Canvassing, a very ancient practice, fell often into the hands of the Central Committee of the Association, who relieved the candidate of much of his work; but it was not until 1867 that the full Caucus system, as it was derisively called, developed in Birmingham. In that year Birmingham received thirty thousand new voters. It was suggested that the City should be divided into wards, and the Central Committee be made up of elected ward representatives. They took upon themselves, more particularly where the minority clause was in operation, to tell the electors for whom to vote; each elector receiving a ticket with two names on it.

By the last Act, Birmingham had received three members, but the elector had only two votes. By a skilful allocation of the votes in each ward, the total votes in the City could collectively produce a majority for each Liberal candidate, and the machinery for ensuring minority representation was thus defeated. This device was very largely the work of Chamberlain—it depended, of course, for its success on the voters obeying the directions of the Caucus. They did so loyally, and the result was three Liberal members for Birmingham. The Caucus had justified itself.

A similar device was tried in Birmingham to defeat the cumulative vote at the first School Board election, but here the results were less successful. In 1873 Chamberlain was elected Mayor of Birmingham, with him was associated Schnadhorst, the Secretary of the Liberal Association, and between them they organized an all-powerful organization. They felt none of the qualms of John Stuart Mill with regard to minorities. They were advanced Radicals of the new collectivist type; their purpose was to capture the Municipality and the State in order to use them directly for social betterment and in the former case they were triumphant. Public works to improve the sanitation and buildings of Birmingham were begun, no timid fear of interference with vested rights deterred them. Slums were demolished, new streets built, libraries, public baths and hospitals opened, and the town acquired its own water and gas. There was a local social revolution; *laissez-faire* was overthrown—all this was made possible by the astuteness of Chamberlain and his Liberal Association.

Party membership was now open to every burgess, whether elector or not. The ward committees were reorganized, they elected an executive committee for the town to which thirty members were added, elected at a public meeting from the general committee. There were nearly six hundred in all, the cream of Birmingham democracy, needless to say, all devoted to their mayor. Many of them were on the Town Council and engaged in active public work.

After the Liberal defeat in 1874 (when Gladstone retired from the leadership), it was generally considered that the Birmingham principle would be universally adopted. A National Federation of Liberal Associations came into being and the great Gladstone himself came to Birmingham to bless it. The excitement was great—a new portent had arisen. It was Disraeli who gave to the new national organization the American name of Caucus. After deliberation the Federation at Birmingham thought that it would be "better to accept the word while trusting to time and experience to attach new and more attractive meanings to it".

It would appear to be the Nemesis of progressive governments that they are as likely to fall by disappointing their advanced supporters as by the attacks of opposition. In no other way is it possible to explain the failure of the Liberal Party in 1874.

The republican movement in France, and the continued seclusion of the Queen at home, had made the monarchy unpopular—on the proposal to give the Princess Louise a marriage dowry of £30,000, Fawcett Dilke and Taylor had dissented. The Duke of Cambridge, as Commander-in-Chief, was attacked by Trevelyan, a member of the Government, and eighty-three members supported his views with their votes. In 187 a "republican" conference met in Birmingham, but the Prime Minister was horrified at such disloyalty; this new attitude towards the Crown perplexed him and the older Liberals, they did everything to discourage the Radical elements. There arose a general disintegration. Both of the Budget and in liquor licensing, the Government showed they had no coherent policy. Harcourt, who was one of the most important of the younger Liberals, frequently attacked the Government, and in particular its leader. He moved against them a resolution paraphrastically borrowed from Dunning, that the national expenditure had increased, was increasing and ought to be diminished. He denounced the Home Secretary's Licensing Act, which limited the hours during which public-houses might be open, on the ground that it was an interference with liberty. Emphatically he was not a member of the new collectivist school! "I don't admit a grand maternal government which ties night-caps on a grown-up nation by Act of Parliament," he said. "The policy of the Liberal Party has been for generations a policy of emancipation from restriction, and it now to begin to forge fresh fetters for the free?" That, indeed, was the question.

On March 12th, 1873, Gladstone had been defeated by three votes on an Irish University scheme, the Irish Catholics opposing. He resigned but on Disraeli refusing office, resumed a few days after; the incident did nothing to rehabilitate the Government. Not long after, he was inveigled into a speech against disestablishment in England which increased his disfavour with the Nonconformists. On the resignation Lowe, he himself took over the office of Chancellor of the Exchequer. The question was raised, must he resign his seat? It was a technical point but, like the cases of Sir John Collier's appointment to the Judicial Committee and the Ewelme rectory qualification, it was used to annoy and discredit him, the object being to represent him to the country "Jesuitical".

The adverse judicial interpretation of the Conspiracy Law as relating to Trade Disputes produced a declaratory Bill which Harcourt piloted through the Commons, only to be defeated in the Lords. Next year was carried by Disraeli.

Yet, while politically the Government was sinking, the country was prosperous and not indisposed to progressive measures. The Trade Unionists, little placated by a Bill in 1871 legalizing their funds (which was coupled with another which imposed great liabilities in Trade Disputes) had found that it was easier to obtain shorter hours by threatening strikes than by political methods. Wage increases had been secured through the organization of the agriculture labourers, remuneration pitifully small as judged by modern standards. The Trade Union Congress, representing nearly all the Unions, was increasing in power and endeavouring through its Parliamentary Committee to put pressure upon the Government, more particularly to amend restrictive Trade Union laws. The Radicals and workers generally were becoming restless, they had ceased to have confidence in the Government. Radical measures —a Burials Bill to enable dissenters to officiate in parish churchyards, a Bill to carry a much-needed reform of local government in London, a Bill to abolish the government of counties by Justices and to set up County Boards—were all rejected by a ministry fearful of antagonizing the House of Lords and the powerful landowning classes; "Exhausted Volcanoes" was Disraeli's description of an administration bankrupt of initiative. Moreover, the Queen had turned against Gladstone. His attitude towards the High Church offended her—"Protestant to the heart's core," as she described herself. The royal suggestion that the War Office administration should be chosen to please the Duke of Cambridge as well as the Secretary of State was difficult of acceptance. In the end she did not hesitate to show herself pleased when Gladstone asked for dissolution.

By 1874 the Tories had followed the Liberals in devising a national organization, planned by Eldon Gorst. In January that astute electioneerer had estimated a Conservative majority of three. When the seats were counted their majority was found to be fifty. In reality the situation from a Liberal point of view was even worse, for the Irish came back as an independent organization, fifty-eight strong, under the name of Home Rulers; there were only about a dozen Irish Liberals. In the counties and in the boroughs alike the Conservatives were victorious. In Great Britain alone it was estimated their majority was eighty-three, but the uncertainty of Irish distribution led to a net estimate of fifty; in reality, to quote Gladstone, "it was of much greater strength". The era of Disraelian Imperialism had begun.

One of the most noticeable social features which marked the middle of the nineteenth century had been the growth of organized societies of every kind; some recognized expressly by law (as in the case of limited liability companies first constituted under the Act of 1855; Trade Unions in 1871 and the earlier Friendly Societies), others incorporated by Charter for scientific and philanthropic purposes, and yet others, such as political associations, constituted on an entirely voluntary basis.

These last so completely entered into political activity as to produce a revolution in the method of parliamentary and local government representation, a transformation of power which at the time passed almost unnoticed.

The discipline of the contending forces, now drilled for battle, was greatly increased; individual resignations and hostile votes against party became far more rare. Programmes were prepared for the acceptance of the candidate and legislator, and individual initiative in all party issues regarded as disloyal. In the House the Whips assumed a coercive tone. Agents, acting under an agent-general, reported opinion in the provinces, the machinery of propaganda by poster and by Press was strengthened. In all this we see the beginnings of a great machine, unknown to the constitutional lawyer, but which, in fact, in the hands of a few competent controllers governed the party and thus, if successful, ultimately controlled the nation.

E

At Birmingham, so powerful had the association become that Conservatives (now openly called the "enemy") were practically driven out of public affairs; even the holding by them of public meetings became difficult. The Liberal victory in 1868 had been largely due to the adoption in other constituencies of the "Birmingham Plan". Schnadhorst went about the country hawking model associations and Mr. Gladstone himself praised them. "It is Liberal," he said. But he went on, significantly: "At Birmingham they are tolerably advanced, but they don't attempt to exclude the most moderate". (*Speech at Nottingham*, September 27th, 1877.)

There still existed, however, the old Central Liberal Association, controlled by the Parliamentary Leaders and Whips—it was Whig through and through, and regarded the new Federation with undisguised alarm. Lord Hartington, who had temporarily succeeded Gladstone as leader in opposition, was of the old school; Bright, now daily becoming more moderate, supported him.

When Gladstone reappeared in 1876 to fight the case for the eastern Christians against the Turk, the Federation stood behind him—no less than thirty thousand people were organized to hear the orator denounce Disraeli and the Turk at Birmingham. Hartington, on the other hand, unwisely declined to address the first annual meeting of the Federation. He attacked the organization as "American"; he declared it to be solely Radical, which Chamberlain would not admit; the meeting was held without him—again the official party was defeated.

In 1876 Chamberlain had been returned to Parliament at a by-election. On Gladstone's motions demanding that no material or moral support be given to Turkey, but that local government in the disturbed (that is, Christian) provinces be accorded, he found Chamberlain on his side. But the attempt of the Whigs to whittle down the Liberal attack to the denial of arms or a declaration that Turkey had forfeited all claim to British support induced Gladstone, to Chamberlain's disgust, to limit his resolution.

Gladstone's sentiments, however, embodied in pamphlet form and in great meetings was transparently clear. The Turks should be "cleared out from the provinces they have desolated and profaned, bag and baggage". For the moment he and the Radicals, save a few who hated Russia even more than Turkey, were as one.

The Constantinople conference, where Salisbury represented the Government, had failed to stop war between Russia and Turkey—it was then that the famous resolution was tabled. Gladstone, after his speech, was defeated by one hundred and thirty votes. In 1878 Russia entered Adrianople, and was drawing in on Constantinople. The Cabinet asked for a special vote of money, the British fleet passed the Dardanelles. The Russians replied by approaching to within thirty miles of the Turkish capital. Patriotic sentiment in London was intense—Gladstone's windows were broken, the "Imperial country" which Disraeli had proclaimed was reverting to a Palmerstonian condition. The purchase of the Suez Canal shares in 1875, the proclamation of the Queen as Empress of India, and Disraeli's general success in converting the Tories to the "vision of Empire" had roused the people to an excitement against Russia comparable to that which produced the Crimean War.

The Russians had freed Bulgaria from the Turks, but the Tories and the "Jingoes", as they came to be called, regarded that Christian province as merely under Russian vassalage. Austrians and Russians were in competition for the south-east of Europe. The German Chancellor had it in mind to destroy France first; that failing, he worked to help Austrian power in the Balkans, the policy being that the loose federation should become his dependant. It suited him to side with Disraeli and call a halt to Slavonic ambition.

There followed the Treaty of Berlin, which, though hailed in England as "Peace with honour", in fact aggrandized the Germans. Not for many years, however, was this realized. Russia had been held, Constantinople was still Turkish; that was all that concerned the British patriot. Even Gladstone was satisfied; Rumania, Servia, Montenegro and southern Bulgaria were free; it was for a later generation, at Serajevo, to realize how greatly Teutonic ambitions had been served by this inappeasable British fear of Russia. While Germany was increasingly menacing Europe, England persisted in regarding the distant Russia as her foe. To the Tories, her claims in the Balkans affronted patriotic sentiment; to the Liberals, Russian despotism was an iniquity.

As the time for the General Election drew near it was clear that Gladstone must again return, but still the Radicals under Chamberlain and Dilke had their many contentions with their nominal chief in the Commons, the Whiggish Hartington. On flogging in the army, Bright, Forster and Trevelyan all regretted the Whig complacency with existing discipline; it was evident that Hartington could not count on the support of the live elements in the Liberal Party. If Beaconsfield were defeated, Gladstone would have to be the Leader again.

Yet in matters economic the Radicals were almost as loath to advance as were the Whigs. Chamberlain alone protested against the Government Bill which restricted the borrowing powers of municipalities—the Liberals as a whole were still fast bound to *laissez-faire*. Indeed it was on the Conservative side that a recognition of the "condition of the people" questions was chiefly to be found; the Artisans' Dwellings Bill of Cross, the Home Secretary, inaugurated housing legislation. It sought to do for the country as a whole what Chamberlain had achieved in Birmingham—to enable local authorities to remove insanitary buildings and erect new ones. Fawcett, the Radical, characteristically opposed this invasion of proprietary right, and he was not the only one. Next, Friendly Societies received attention, their solvency being made capable of investigation by the State. A new Conspiracy Act removed doubts which were still held about the effect in the criminal law of Gladstone's Act of 1871 dealing with trade disputes. For this measure the Government was thanked by the Trade Union Congress. The one "Labour" member, MacDonald, nominally a Liberal, must ruefully have compared the failure of his own party to deal with social injustice contrasted with the activity of the more enlightened Tories.

Agricultural tenants now received that compensation for removal which Gladstone had only conceded to Ireland. In the same year, 1875, a great Public Health Act was passed, and in 1878 Lord Shaftesbury had he satisfaction of seeing a consolidating Factory Act enacted by which he hours of labour for women and young persons were reduced to fifty-six a week or ten-and-a-half a day—this also was opposed by Fawcett and no less than seventy-nine Liberals! In 1876 merchant shipping was protected by statute and the lives of the sailors made more safe.

Thus the great change over from Individualism to Collective Action, of which so many publicists have written, took place under Conservative auspices. In the face of history it is vain for the Liberals, other than the followers of Chamberlain, to claim the credit; yet, once the Rubicon was crossed, we do not find that there was any longer any notable cleavage between the two parties on this issue—both were now prepared to ameliorate conditions by public action, while at the same time neither desired to interfere with the processes of profit-making and capitalist finance. But already John Stuart Mill, in his later writings, had passed over to a collectivist position; the Socialist criticism of monopoly in land and capital was slowly seeping into the minds of the working people and the less conventional intellectual classes. The Trade Union Congress, which had been founded in 1869, afforded a platform for the new idea. Even the less revolutionary Trade Unionists now demanded laws for compensation in case of industrial accidents and an increase in the number of factory inspectors.

The congress were active in obtaining the 1875 legislation, freeing Trade Unionists from fear of criminal prosecution in combining in trade disputes, being advised in particular by Professor Beesly and Frederick Harrison the Positivist, and they were much concerned to assist to promote the Employer's Liability Act of 1880. Later, they came actually to participate in government in the person of Broadhurst (once Secretary of the Congress Parliamentary Committee), and Mundella, the President of the Board of Trade, who had for so long advised the Congress. But this was not achieved until 1886. About this time Herschell, the Lord Chancellor, and Trevelyan, in the Duchy of Lancaster, first appointed "workmen magistrates".

For the time being, however, active Liberal sympathy with Labour was conspicuously absent. The excitement shown by Gladstone at the introduction of the Public Worship Regulation Act to "put down Ritualism", though important to the ecclesiastical mind, merely bewildered the mass of the people on whom the Liberals relied or, if they were Low Church or Nonconformist, annoyed them. His campaign against "Vaticanism" did nothing to allay the suspicion which most Progressives felt (and feel) towards those who hold sacerdotal or sacramental principles. All this was before his whirling campaign in support of the Balkan Peoples. In that enthusiasm, his foibles (as the people saw the deepest part of his convictions) were overlooked.

But the most serious innovation in political life of the time has still to be mentioned; for now there appeared a party in Parliament who asked, not so much for the redress of grievances or the maintenance of rights, as to be allowed to depart altogether—the Irish Home Rule Nationalists.

Gradually, it will be found, all other divergencies between parties come to be aligned according to their treatment of this matter. That a small and depopulated island should throw the whole machinery of British government and the prospects of social progress into confusion may now be considered absurd—nevertheless, it so happened. It is not too much to say that for fifty years from this time Parliament and politics were dominated by what came to be called "The Irish Question".

CHAPTER VII

THE GREAT SCHISM

THE inability of the Queen to appreciate the forces which had united to produce the great Liberal majority in 1880 was never more clearly shown than in her endeavours to exclude the organizers of victory, Gladstone and Chamberlain, from the direction of affairs. In April the Queen saw Lord Hartington and asked him to form a Government; actually the Leader of the Party at the time was Granville.

The Whig statesman replied that he did not think that a Government could satisfactorily be formed without Gladstone, who would only come in as First Minister. On April 23rd Hartington saw Gladstone and stated that he and Granville had advised the Queen that Gladstone should be sent for—they both agreed to serve under him, Granville to return to the Foreign Office. After the Queen had stated that "some expressions of his had caused her concern", he kissed her hands and prepared to form a Government.

At the outset there were difficulties over Radical participation, for Forster had quarrelled with the progressive wing over Education and another advanced man was needed. The Prime Minister sent for Dilke, who refused to serve unless Chamberlain was in the Cabinet. After much protest, Gladstone surrendered; he was as loath to have the great democrat as the Queen was to have himself. A Cabinet half composed of Whig peers was scarcely such as the new Liberal Federation could approve. From the outset Chamberlain found himself in suspicious, if not hostile, company; in the past he had fought nearly all of them. Dilke, his particular friend, had been excluded from the Cabinet. Bright was fast becoming an uncritical Gladstonian, Harcourt was Chamberlain's only ally—and he was not very dependable.

Outside Downing Street, however, the social reformer had both Press and political machinery on his side. The *Daily News*, the *Pall Mall Gazette* (with John Morley as Editor) supported him; the *Birmingham Daily Post* was his, the *Manchester Guardian* sympathetic. In the outer government, Dilke had great popularity among the intellectual forces of Progress. But above all, the great Trade Unions were behind Chamberlain. He was a powerful man to tackle, more particularly now that he was inside the citadel. Meanwhile there was nothing to be done but to wait upon events.

The House now consisted of three hundred and forty-seven Liberals of various shades, two hundred and forty Conservatives and the new independent Irish Nationalist Party, some sixty-five in all. In personnel, the Radicals were powerful; Labouchere and Bradlaugh had been returned for Northampton. Firth (the advocate of a general Municipal Council for all London), Thorold Rogers, the economist (who did so much to break down the narrow views of the classical writers and draw attention to economic justice as a part of democracy), Jesse Collings, the friend of Chamberlain; and two specifically working-class members, Burt and Broadhurst, were all in the House, yet, counting heads, the majority of the Liberals were rich industrialists, bankers, brewers, shipowners, together with the remnant of the old Whig families and the inevitable lawyers. Both in the Government and in the House it was a most unstable coalition.

The only Bills passed in 1880 of any real value emanated from Chamberlain's department or owed their passage to his support. He safeguarded seamen's wages and legislated for their safety in his Grain Cargoes Bill. The juridical doctrine that, as workmen elected to go into danger by working with negligent fellow-men, they could not get damages from their employers—the principle of Common Employment, "a most unfortunate example of judicial legislation"—was partly overthrown by the Employers' Liability Act of 1880: it started a movement which finally resulted in the Workmen's Compensation Acts. This, as has been said, was one of the measures which had been demanded by the Trade Union Congress and was an instance of the utility of its Parliamentary Committee. The usual protest that the Bill would interfere with freedom of contract, rights of property and the like came as much from the Ministerial as from the Opposition side of the House. It was evident that they were far from accepting Chamberlain's notion of making the Country as reformable as Birmingham. A Burials Act, to enable Dissenting ministers to bury their people in churchyards, won far more general Liberal assent, though probably it was distasteful to the ecclesiastical layman who led them.

The Bradlaugh agitation may be shortly dismissed; his claim to affirm, instead of talking an oath, was rejected by a majority of one in a committee appointed to enquire into the matter. Thereafter, in the House, by 275 to 230 it was decided that Bradlaugh should not be allowed either to affirm or swear. Though Gladstone made a great speech for toleration, declaring that he had no fear of atheism in the House, the Affirmation Bill was rejected by three votes; it was not until 1885 that Bradlaugh was allowed to take the oath—in 1891 the record of 1881 was struck out and the Affirmation Bill finally passed in 1888.

In Imperial affairs this pacific Government was also unfortunate. The Conservatives had reversed the Liberal renunciation of the Transvaal (which had been accorded in 1852) by annexing it to the Crown, and though Gladstone had criticized this act of aggression he did nothing to reverse it, for he, Bright and Chamberlain had been overruled by the Liberal Imperialists. In 1881 the Boers revolted, defeating the British at Laings Neck and Majuba. In the end, a vague assertion of British supremacy was made, later in 1884, to be abandoned; the Boers thus resumed their independence. The prestige and honour of the Government and the Country had suffered a severe loss. At the northern end of the

African continent, Gladstone, contrary to all his principles, allowed himself, under financial pressure and commitments of the previous Government, to refuse recognition to the first Egyptian Nationalists. It was said that the Khedive must not be deserted. In 1883, the French refusing to use armed force, the British appointed a monetary adviser, and by 1885 they had obtained control over the finances of the country. That year, after the Gordon disaster, the Government barely escaped censure by fourteen votes. Only in Afghanistan, where they had made friends with the Ameer, was a withdrawal consistent with Gladstonian principles possible—for the rest, throughout this uneasy period it was Ireland that held the stage.

In May, 1870, partly as the result of disestablishment which had enraged the Irish Protestants, there had been founded an Irish "Home Government Association". Its purpose was to gain for Ireland the management of internal matters, leaving Imperial affairs to Westminster. Its name was soon changed to the Home Rule League, and an association for the same purpose was set up in England. The sixty-odd members, of whom mention has been made, were returned in 1874, pledged to the programme of the League. Its leader was Isaac Butt, an erstwhile Conservative lawyer, but under him were Fenians, advocates of Tenant-Right and even Orangemen! He himself, unlike many of his followers, was urbane and conciliatory. Every year he presented his Bills to give tenant right and to institute Home Rule, but without any success. It was not, however, until 1879 that the people in England took any active interest in Irish affairs. In that year Davitt, who had been imprisoned as a Fenian, returned to Ireland, passionately concerned for the amelioration of the Irish tenant. Famine was increasing and, under his guidance, a Tenants' Defence Association was formed to press for a general reduction of rents. In October a conference of Nationalist politicians and land reformers met, and an Irish Land League formed with Parnell at its head.

The Fenians did not believe in parliamentary action; some were for the use of physical force, but to this recourse Parnell was always opposed —many, however, were prepared to tolerate the obstructive tactics which he, following Biggar, had introduced at Westminster; a device to talk at great length on every sort of measure so as to make legislation difficult, if not impossible. These tactics had been used by the advanced Nationalists as early as 1877, when, on a protracted obstruction of the Mutiny Bill, Butt was foolish enough to reprove the younger men.

In Ireland it was his ruin, Parnell became a hero; he had worsted the British Lion! In May, 1880, he was elected Chairman of the Irish Party in Parliament.

A promise was made by Forster, the Irish Secretary for the new Government, that a Commission should be appointed to enquire into the working of the 1870 Land Act; meanwhile a Bill, authorizing compensation for disturbance, was thrown out in the Lords, a number of Whig Peers being in the majority. Dillon advised the tenants to pay no more rent till "justice was done". By September fifteen thousand persons were threatened with eviction. Parnell advised "Boycotting"—Captain Boycott to be the first to be "sent to Coventry". An agrarian conflict had started. It did not stop at boycotting; murder became frequent. At last Parnell was tried for conspiracy, but acquitted; the ordinary processes of law had proved useless.

In the result, the Government introduced a Coercion Bill. After a debate of forty-one hours, the Speaker, of his own authority, put the question. At the beginning of March it passed into law. The measure was disliked by many Liberals—as in the case of foreign affairs, once more Gladstone had been forced to deny his own principles. The support of Lord Salisbury, the Conservative Leader, did not increase its popularity with the Radicals. Conciliation, he said, to which the fortunes of the Irish landlords had been sacrificed, had failed.

The Land Bill, soon afterwards introduced, found more favour. The measure set up a Court to decide what was a fair rent, free sale and fixity of tenure, the "three F's" were all conceded by Gladstone to be necessary—in 1870 he had objected to them as an invasion of private proprietary rights. The Irish were gratified, but would not admit it. They now declared that they required complete peasant proprietorship. Parnell had half accepted the Bill, the Fenians would accept nothing. On October 2nd, 1881, Forster, pressing for that act of authority, again decided to arrest Parnell. When, in the following May, the suspects were released—even Tories had argued for this—Forster resigned, and Lord Frederick Cavendish was appointed Chief Secretary.

A few days afterwards he and the Under-Secretary, Burke, were murdered in Phœnix Park. Parnell, who was horrified, offered to resign. Gladstone, believing Parnell to be "sincerely anxious for the pacification of Ireland", refused to countenance the offer. A further Coercion Act was passed in 1882, and Spencer and Trevelyan, as Viceroy and Secretary, proceeded to Ireland. Ireland, to quote a well-informed contemporary, "seemed literally to be a society on the eve of dissolution". Even the Constabulary were disaffected.

To Chamberlain it appeared that the Irish "want to destroy their Government. . . . They also want to make all Government of Ireland by England impossible; all our people", he declared, "Radicals included, will resist them to the death". "They have great practical wrongs and grievances and one sentimental one, the Union." "The latter is one on which we cannot and will not yield." In these words, written to Morley in December, 1881, we hear the first murmurings of a storm which was eventually to wreck the Liberal Party.

The New Crimes Bill, as the Coercion Act was called, suspended juries and gave to the police complete powers of search and arrest on suspicion. Three judges could deal with murder, treason and crimes of violence whenever the Lord-Lieutenant thought that an impartial trial could not be obtained by ordinary law. There was a right of appeal. The Bill was not popular, but Harcourt, who was in charge, persisted. Gladstone, he suspected, was lukewarm, but the Home Secretary threatened to resign if the Bill were altered in principle. Chamberlain, then in touch with Parnell, also objected to Harcourt's attitude, but Dillon's violence converted many waverers, and in the end the Bill became law, after much obstructive debate.

Parnell was now in comparative favour with Gladstone; an Arrears of Rent Bill became law, much in the form which the Irish Leader had suggested, and for the time being, whether because of the strong action of Lord Spencer, the operation of the Crimes Act, or because of a reaction after the Phœnix Park murders, things became quieter in Ireland. There were still some murders to chronicle and there was trouble in the police force, six hundred temporarily resigning in Dublin; but the Cabinet, exhausted, turned to other matters.

Agricultural Holdings Acts were passed, to compensate tenants for improvement and prevent "contracting out"; the Factory Acts were extended to cover those working in dangerous trades. After Dilke became President of the Local Government Board, women inspectors under the Poor Law were appointed; a Royal Commission sat on the Housing of the Working Classes. At the Board of Trade, Chamberlain had produced and carried a Bankruptcy Act which "distinguished between the judicial and administrative aspects of Bankruptcy"; a Bankruptcy department of the Board of Trade was constituted and Official Receivers appointed to act in the large towns. In addition, a new Patents Act was passed with a central office properly equipped with experts. Finally came the Merchant Shipping Bill, violently attacked by the shipowners, most of whom were Liberals. The Cabinet were embarrassed, they did not wish to offend their wealthy supporters—it was a test case, for the preventible death at sea was very great. Chamberlain was defeated, and his Railways Regulation Bill, designed to protect the workers, was withdrawn. It is not surprising that the more advanced of the Trade Unionists, seeing the power of independence in the case of the Irish to extort legislation, should be coming to the conclusion that the Liberal Party was the stronghold of wealthy interests, and begin to think of forming their own organization, but before the time for action had come Chamberlain had left the Liberal Party.

Nothing daunted, the National Liberal Federation prepared for a new Franchise Bill; they realized that the only way to menace plutocracy was to get a new type of member elected and that this could only be done by getting more of the workers on to the register.

A Radical programme appearing in the *Fortnightly* demanded adult suffrage, payment of members and equal electoral districts. A great conference at Leeds began to speak of schemes for Bills rejected more than once by the Lords becoming law in their despite. Their demands were rejected. On February 28th, 1884, Gladstone introduced a new Franchise Bill. It was said that an increase in the electorate of two millions was involved; on June 26th it obtained a third reading. The Conservative opposition had been very perfunctory. In the Lords the usual policy was adopted of threatening to hold up the Bill until a redistribution scheme was introduced by the Government. This was carried as an amendment, and a serious political crisis arose, Lord Salisbury describing the Lower House as Mr. Chamberlain's "registration machine". In one sense he was right, Chamberlain certainly was the spear-head of the Radical attack. As to the Peers—"Mend them or end them", cried John Morley.

The attack now fastened on the House of Lords; not an instance of their illiberal past, and there were many, was forgotten. The violence of the Radicals, now infuriated, alarmed both Mr. Gladstone and the ageing Queen. Chamberlain was notified of the Queen's displeasure:

E*

"This was no true Liberal feeling", she wrote, "but destructive". She called on Gladstone "to restrain, as he can, some of his wild colleagues and followers".

A riot at Aston forced the Queen to even more active protest—she accused Gladstone of approving the "disgraceful riot at Birmingham". It had been caused by the Tories holding a great meeting in Aston Park, a sacred place, ordained for Radical assemblies. Two great crowds fought one another and Randolph Churchill had to flee. He used the occasion to move a vote of censure on Chamberlain. It was rejected by only thirty-six; it was evident that the Whigs also were becoming thoroughly frightened.

At last negotiations took place on redistribution; single-member constituencies were to be the rule and not the exception. Minority representation was to go. "Not bad for a Tory Bill", commented Chamberlain to Morley. He had reason to approve; all constituencies with under fifteen thousand electors were to be disfranchised, all two-seated places from fifteen thousand to fifty thousand to have but one member. There was to be no reduction in Irish representation.

The Conservatives gained nothing by their delay and compromise, but it did mean the final end of Whiggery, still ensconced in a certain number of small boroughs. Thereafter, had the Radicals stood together, their triumph would have been assured.

In its final form the new franchise reposed uniformly on a £10 yearly value of household, lodger or service qualification. Two million new electors were created and London obtained thirty-seven, Liverpool six, and Yorkshire and elsewhere, thirty-one new members.

One of the consequences (which the Conservative Party in the House of Lords had tried to prevent during the passage of the Franchise Act) was greatly to increase the power of Parnell and the Nationalist Party in Ireland. It will be recalled that the number of seats accorded to that country was not to be affected by redistribution, and the voting power now given to the agricultural poor ensured that Nationalism outside Ulster was without a rival. The General Election in 1885 resulted in the return, mostly unopposed, of no less than eighty-six Home Rulers.

Meanwhile, Parnell, dropping the Land agitation, conceived a new plan whereby to win Home Rule; he determined to tempt the two British parties to outbid one another for the Irish vote.

By the end of 1884, after years of sterile attempts at coercion, a feeling was growing that a solution did not lie that way. Chamberlain and Dilke were prepared to favour an Irish National Council which would govern Ireland in domestic affairs, it being understood that Imperial concerns should continue to be directed from Westminster—there must be no "separation". These proposals were regarded by Parnell as a mere instalment or, possibly, only as an offer, to be contrasted with whatever might come from the Conservative side. However this may be, the Radicals in the Cabinet presented them to Gladstone sincerely as a means of final settlement; owing principally to the unreliability of the go-between, O'Shea, the Irish and English reformers were really never *ad idem*.

Notwithstanding the approval of Gladstone, the peace proposals of

Chamberlain (which included a modification of the Crimes Act) met with scant approval from the Whigs. Spencer, the Viceroy, would not agree to a National Council; he would concede more Land Purchase, but insisted that the Crimes Act must be maintained in all its vigour. In April, 1885, the Viceroy declared that he now "leaned to some Central Board, but the difficulties are very great". Cardinal Manning said that the Catholic Church would support Parnell if he would accept a scheme of local government. In May, Harcourt gave the scheme his support, but Hartington and all the Peers in the Cabinet, except Granville, opposed—a deadlock had arisen.

Chamberlain and Dilke threatened to resign—at most they would not tolerate a new Crimes Act for more than a year; Land Purchase they regarded as mere "tinkering". In the end Gladstone introduced a Bill to renew the Coercion Law, saying that in that session it was not possible to proceed either with land purchase or local government. Dilke, and then Chamberlain, resigned, and Gladstone at last, without consulting them, introduced a Land Purchase Bill, to which, he said, he understood that the Radicals had agreed.

At this juncture, Lord Randolph Churchill declared that he also was opposed to coercion. Parnell, foolishly, placed more faith in him than in the Radicals—he forgot that the Conservative Party, from whom Churchill derived what little power he had, was far more hostile to Irish and even more concerned to maintain Imperial unity than any Whig. For the moment, however, Churchill was in opposition. In a debate the previous November about murders at Maamtrasna, where Lord Spencer had refused an enquiry, he had supported the Irish demand—Parnell jumped to the conclusion that it was time to try the Tories.

On an amendment to the Budget (in which on a question of beer duty the Cabinet were divided) the Nationalists cast their vote for the Opposition and the Government were defeated by twelve votes. This was on June 8th; on June 11th, after some correspondence with the Queen, the Prime Minister resigned and Lord Salisbury was called upon to form his first administration.

The declaration of the new Government's Irish Policy was left to the new Viceroy, Lord Carnarvon; he pointed out that Ireland had been under exceptional laws with few intervals since 1847, and said, amid general astonishment, that the Government were prepared to risk the dropping of the coercion laws. In the Commons, Spencer was denounced by Churchill, to the agitation of the Queen, for his severe administration. This alarmed the Tories generally; it was pointed out by one of them that Lord Spencer had risked his life in upholding the law, with the approval in particular of the Conservative Party. Chamberlain, while not dissociating himself, approved the abandonment of coercion. Lord Salisbury also, to mark his dissent from the attacks of Churchill, Gorst and others, eulogized Spencer.

But a greater difficulty to Lord Salisbury was the approval which Home Rule had won from his own Lord-Lieutenant, Carnarvon.

It is not easy to say what took place. When at length Carnarvon, in the summer of 1885, had an interview with Parnell, according to the Irishman the Viceroy had told him that the Conservatives would offer to Ireland a statutory legislature if they had the power. Carnarvon subsequently denied that he had spoken with the authority of the Government—certainly Salisbury was, in fact, always opposed to any concession.

Meanwhile, it was clear that Chamberlain and Dilke had been deceived. Manning refused an introduction to the Irish Bishops, and the Irish Press, controlled by Parnell, attacked them as mere users of Ireland for British Radical purposes. Finally, Parnell, on August 20th, openly stated that he would fight the election on legislative independence for Ireland—all question of National Councils was at an end.

In July, Herbert, Gladstone's son, declared at Leeds for full Home Rule, and in the middle of August, about the time of Parnell's declaration, Parliament was dissolved.

A new conception of democracy is noticeable in the Radical election appeals. "New conceptions of public duty, new developments of social enterprise, new estimates of the natural obligation of the members of the community to one another, have come into view and demand consideration", appeared in Chamberlain's preface to the "Radical Programme". Their proposals, written with Chamberlain's approval it was said, "sound the death-knell of the *laissez-faire* system".

The Radical Leader himself spoke of the "social evils which disgrace our civilization and the wrongs which have cried vainly for redress", and added significantly, "if we cannot convince our allies (the Liberals) of the justice and reasonableness of our cause, we must part company". From the Collectivists he had taken heart to say: "We have to account for, and to grapple with, the mass of misery and destitution in our midst, co-existent as it is with the evidence of abundant wealth—it is a problem put aside by references to the eternal laws of supply and demand, to the necessity of freedom of contract, and to the sanctity of every private right of property. These phrases are the convenient cant of selfish wealth".

But with these socialistic sentiments he remained resolute to defy Parnell, saying that he would not enter into a competition with the Tories to secure him an independent Parliament. "I will not allow that five million Irishmen have the right to govern themselves without regard to the rest of the United Kingdom, any more than five million inhabitants of the Metropolis." That was his case; for it he destroyed in the social field all hope of achieving his ambitions.

Although Chamberlain and his followers were denounced as Socialists, it is clear that in the 'eighties progressive public opinion was divided between those who had merely come to doubt the old idea that each individual should be free to work out his own destiny without State interference, the reformers who were not prepared to deny that there were occasions when the State might usefully protect the weak (taking the view expressed by Jevons in 1882 that "it is futile to attempt to uphold, in regard to social legislation, any theory of abstract rights, it is all a question of probability and degree"), and the avowed Socialists, who found representation in the Social Democratic Federation and the Fabian Society, and asked for the "Nationalization of the means of Production, Distribution and Exchange". Of these the "Radical Programme" inclined to the more moderate view. Despite the denunciation of its Leader as "Jack Cade", "Dick Turpin" and the like, Chamberlain was only a Socialist in the sense that Harcourt had said "we are all Socialists now". He repudiated the dead hand of *laissez-faire*, it is true, but the Tories had never accepted it—all he asked was that there should be no prejudice against the employment of the State and Municipality to redress specific abuses. At the same time he and his school set no limit, save that of expediency, to possible collectivist activity.

In particular the Radicals sought to appeal to the new county electors, promising the labourer treatment such as had been given in Ireland— "Three acres and a cow", as a Conservative derisively said—and, for the wealthier country dweller, the benefit of a simplification of land transfer. Both sides seemed to think that the time had come when the Government of the counties should be taken from the magistrates and given to County Boards. On Ireland, Lord Salisbury was reticent, though Parnell campaigned actively on his behalf, or rather against the Liberals. The large Irish vote in the industrial towns was told to turn Tory, and to a great extent obeyed; Parnell was seeking to produce a situation in which he could conduct an auction. Yet Salisbury had declared unequivocally against Irish parliamentary independence; even in local government a hint was given by him of the peculiar dangers in Ireland where "the population is on several subjects deeply divided". This is almost the first reference to the Ulster problem which afterwards became so important.

The Irish, throwing their vote in with the Tories, did much outside Birmingham to weaken the Liberals in the towns; probably also the shopkeeping class were beginning to be alarmed at Chamberlain's appeal to the working people. In the result, in the boroughs the Conservatives had a majority, but the counties told a different tale—the final result was three hundred and thirty-five Liberals, two hundred and forty-nine Conservatives and eighty-six Home Rulers.

Parnell had succeeded in holding the balance. Whether his tactics had been wise, time was to show.

Gladstone now endeavoured to come to some understanding with Salisbury for an agreed measure; this would perhaps have defeated Parnell, saved England from much acrimony, and in the end trained the Irish to self-government. It might even have satisfied Chamberlain; but it was not to be.

While Balfour, Salisbury's trusted nephew, was at Eaton, staying with the Liberal Duke of Westminster, Gladstone came over from Hawarden; the old man said that if some concession were not made to Parnell the Irishman would possibly resort to violence in England. "We are to be blown up or stabbed if we do not grant Home Rule by the end of the next Session?" asked Balfour. "I understand", said Gladstone, "that the time is shorter than that." The younger statesman reported to his uncle that Hartington, Goschen, Chamberlain and Dilke were all anti-Parnellites. He adds in his letter to Salisbury, and this may explain much, "Chamberlain finds it impossible to forgive the Irish Party for the way in which they have treated him and his Radical following".

Lord Salisbury, undeterred, repudiated all idea of Home Rule and, while a fresh Coercion Bill was being secretly prepared, a rural reform motion opposed by eighteen Whigs and seventy-eight other Liberals was carried as an amendment to the address by seventy-nine votes, and Salisbury resigned.

Before this, however, Granville, Spencer, Hartington and Rosebery had all become acquainted with the desire of Gladstone to concede a statutory parliament to Ireland, "Union of Empire and the supremacy of the Imperial Parliament being maintained". The reaction of Chamberlain was to say, "Mr. Parnell has appealed to the Tories. Let him settle accounts with his new friends". In substance he favoured leaving the Tories in office; it was a suggestion not very different from that which Gladstone had made to Salisbury through Balfour.

Parnell now, at length, discovered that his plans had failed; the Conservatives would rather relinquish office than give him Home Rule —all his labour to put them in had proved futile. His sympathizer, Carnarvon, while the Conservatives were still in power, and the Chief Secretary, Hart Dyke, had both resigned; but this was not generally known until the middle of January, 1886. As has been said, a new Coercion Bill had been prepared on the 27th; when the new secretary, W. H. Smith, brought back his Bill from Dublin, the Government had already resigned.

Despite the sympathetic treatment which Chamberlain has received at the hand of Garvin, his biographer, it is not easy to believe that personal resentment did not take a large part in his subsequent attitude. Beyond all question he had been basely treated by Parnell, O'Shea, and the Irish Party generally. He had resigned from the Cabinet because they could not carry the most advanced proposal for a National Council with domestic supremacy which had yet been proposed, and he had refused to tolerate indefinite coercion; by way of gratitude he had been reviled by Parnell and the whole Irish vote thrown against him and the other Radicals. Undoubtedly he was full of indignation. Nevertheless, knowing Gladstone's views, he re-entered the Cabinet. He took the Local Government Board. Harcourt was Chancellor of the Exchequer; Rosebery Foreign Secretary, and Campbell-Bannerman Secretary for War. Most significant, Morley, who had always supported Irish government of a "colonial type", was made Irish Secretary. Hartington, Goschen and Derby declined to serve; the rumours of the intentions of Gladstone, ever since the statement on December 6th in the *Leeds Mercury* that he wished to establish a Parliament in Dublin for dealing with purely Irish affairs, though dismissed at the time as "merely a speculation", had alarmed them.

The relations between Chamberlain and the Prime Minister, always strained, had not been made the more easy by the offer to him of the Admiralty, Gladstone's objecting to making him Colonial Secretary, and by an abortive attempt to reduce the salary of his friend Collings.

Yet, in so far as Chamberlain was willing to take office, albeit with "unlimited liberty of judgment and rejection" of Irish proposals, he showed a desire to avoid a breach. The difficulty is to see in the difference between an acceptable National Council, such as he had suggested, and a local Parliament, such a divergence as would justify his subsequent conduct. "He was willing", says Garvin, "not to go beyond a subordinate legislature compatible with Home Rule all round." (*Life of Chamberlain*,

Vol. 2, p. 179.) "He would not go beyond a point" (*ibid.*, p. 180), but what was the point beyond which he would not go? This neither Garvin nor any other writer has made clear. Chamberlain's honesty is beyond question. He knew, as he told Morley, that he would be left almost alone for a time. "I cannot of course work with the Tories", he said, "and Hartington is quite as much hostile to my Radical views as to Mr. G's Irish plans."

The crisis came on a proposed scheme of the Prime Minister to buy out the landlords in Ireland for £120,000,000 at twenty years' purchase. Chamberlain insisted that before he agreed he should be told the contents of the Home Rule Bill—Harcourt apparently already knew them. Then it came out—a separate Parliament for Ireland with full powers to deal with the Irish affairs. This differed only from the National Council scheme by abolishing representation at Westminster, but for this double representation Chamberlain never before had pressed.

Chamberlain thereupon said he must resign, Trevelyan took the same course. A scheme comparable to the "States basis in the United States", Chamberlain said, could have been discussed. On March 26th, Gladstone replied to Chamberlain's questions: Irish representation at Westminster was to cease, taxation in Ireland would be given to the Irish Parliament, they were to appoint the Judges and have authority in matters not excluded. On this Chamberlain and Trevelyan withdrew. Had the second condition been called Local Taxation, Chamberlain had already agreed to it in his own scheme. The last was a mere matter of exclusion by Schedule, a drafting point. The appointment of Judges had not been considered in the Irish Council scheme; in any case, as there would be an appeal to the Privy Council, it does not seem a sufficient reason for the rupture.

Outside the Government, Randolph Churchill now abandoned his coquetting with Parnell, and stirred up the Ulstermen; rioting occurred in Belfast. "Ulster will fight and Ulster will be right", he cried. Not long before, the Ulstermen in Liverpool had forced him to abandon a meeting on account of his suspected alliance with Parnell! Finally, he invented a name for a new party, the "Unionist", and asked the dissentient Liberals to join it. He succeeded in working the country into a state of anxiety and alarm.

Chamberlain was now asked to join the Tories, or the Whigs; by the Radicals he was petitioned to save the Liberal Party. Under pressure he even went so far as to say there must be a legislative body or bodies in Ireland. The Prime Minister, to meet him, gave up the claim that Ireland should have control of Customs and Excise; but this did not content—there remained the cessation of Irish representation at Westminster and the appointment of Judges to divide him from Morley and the other Liberals. In the debate on introduction—April 8th—for almost the first time Chamberlain said "Ireland is not a homogeneous community—it comprises two races and two religions". It was Churchill's argument, but in the past it had not prevented either of them from seeking an understanding with Parnell, nor did Chamberlain's proposed National Council for all Ireland recognize the division as an insuperable difficulty.

"Even now", he writes to Gladstone, "the differences may be further reduced when the second reading is taken." On the debate on the Land Bill he contended that if there were to be a legislature in Dublin there would have to be another one in Belfast; yet he admitted that the Bill had been much modified to meet him. Friends and enemies alike were confused as what he really wanted or to what he took objection.

At Birmingham, after a fierce fight, he defeated Schnadhorst, and the Caucus supported its member; but later, in London, the general committee of the Federation carried a resolution expressing confidence in Gladstone. The motion of Birmingham, asking for Irish representation to remain at Westminster, was defeated, and Chamberlain resigned from the national body.

The vital matter, he now said, was to maintain the Irish at Westminster; if this were granted he would vote for the second reading. As the Bill now stood there would be an Irish Executive, with Law and Police under its powers, it would pay one-twelfth of the taxes collected to the Imperial Treasury. This provision alone showed that its autonomy was limited; establishment and endowment of religion was also excluded. Chamberlain raised the question of Irish control of the declaration of war and of the armed forces. Salisbury declared the Irish were incapable of self-government; it was the prevailing opinion in England.

At last Gladstone announced that he would compromise on the retention of Irish members at Westminster. How, after this, Chamberlain could continue his opposition except upon Harcourt's supposition that "he has no thought but war to the knife", it is not easy to understand. Salisbury and Hartington appeared together at a great meeting, and Gladstone was socially ostracized. But Chamberlain had never been in Society; such exhibitions of bad manners in the ruling class meant nothing to him; he had won the concession, declared by him to be vital. He showed his teeth; refused to attend a meeting of the Liberal Party and summoned one for May 31st, the next day, of his own group. All depended upon him—if he abstained the Bill would get a second reading; if he voted against it, it meant defeat. Parnell, if he were capable of admitting error, must have regretted the day when he betrayed Chamberlain and was in his turn disowned by Churchill.

In the end, when his party meeting was held, Chamberlain refused to give them advice. He stated the case both ways, but concluded by reading a letter from Bright, saying that he would vote against the second reading. That decided them; the fifty agreed to oppose the Bill.

On June 1st Chamberlain spoke in the House. He denied inconsistency, but now declared that he could not see that the amendments suggested by the Prime Minister would meet his objections in any considerable measure; but the old statesmen had the last word—taking up Chamberlain's statement that a dissolution had no terrors for him he went on to say, "I do not wonder at it. He has trimmed his vessel and touched his rudder in such a masterly way that, whichever direction the winds of heaven may blow, they must fill his sails".

When the tellers came to the table it was seen that Home Rule had been defeated by thirty (343 to 313)—forty-six of the malcontents had followed Chamberlain, the remaining dissentient forty-seven Liberals were Whig.

A new organization, the National Radical Union, supplied Chamberlain with opportunities for meetings all over England. He spoke much of his conscience and his honour. He spoke of British courage and British pluck in a manner worthy of Randolph Churchill himself; he spoke of cowards quailing before the assassin and the dagger, but he did not explain how it was that, when terrorism was at its height in Ireland, he had been willing to hand over to the assassins or their friends the whole internal government of that country.

CHAPTER VIII

IN THE WILDERNESS

THE defection of Chamberlain, for reasons which must, it is suggested, having regard to the slender grounds of difference, be deemed insufficient, had the most far-reaching effects upon political development. It is at least possible, had he remained to lead the Radicals, that the Labour Party, which ultimately undermined the confidence of the working people in Liberalism, would never have come into being. The gradual absorption of the Whig elements into Conservatism was inevitable, but Chamberlain stood in quite a different position—indeed the departure of Hartington, Goschen and other territorial and city magnates could only have strengthened his control over the party at large. Almost certainly he would have succeeded Gladstone as Prime Minister. In that office, in control of the party machine, the first political leader in whom the trade unions and reformers generally had confidence, he might have proved irresistible. The academic shibboleths of Socialism would not have bound him, as later they did the Labour Leaders, nor would that doctrine have embarrassed him in soliciting the votes of such of the middle classes as were not wedded to materialist economics—instead, he came gradually to abandon his own programme. Apart from intermittent incursions into that province of social reform which he had made peculiarly his own, he sank back into the acceptance of a plutocratic imperialism, never more clearly indicated than in his acceptance of the Boer War.

Meanwhile, Home Rule was dead; not the Lords, but the people's House, had rejected it. If the interested Irish vote were deducted, the opinion against the proposal was irresistible. In the new Commons, after the General Election, the hostile majority was one hundred and eighteen. The Conservatives had a majority of over forty against Gladstone and Parnell; in the whole House they were in a minority of twenty. Thus they were driven to depend upon Chamberlain and Hartington.

There was, however, no real fear of defeat. Arrangements had already been made before the election for "Unionists" (as they were now called) not to oppose one another; on the other hand, Gladstonian Liberals had not hesitated to fight Chamberlain's candidates—the fissure was already complete.

A suggestion to make Hartington Prime Minister failed, and Salisbury, for the second time, became Premier, Churchill taking the Exchequer—there was to be no open coalition as yet. Soon a crucial test was offered. Chamberlain declared that he would not vote for an amendment "equivalent to a vote of censure on the Government". "I shall do nothing to turn out the Government, so long as the Government which would take its place is committed to a separate policy." Nevertheless, he still asked that the tenants of Ireland should be given land through State purchase.

A crisis nearly arose over the proposed new County Councils, a proposal which it was thought would remove the last power of the governing class as magistrates in quarter sessions to administer the counties. As so often is the case, their fears were entirely unfounded; apart from mining and similar industrial areas, the County Councils, when constituted, in nearly every case consisted of the same class of landed gentry who as Justices had formerly ruled the county—indeed their supremacy was even greater, it turned out, than before, for in time Labour men were nominated as Justices in many County areas; the expense of travel, the cost of contest and general inertia often had the result that no single member could be said by any reasonable interpretation directly to represent the working class on the new Councils.

All this, however, was not realized in 1887. It was reported to Chamberlain that the new Councils were to be filled in part by *ex officio* members. Salisbury was told that Chamberlain insisted as the price of his support that they should be wholly elective. The Government compromised, aldermen elected by the Council were to be created, following the borough tradition; the police to come under a joint committee of magistrates and councillors—in such form the Local Government Act of 1888 was passed. As time went on considerable powers and duties came to be entrusted to the Councils, and to County Boroughs who had the like powers. The advance towards collective action in matters of Health, Roads, Housing and the like increased yearly as more activities were entrusted to these local governing bodies. The staffs grew ever greater and more competent; alone in the personnel of the elected members there was practically no change. In the result the governing of most counties fell into the hands of the chairman and a few colleagues, but administration was controlled by officials to a far greater degree than it was in Parliament, for opposition in the Council Chamber was, in most cases, non-existent.

Nevertheless, though it was not then recognized, the establishment of County Councils was greatly to encourage socialistic experiment. The Fabian Society, under the skilful guidance of Sidney Webb, realized the opportunity. The Bill which became law on August 13th, 1888, made London into a new county, though the City retained many of its peculiar privileges. An advanced party, calling themselves Progressives, set out to rival Birmingham in municipal activity. The election of Lord Rosebery as first Chairman was carried, a few Radicals only objecting, and he certainly did much to give the new body a feeling of corporate dignity. The vigour of the London Progressives and the healthy state of Liberalism therein was in marked contrast to the confusion at Westminster, where Whigs and the followers of Chamberlain combined to force a feeling of inadequacy and frustration upon the followers of Mr. Gladstone.

The sudden resignation of Churchill on the most unconservative of issues—a complaint of the undue size of the service estimates—robbed Chamberlain of his most advanced Cabinet associate. It was at this time that he made a suggestion that a round-table conference between himself and the Gladstonians might even now end the discord: "A frank conference on the part of the members with him and those who disagreed with his line of action with reference to the Irish question". Harcourt agreed cordially—Gladstone concurred. Hartington, however, stood aloof; to him Chamberlain stated that he would never agree to a Parliament in Dublin with an executive dependent on it. On land and local government, he thought, there was room for compromise. The Conference met three times in January and February, 1887. Chamberlain declared that he would consider Home Rule on the Canadian basis, but Ulster must receive separate treatment. As to representation at Westminster, Harcourt was in favour, Morley against. In the end nothing resulted. "All hope of a reunion was abandoned" is the entry in Chamberlain's memorandum, made shortly after the February meeting.

In that year he supported by his vote the Tory address to the Crown, as did Hartington and Bright. He took no objection to the new Crimes Act which occupied Parliament from March until July. It was piloted by Arthur Balfour, the new Irish Secretary, with great skill amid constant Nationalist obstruction. To two matters the Liberal Unionists objected: the holding of trials for Irish offences in certain cases in England and the proclamation of the National League. In the latter case, though Hartington supported the Government, Chamberlain voted in opposition —the proscription of the League was carried, however, by seventy-seven votes.

The severity of Balfour's methods of coercion was greater than anything Harcourt had formerly countenanced. In the earlier days the eviction of tenants had not played a principal part in the disturbances, but now they could no longer pay the rents which had been fixed by the Land Courts, or would not. Chamberlain and Churchill demanded some concession and the Government surrendered, giving power to the Court to revise the rents originally fixed.

Parnell had introduced a Bill which would have halved all rents. On this being rejected, the tenants were advised by their leaders to pay only a part of their rents into a pool, which, if the landlord refused, was to be used for "defence", a term often including boycotting and terrorism, though to the latter method Parnell had always objected. This scheme was called the "Plan of Campaign"—the Liberals were ambiguous about it, some even went to speak in support. In the end there was a general consensus that the system of dual ownership was a failure, the only solution was to buy out the landlords; in effect this was the only matter on which all parties agreed. Prosecution and Proclamation failed to stop the Plan of Campaign, and murder and violence continued. Nevertheless, in 1889 Balfour introduced Irish Drainage Bills and, in 1890 (taking money from the disestablished Church surplus of £41,000 a year and £84,000 from the Fishery Loan Funds), he took over the Congested Areas (places where the land could not support its inhabitants), using the money for assistance and development: weaving, improving stock and implements, providing seed potatoes, and the like.

Another Conservative measure was the extension of land purchase—£33,000,000 to be guaranteed by the Government to support loans to enable the peasants to buy new land. Harcourt opposed on the ground that the Bill made the British taxpayer advance moneys on Irish land at a price that could not be obtained in the market and to receive on it a rent of 20 per cent less than it now yielded. Chamberlain, who had opposed Gladstone's Bill on the principle that British credit should not be pledged for Irish landlords, now supported Balfour who sought to do that very thing. Indeed, by now, as regards Ireland at any rate, personal rancour and political opportunism had excluded all consistent principle.

But an event more important than these squabbles had occurred. On November 27th, 1890, a fortnight after the O'Shea divorce had been granted in the Courts, only twenty-five of the Irish followed Parnell into the Opposition lobby. In the Judicial Commission, which among other things had inquired into his alleged approval of violence in Ireland and pronounced Piggot's letter (approving Burke's murder and imputed to Parnell) a forgery, he had obtained a great victory, but on his citation as co-respondent in the divorce case, Gladstone, after hesitation, wrote to Morley saying that Parnell's continuance as Leader of the Nationalists would render his own leadership of the Liberal Party almost a nullity.

Parnell refused to retire, and Gladstone's letter was published in the recess. The Irish were divided and acrimonious. In the end, forty-six with whom Gladstone continued to work deserted Parnell; twenty-six supported him. The effect was to break that power of the Nationalists in the House which Parnell had so laboriously built up with so little practical result.

On October 6th Parnell died and was succeeded by John Redmond—even then the two groups, though seeking precisely the same object, were not reconciled for several years, but the general improvement in parliamentary manners was marked. Balfour carried his land purchase schemes. As they finally emerged, if the landlord would sell, the whole purchase money would be advanced by the Exchequer up to £30,000 and after forty-nine years the tenant would become owner. On the death of W. H. Smith, Balfour became Leader of the House and First Lord. Hartington soon went to the Lords and Chamberlain became leader of the Liberal Unionists in the Commons.

Other measures which the Government sponsored were supported by the Liberals: a new Factory Act in 1891, limiting hours of labour for women to twelve a day with an hour and a half for meals, controlling of sub-contracting, and raising the minimum age of employment for children to eleven. Education became free and a Small Holding Act was passed. In all these measures, it is interesting to note, the old Liberal opposition on the ground of objection to State interference was notably absent.

It was evident that collective action, as such, was no longer regarded as objectionable in principle; a new Board of Agriculture testified to a growing interest of the State in that great industry. We already detect a feeling that the future problems of reform were likely to be more social than merely electoral. There was still a feeling among the masses that the Liberals rather than their opponents were likely to deal with these matters, though a dispassionate examination of the Statute Rolls would have shown them that the contrary was the case. In reality a new cleavage between Plutocracy and the masses was arising which threatened to overrride the old political divisions, but the time for the recognition of the fact was not yet come.

In 1891, before the General election, the advanced Liberals drew up a manifesto known as the Newcastle Programme. It included proposals for the taxation of land values, the abolition of entail, extension of small holdings, the building of rural cottages, payment of members, District Councils, Local Veto in the drink trade, disestablishment of the Church and reform of the House of Lords—a medley of proposals designed to satisfy different interests. The great dock strike of 1889 and the formation of socialistic Trade Unions alarmed the wealthier Liberals; the articles in the programme proposing still further to shorten hours of work and extend compensation for accidents seemed to be directed against their financial interests. The disestablishment proposals affronted some of the more Erastian Church people, the local option scheme enraged the publicans, who in any case were inclined to join the Church in supporting the Tories. Gladstone himself approved the programme, though in fact caring for little at this time but Irish Home Rule. When the election came the Liberals found that, even with Irish Nationalist support, they had a majority of only forty for Home Rule. It was at this election that Keir Hardie was returned as Independent Labour candidate for West Ham; the other fourteen working men returned were not prepared to assume such a position: they ranked as Liberals or Liberal-Labour.

In this Government the chief new-comer was Asquith. In 1889 he had declared himself in favour of Home Rule all round, with the unimpaired supremacy of the Imperial Parliament, a position not easily distinguishable from that of Chamberlain. He agreed with Rosebery in the now popular cry for supporting imperial expansion and the maintenance of the Egyptian protectorate. In domestic affairs he was associated with Haldane, Buxton, Ferguson and Acland; they tended to form a Radical element.

Salisbury decided to meet Parliament: the Liberal Unionists had fallen from ninety-four to forty-seven, and Asquith, in moving the amendment to the address, predicted their early extinction. He said that the Conservatives, to placate this little group, had inaugurated some Liberal measures in which they did not believe and he asked the House to reject the address, which they did, whereupon Salisbury resigned. Haldane was not found a place, but Grey became an under-secretary at the Foreign Office.

The second reading of the Home Rule Bill was taken on April 4th, 1893. Chamberlain was reminded how in 1885 and 1886 he had been prepared to hand over the government of Ireland to the Nationalists. It was said that the present Bill guaranteed imperial supremacy by

retaining eighty Irish members at Westminster and by inserting a clause
as to the Imperial Suzerainty in the preamble. The second reading was
carried by three hundred and forty-seven votes to three hundred and four.
In September the third reading was agreed by thirty-four. In the Lords
the voting for rejection was four hundred and nineteen to forty-one.

It had been said by Lord Kimberley, a Liberal, that there was "No
enthusiasm for Home Rule in the Party", and the indifference seemed to
have infected a large part of the Cabinet. Morley has declared that only
Asquith and he shared Gladstone's belief in Home Rule. Harcourt,
Gladstone said, "hated Home Rule as a Britisher hates those whom he has
ill used". At any rate the Cabinet would not agree to a dissolution on
the action of the Lords. Writing in 1897 in *Essays in Liberalism* six young
Liberals declared that: "A dissolution would have been the best course—
the Ministry had a real cry with which to go to the country". It was not
until March, 1894, that Gladstone finally retired, but before that he also
had come to the conclusion that dissolution on the rejection of the Home
Rule Bill would have been the right course. The Lords had so maimed
an Employers' Liability Bill as to force its abandonment, and they had
wrecked a Local Government Bill for parishes. On all these matters,
but particularly on the Home Rule Bill, Gladstone, aged eighty-five, was
prepared to go to the Country; he suggested dissolution in January, 1894,
but, to quote his own words, "received by telegraph" (he was in Biarritz)
a hopelessly adverse reply". In Asquith's words: "We all agree that this
is madness". Not until 1911 was the issue with the Lords faced; not
until 1912 was another Home Rule Bill to be introduced.

The real cause of Gladstone's resignation was a growing disagreement
with the majority of his colleagues on the question of armament. He
objected to the increase of three million pounds odd which Spencer and
his advisers thought necessary for the Navy; nevertheless, had his advice
been sought, he would have recommended Spencer as his successor. It
was not. The Queen offered Lord Rosebery the premiership. The new
Prime Minister startled the Radicals in his first speech by declaring that he
agreed with Salisbury that, before Home Rule was granted, "England, as
the predominant member of the partnership of the three kingdoms, would
have to be convinced of its just.   . This presumably was a reference to
the fact that in England there was a hostile majority; it was a new
constitutional doctrine so to divide the United Kingdom, but Lord Rosebery did not explain how he came to remain a member of a Government
which had treated the three parts as one for the purpose of obtaining a
parliamentary decision.

In the Commons, however, great things were stirring. In the Budget
Harcourt sought to equalize the charges on personal and real property at
death—the duty was now to be paid on the whole estate at the selling
value in the market. It was to range from one to eight per cent. By a
majority of fourteen this was carried, the Lords not daring to interfere.
Without exaggeration, this duty may be said to have done more to
change the social complexion of England than almost any recent legislation. The need for the money had come through the demands of the
Navy. To Harcourt it was a good expedient, but upon the landed
aristocracy the cumulative effect of the taxation was to prove
disastrous.

The temptation to increase the yield was too much even for Conservative Chancellors of the Exchequer. In a quarter of a century the yield had risen from four to forty million. "The consequence of cutting off something like a third (in 1942 considerably more) of each big estate whenever the owner dies has reduced the aristocracy of England to the position which the remains of the ancient régime occupy in France", writes Hamilton Fyfe. (*Liberalism.*) It is to be marked how, with failing economic resources, the political power of the old families had died away. Yet if Harcourt had been told that his was the axe which felled the family tree, he would have been astounded.

Rosebery sent Harcourt "an elaborate memorandum directed against the Budget generally, and the graduated death duties in particular". The Chancellor pointed out that the fear of taxation of capital is out of date. "At present", he wrote, "capital is not in deficiency, but superabundant." As to the break-up of large properties, he predicts they will be kept together by the prudent. The Prime Minister's suggestion that properties should be held, irrespective of the character of their possessors, is denounced as "very fine old Tory doctrine". Rosebery withdrew his objection, but Goschen and Chaplin marshalled the City and landed interests in opposition. The publicans and brewers objected to a tax of 6d. per gallon on spirits and beer. Fortunately, the Irish were now divided, the Parnellites, as they were still called, voted in opposition, but the other Nationalists supported Harcourt. The principle then won has never since been disturbed.

The foreign issue between Harcourt and Rosebery has still to be considered; it was one which threatened the integrity of the whole party. There is no doubt that the prosperous classes were seeking for an outlet for their capital abroad—a spirit of gambling and speculation was afoot and the old respectable city merchant was giving way to the more modern type of financier. The game of manipulating shares and limited companies was found to be more remunerative than the manufacture of commodities, and the cautious instincts which moved the old Manchester School were fast disappearing. The discovery of gold and diamonds in South Africa brought into the powerful classes a very undesirable element. Murmurs were heard that the Jews were polluting public life. Of a section of that race whose restrictive pressure of environment had produced a marked concentration of character and purpose, not attractive to the easy-going English, it was true to say that they stimulated the worship of money—their interest in its expenditure on art and public benevolence did not wholly reconcile their competitors and neighbours. From the time of the Boer War it is perhaps true to say that anti-semitism, though not virulent, became a conscious force.

Apart, however, from the ambitions of the plutocrats, there were other influences at work which operated to end the dominion of that individualistic pacific outlook of which Gladstone, Harcourt and Morley were surviving representatives. The new conception of the Kingdom and Empire as an estate, new, that is, since the Industrial Revolution, had shown itself in the disappearance of objection to the use of the State in internal betterment, but this was only half the story—if the State was once more to be regarded as an entity in the domestic sphere, so also, figuring as the Nation, it had come to claim a new vigour in Foreign

Affairs. Disraeli was, perhaps, the first statesman to realize and encourage this fact—in Palmerston the external aspect had absorbed all his energy and interest, but by the time of the new *Imperium et Libertas* the two functions had become complementary.

The Germans under Bismarck had led the way; he foreshadowed a State strong within and without. Conscription demanded a healthy army. In England, where conscription was advocated only by a few enthusiasts, the same considerations were subconsciously at work. The day of Protection had not yet come, but it also ultimately arose out of the same influences. The Nation, as it is said, had "found itself"; whether in the process the individual has not been lost is still to be discovered.

Poets, romantics and adventurers swelled the imperialist enthusiasm; it was left for Will Crooks to point out in answer to the claim that on the British Empire the sun never sets, "in our alley it never rises".

To return to the situation which arose on the resignation of Gladstone, there is no doubt on which side Rosebery stood. He was an Imperialist. Why the pacific Gladstone had entrusted him with the conduct of Foreign matters it is not easy to understand. As early as 1874 he had spoken of the great stream of emigration from England being an "affluent of giant Commonwealths and peaceful Empires that shall perpetuate the best qualities of our race". As the years went by, his passion for Empire did not abate. It was dislike for Turkey which brought him on to Gladstone's side; for that reason he objected to the Treaty of Berlin which had saved that "impotent" country. He joined in the great Midlothian campaign and acted as host to the old leader, and in 1881 joined the Government as Under-Secretary to the Home Office, but in June, 1883, he had retired. In the Franchise fight, when Salisbury sought to hold up the Bill until redistribution had been effected, he fought in the Lords from the Liberal benches, attacking in particular the Whig Argylle; yet, from the Liberal view, his imperialist heresies were still about him. In 1884 he addressed the Trade Union Congress on Imperial Federation. He demanded a stronger Navy and opposed the evacuation of Egypt. He would not surrender that country to any other Power.

When the Liberals returned dependent upon the Irish vote, a crisis arose for Rosebery; he declared that "though they might kill Mr. Gladstone's Bill they could not kill its policy". He was not prepared to follow Chamberlain, but his real interest was not in the Irish question at all. In 1886, Granville, having patently failed in Foreign Affairs, Rosebery was appointed in his place. Unlike Granville he claimed much independence. Gladstone supported Russia against Turkey, with France he was not unfriendly; Salisbury feared Russia and desired an alliance with the new German Empire. The new minister admired the new Germany the Russians he did not trust. As to France, he regarded their Government as dangerous and jealous, while Gladstone was almost entirely absorbed in Irish questions. Undoubtedly Rosebery altered the whole trend of Liberal foreign policy. He had a dispute with Russia over Batoum; he succeeded in settling the Afghan frontier and in pacifying the relations between Turkey and Greece. In the Lords he was congratulated by Salisbury, who uttered these momentous words: "The policy which this country is pursuing (in foreign affairs) is not that of one Party or Government, but of all Parties in the State".

When Rosebery returned to the Foreign Office, in 1892, he insisted that Egypt should not be evacuated, as Gladstone had promised during the election, and had his way; generally he refused to disturb the policy of his predecessors—in this policy Grey, his Under-Secretary, agreed. In time this departure from active parliamentary criticism of foreign affairs produced very far-reaching effects. For the moment even Radicals seemed to acquiesce in the withdrawal of this, the most important of all public functions from popular public information and control. At the end of 1892 the Foreign Office dictated to the young Khedive whom he was to choose to be his Prime Minister. The French protested, and Cromer demanded that the Egyptian garrison should be strengthened; then at length the French gave way.

The statement of Rosebery to Cromer that he was to "inform the Khedive in case of his refusing to take your advice, that he must be prepared to take the consequences of his act", and in his warning to Paris that "as long as the British flag was in Egypt and British forces in occupation, the whole Administration could not be reversed at the whim of the Khedive", was far more in the Palmerstonian tradition than in that of Gladstone. So also the declaration of a British Protectorate over Uganda in 1894 was proclaimed against the wish of Gladstone and Harcourt—it was evident that a real cleavage on foreign policy was arising.

His accession to the Premiership accentuated the differences—the unfortunate reference to the need for British approval of Home Rule has already been noted.

Although Harcourt was Leader in the House of Commons, Kimberley, who had succeeded Rosebery at the Foreign Office, failed to give him adequate information on international matters. Thus Harcourt protested in terms on the failure to communicate with him about the Anglo-Belgium treaty which transferred to Belgium a sphere of British influence on the Upper Nile, its object being to keep out the French. He declared to Kimberley that the matter had assumed a most serious aspect, for Harcourt opposed British intervention in foreign affairs; true to the Gladstonian tradition, he hated Jingoism and "prancing proconsuls".

Rosebery, on the other hand, was one of the promoters of the new Imperialism, but both men understood how everything else; finance, defence, domestic politics, all depended on our relations with foreign Powers. It was their methods of dealing with the problem which were irreconcilably divergent. Experiments such as the Belgium understanding, which antagonized both Germany and France, were wholly deplorable from Harcourt's standpoint.

Germany, which was now in alliance with Austria and Italy, disliked Gladstone's pro-Russian policy. The wealth of the British Empire was beginning to cause envy abroad. The claims now being made in Africa intensified the feeling. To the last, Harcourt deplored the developments he saw going on around him; to use modern jargon he was an "isolationist"—in his own time he would have been called a "little Englander".

In March, 1895, Grey had said in the Commons that the whole Nile was under British influence; he objected to French encroachments, and spoke of them, to Harcourt's disgust, as unfriendly actions. Harcourt did his best to save England from being involved in the growing European complications, for he was a good Liberal of the old type. "Is there no pie in the world out of which we can manage to keep our fingers?" he vainly asked.

The policy of Rosebery caused a demand for more expenditure on the armed forces. A reorganization of the War Office was effected, resulting in the resignation of the Duke of Cambridge from the office of Commander-in-Chief which he had held for nearly forty years. The megalomania shown by pan-German and pan-Slavonic movements, the notion of "Will to Power" and the horrible idea that "the good war justifies every cause", emanating from Nietzsche, the desire for a "greater Servia, a greater Bulgaria, a greater Greece" and other nationalist demands had reduced Europe to that condition of alternative armistice and war from which she has never since recovered. In this country the disease took a milder form. Dilke spoke of the "grandeur of our race, already girdling the earth, which it is destined, perhaps eventually, to overspread"—a "greater Britain". These words, it is to be noted, came from an advanced Radical. Chamberlain, increasingly, was of the same way of thinking, and Rosebery was not far behind. Kipling was their lyrist; the Diamond Jubilee their occasion.

In all these circumstances it is not surprising that when the Government were defeated—significantly on a War Office vote—and resigned in June, 1895, that the Conservatives should come back with the great majority of one hundred and fifty-two over Liberals and Nationalists combined.

This time Chamberlain, with little hesitation, joined the Government as Colonial Secretary. He was now an ardent Imperialist. Far more than Salisbury or Balfour (who had become Prime Minister), he guided the rising national vainglory until it was involved in war, the certain end of all such amoral ambition. It was his own choice; from henceforth Imperialism looked to him for guidance.

Balfour became First Lord, the Prime Minister took the Foreign Office, Hicks Beach the Exchequer. The other Liberal Unionists in the Cabinet were Whigs—Lansdowne at the War Office and James at the Duchy of Lancaster. Austen Chamberlain was Civil Lord of the Admiralty.

Chamberlain began with small things; the King of Ashanti was told to accept a British protectorate. He refused. His capital, Kumassi, was occupied, and Ashanti annexed, but trouble in Africa was not over —bigger problems soon arose.

It was the desire of the Boers in the Transvaal to obtain access to the sea, a reasonable ambition it would be thought. It had been said by Lord Ripon that for them to obtain a port was unfavourable to the interests of the paramount Power, a claim which the Boers would never admit. In the negotiations in 1884, in which Chamberlain had taken an active part, the title of South African Republic had been acknowledged to the Transvaal and the claim to British suzerainty removed from the preamble of the Treaty. It was clear that in law the claim of Ripon to

Imperial paramountcy was at least doubtful—but this was not all. The non-Boers in Africa had complained that they were excluded from public government (with perfect propriety according to international law if the Transvaal was to have its own independent government), and domestic autonomy on any view had been conceded without question in the treaty following Majuba. It was said that the Boers were unprogressive and that they needed the new blood of the "Outlanders" who already were busy extracting gold from the Rand.

Meanwhile, Kruger had obtained a seaport through the opening of the railway to Delagoa Bay from Pretoria. He unwisely proclaimed that the fords across the Vaal river would be closed to goods imported from Cape Colony; he negotiated with the Germans. All this made Rhodes, the pioneer of Empire development in South Africa, turn to revolutionary methods. Chamberlain pointed out that the closing of the fords was unfriendly and a breach of the London Convention of 1884. He notes in the autumn of 1895 that "the representatives of the Chartered Company (i.e. Rhodes and his friends) were convinced that unless the Transvaal Government made some concessions there would be a rising in Johannesburg". At this time, in fact, Rhodes was conspiring to bring about such a revolution. Rifles and guns were to be bought in England, the de Beers company was to smuggle them into the Transvaal capital.

Kruger had given way on the importation over the fords and the Outlanders were in a state of exultation. It appears probable that Chamberlain knew of the preparations for the raid, but he did not expect that Jameson, who was in command, would so soon act.

On December 28th, Jameson started to advance on Pretoria with a few hundred men; on January 2nd he surrendered—two days before Chamberlain had instructed Sir Hercules Robinson to denounce the raid as "an act of war, or rather filibustering". A proclamation was issued forbidding all British subjects to aid Jameson. Next day the Kaiser telegraphed to Kruger, congratulating him on having succeeded "in establishing peace against armed bands" without calling on the aid of friendly Powers. This fact of course saved Jameson and, perhaps, Chamberlain. Both became popular heroes. It remains to consider the action of the Liberal Party during this tumultuous time.

It must be remembered, in the first place, that England was in the throes of a gold fever, and that the suppression of the Boer Republic would, it was thought, increase the profits. Next, there was a bitter feeling among the older people arising out of the defeat of Majuba and Gladstone's consequent 'humiliation', as it was construed; a surrender in which Chamberlain, it was conveniently forgotten, had taken an active part. Austin, the poet-laureate, praised Jameson in a doggerel beginning: "There are girls in the gold-reef city", there was much other absurdity of the music-hall type, so easily in times of excitement to be mistaken for patriotism.

At this time, Harcourt writing to Bryce said: "I know that the South African directors have advised that they knew of the intention to organize an armed rising at Johannesburg, and that Jameson was at Mafeking with their knowledge and authority to take part in the rising when it occurred". Harcourt did not accept the view that Chamberlain was involved. The Chartered Company included as directors the Dukes of

Abercorn and Fife, and all Society held shares, which were now worth £9. They all turned on Harcourt, but he was not deterred. In the House he made a great speech. "Stock jobbing Imperialism" was his description of the Company's activities. The Government were forced to concede an inquiry, but Chamberlain would not agree that Rhodes should retire. He was at that time both Prime Minister at the Cape and Chairman of the Chartered Company, and by far the most powerful Englishman in South Africa. "He was necessary to South Africa," declared Chamberlain, "for he had the confidence of the whole community."

The inquiry opened in the autumn of 1896 and continued during 1897. Meanwhile, the raiders were tried before the Lord Chief Justice and convicted, but their sentences were light; the real question was the responsibility of Rhodes, and, indeed, of Chamberlain. As to the first, he was proved to have consented to everything except the exact hour for Jameson's action. Nevertheless, nothing was done. He remained a member of the Privy Council, and Chamberlain went so far as to say that there exists nothing which affected Mr. Rhodes' personal honour. "If a man goes into a revolution, it follows as a matter of course that he must deceive other people." With this example of the decay of moral judgment in this acquisitive period we may leave the matter. From that time, war became inevitable.

The conflict, when it happened, is here only to be considered in so far as it affected the fortunes of the Liberal Party. Before it came, Rosebery had resigned the leadership on the ground that he could not follow the veteran Gladstone in a crusade against the Turk after the Armenian massacres. He feared, and with reason, a general European conflagration. Gladstone proposed that England should at least withdraw her ambassador. Most naïvely Rosebery replied that the British Empire had increased by 2,600,000 square miles in twelve years, and that with this mass of "undigested Empire" peace was essential.

The Radicals were infuriated; they saw an affront to the beloved Grand Old Man in Rosebery's refusal, and possibly also some electoral advantage lost. On October 8th, 1896, Rosebery wrote to his chief Whip saying: "The leadership of the Party, so far as I am concerned, is vacant". On September 24th, Gladstone had urged independent action on England's part against the "infamous Turk", but Rosebery would not take the responsibility of fighting one who, he said, "so long as he lives will always be the real leader of the Liberal Party".

At this time the division among Liberals as to Imperialism was growing wider; Harcourt was content to remain Leader in the Commons, but Rosebery had already expressed to Asquith a hope that "you very soon will replace me". There was reason in this; as the biographers of Lord Oxford and Asquith wrote: "His leaning in this and similar conjunctures were on the whole Roseberyite." (*Life*, I, p. 115.)

In 1898 Kitchener conquered the Soudan, and the dispute with France at Fashoda produced a diplomatic crisis. The Liberal Imperialists joined with the Government in demanding the withdrawal of France. Harcourt expressed the hope that we should all abstain from language "of vulgar swagger or provocation or menace which might embarrass their conduct or precipitate their action". It was a wise caution, having regard to the marked increase in Jingoism which was now so universally rampant.

That the party was "rent by sectional disputes" was the reason why Harcourt declined any longer to attempt to lead—this was in December, 1898.   In January of the next year Morley also resigned his official position—he would not "sponge off the slate all the lessons Mr. Gladstone has taught us".   Next month, Campbell-Bannerman, who then occupied a central position between the disputants, was elected Leader without opposition.

By May, Rosebery had suggested the formation of a new party to include "the factor of the larger patriotism which I have called Imperialism". Harcourt replied: "What is this Imperialism which, in the slang of the day, is paraded as the highest form of patriotism?"—"If it was to relieve distress and raise the standards of comfort for all the subjects of the King, he was an Imperialist", he declared; but, "there is another and exactly opposite view of imperial policy—it is to postpone and subordinate all these objects to vanity, to the acquisition of fresh populations, the adoption of additional burdens. To these ends social reforms are neglected—to talk of social reforms is ' parochial' and that what we ought to occupy ourselves with is this inflated Imperialism".

So far, therefore, from Rosebery's retirement easing the position, as Harcourt had hoped, it accentuated the divergence. Asquith, Grey, Haldane and Fowler were all sympathetic in varying degrees to the Rosebery policy. E. T. Cook, the editor of the *Daily News*, was an enthusiastic supporter of Liberal Imperialism. In the country the Jameson raid, so far from disgusting people with the 'new order', had increased their patriotic zeal, nor was the benevolent treatment of Rhodes, the prime conspirator, by the Government anything but popular. What the Liberal Imperialists failed to understand was, that if the nation wished for a swashbuckling Government, they would look for it on the Conservative and not on the Opposition side of the House.

In South Africa the position became ever more acute. Milner, who had succeeded Robinson as High Commissioner, was truculent. In May, 1899, he telegraphed to Chamberlain of "thousands of British subjects kept permanently in the position of helots". He demanded action. In a conference, Kruger offered the franchise after seven years' residence. This was refused. Campbell-Bannerman deprecated military preparations on this side, but by July the Government had already started to mobilize their forces. Kruger then offered a five-year qualification—by this time the seven-year condition was law—if Britain would no longer interfere in the affairs of the Transvaal and abandon her claim to suzerainty, further disputes to go to arbitration—a most reasonable demand. Chamberlain, who in earlier years had agreed that the suzerainty claim should be dropped—though this was before the days of the Kaffir-market and gold interest—insisted on it. Now that the franchise had been granted it was the only issue outstanding. In October, fifty thousand Outlanders left the Rand. England moved troops up to the Transvaal border. The Boers then sent an Ultimatum, demanding the withdrawal of the British army from the frontier, and a stop to be put to the landing of troops from England.   This was refused, and on October 11th they crossed into Natal and surrounded Mafeking and Kimberley. The War had begun.

The effect upon the Liberal Party was disastrous. Harcourt had said that the Boers were right on the suzerainty dispute; Sir Edward Clarke, another considerable lawyer, though Conservative, took the same view. Morley declared against the yellow Press that "you may give greater buoyancy to the South African Stock and Share Market. You may send up the price of Mr. Rhodes' Chartered. Even then it will be wrong". This was on the eve of war. Asquith, with Grey and Haldane, was on the Government side.

Bryce and Reid agreed with Harcourt and Morley, as also did the young Lloyd George. In the end one hundred and thirty-five Liberals voted on an amendment "disapproving the conduct of the negotiations which had involved us in hostilities with the South African Republic". Campbell-Bannerman's position was intermediate between the Imperialists and those who came to be called "pro-Boers". He thought the Ultimatum had made war certain, but believed that Chamberlain, by nominating a friend of Rhodes as High Commissioner, by exonerating Rhodes for the raid itself, and by harping on suzerainty was at least *particeps criminis*. His constant criticism of the past action of the Government soon made him associate with the Harcourt side; indeed, apart from his laudable desire to preserve the party from further disruption, that was obviously where his heart lay.

In reality, it made little difference. The Country and the Government, smarting under early military defeats, abused all Liberals indiscriminately as traitors. The Imperialists asserted their patriotism, the pro-Boers declared that the party must stand aloof from Jingoism. Still the leader tried to keep a middle course. He refused to attack the Boers as evil men; on the other hand, on the question of annexation, he disagreed with Asquith who had spoken against it—he saw that annexation must follow victory in war.

At home, the institution of London Borough Councils was opposed to some extent by Liberals, more particularly as it left the ancient rights of the City unaffected. An Act to relieve the Clergy of rates on tithe, costing £87,000 a year, angered the Nonconformists, and Sir William Robson, afterwards Liberal Attorney-General, obtained an Act raising the school age to 12 years.

An amendment of censure on the King's speech, when Parliament met early in 1900, regretting "want of foresight in the conduct of South African affairs since 1895 and in their preparations for the war", was officially moved by the Liberals. The Imperialists and "pro-Boers" again disclosed their differences; the Leader taking a middle course. In the end there were abstentions, but no serious cleavage was as yet exhibited. The question of annexation now came to the fore, for the military position was improving. Campbell-Bannerman from the outset took the view that the proper course was to annex and then give a Liberal constitution to united South Africa. This, in 1906, he was able to achieve; it was his greatest work.

During the election of 1900 the Liberal Imperialists suffered more than their party opponents. The whole party had been attacked with equal violence. Just before the election the Government had put through the Commonwealth of Australia Bill, which had generally been approved. From now on Australia had the same dominion status as Canada; even the anti-Imperialists could not deny that this measure was unobjectionable. By the nation as a whole it was regarded as Chamberlain's personal triumph.

Circumstances had made him by far the most important person in the Cabinet, yet, notwithstanding his abusive speeches, the Government only gained four seats—the remark of Chamberlain that "every seat lost to the Government was a seat gained by the Boers" was an example of his manner—the result was to infuriate the Imperialist Liberals and to make the prospects of Liberal reunion the brighter.

Milner now wished to suspend the Constitution at the Cape, though the Colonial Secretary had announced for the Government that the Republics would be incorporated into Her Majesty's dominions. The time seemed not far off—in May the British were in Johannesburg To the gratification of the Liberals, Chamberlain hinted at an ultimate constitution leading to self-government. Campbell-Bannerman was surprised at a speech "very much more favourable to our object than I had anticipated". But he was premature; in answer to his speech on the address in the new Parliament that the Boers should be told that "by and by, when things have settled down and there is safety, they will have their share in the full rights of self-government", Balfour, the Prime Minister, replied that "he knew not how long the delay might be, it might be years, it might even be generations". It soon emerged that the Unionist policy towards the Boers was unconditional surrender.

In truth, despite the assurance at the election that the war was practically over, guerrilla warfare was still universal in the Transvaal. The military decided upon more punitive methods. They put the women in concentration camps, and burned the farms which were often centres of resistance. It appeared that both Kitchener and Milner had objected to the method of conciliation, and the proclamation promising the Transvaal self-government was not issued. Thousands of women had been driven out on to the veldt, and an unfortunate proclamation made, though afterwards withdrawn, that "the Boer women should apply to the Boer commandant for food", enraged Campbell-Bannerman and the "left" Liberals. In June, 1901, he denounced such proceedings as "methods of barbarism". In the House he repeated his accusation, to be at once reproved by Haldane. On a motion for adjournment by Lloyd George to call attention to the whole punitive system, fifty Liberal Imperialists, including Asquith and Haldane, abstained from voting. The temporary truce was again broken.

In June, the Leader called a meeting of the Party and received a unanimous vote of confidence from Liberal Peers and Commons. Thereupon Rosebery declared that he would "never voluntarily return to the arena of party politics", he would "plough his own furrow alone".

Rosebery had gone too far, the other Imperialists did not follow him; indeed Asquith shortly afterwards, while claiming the right of his opinions that the war "was neither intended nor desired by the Government or the people of Great Britain, but that it was forced upon us", went on to say that he desired "the fabric of a free, federated self-governing South African Dominion".

Next, Rosebery delivered himself at Chesterfield. In his speech Liberals were exhorted to "put away their fly-blown phylacteries", though what was to be discarded was not very clear. At any rate, he meant to insult the past traditions of Liberalism, presumably in their dislike of foreign commitment and Imperial expansion. Fowler, Grey and Asquith were all upon his platform. "The efficiency" which he recommended was something other than Liberalism as it had so far been understood. Campbell-Bannerman went to see him; all that emerges was that they could not co-operate. Grey demanded, as the price of his allegiance, that the Leader should accept Rosebery's views on the war; this the genial Campbell-Bannerman described in a letter to one of his friends as "damned egoism and impertinence". It was clear that the Imperialists wished the Leader to abdicate or surrender, but the skilful Scotsman was not to be intimidated. Soon Rosebery became more lucid; he said he was opposed to Home Rule for Ireland, though favouring devolution. "I am outside the tabernacle," he declared a little later. The followers of Rosebery treated Campbell-Bannerman with contumely; when he spoke in the House, the author has been informed by a Radical member then in Parliament, it was the habit of the Imperialists on the front bench to withdraw.

They were evidently scheming to make his position intolerable. The Liberals in the country, however, were quite of another opinion. On February 19th, when Campbell-Bannerman repudiated the Rosebery "clean slate" and declared his belief in Home Rule, he received from the National Liberal Federation a call on all Liberals to support him.

Thereupon the Rosebery faction formed a Liberal (Imperial) League with that nobleman as President; Grey, Asquith and Fowler were vice-presidents. Harcourt alone stood behind the Leader. The journalist, Harmsworth, daily attacked him and tried to persuade Liberals to put back Rosebery. Still the bulk of Liberal opinion in the country trusted him rather than the brilliant nobleman and lawyers who were busy reconstructing Liberalism on an Imperial basis.

All this, however, became very stale once the War was over. New interests arose which united Liberals once more; the League and its President were alike soon forgotten.

This unifying influence came in the first place from opposition to the Government's Education Bill of 1902. In July, 1902, Salisbury had resigned and Balfour became Prime Minister. He it was who insisted upon rate-aid for Voluntary Schools against the advice of Chamberlain and the wise old Lord Salisbury, but the Cabinet was persuaded. The trouble had arisen from a legal decision that, under the existing law, School Boards could not use rates outside the very restricted definition of elementary education in the earlier Acts. The vast majority of the Voluntary Schools were Anglican, and any final assistance to them out of the rates was objectionable to the Nonconformists. In country districts, "single school areas" as they were called, where the school had often been built by the Squire and the pupils taught by the priest, though a Wesleyan child might be withdrawn from the religious teaching, it would be at the cost of being left without any religious education. Money, however, was the difficulty; the Church school did not receive the assistance of the local rates, but only a small grant. Unless fresh subscriptions could be raised, the Church people could not always maintain their buildings or furniture or pay proper salaries to teachers. They were in constant fear of condemnation by the inspector.

The promotion of Welsh disestablishment by the Liberal Party in 1892–95 had made most parsons Tory agents, they now asked for their reward. But times had changed—dogmatic religion was rapidly losing its hold, particularly on the urban population. Not one-fifth of the people of Birmingham, said Cadbury, entered any church or chapel. The same was true of other towns. It followed that a Bill which would take State money to satisfy Church people must antagonize not only Nonconformists but also the immense hosts of voters who were without any religion at all.

In 1896 the Duke of Devonshire, who was then President of the Council and so, indirectly, Minister of Education (for there was no special department at that time), and his representative in the Commons, Sir John Gorst, sought to make each county the supreme education authority for its area. The Government was to stimulate secondary education by grants and the founding of new institutions and also to give grants to School Boards and to Voluntary schools, where attendance was compulsory, in single school areas. Thus the Church would benefit by receiving rate aid, while the Radicals were to be pleased by raising the school age to twelve, and the increase in staff.

The Bill was withdrawn, but many of its proposals found expression in the measure of 1902. In 1899 the Board of Education had been established; the old Education Department and the Science and Arts Departments were absorbed into it, and also the educational functions of the Charity Commission. To all this there was no objection; and an increasing interest in education generally, stimulated in part by fear of German rivalry, was arising. Then came the decision above mentioned that the grants from the Central Authority were only available for technical education. It was at this point that the Socialist Fabian Society raised the cry that in each district of convenient size there should be only one education authority. They attacked the whole notion of special School Boards. The contention was not very inconsistent with what had been accepted in the 1896 Bill. In 1902 the Government decided to clear up the whole muddle. Gorst was enthusiastic, the Duke of Devonshire lugubrious. Sir Robert Morant, the private secretary of Gorst, was an intimate friend of the leading Fabians, in particular of Sidney Webb, who combined with his advocacy of "Evolutionary Socialism" practical experience of local Government on the London County Council, where he sat as a Progressive. He had also a great knowledge of the history of the subject.

Sir William Anson had taken the place of Gorst; he was a juridical expert, a fellow of All Souls, and a member for the University. The Bill, as it passed, abolished the School Boards as the Fabians had sought; the county councils and county boroughs took over their functions, and certain larger urban districts were given education committees. So far the objection was expert and technical; but the other part of the measure, that which dealt with the Voluntary schools, united the Liberals in opposition and in the end proved most damaging to the Government.

F

The Voluntary Schools, now for the first time were to receive assistance from the rates. They had to set up a Board of Managers (on which sat representatives of the foundation trust and of the local education authority). The Board were to see that the religion taught agreed with the views of the founders.

From March till December the Bill was fought in the Commons. The abolition of the School Boards was called an attack on the people's rights, the presence of co-opted members on the Education Committee of the Council being the justification for their indignation. All were united: Imperialists, little Englanders and Nonconformists agreed that it was an outrage.

The Nonconformists, led by Dr. Clifford, denounced the financing of Church Schools out of public funds; that they had long received State grants, though not rating assistance, was generally overlooked. The cry, "the Church on the rates", the passive resistance of several thousand people, including in Wales a County Council, added to the excitement. Campbell-Bannerman addressed the National Free Churches Union, describing the measure as a Church Bill in disguise. Even Rosebery came out of his solitude to condemn it, yet, to-day, no impartial person can deny that the educational work of the Councils has been one of the most successful of their enterprises. The new secondary education proved invaluable. In the school year before the passing of the Act there were but three hundred and forty-one secondary schools; in five years the number had risen to six hundred and eighty-nine, and the increase, both in numbers and efficiency, has continued ever since: never were the Liberals less justified than in their attack upon this measure as doing nothing for education. The truth is that the Dissenter had largely captured the old School Boards and the Anglicans controlled the majority of the county Voluntary schools. By-elections were being won on the issue.

It was, in part, the fear that they would lose their power in urban areas which caused the Liberals to lament the extinction of the School Board—in reality their abolition was but one instance of the general tendency to eradicate special *ad hoc* authorities, to "use a convenient barbarism" as Sir William Anson, in his academic manner, had said in introducing the Education Bill. When Government intervention was occasional and irregular, as in the earlier portion of the nineteenth century, it was natural that Parliament should appoint specific Boards to deal with particular difficulties; now that the notion of collective action in the social sphere was coming to be accepted, the multiplication of authorities would make the further specific endowment of powers for stated purposes impracticable. Gradually they were absorbed into one general governing body. The Highway, Sanitary and Burial Boards had already gone; there was everything to be said from a constructive point of view for the elimination of the School Board also—the Liberal opposition on this occasion was in reality obscurantist and unimaginative. Moreover, on the sectarian objection to endowed Church schools, the clamour was without substance. Already, as has been said, the State was helping them. Whether their assistance was to come out of taxes or rates was a matter which could raise no sort of principle. In fact the power of Councils to take them over or supplant them was greatly increased by the 1902 act. Regarding the whole matter dispassionately, it must be confessed that the Liberal agitation was unfortunate.

In May, 1903, however, a far greater excitement arose out of the declaration of Chamberlain at Birmingham in favour of preference in import duties for Colonies, and in his more or less overt advocacy of a return to Protection.

The matter had been touched upon in the Imperial Conference resolutions in 1897, and in a more marked form in 1902. Among the latter appeared a specific request for preferential treatment for the Colonies, either by exemption from or reduction of duties. At that time there existed a very slight Corn Tax, and Chamberlain, who was visiting South Africa, desired an assurance that the existing shilling duty on corn should no longer apply to the Empire. According to the Prime Minister, this was agreed to in the Cabinet. Nevertheless in the Budget, Ritchie, the Chancellor, an irreconcilable free-trader, decided to repeal the whole tax. Hicks Beach supported its abolition, and a "Free Food League" was instituted on the Conservative side to fight food taxes. In September the Free Trade ministers, Ritchie, Lord George Hamilton, and Lord Balfour, resigned, and shortly afterwards the Duke of Devonshire joined them. On the other side Chamberlain also went, but his son Austen, who was a Protectionist, remained, and the Prime Minister tardily declared himself in favour of "safeguarding industry but using tariffs only for purposes of negotiation". Clearly he was prepared to go further if the country would support him.

That the old Liberals should fight was intelligible, but few people at the time saw the anomaly of the Imperialist Opposition taking up the same position. From an Imperial point of view the argument of Chamberlain that preferences would have pleased the people overseas and strengthened the bonds of the Empire was strong. Why Lord Rosebery, Grey, or Asquith, remained such inflexible advocates of Free Trade is not clear; was it not one of the "fly-blown phylacteries" which Rosebery had denounced?

The attitude of Campbell-Bannerman and his school was logical and consistent. They saw that the growth of aggressive nationalism was bound to lead to a demand for economic autarchy such as is now seen in its extreme form in Fascist countries. In a sense it was a military rather than an economic requirement which condemned free importation and general unfettered trade between nations. It was a necessary part of the Cobdenite conception of nations and their peoples as trading entities peacefully exchanging goods and services for the benefit of the whole world—a "bag-man's millennium", as that early Fascist, Carlyle, called it. But the new Liberalism had pledged itself under the name of Empire to Nationalism; such an ideal was bound sooner or later to lead to a demand for the re-introduction of Protection.

Much contention ranged whether the consumer was to bear the duty, but this was a minor point; the real question was whether the abandonment by England of Free Trade would increase the isolation and bellicosity of nations or help towards international comity. That issue was never fairly stated by either side, perhaps it was not yet understood.

Yet international matters were approaching a crisis. One of the last acts of the Tory Government, accomplished with Liberal approval, was in effect to make an alliance with France. That country was clearly falling into weakness, her population was declining; conversely, her neighbour, Germany, was daily increasing in numbers, power and truculence. The creation of the Committee of Imperial Defence in 1904 showed how little confidence was felt in the stability of Europe. The alliance with Japan was made to safeguard the eastern position. King Edward, who disliked his nephew, the Kaiser, insistently urged an understanding with the French. There is now little doubt that secretly, at this time, 'conversations' between the military staffs of England and the French Army were started. It was with reluctance that Balfour abandoned the Salisbury tradition of regarding Russia as the potential enemy and began to watch the Kaiser. The defeat of Russia by the Japanese in 1905 weakened Britain's fear of that country. Undoubtedly the Germans were becoming very unpopular in England. Ever since the Kaiser's telegram to Kruger relations had been precarious. The doubling of the German Navy, following a failure of the attempt to come to an understanding, helped on the undefined French alliance.

Nevertheless, the understanding with France, as has been noticed, was welcomed by the Liberals, Lord Rosebery alone dissenting. He urged the Opposition to be more cautious in agreeing with the new policy; he spoke of "violent polemics with Germany"; he protested that cordial relations with France should not mean animosity with her neighbour— yet all informed persons knew that it was fear of the Teuton which had forced France to come to terms with her ancient enemy, England.

At home there passed a Licensing Act, providing that licences should not be refused to public-houses except for misconduct or other special reasons and setting up a Compensation Fund, all of which greatly increased the value of the public-houses by practically giving them a freehold; and an Irish Land Purchase Bill, easing the rental for the tenant and giving him a fee simple subject to a small rent-charge—a Bill approved by the Liberals as a whole. After disputes among the Conservatives as to what part Tariff Reform should take in the election, Londonderry saying it was moribund and Austen Chamberlain describing it as a foremost issue, the Prime Minister equivocating as he had done in the House for a long time, on December 4th, 1905, Balfour resigned. Not until 1922 was a Conservative ministry again in office.

CHAPTER IX

THE LAST LIBERAL ADMINISTRATION

DESPITE a number of attempts, no very convincing explanation has ever been given to account for the very great turn-over of votes which took place at the General Election of January, 1906. The Liberals returned three hundred and seventy-seven members, the Conservatives were but one hundred and fifty-seven, of which about a dozen were free-traders. Some thirty Labour members pledged to independence, and the odd eighty Irish Nationalists completed the tale.

From the Conservative side, Mrs. Dugdale, the biographer of Balfour, suggests as causes of defeat the Education Act and the Food Tax cry. She adds the agitation against "Chinese slavery". The Liberals certainly used all these matters as arguments against their opponents. On the other hand, their commitments to the Irish (now at the height of their unpopularity owing to their dubious loyalty in the Boer War), an obligation denounced on the eve of the election by Rosebery; the almost universal antagonism of the landed and commercial classes, and the great weakness of support in the Press must all have told in favour of the outgoing Government. The Liberals themselves expected no more than a working majority. It is suggested that the reasons for their unique victory are to be sought in more profound sociological changes than most political historians have been willing to suggest.

Since the Liberals were in power in the 'nineties there had been a constant movement, more particularly in municipal activity, in a collectivist direction. Apart from those who held that, ultimately, all industry should be socialized, there were many who saw no objection to State activity to deal with specific social ills, or even, in certain cases, to embark upon direct trading. The rich and self-interested objected to anything approaching commercial competition from a civic source; they opposed the increase of rates which might follow the development of non-productive corporate activity, but their objection, though often pushed to extreme lengths by ratepayers' associations, was now frankly opportunist. The old Benthamite objection to State action as such (of which Herbert Spencer had been the last forceful exponent) was dead.

It followed that the electors now looked for a political party who would utilize the machinery of government for their advantage. Judged from this standpoint, the record both of Tory and Liberals in the past had been woefully insufficient; even old age pensions, long promised, had not been forthcoming; the compensation laws were still inadequate—the Statute Roll had been shrinking to very meagre dimensions. There was much to be accomplished, and it could only be achieved by a party which had no objection to use the machinery of legislation for social betterment.

This view, in its extreme form, accounts perhaps for the appearance and return of independent Labour members. Their power and significance have been much exaggerated. A few were conscious Socialists, but the majority were leaders of Trade Unions, who did not object in theory to the broad collectivist resolutions which were passed by Congress, but had little practical interest in them. Indeed, the structure of the Trade Unions which they administered assumed a continuance of capitalism and collective bargaining between employer and workman.

Moreover, nearly all of them were, in part, returned on Liberal votes in two-membered constituencies or crept in through a three-cornered contest—it is doubtful, outside the coalfields, if half a dozen held their seats by absolute majorities.

There were, it is true, among all the Liberals, some old-fashioned

Individualists who deplored all collective action. The Prime Minister was not one of them. His sympathy with the Labour leaders was strong. Keir Hardie, one of the least easily reconcilable, declared that "Sir Henry deserves all the praise that has been heaped upon him; where the Liberal Party falls short of its promises, the blame will not rest with C.B." The attempt of the Liberal Imperialists, led by Grey, to force the new Premier into the Lords, had it succeeded would have been most unpopular. It was the weakness of this little group of highly intellectual gentlemen, Grey, Haldane, and Asquith at their head, that they failed to recognize that the days of Whiggery were over, and that select government by a small clique had become as objectionable if it emanated from Oxford, as if it were limited to large land-holders.

The circumstances of Grey's action have been so frequently recounted that they do not need repetition. His behaviour to Campbell-Bannerman at the time of the Cabinet construction was entirely inexcusable. The demand of Asquith that Haldane should be Chancellor also showed that the Imperialist Liberal believed they possessed a power which was far from existent.

There is little doubt that the Prime Minister, had he been a vindictive man, could easily have formed a government from his loyal friends, and abandoned the whole of the Leaguers, as in fact he did in the case of Rosebery, where the gulf was unbridgable; but his noble character inclined always to the healing of differences rather than to the hardening of them. In the matter of the Woolsack, however, he was obdurate. Reid, his old friend, not Haldane, whom he had never trusted, was to be Lord Chancellor.

On December 21st, 1905, the Cabinet being formed, the Prime Minister laid down his programme in the Albert Hall. If the views here expressed are correct—that the electors were waiting for a bold programme of reform—that speech contributed very largely to the subsequent Liberal success at the election. He declared the country to be tired of 'tactics'; he said that "we desired to develop our undeveloped estates, to colonize our own country". Already the researches of Booth and Rowntree had disclosed the frightful poverty which had followed unregulated commercial competition. There followed these memorable words: "We wish to make the world less of a pleasure ground for the rich and more of a treasure-house for the nation". The land system and the rating system should be reformed, so also the poor law. He warned his hearers that we are fighting "powers, privileges, injustices and monopolies which are unalterably opposed to the triumph of the democratic system". It was on this broad issue, rather than Chinese labour, trade union law, or even education, that the ordinary elector responded to the Government's appeal.

Abroad, the situation rapidly worsened. Again the Germans were the disturbers of the peace. In 1904 Germany had not overtly objected to the Anglo-French arrangements in Morocco. In 1905, however, the Kaiser intervened. He landed in person at Tangier and declared that he would never permit any power to step between him and the Sultan of Morocco. Delcassé, the French Foreign Minister, who had settled the *entente* with England, was forced by threat of war with Germany to resign—a most disgraceful French humiliation. The German Navy increased in power, and Teutonic threats both to England and France became very gross. Up to now the Germans had been restrained by fear of Russia, but Russia was now prostrate, and they felt they could safely resume their old policy of hectoring aggression.

The Balfour Government had already pledged England to help the French against German claims in Morocco. Grey was asked by the French where he stood. He replied that he had no hesitation in affirming Lansdowne's policy of *entente*. He did not dissent from the Gallic proposal that "unofficial communications between our Admiralty and the War Office and the French Naval and Military attachés should take place". On January 31st the French Ambassador asked Grey in terms: "Whether France could count upon the assistance of England in the event of an attack upon her by Germany"; he answered that, as a personal opinion, in the event of an attack by Germany on France, "public opinion in England would be so strong that no British Government could remain neutral". Grey also stated that if a defensive alliance was formed, though it could be concluded without the consent of Parliament, it would have to be published afterwards!

These words illustrate very clearly the way in which the Foreign Office—even under a Liberal minister—was seeking to escape from parliamentary control. Grey certainly did not commit the Government, but equally he made it clear that if they wished to do so, they could make treaties without previously consulting Parliament. In the end a settlement was effected at Algeciras, and the Kaiser accused the French of 'nerves', but those in the centre of things realized how nearly both countries had been to war; thereafter, until 1914, the peril of hostilities was never absent from the minds of men responsible for the ordering of the foreign relations of this country.

But even now, hopes of an understanding with Germany were not abandoned. Haldane, as Secretary for War, visited Berlin; Campbell-Bannerman, despite the laudation of militarism by the Kaiser, was never inclined to abandon a hope of understanding with that imperious neurotic.

In Russia a democratic movement, centering round the new Duma, complicated foreign relations. The Liberals in England naturally supported the Russian developments. At the same time a fear that the Czar might make an alliance with Germany made them fearful of offending him. The Czar dissolved the Duma, and the hatred of him by Radicals and Labour Party members increased. The Prime Minister's speech, "The Duma is dead, long live the Duma", while pleasing them, was considered in St. Petersburg to be a censure on the Czar. The Germans, fishing as usual in troubled waters, stirred up the Turks to come to the Suez Canal from the east; doubtless the German General Staff were behind them. A British ultimatum was sent to Turkey and they withdrew. Nevertheless, it was clear that the new Government could no longer say, as had the Prime Minister at the Albert Hall, that "the outlook abroad was most pleasing".

From the outset of their legislative career it was evident that a great conflict between the two Houses could not be avoided. With the breakdown of territorial aristocracy, the House of Lords had increasingly become the stronghold of the new wealthy class, who, if they succeeded in acquiring a great amount of capital, were almost always ennobled.

Brewers and bankers had long been there, but now the proprietors of cheap newspapers were given seats. Moreover, now that nearly all rich men were on the Conservative side, it lay in their power to kill any Liberal Bill they disliked. If they allowed some legislation, like the Trade Disputes Act and the Workman's Compensation Acts, to pass, it was because, as a matter of party tactics, they deemed it expedient not to quarrel with organized labour. Their behaviour was quite without principle; if there ever was a measure which might reasonably have been rejected, it was the Trade Disputes Act, which gave a complete immunity to Trade Unions for all wrongs committed by them, not even limited to those done during a Trade Dispute: it was not even a Government Bill, yet the Conservatives, despite the protests of their lawyers, let it pass. The Education Bill (which would have transferred the non-provided schools to the local authority with provision for special religious teaching, the local authority to take over the fabric—a most sensible solution of the problem of inefficient non provided schools) the Lords so fundamentally amended, conceding even in council schools the option to give full denominational teaching, that the Government declared they would not go on with the measure—as amended, it was indeed almost exactly the contrary of their own in its effect.

The King was concerned at the signs of coming conflict. The Lords passed the third reading of the amended Bill; time was spent in conference between Lords Lansdowne and Cawdor on the one side and the Minister, Mr. Birrell, and Lord Crewe on the other. In the end Lansdowne moved that his House insist on its amendments, which was carried by one hundred and forty-two to fifty-three. The minority vote was about representative of the strength of the Government in the Lords. The Prime Minister declared it intolerable that a "second chamber when one party is in power, should be its willing servant, and when that party has received condemnation in the country, be able to thwart the policy of which the electors show they approve". He went on in minatory manner to say: "The resources of the House of Commons are not exhausted".

Next, the Lords destroyed the Plural Voting Bill. The Liberals, on the whole, were against dissolution, but they demanded some reform whereby, it was said, "the will of the people as expressed through the House of Commons must be made to prevail".

The recognition of an "expeditionary force" in the Army Bill of 1907 pointed the way in which the Government saw the foreign situation. Haldane's reforms, generally, were carried, though the "patriots" on the Conservative side, Brodrick, Arnold, Forster and Wyndham, did not hesitate to obstruct his work so far as they were able. Behind the scenes, the Committee of Imperial Defence was considering the whole position on the assumption that war was not unlikely in the near future. The Prime Minister had hoped that some limitation of armaments might arise from the Hague conference, an international congress originally summoned at the suggestion of the Czar, but the Germans were determined that the question should not arise. They professed to see in its advocacy, coupled with the reorganization of the English Army, some subtle conspiracy, though in their own interest, they were very willing to have declared the immunity of private property at sea. In view of their later record in destroying neutral shipping it seemed a cynical request. England, as a great maritime power, refused to concede the demand.

In May, 1907, at length the inescapable question of Home Rule was once more raised. Mr. Birrell, the Irish Secretary, introduced a Bill for a representative Irish Council. As it was promptly opposed by a National Convention in Ireland, this method of conciliation by stages had to be abandoned; it was clear that Redmond, like Butt before him, who had been willing to give the measure consideration, was being overborne by a more intransigent policy.

In South Africa, Home Rule had a happier passage. At the end of 1905 a form of Crown Colony government had been suggested for the Transvaal. There were to be both nominated and elected members, the Governor to have great powers of rejection of Bills. The Executive would still be under the Governor—this was all the Conservatives would concede, but the Liberal Cabinet, by February, 1906, had decided in favour of complete self-government. When the proposals were known they were violently attacked; "Dangerous, audacious and reckless" was Balfour's description of the experiment. Lansdowne and Milner predicted a Boer Government which would evict the whole British civil service. If the matter had depended on legislation, the Lords would probably have rejected it, but the new constitution was issued under Crown Patent, it was to inaugurate "immediate responsible government for the Transvaal". On December 17th the House of Commons, by resolution, approved the new democratic charter. It was the crowning achievement of Campbell-Bannerman's career.

There remained the scheme for dealing with the Lords. A Bill passed three times in the Commons was to become law after six months (afterwards in the Parliament Act, two years were to elapse between the first rejection and legislation). There was no such provision as to Money Bills as appeared later, for no one then conceived the possibility of the Lords rejecting such measures. A long debate followed the introduction of the proposals. The Labour Party moved that the House of Lords ought to be abolished, but this, of course, was not at the time a serious suggestion.

The resolution approving the scheme was carried in the Commons by four hundred and thirty-two votes to one hundred and forty-seven. It was clear that Irish support would also be forthcoming. They saw in the Liberal proposals the only way to Home Rule.

This was almost the last public work of the Prime Minister; he continued to preside at the Cabinet until February of the next year. On April 22nd, 1908, he died. He was the first leader, since Fox, in whom advanced Liberals could expect to find full understanding, sympathy and confidence.

The passing of the great Radical statesman at a comparatively early age had consequences, it would seem, decisive for the future of the Liberal Party. Asquith, his successor, educated in the formal atmosphere of classical Oxford and the Inns of Court, though possessed of an eminently honest and judicial mind, lacked that foreseeing genius which is the endowment of so few politicians. That the commercial assumptions of Victorian England had resulted in the subordination of life to the pursuit of profit was not to him a distasteful notion. The accumulation of so large a share of national wealth in the hands of a very few people (and they often of an undesirable kind) gave him, it would seem, very little concern; in his view the diversion of the employment of surplus wealth from public necessities to luxury was inevitable. Retrenchment, the old panacea, the lifting of taxation from the capitalist, seemed, save in case of urgent necessity, to be the prime purpose of financial administration. The social services must be curtailed rather than taxes should unduly rise. He did not discriminate between the growing monopolies and price-fixing combinations of his time and the old, small, competitive businesses which Liberalism, through a perverted reading of the fashionable doctrine of the survival of the fittest, had thought to be inevitable, and indeed excellent.

All this was to say that, in essentials, he repudiated his predecessor's dictum that England had become a pleasure-ground for the rich. He had little sympathy with the now active and popular socialistic opinion.

Although the Labour Party had been blamed by their adherents for their constant support of Campbell-Bannerman, it might at least be urged on their behalf that they knew instinctively that he was on their side; the same could not be said of the new Prime Minister.

For the time (still being Chancellor of Exchequer), he made himself popular by introducing an Old Age Pension scheme giving 5s. a week to persons over seventy who had no more than 8s. a week of their own. The Tory Lords and Rosebery opposed it, the latter declaring that "it would deal a blow at the Empire which might be almost mortal"—a form of Imperialism which the most ardent must have found disquieting. The Opposition attempted to amend the Bill in Committee, but the Speaker ruled their efforts out of order, and the Lords submitted. It was an indication what they would be likely to do with a distasteful budget.

A further attempt to solve the education impasse was made. A second Bill, which would have stopped the rate grant to denominational schools, while permitting specific religious teaching to be given in council ones, at one time seemed to offer hopes of conciliation, but, again, theological acrimonies prevented all chances of legislation by consent. Looking back, as the Council schools were continually encroaching on the non-provided, it would seem that the Church were very ill advised in refusing the right of entry into the public schools which the Bill gave them.

In June, 1908, Austria formally annexed Bosnia and Herzegovina, which she had controlled since the Treaty of Berlin, and the Russians took umbrage at the act. It became clear that the Germans were behind Austria in their action. The Russians by now had an alliance with France, and the alignment of forces, which some years after made peace impossible, was already ominously apparent. The Turks, who had been affronted by the annexation, received from Austria the Sandjak of Novi-Bazar and certain financial compensation. Germany threatened Russia that if she did not recognize the annexation she would allow Austria a free hand. The Serbians, who had claimed access to the sea, were reluctantly abandoned by Russia; she was ill-prepared for war and, in the end, the Teutonic powers undoubtedly increased their influence over Eastern

Europe. What is more significant is that they had achieved this by little-disguised threats of war. The Kaiser was evidently intending to use force, or the fear of it, as his prime method of diplomatic action. Thus the seeds were sown of which the full harvest has not yet been gathered.

All this necessarily meant an increase in the service estimates which the Admiralty very properly demanded. Curiously, in the light of subsequent history, Winston Churchill was found to be supporting Lloyd George, now Chancellor, in his demand for economy; but in the end, largely owing to public agitation, the Admiralty won, getting eight new capital ships. It is to be noted that the German menace was now very clearly recognized by the whole nation.

To raise this extra sum and, generally, to implement Liberal pledges, Lloyd George, in his famous Budget, introduced a scheme for the taxation of land values with duties on undeveloped land and increment. For years the land round great cities had passed from agricultural to building-site value, and the owners had thus reaped immense capital gains through the necessity of the community to acquire more houses near their work. Even Asquith, supposed in his own language to be "a financier of a respectable and more or less conservative type", thought the taxation of the added value to be consistent with natural justice that "the State should from time to time levy toll"; a guarded defence—it was evident that his approval of the Budget was not enthusiastic.

A Budget Protest League was formed by the Conservatives. They seemed to have lost all sense of proportion, and Lloyd George, by very offensive remarks about Dukes and Peers, exasperated them still further. Regarding the matter with the soothing tranquillity of time, the whole dispute seemed a little absurd. On the Progressive side the tax did really almost nothing to cope with the fast accumulating and surplus wealth of the rich; the uncontrolled language of the Opposition, which daily described the proposed taxes as confiscation and robbery, helped only the growth of opinion that the Lords were utterly self-regarding and that the abolition or the curtailment of their powers was essential to the national interest.

The other taxes (apart from the 20 per cent unearned increment on land payable on sale or death) were a larger income and a new supertax, and increased duties on spirits and tobacco. The biographer of Lord Balfour says, somewhat naïvely, that the Conservative decision to oppose the land taxes "sprang from the irresistible instinct of self-preservation in the class from which the Party derived its tradition and much of its strength. The land taxes and the land valuation clauses were a death blow to the landed gentry". (*Balfour*, Vol. 2, p. 55.) Whether they or the speculative builder were most affected may be disputed, perhaps by then they were indistinguishable. On November 16th Lord Lansdowne moved in the Lords that: "This House is not justified in giving its consent to the Bill until it has been submitted to the judgment of the people". Balfour, next day, approved this action; on the 30th Lansdowne's motion was carried by three hundred and fifty to seventy-five votes.

This division showed the growing contempt of constitutional propriety and usage which was steadily growing in the Conservative Party, soon to be exemplified in Ulster. It was very many years since the House of Lords had tampered with finance, the raising of which is constitutionally the principal reason for the summoning of the Commons. In the King's speech this is recognized when he directs the financial part to the House of Commons alone. The Conservative Party had inaugurated a constitutional revolution.

On December 3rd Parliament was dissolved; the Peers had for the moment succeeded, but their victory was to prove a costly one.

The issue at the election was expressed in the resolution, carried in the expiring House of Commons by 349 to 134 votes, that "the action of the House of Lords" in refusing to pass into law the financial provision made by this House for the service of the year is a breach of the Constitution and an usurpation of the rights of the Commons. During the election Lord Rosebery took occasion to say that he had "long since ceased to be in communication with the Liberal Party". It was the end of the Liberal League.

The outgoing Parliament had much legislation to show to its credit; among other things the establishment of the Union of South Africa. On one matter, the exclusion of the negroes from the franchise, Asquith reluctantly had to give way. At this time he was approving more of votes for the African natives than for women at home—so inscrutable are the processes of the human mind that no explanation for this outlook will be here attempted; it is sufficient to record the fact. Milner and the Opposition generally had been hostile, their Imperialism seemed to stop short at the African continent; but Balfour, in the House, generously admitted that the South African Act was a "wonderful issue out of the horrors of war. I do not believe the world shows anything like it in its history", he concluded.

It appeared that the Tariff Reformers and Chamberlain had incited the Lords to throw out the Budget; for the reason, said Asquith, that it provided a sound substitute for their schemes, rather than because it was socialistic; it was evident that Socialism, whatever it had meant to Harcourt, was most distasteful to the Prime Minister.

The Government majority after the election was only one hundred and twenty-four; without the Irish and Labour Party they could not have survived. It was uncertain what line the Irish would take. Redmond was suspicious, the Irish had objected to the spirits duty in the last Budget and, if they again opposed, the Government might fall. The Government refused to withdraw these duties, and at the end of April the Irish voted for the same Budget as the rejected one; the next day, the 28th, it was accepted by the Lords—they had won the first, but lost the second round.

Meanwhile, in March, resolutions, afterwards embodied in the Parliament Bill, had been passed. Save that it contained the clause that a Bill certified to be a Money Bill by the Speaker was one with which the Lords could not interfere, it followed the Campbell-Bannerman scheme, extending only, as has been said, the period for which the Lords could delay the measure. Further, the life of Parliament was to be limited to five years.

In June, King Edward VII had died, and a Conference with the Conservative leaders to discuss the relations between the two Houses was inaugurated. The Labour Party were not represented and, apparently, made no protest. Home Rule and other constitutional matters were sought to be excluded from the Parliament Bill, but this was 'tactics' again—of course with such a concession the Irish would vote against the Government—in any case it was impossible to draw any such distinction. The Conference broke up and the Prime Minister saw the new King, who promised, that if the election supported the Government he would "use the constitutional last resort to prevent it being stultified in the subsequent Parliament". This was to be kept secret, and even the Opposition leaders did not know of the royal assurance until the following July.

In the event, the election made practically no change in the balance of parties; owing to the foolish manœuvres of the Conservative leaders the curtailment of the powers of the House of Lords could no longer be avoided.

When, on July 18th, Lloyd George told the Conservative leaders that the King had agreed to create peers sufficient if need be to carry the Parliament Act, great differences of opinion were expressed among them as to what course they ought to take. With these disputes a history of Liberalism is not directly concerned. It appears that in 1910 Lloyd George had approached Balfour in view of the danger of war to form a coalition. The proposal was laid before the inner Cabinet—it included suggestions for a settlement on the questions of Second Chamber reform, Home Rule and National training for defence, together with an impartial enquiry into the fiscal system. How far the further proposal that Asquith should go to the Lords (which would have meant his withdrawal from the office of Prime Minister) was known to him and his friends it is not possible to say—it certainly did not appear in Lloyd George's memorandum. The authority for it is Mrs. Dugdale in her *Life of Balfour* (Vol. 2, p. 79), where she quotes J. Hill's diary to that effect. In the obituary notice of Lord Balfour in *The Times* of March 20th, 1930, it is said that "a common programme was laid down, Mr. Asquith being excluded." Balfour, however, declined participation in the intrigue". If Asquith knew of this, he behaved subsequently, during the Marconi troubles, with extraordinary forbearance and loyalty—in any case, whatever discussions there were came to nothing. The position of Balfour himself was not strong; the Tory Party was enraged at the counsel of submission given by its elder statesmen, for both Lansdowne and Balfour were in favour of surrender. A violent campaign was launched against their philosophic leader, and in November, 1911, he resigned, his place being take by Bonar Law.

The most important legislation of that year was the National Health and Unemployment Insurance Act introduced by Lloyd George. It contained features which have left a lasting mark upon the policy of this country; in the first place, in order to carry out its provisions it gave to the Minister great powers of a novel order, to legislate by order and regulation, under the Statute, without further consultation with Parliament —a power found so attractive to the Bureaucracy and so speedy in its operation that nearly every Government Department exercising administrative functions is now endowed with similar authority. In the end it may operate to displace parliamentary control of the executive. It was not content with administrative regulation; the Bill also in effect excluded the Courts from nearly all jurisdiction to decide whether a particular person was or was not entitled as a matter of law to receive benefit.

The third new feature was that the measure imposed obligations on limited classes of persons not arising out of their occupational function, as does, say, the Army Act, but the extent of its operation was solely dependent upon income—broadly, only the poor were affected. This exclusive compulsion on the humble, said Belloc, was the institution of the "servile state"—the argument was too philosophic, perhaps too inconvenient, to be understood by politicians. The Labour Party, who, as a whole, supported the Bill, had a minority who objected to the scheme being contributory, but no one took the point in the House that it was only compulsory on the poor. Lloyd George subsequently spoke of the staunchness and loyalty of the Liberal members—no thanks were accorded to the Labour Party for taking their share in the considerable obloquy which followed the passage of the Bill. Attacked by their own following for their subservience to the Liberals, by the Liberals they were treated with contempt. The time was to come when Liberals would vainly seek an alliance with the then despised forces of Labour.

The year 1912 witnessed the last Home Rule Bill before Parliament. No one foresaw that when the Irish question was eventually settled the representatives of that country would appear as Plenipotentiaries, speaking of treaties as between independent nations. It may have passed the minds of some old Conservatives of long memories, with the example of South Africa before them, that they would have been wiser to have compromised with Gladstone; certainly from an Imperial point of view, nothing sort of complete secession could have been worse than the settlement to which the English Government was ultimately driven, but for that the Liberal Party was not responsible.

Indeed their days of responsibility were rapidly drawing to a close, perhaps for ever. Meanwhile, Home Rule and Welsh Disestablishment still awaited consideration.

It was decided to include all Ireland in a Bill, allowing that Ulster's case might be met by amendment. The measure was welcomed by a National Convention in Dublin. Peace and war, treaties and customs, were reserved for the Imperial Parliament, where forty-two Irish members were still to sit. There were transitional provisions affecting the Irish constabulary, and restrictions on the imposition of religious disabilities.

In January, 1913, the Bill had its third reading in the Commons; to be rejected in the Upper House by a majority of two hundred and fifty-seven.

Meanwhile, under the stimulus of Sir Edward Carson, a so-called "Provisional Government", with armed forces, was established in Ireland. Another lawyer, F. E. Smith, joined him as aide-de-camp. The Government did nothing to prevent these flagrant illegalities. Whether they were wise or not in the action they took is questionable. Discontent was general. In 1911 no less than nine hundred and three big strikes and lock-outs were raging. In 1913 the number had risen to an average of one hundred and fifty a month. Tom Mann, the revolutionary trade union leader, was treated less leniently than Carson—he was imprisoned for inciting the troops to mutiny. The contrast between them should have given the Labour Party its opportunity, but under the hesitant leadership of MacDonald nothing was done, and a supine support was given to the Government in nearly all its doings and omissions, though Henderson in 1910, speaking generally, had gone so far as to say: "The Labour Party is not always treated with that consideration and fair play to which it is entitled".

Women's suffrage was another issue. The Labour Party were pledged to it, the Liberals were not. Prices were rising, for gold was becoming cheap; the pound of 1900 was now worth only sixteen shillings. The miners were demanding a minimum wage for workers in bad places, which rapidly spread to a movement for an all-round minimum.

The railways had a dispute as to the recognition of their unions, which in the end reluctantly was accorded. In March, 1912, Asquith very hesitantly agreed to the fixing of the miner's minimum wage. The principle had already been recognized in the case of sweated industries, yet to the old *laissex-faire* mind of the Prime Minister, to fix wages by statute was almost heretical.

The failure both of the Government and the Labour Party to meet the industrial crisis with any more resolution than they had shown in the case of Ulster, led to the growth of Syndicalism and a clamour for striking, not merely to obtain better conditions in a particular trade, but as a means of reconstituting the whole social fabric and destroying Capitalism. The activities of Mr. Osborne to prevent trade union funds being spent on parliamentary candidates, though successful in the Courts, by putting further obstacles in the way of parliamentary representation, actually strengthened the hands of the Syndicalists.

A compromise in 1913, not disturbed until 1927, enabled individual trade unionists to withhold their subscriptions from political objects. It was no great victory for the Labour Party, but it was almost the only one to be recorded before the Great War.

The Irish position became worse; attempts at settleme were made by the King and by direct contact between the Leaders (Labour, as usual, being omitted from all consideration). They allowed these great decisions to be taken without any recognition being made of their existence. This is not a history of the Labour Party, and it is not directly relevant to trace that sense of inferiority which prevented any degree of self-assertion. It was useless for them constantly to proclaim their independence; in Parliament they behaved in a manner far more subservient than did the old Radicals. The selection of MacDonald as leader, in place of Keir Hardie, accentuated their feebleness. What is important is to note that few in the Liberal Party had the imagination to realize that, nervous and fumbling as the Labour leaders were, the working-class movement who sent them to Parliament was rapidly coming into its own heritage. In the industrial field it had taken the offensive; if Liberalism was to become anything but an outmoded middle-class and Nonconformist coterie, it behoved its adherents to be generous to those who were at least prepared to support any reformist proposal which went in the direction of social democracy.

In the result, as is known, the new movement of Labour was ignored and its aspirations mocked at by the old-fashioned Liberals. The error of underestimating the forces behind Labour, subservient as might be its political behaviour at the moment, was in the end to destroy Liberalism as a potent political force.

From the problems of Ulster and industrial dispute the country passed to that of war. In July, 1914, an attempt by non-party conference to define the area to be excluded from the Home Rule Bill had failed. In September, the Home Rule Bill and that dealing with Welsh disestablishment which had passed the Commons in 1912 were to be placed under the Parliament Act, but with a suspensory clause providing that they should not come into force for twelve months, or, if the war still continued, until a date to be fixed by Order in Council.

In the case of Ireland, Parliament was to be given power to pass an amending Bill excluding Ulster. Bonar Law and his party took the occasion of the debate to insult the Prime Minister, comparing his conduct with that of the Germans in entering Belgium—they walked out of the House, though the war was then at a most critical stage. The failure to settle the Irish measure may well have assisted the revolutionaries in 1916; in any case it was a poor return for that Nationalist loyalty to England which later caused the political ruin of Redmond and his followers.

As the war developed, the impatience of the Conservatives at being kept out of office, where they might hope to participate in and influence the control of the war, increased. They suspected a shortage of munitions, and were very uneasy at the resignation of Fisher from the office of First Sea Lord. It was Lloyd George who forced the matter—Bonar Law and he had been in contact. He knew that the shell shortage was known to the leaders of the Opposition and he believed that the only way out to avoid recrimination in public and to fortify the future was a national coalition. He threatened to resign unless Bonar Law could come to Downing Street. Of all this Balfour knew nothing, but soon all was settled; a coalition government was formed, Balfour became First Lord of the Admiralty, McKenna Chancellor of the Exchequer, and Lloyd George went to the new Ministry of Munitions. The Liberal Government was at an end. It is only necessary to add that Labour was contemptuously thrown a sop in the appointment of Arthur Henderson as Minister of Education, an office which, by common consent, beyond the barest routine administration, scarcely functioned in war-time.

This was in May, 1915; after much dissension about conscription, during which dispute Lloyd George threatened to resign, compulsory service was imposed. But divergences still existed in the coalition; they culminated in a demand by Lloyd George, now Secretary for War, that the Prime Minister should cease to be President of the War Committee. According to Churchill (*The World Crisis*, 1916–1918, Part I, p. 249), Asquith was at first prepared to agree, but later refused, whereupon Lloyd George did actually resign. This act brought down the Government; the Prime Minister, in his turn, proffered his resignation, and Lloyd George became Prime Minister. Henderson still represented Labour in this, the second coalition.

．　　．　　．　　．　　．　　．　　．

It is now nearly thirty years since Asquith ceased to be Prime Minister in a Liberal Government; from that time the Liberals have never comprised a quarter of the House. In 1918, after the election, when Lloyd

George and his followers and the Conservatives went to the country as one, the independent Liberal representation fell to thirty-three, that of Labour was just over sixty. Asquith himself lost his seat. An offer by him to assist at the Peace Conference was not accepted by the then omnipotent Lloyd George. When he, in his turn, was overthrown by a Carlton Club 'palace revolution', some of the 'National Liberals', as they called themselves, being without an organization and attacked by the Conservatives, tried to return to orthodox Liberalism, but most of the local independent associations decided to oppose them. In the result, sixty-four Independent and fifty-three 'National Liberals' were returned. Together they were outnumbered by Labour, who were now one hundred and forty-two strong.

The Conservative Government lasted but a short time; in November, 1922, Baldwin again went to the country—Protection being the issue. Now was the time for the Free Traders to come to some accommodation. Lloyd George and Asquith issued a joint manifesto which had the result of raising the total Liberal membership to one hundred and fifty-eight; Labour was one hundred and ninety-one and still officially pledged to Free Trade, though many of its younger members no longer held passionate convictions about that ancient dogma. In the event MacDonald took office, depending on the Liberals for his majority.

The author of this book was a member of the MacDonald Government, and it is his opinion that the Liberals were prepared to consider a joint programme which might have led to great social benefit for the poorer classes. Although some of the Labour Party were committed to Socialist theories (some, like the writer, inclining more to the method of the mediæval guild), there was a great amount of legislation on which they and the advanced Liberals could have agreed. There was suspicion on the part of some of the Labour politicians of any "fraternising" with Liberals, but such an adroit politician as MacDonald could, perfectly honourably, have come to a private understanding as to the promotion of selected measures, by methods known to every member of Parliament, without any overt proclamation of alliance.

In fact he did no such thing; from the outset he held himself markedly aloof from those on whom he depended for his power. This was an impossible situation; had he not wished to work with the Liberals, he should not have taken office. To expect support without some degree of concession was ridiculous. As is said by the biographies of Lord Asquith, for "lack of touch between the two parties, the life of the Government seemed always to be in danger".

A Housing Act was passed with Liberal support, but on Asquith suggesting a committee of enquiry into the "Campbell case" (a withdrawn Communist prosecution), MacDonald, though there was ample precedent for a government remaining in office in such circumstances, very impetuously resigned. At that election, at which a proposed treaty with Bolshevik Russia was used to alarm the voters, the Liberal representation fell to forty; Labour, although its number of seats was less than before, actually increased its total vote by over a million.

Asquith was defeated at Paisley, and shortly afterwards took a peerage. It was evident that the leadership in progressive politics had passed away from the Liberal Party.

Even then, small as they were in numbers, they were divided; there was, as ever, a Radical and a Whig wing. The divergence came out very clearly at the time of the General Strike in 1926, roundly condemned by Asquith and Simon, but sympathetically treated by Lloyd George in the sense that he realized that there were grievances to be redressed and that the Government was not free from blame.

The same cleavage was witnessed when, next year, the Government introduced their Trade Union Bill to make large-scale striking, affecting the community, illegal. On the whole, Sir John Simon lent the weight of his authority in support of the Government. Lloyd George and Mr. Harney, a K.C., supported the Labour Party in opposition. Moreover, Lloyd George insisted on keeping his party fund distinct from that of the Chief Whip, which was held in trust for the whole organization. The National Liberal Federation sought to raise a new revenue from a "Million Fund Appeal", but the results were not enough adequately to finance a general election. Liberal reunion, to quote Lord Oxford, "has turned out to be a fiction, if not a farce". Lloyd George insisted that his fund was at his personal disposal; Asquith was unwilling to wrangle with him about money—in October, 1926, he resigned the leadership of the Party.

Poor as was the representation of the Liberal Party in Parliament, their condition was even worse than their numbers would disclose. Broadly speaking, the rural and suburban areas were Conservative, the industrial ones inclined to be Labour; it was only on the "Celtic fringe", as it was called; in Wales, Scotland and Cornwall, that an old-fashioned type of Nonconformist Radicalism held its own, and even there the growth of collectivist assumptions was at last penetrating even into the agricultural industry. The labourers' trade unions and minimum wage, the application of scientific methods to farming and the urbanizing influences of the cinema, the etherial activities of the broadcasting corporation and, above all, the motor omnibus, were fast breaking up an age-long rural self-sufficiency.

Dogmatic theological politics were ceasing to attract the young, who, conveyed in their childhood to neighbouring towns for education under the Hadow scheme, were becoming secular in outlook. Gradually the country, like the towns, was becoming ranged as Conservative or Labour, the latter slowly winning the labourers' assent. The Liberal farmer, in perplexity, taking refuge in pluto-conservatism, the modern substitute for old Tory.

But another reason, even more deadly, was sapping the last strongholds of Liberalism. By 1930 it was recognized that the hope of a Liberal Government being returned within the lifetime of its remaining supporters was very slender. No one joining it could hope to receive the fruits of patronage in Government, Church or Law. To adhere to the Party entailed an abnegation which few would care to accept. Even the laudable desire to serve the State in office would be frustrated. The Party retired to the fastnesses of Summer Schools and Universities—there they prepared schemes for the regeneration of Society by Liberal principles. Their views obtained a hearing in the Press, who, having no real fear of Liberalism, hoped to embarrass Labour by causing disharmony as to ends and method by popularizing the rival schemes of other progressives. This gave to the Liberals an unreal importance. The electors as a whole did not read the reports of the young Liberal intellectuals; in the testing times of elections they proved impotent to sway votes.

Yet, at bottom, a great matter was at stake. In their several ways both Conservative and Labour were inclined to be authoritarian. They looked to the State and its power to control the individual citizen, whether in matters military or social. The necessity of war had brought about conscription, and it was then to be noted that academic Liberals, such as Sir John Simon, were more reluctant to introduce it than were the Trade Unionists who, at least, did not dislike a compulsion which, in theory at any rate, was to be imposed without distinction of persons.

The many Liberals who, after the first German War, drifted over into the Labour Party—Haldane, Ponsonby, Trevelyan, Lees Smith, Kenworthy, Benn and others—were all ready to accept Collectivism. The greatest of them all, Haldane, who became Labour Chancellor in 1924, had been offered the Board of Education by MacDonald. He was never a Socialist, but had no prejudices against collectivist activity. He was an Hegelian and looked upon the nation as a corporate entity—why he ever joined the old individualistic Liberal Party is more difficult to explain than his association with Labour. At the end he desired "a progressive party more wide in its scope than any we have seen".

He thought the old feud between Liberal and Labour could only end in futility—now that the Liberals were fast abandoning their individualistic prejudices, the hostility was not only absurd, but fatal to social advancement.

As Lord Haldane said in 1925: "The mistake Tories and Whigs alike made was in failing to see that as the franchise was extended, and as education permeated further and further, it became vital for any political party which desired to remain effective to be in the closest contact with the people. Labour is the only party that has so far succeeded in giving this faith to its supporters".

Despite these endeavours to promote reconciliation among Progressives, the Liberal Party went to the poll in 1929 in opposition to Labour, returning only fifty-eight strong, while the Labour Party became the largest in the House with two hundred and eighty-eight members; the Conservatives numbering but two hundred and sixty.

For two years the Liberals were reduced to the same position as Labour had sustained between 1906 and the War, supporting them in the lobbies without any real share in determining policy. During this time useful legislation in housing, road improvement and electrification was passed, but the real problem was unemployment—here all devices in the way of public works and relief proved utterly insufficient.

The Labour Party had never given serious consideration to the third element in their credal triad, the nationalization of the means of exchange. The Socialists, as a whole, had been most unwilling to study the more modern aspects of economics; Snowden proved himself in office to be an orthodox Gladstonian Chancellor—Banks and Credit were sacred, not to be touched by any collectivist principle. The notion that credit controlled industry, that mere nationalization did not touch the real problems of wealth production, was an idea which developed later than the time when Snowden, MacDonald and their contemporaries had come to their ideas, nor did the advanced Liberals take the problem of credit into their consideration. In a work entitled the *Liberal Way*, published in 1934, issued with the authority of the Liberal Federation, under the heading "Finance", all that is proposed is that the Board of Direction of the Bank of England should include representatives of Government, industry, trade and labour; otherwise the ancient refuge for the confused, the dilatory method of a Royal Commission, was suggested (p. 120). They admit that £463,000,000 was spent in 1930 on social services, which vast sum went mostly to poor people in the form of pensions, unemployment and sickness benefit and the cost of education. Nevertheless, they think that the only remedy for the "crippling weight" on industry is to "free trade from its shackles", which, if it mean anything, is but the old plea for free importation. For the rest, the demand of the workers for a share or the control of industry, as exhibited in the desire of the Miners' Federation to co-operate with the State in organizing their industry—a desire now fast spreading to other industries—is ignored. Poverty, insecurity of livelihood and unhealthy conditions of life are cited as the causes which most seriously restrict true liberty" (p. 187). The dissolution of the Poor Law and the distinction made in the Unemployment Acts of recent years, distinguishing between insurance and relief, is praised, but there is a complete lack of recognition of the fact that the immense wealth which plutocracy had gathered into its hands before the second great War had made cultural and social freedom for the dispossessed impossible. The danger to liberty of great State enterprises is emphasized, and the evils of the programme of the Labour Party in this direction exposed, but of the no less, and far more sinister, powers of uncontrolled trusts and combines, working for dividends, and not even in theory for Society, little is said.

Thus, until the Coalition of 1931, formed in the financial crisis of that year, when once again the Liberal Party was split asunder, the Party either grudgingly assisted Labour or aided the Conservatives. In either case the Liberals did little to revive that belief in the sanctity of individual right which is the fundamental justification for their continued existence.

Though many Liberals, such as Sir Herbert Samuel and Sir John Simon, had joined MacDonald's Coalition Government, the prevailing tendency of the administration to favour Protection produced much uneasiness. At the annual meeting of the National Liberal Federation in April, 1932, much disquiet with the position of the Liberal ministers with regard to Free Trade was expressed, but no action was taken. In January of that year, Samuel, Maclean and Sinclair had already declared themselves "inflexibly opposed to the imposition of a general tariff". The Cabinet, nevertheless, agreed to support the proposal of a committee for a 10 per cent duty on many imported goods, leaving the Free Trade dissentients at liberty to express their dissent by word or vote—a most extraordinary departure from the doctrine of collective ministerial responsibility; as a result Samuel, in February, attacked the proposals of his own Government, pointing out that they wished for general Protection. In September he and Sinclair; Foot, Hamilton and Lothian resigned; Simon, Hore-Belisha and Brown remained. The immediate cause of the resignation of the more orthodox Liberals was the Conference at Ottawa, whereat it was agreed to add to the existing preferences to Dominion products taxes on foreign meat and specified minerals. In return, the Dominions consented to lower their tariffs against certain British manufactured importations.

This was too much for the Free Trade Liberals, even under the "agreement to differ". Snowden associated himself with them in resignation. The remainder of the Liberals, constituted as National Liberals, continued in or in support of the Government, but their existence as an independent party was very precarious. Most of them depended upon Conservative benevolence for their continued existence, as was also the case with the so-called National Labour Group. Both these were now protesting that their continued existence was in the national interest, but many Conservatives and the impartial historian alike must confess doubts whether the country would not have been just as well off without them. They represented no real public opinon.

The total Opposition vote was now under ninety; the National Liberal and Labour sections but confused the issue—possibly this is why their services were retained in Government.

The Liberal Federation met on February 6th, 1933, when Samuel attacked the Government's policy on tariffs. Next day the Parliamentary Liberal Party decided to support a waiting policy, Major Nathan alone deciding to go into opposition; shortly afterwards he joined the Labour Party. By May, when the annual conference met, it was clear that the Party as a whole was no longer willing to abstain from opposing the Government particularly for failure to succour the unemployed or to utilize the League of Nations; again they deplored the official tariff policy. But in the end, Samuel was still allowed a free hand in Parliament; finally, however, in November, the Liberals decided to go into "full opposition". They were to resume the "fullest independence", but even now were not prepared to come to an understanding with the Labour Party.

The programme, set out in a book compiled by Mr. Ramsay Muir, called the *Liberal Way*, was declared to the Federation by Sir Archibald Sinclair on May 4th, 1934, to be "an authoritative exposition of the principles of Liberalism"—again it was decided not to come to an agreement with the Labour Party. In September, a suggestion by Sir Charles Hobhouse that at the next election the Liberal Party should only contest those constituencies "in which it had a reasonable hope of being successful", was rejected in favour of "fighting along the widest front". The more timorous proposal would have meant restricting candidature to about one hundred constituencies.

In November, 1935, MacDonald resigned the Premiership and a greater sense of reality in politics followed when Baldwin, the leader of the one and only party really in power, the Conservative, again became Prime Minister. The pretence of non-party government was over.

The formation of the Coalition Government of 1931 is not easy to explain; the Liberals in any case played a very minor part in it. On August 22nd of that year, MacDonald, though refusing to meet his colleagues on the financial situation, had been visited by Baldwin and Neville Chamberlain. The proposal to cut unemployment pay was refused by the Labour Government; whatever economies were sought it should not be there—at length MacDonald suggested that his colleagues should resign if the unemployment pay be cut—the Cabinet for the most part declined to follow him and he resigned to lead a new Ministry; it was in this manner the new National Government had been formed.

For all this plot and counter-plot, the Liberals, as such, bore no responsibility. The loss of all Labour seats but fifty-two in the election of 1931 did nothing to strengthen the Liberals; disguised as a national triumph, it was in fact a Conservative victory—Protection, among other things, was the natural outcome. In 1935, after the election, the Independent Liberals were still negligible in number, and the holding of a National Liberal Conference in June drew attention to the divided state of the Party. Sir John Simon and Runciman declared that they were remaining true to Liberal principles in supporting the Government and influencing it in a Liberal direction. To this the editor of the *Annual Register for 1936* comments: "Whatever measure of truth there may have been in that statement, there can be no doubt that the National Liberal ministers acquiesced in many things that were quite contrary to the spirit of Liberalism" (p. 55). Indeed, Baldwin prophesied that they would all soon become Conservatives.

The Independent Liberals, now organized in a Liberal Assembly in place of the Federation, declared that nobody supporting the Nationals could be in the Liberal Party organization; they condemned the withdrawal of sanctions against Italy, which policy had been defended by Sir John Simon in Parliament. So matters continued until the resignation of Chamberlain in May, 1940, when the whole Liberal Party agreed that their Leader, Sir Archibald Sinclair, should join the Government. Under the exigencies of war, the issue between them and the National Liberals as to the participation in a Coalition Government was ended.

In September 1942, notwithstanding their participation in the War Government, the Liberals at their Assembly carried a resolution endorsing a specific programme entitled "The Liberal Goal". It is very similar in scope and intention to the formulations of Mr. Ramsay Muir; while refusing to commit itself to anything like Socialism—there is no demand even for national control of monopolies or trusts—yet the Liberal Party wished to use the State "to do whatever is necessary to overcome the evils of ignorance, squalor, idleness and want". There is proposed an "Economic General Staff to advise the Cabinet on economic problems" —it will be observed that no direct powers are to be accorded to the State as such over the conduct of industry—indeed, anything like a "planned national economy" is "utterly opposed". For the rest, the programme supports a social order in which "there shall be neither poverty nor privilege". Believing that the paramount test of all policy must be a moral one, it repudiates "unbridled individualism and the tyranny of collectivism". It would appear that no specific remedies to cope with after-war confusion are envisaged.

This economy of detail may be wise, but at the same time it is likely that the electorate will demand some guidance other than that of abstract aspiration. Already a significant drift away from the Party has been disclosed in the departure of Sir Richard Acland to form his Common Wealth Party—one which directly attacks the holding of property for purposes of individual exploitation—and seats have been won for his cause which would scarcely have gone to Liberalism. Mr. Quintin Hogg and his school of young Tories have produced a policy which, while preserving the essential features of capitalism, is far more concrete in its specific remedies for social maladjustments. Indeed, compared with these pronouncements and the complementary ones of the Labour Party, there is an academic and aloof atmosphere about the current publications of Liberalism which make them appear to be more suited to study circles and places of ethical improvement than to those demands which the consequences of protracted modern warfare are likely to impose upon future government and administration.

Thus, while insistent upon the value of personal liberty, little is said about the very real menace of the supersession of the Law by bureaucratic ordinance and decree. The peril (from a Liberal point of view) of industrial conscription being continued in times of peace is not considered. The uncritical acceptance of the *Beveridge* proposals (themselves containing potential limitations of freedom) by modern Liberals must, to an old-fashioned individualist, prove disquieting, nor is there any recognition of the growing danger of central control of local authority by nationally appointed regional officers or otherwise.

Indeed, the modern Individualists, represented by their league under the guidance of Sir Ernest Benn, are no longer apt to look to the Liberal Party, as their predecessors in the days of the philosophic Radicals were wont to do, for the natural political expression of their views. It may be that the new dispute between Liberty and Authority—perennial, but now destined under modern mass conditions of production of goods and thoughts to be acute—will destroy the old party cleavages. The influence of a victorious Russia in Europe is incalculable; the future ideals of Europe are uncertain. It may well be that politics, as they have been understood for so many years, will cease to have meaning or interest for future generations—for the time being we have to note, reluctantly or not according to our temperament, that the days which were favourable to a middle class, petty commercialism are apparently over, and to recognize that it was in such a period of English history that Liberalism flourished.

* * * * * * *

Three reasons, perhaps incompatible, have been advanced to account for the disappearance of the Liberal Party as an effective force in politics. The first, and more superficial, is to assert that the purposes for which the Whigs and their successors stood have been fully achieved: the relations of Crown and Parliament have been finally determined, the rule of Law has been irrevocably established, and the Commons, under adult suffrage, have been finally accepted as the rulers of the nation, to govern according to the people's will; there is nothing more for Liberalism to do. They have perished of success; their work is done.

Another explanation for their failure to continue as a party with any reasonable prospect of power lies in the assertion that the ideal for which Liberalism contended is spent. Sociology, it is said, has exploded the notion of the free autonomous individual—man is but the creature of his race and environment; the exact influences of each may be a subject of dispute, but essentially he is but a unit in society—we are back with Plato and Hegel.

In this latter view, planning by competent authority must be the prime concern of governments and society. Irresponsible plutocrats are to be condemned as much as eccentric anarchs; both distract the community from its essential purpose, to breed, educate and sustain functionaries to serve and fight for the Nation—all else is futile and may be dangerous. Liberalism is negative, it relies upon the notion of Liberty; social purpose, not freedom, is the modern ideal; from this standpoint, Fascism and Communism are but extreme illustrations of the good life —even a religious sanction can be found in the notion of uncritical dedication to service.

Whether, therefore, a resurrection of Liberalism is probable may depend upon the possibility of the recapture of the vision of the basic invaluable quality of personality. If the present collective outlook persists or develops, the very notion may be incomprehensible to future generations. Recurrent war has done much to destroy Liberalism. It is not an accident that Asquith, the last Liberal Leader, was unable to weather the upheaval of 1914. As has been said, his prejudices against conscription and compulsory labour delayed the passing of the Military Service Acts.

As to the Common Law, for which the first Liberal parliamentarians contended, ever since the introduction of the National Insurance Acts, one civic function after another has been withdrawn from juridical determination. The decision of the House of Lords in a recent case, that a minister has but to state that he has reasonable grounds for the exercise of his powers under some statute or regulation to justify detentions without trial, opens up a possibility of autocracy which need not necessarily be confined to the exigencies of war.

The decay of party government may assist the progress of benevolent surveillance; in the Middle Ages, the cities of Italy won their freedom through the contending claims of Pope and Emperor—when all are agreed how to organize and educate the citizen, his prospects of independence are poor.

At the same time it must be confessed that the present programme of the Liberals, as exemplified in the publications of Ramsay Muir, their political philosopher, is very inconclusive. In 1920, under the title, *Liberalism and Industry*, he wrote: "Real liberty is not mere absence of restraint, it is security in doing, of a man's free choice, all or any of the things that are worth doing and that are not harmful to his neighbours— first and foremost the Liberal concern is to preserve or increase human liberty—Liberalism attaches an infinite value to human personality" (p. 21).

This is very fine, no instructed civilized man could dissent from it. He goes on to point out how nineteenth-century Liberalism, in its limited advocacy of the mere removal of restriction in the economic sphere, meant that "the rich were left free to employ the power that their riches gave them over the unprotected poor" (p. 29).

"Liberals, nevertheless," he declares, "believe in a man being allowed to save what he earns" (p. 49). "Far from agreeing to the abolition of the ownership of capital, the Liberal would desire to extend it more widely. In the ideal Liberal State everybody would have the chance of creating capital by thrift (*Ibid*). This kind of capitalism, it appears, Liberals still defend. In conclusion, the author, not very convincingly, asserts that "modern Liberalism is not merely helpless and bewildered in face of the problems which surround us" (p. 193). Those not in the Liberal Assembly may be less sure.

Yet a third suggestion which has been advanced to account for the fact that in this present age few boys and girls are 'born little Liberals', (or become so) is that Liberalism has so converted the other two parties that the modern Conservative and supporter of Labour alike accept all Mr. Muir's assumptions. There is much to be said for this view. If it be correct, the fall of the Liberal Party is but an incident in the general acceptance of libertarian ideals; if it be false, the failure of Liberalism may prove to be an unqualified disaster.

INDEX

Date Due

The Postpartum
Survival Guide

The Postpartum
Survival Guide

Everything You Need to Know about
Postpartum Depression

PAUL MEIER, M.D.
TODD CLEMENTS, M.D.
LYNNE JOHNSON, R.N.

Tyndale House Publishers, Inc.
Carol Stream, Illinois

Library of Congress Cataloging-in-Publication Data

Meier, Paul D.
    The postpartum survival guide : everything you need to know about postpartum depression / Paul Meier, Todd Clements, and Lynne Johnson.
    p. cm.
    Includes bibliographical references and index.
    ISBN 978-1-4143-1283-5 (sc : alk. paper)
    1. Postpartum depression—Popular works. I. Clements, Todd. II. Johnson, Lynne. III. Title.
    RG852.M45 2009
    618.7′6—dc22   2008048799

Printed in the United States of America

15	14	13	12	11	10	09
7	6	5	4	3	2	1

CONTENTS

ACKNOWLEDGMENTS

I (Dr. Meier) would like to dedicate this book to several significant individuals in my life. They all contributed to making this book a helpful and practical one that will let women experience postpartum delight instead of postpartum depression.

First and foremost, I want to thank my wife, Ann, who gave me love, prayers, and encouragement during my long hours of hiding away in my study writing my portion of this book. She also came up with many creative ideas to include.

Second, I thank my very sweet and beautiful daughter Alana Fones (2007 runner-up in the Mrs. Florida contest), who presented Ann and me with our first grandchild, Vance. We also dedicate this book to him. We practiced all of our advice and techniques for postpartum delight on Alana and her devoted husband, Don, whom we also appreciate.

Thank you to Cheryl Lamastra, a Christian therapist in the Dallas area who at one time worked with me at the Meier Clinics in Dallas, and even helped me do radio broadcasts. To spend more time with her family, she has gone into part-time practice closer to her home, yet she still spent many hours searching psychiatric research to assist Dr. Clements and me in making the book scientifically accurate. She offered particular help on the effects of postpartum depression on fathers and children.

More than a decade ago, my awesome number one nurse, Lynne Johnson, was living in the far Northwest. She felt a call from God to move to Dallas. In faith, she and her husband quit their jobs and moved. I already had a wonderful nurse, Kathy, at that time. But just as Lynne arrived in Dallas, Kathy informed me that her husband had been transferred to Wisconsin, so she would have to move. We began to write a newspaper ad to find a qualified nurse compatible with the missions of our Christian, nonprofit clinic. Lynne had already accepted another job when she saw our ad in the paper. She said her dream nursing job would be to work with me, combining her love for psychiatric nursing and Christian principles. She struggled with leaving on the day she was to start her new position but could not turn down her dream job or the call of God. Lynne showed up at the exact moment we needed her, and she has been the most loving, intelligent, and dedicated nurse any doctor could ever hope for. Lynne became a coauthor in this project because she searched all of our records for the past ten years to find the very best cases of postpartum depression to include in the book. She then assisted me in writing up the case stories, disguising enough details to maintain doctor/patient confidentiality. She also interviewed some friends who had experienced varying degrees of postpartum depression. We all owe her a debt of gratitude for making the teachings of this book come alive by letting us see how postpartum depression actually plays out in the lives of individuals.

Paul Meier, M.D.

INTRODUCTION

Before we became psychiatrists, Dr. Todd Clements and I first had to become general physicians. We practiced medicine, assisted in surgeries, and were trained in almost every major field of medicine. But the most exciting time of my entire thirteen years of college, graduate school, medical school, and psychiatry training was the period when I studied obstetrics and gynecology. I personally delivered twenty-three babies, and watching live, human bodies and souls emerge from their mothers often brought tears of awe and joy to my eyes. An eternal soul was born—an eternal soul with thirty trillion cells, each having thousands of components and thousands of indispensable enzymes. I witnessed a living miracle every time I delivered a baby.

When you were conceived, three hundred million sperm were probably released—enough to repopulate the entire United States of America. Those three hundred million sperm then raced up your mother's fallopian tubes to the recently released egg, one of thousands of eggs produced by her ovaries. Only one sperm was smart enough and a fast enough swimmer to beat all two hundred ninety-nine million others, and that egg and that sperm united to become the miracle that is you. Whether your parents planned you or not, God did. And no matter how they treated you growing up, you are an eternal soul worthy of loving and being loved forever. Your child—whether already born or still growing in the womb—was also planned by God and is deeply loved by him.

There's no question that children are an incredible gift from God. Yet the fact remains that having a baby brings an immense

amount of change to a family. All significant changes are stressful, even good ones, like getting married or taking a job promotion. For some women, the added responsibility, new routines,
and surging hormones after childbirth combine to give them
some form of what is called postpartum depression. In fact,
80 percent of women deal with some degree of postpartum
depression, ranging from a light case of what is sometimes
called "postpartum blahs" or "baby blues" to the rare, worst-
case scenario of postpartum psychosis.[1] The most likely time
to develop postpartum depression is within a few days after the
birth of the baby, but it can come during pregnancy or even
weeks after the baby is born.

Despite how common this is, it's not discussed very frequently.
Many women feel isolated and alone in their experience, even
ashamed. In fact, it's been estimated that approximately two-
thirds of women who experience depression during pregnancy
are afraid to tell anyone, and two-thirds of women with postpartum depression still do not get any help.[2]

We want to change this. Our goal is to help you understand
that postpartum depression is normal and treatable. It doesn't
signify a spiritual problem or a lack of gratitude for your baby.
It's a stress-related, hormonal problem, and it can be corrected.
There is hope!

We cannot guarantee totally preventing postpartum depression, of course, because there are a host of complicating factors,
from thyroid abnormalities to hidden nutritional deficiencies
to buried spiritual and emotional secrets that need to be dealt
with. But we feel really good about the fact that the information in this book will either prevent or lessen postpartum
depression in thousands of women for many years to come.

Our perspective on this topic is a distinctly Christian one.
At the Meier Clinics, we integrate biblically based, Christian

beliefs with psychological principles to treat the whole person—emotional, physical, and spiritual. We believe in God's ability to change and heal, and you'll see examples of that throughout this book.

As a team of two psychiatrists and a nurse, we have seen too many women suffer from this condition. We have also seen the effects of postpartum depression on the husbands, children, parents, and friends of the suffering victims of this painful disorder. So it is with great delight that Dr. Clements, Nurse Lynne, and I aim to show every woman how to prevent postpartum depression and turn the birth experience into postpartum delight.

Practical Tools

The postpartum period doesn't have to be a low point. In this book we'll talk about the root causes and risk factors of postpartum depression. We'll look at treatment options. We'll also give you highly practical tools to help your family adjust to a new member with the least amount of difficulty for everyone. And we'll share stories from our own case files so you can see how postpartum depression and recovery have happened in the lives of some specific families.

Scientists who have desperately tried to nail down the causes of postpartum depression have thus far been unsuccessful. That's because as human beings with minds, bodies, and spirits, we are not one dimensional, but rather three dimensional. Likewise, postpartum depression is a three-dimensional problem resulting from spiritual factors, emotional factors, physical factors, or any combination of the three. In this book we'll examine all three factors and the role each one plays.

Grandparents, as well as other relatives and friends of expectant or new mothers, will become more helpful to their loved ones by reading this book. But this book is primarily for current or expectant mothers. You are the ones in the trenches, in terms of pregnancy (except in cases of adoption), childbirth, and often the lion's share of hands-on care in the newborn stage. You are the ones with immense hormone fluctuations in the immediate postpartum stage. So you're the ones most often affected by postpartum depression. But the book is also for husbands, who play a huge role in helping depressed mothers get back on their feet. The more you know, the better you can help. In the second half of the book, you'll find discussion about postpartum depression for men, how postpartum depression affects families, and how to make family relationships stronger during the transition to a new family member.

Postpartum psychiatric problems should be used to rally a family together and bring them closer. The apostle Paul says in Romans 8:28 that God can use any situation for the good of those who love him. God will never abandon his followers, even in the midst of a difficulty like depression.

If you're a pastor, counselor, physician, social worker, hospital staff member, or law enforcement officer, this book is not written to you, but you can benefit from it. You will undoubtedly deal with families experiencing postpartum depression. When that happens, will you recognize it? Will you know what to do? We sure hope so, and we want to equip you. The more truth people know about these conditions, the less pain and suffering they will cause us. Our prayer is that this book spreads truth—because after all Jesus said, "The truth will set [us] free" (John 8:32).

Learning the Basics

An Overview of Postpartum Depression

You've seen the Hallmark cards, the television commercials, and the magazine ads. Beautiful, glowing, rested women gaze adoringly at their tiny new babies. Babies who are never crying, never need clothing changes because of a diaper blowout, and never spit up. Mothers who look perfectly fulfilled after spending a whole day alone in the house with a little being who is constantly needy and who communicates virtually no gratitude or affection. Mothers whose houses are still surprisingly immaculate. Parents whose every dream is complete now that they have their new bundle of joy.

Those are the ideals, and certainly there's some truth to them. Having a baby does fulfill a desire for many people, and it's enriching and includes moments of genuine, heart-filling joy. But as in every area in life, perfect doesn't exist. Parenting will bring challenges, messiness, and exhaustion. And while most experienced parents will tell you that eventually the joy overcomes the challenges, in the first few months of adjustment—months in which your baby perhaps needs you more than he or she will at any other time—challenges are significant. Some

amount of ambivalence about these huge life changes is perfectly normal—but many women are ashamed of having any
negative feelings.

That's why it's no surprise to us that up to 80 percent of postpartum women develop some level of depression.

The Good, the Bad, and the Ugly

Thankfully, the majority of postpartum depressions are mild
"baby blues" that only last a few weeks. And there is good news
about all of the postpartum mood disorders: they are almost
100 percent treatable. Researchers and physicians are learning
more about why they happen, who's at risk, and how to better treat them (all subjects we'll cover in this book). People
in this country and across the world are also becoming more
aware of and educated about postpartum disorders. We see more
people coming for treatment. We have learned from our years
of experience practicing psychiatry that many women will suffer
silently for years without asking for help, but will seek treatment at a friend or family member's prompting.

Unfortunately, there is still a stigma attached to psychiatric
problems. Many people continue to view them as character
weaknesses rather than medical problems. This keeps many
mothers from admitting that they need help, because they're
afraid that getting help means they are weak. In addition, many
mothers blame themselves for their feelings. This only worsens
their guilt and intensifies the downward spiral.

The more anger and the more guilt a person experiences,
whether or not those emotions are justified, the more serotonin
dumps out of the brain, causing depression. If the depression
reaches a severe enough level, dopamine also kicks in, and
the depressed person eventually breaks into delusions and
hallucinations.

Every week we see patients who feel isolated. They think they are the only people in the world who feel the way they do, and therefore no one else could understand them or help them. You can see the weight of a thousand pounds lifted off of their shoulders when they realize we do understand and can help. Their despair turns into hope, which in itself brings new life. Counseling or medical treatment from a professional is confidential, caring, and corrects the problem in almost 100 percent of cases.

The six months following delivery of a newborn baby is the highest period of risk in a woman's life for developing mood symptoms. The added danger is that not only is a mother at risk, but so is a helpless infant. Unfortunately mood symptoms in pregnancy and the postpartum period are frequently overlooked or downplayed by family members and caregivers.

There is nothing so tragic as a young mother or infant whose life is cut short due to a condition that could have been treated. While suicide and infanticide from postpartum problems are rare, they happen. We have also seen postpartum problems contribute to divorce, financial ruin, and the long-term health issues of mothers and children. It does not have to be this way. All three of us have treated hundreds of women who could have had tragedies had they not come for immediate help when they sensed that they were "losing their minds." Often a person can sense it before it happens.

That's why we are writing this book. The more we can get the word out, the more mothers will realize that it's not their fault and there's no shame in asking for help.

A few years ago, a public feud broke out between two movie stars, Brooke Shields and Tom Cruise. Brooke Shields was vulnerable and publicly admitted taking an antidepressant for a severe bout of postpartum depression. It took a lot for her to do that, because so many women feel falsely guilty for having this problem. She gave women permission not only to be human but to do whatever it takes to restore joy to their lives, even if medications are required in some circumstances. Tom Cruise, on the other hand, essentially told the world of women that they should work out their postpartum depression on their own, without medication. Based on his status and influence, this probably discouraged many women from getting the help they needed, or made those who did turn to medication feel guilty for doing so.

Most bouts of depression, whether postpartum or not, *can* be worked out without meds. But some people run out of "happy juice"—the hormone serotonin—in their brains because of genetic factors, low thyroid, lack of sleep, too much alcohol or marijuana, viral illnesses, or even the stress of having a baby.

Your brain runs on serotonin just like your car runs on gasoline. What would Tom Cruise do if his car ran out of gas? Would he coast to the side of the road and think positive thoughts until the car ran without gasoline? Or would he get up and walk to the nearest gas station to bring back a can of gas to make his car operate normally again? Probably the latter. If a new mom's serotonin depletion is mild, positive thinking and counseling may be enough to get her out of it. But if it is severe, meds are needed to fill up her gas tank of happiness and straight thinking.

A Historical Overview

Postpartum depression has been documented for centuries. We would venture to guess that it has been around for millennia—ever since women began giving birth. Postpartum depression is a normal, natural occurrence, but unfortunately, over the generations it has been misunderstood, ignored, or denied, and therefore remained untreated.

Historians have credited Hippocrates as the first physician to describe postpartum depression—more than four hundred years before the birth of Jesus. Hippocrates and the ancient Greek philosophers knew about the existence of depression but misunderstood its roots. The condition was referred to as "melancholy" and was thought to stem from the overproduction of "black bile" by the spleen, which led to dark and somber moods. Physicians believed that the planet Saturn somehow influenced the spleen's functioning and that black bile overproduction usually occurred in the autumn. They also thought that some emotional reactions of women were due to a "wandering uterus." Have you ever heard anyone say, "She was really hysterical"? The root of the word *hysterical* is actually "wandering uterus"! We may laugh at the ancient Greeks' guesses, but actually, they were not as far off as we think. Lots of postpartum depression comes from "wandering hormone shifts" that stem from changes in the ovaries and brain.

What Hippocrates actually described was a state of "insanity" common in ancient times after the delivery of an infant. The mother often did not recover and died shortly after the emergence of her bizarre behavior. What he was most likely describing was a state of delirium associated with a post-delivery infection.

Until the late 1800s, women commonly died during or soon after a delivery. It was not until Louis Pasteur proved the existence of germs and their role in infections only a couple of centuries ago that the death rate of new mothers plummeted. This was in large part due to the simple action of health care workers washing their hands between patients and sterilizing the medical equipment! In the mid-1800s Dr. Ignaz Semmelweis insisted on this practice in the delivery room and was locked up in an insane asylum for having obvious "delusions" about germs.

It was not until the 1960s, when the term *maternal blues* was coined, that physicians finally began investigating this phenomenon. We see women today in our practice who tell us their mothers and grandmothers experienced the symptoms of postpartum depression years ago, but when they told their doctors about it they were labeled hypochondriacs and told to quit worrying and stop whining. Sadly, many of these godly women who were humiliated and misunderstood by the overwhelmingly male-dominated medical society of that generation never came forward again.

The knowledge and understanding of postpartum psychiatric problems lags way behind our understanding of other disorders in the medical and spiritual community. Sadly, some physicians and pastors today even refuse to acknowledge that depression is real.

In this modern computer age, with billions of dollars spent annually on scientific research, medical knowledge is doubling every five years. Most of the awesome medications we prescribe for patients today did not even exist five years ago. But unfortunately, because of attitudes toward women throughout history, gains in the area of women's health and hormones tend to lag far behind other areas of medicine that are exploding with new discoveries. We intend to do something about that, and we hope you will too, by voting, by volunteering, by giving out books like this one, or even by becoming a researcher yourself to make the needed breakthroughs.

Roberta: Diary of postpartum depression and recovery

As we mentioned in the introduction, throughout the book we will be including case studies of women who have experienced postpartum depression. This first case study is different from most of the others in that it's in the patient's own words.

Roberta kept a diary during her spiral down into postpartum depression and then during her recovery. It's a beautiful, moving account of one woman's experience.

I am realizing how seldom people talk about postpartum depression. It's a stigma. I have it myself right now but have not told a soul except God. How can a woman give birth to a child and not love it? I do love my beautiful baby boy, but I also feel like killing myself. How can it be that the maternal instincts don't just kick in? Why do I want to throw up every time I hear him cry? I can't even care for my own baby that I desperately wanted all my life.

I feel guilty that I may not be taking good enough care of my baby. My husband is having to miss work. My friends and relatives are calling me to congratulate me and to check on me, but I don't even answer the phone. They leave messages, but I don't even call them back, and I feel horribly guilty about this but still don't have the energy to do it. I am too sad to hide my sadness. If I talk to them, they may be able to tell my secret: that I am so depressed I feel like killing myself. My parents are really stressed. I just know in my heart that I will never get over this depression. Death is around the corner. I don't think God will deliver me.

I am scared my husband will become too tired to help me and I will have to care for my baby all alone. I'm afraid that if I stay alive I may have even more children that I cannot take care of. I am afraid that I may turn into a mean and abusive mother like my mom was to me. Becoming like my mom is one of my greatest fears. I would kill myself for sure if I became as verbally and physically abusive with my kids as my mother was with me all my growing-up years. Why do I feel like I have made the biggest mistake of my life by having a baby?

Day 1. *I decided to keep a diary of my experience having a baby, to share with my children someday. My baby boy, Joseph, was born at 2:00 in the afternoon today. Visitors came and went all day. I breast-fed and it went well. I feel happy. I am all worn out, though, and will go to sleep now,* *because the nurse will bring little Joseph back to me in the middle of the night to feed again.*

Day 2. *I looked forward to breast-feeding little Joseph during the night, but it did not go well. I had problems getting him any milk, and then I worried about my failure and I got no more sleep.*

Day 3. *This morning the pediatrician came into our room with the news that the baby has lost too much weight and may have to stay in the hospital. I immediately began crying. I had just spent hours again last night trying to breast-feed—trying to do what so many people told me was best for my baby, and I failed. I was still sobbing when the doctor returned again with even more bad news—my baby needs to be evaluated by a cardiologist. There may be something wrong with baby Joseph. She offered no reassurance that everything would be fine. I cried the entire day.*

Day 4. *(No entry)*

Day 5. *My husband, Jose, and I were able to take our son, Joseph, home today.*

Day 6. *Dear Joseph,*

If I die before you grow up, then I hope you will read this someday so you will know how much I loved you and that I did not want to leave you without a mother. I am trying to stay alive for you. Your daddy and I love you very much. You are the most beautiful little boy I have ever seen. Everyone who has met you agrees. I don't deserve you, and I don't know why I've already let you down.

My pregnancy with you was the most amazing experience of my life until your birth—then that became the most amazing thing that ever happened to me. I felt great the whole time. Not one day of morning sickness, no swollen legs or muscle cramps. Just a huge belly. I read every single magazine, book, and Web article I could find to prepare to be a good mother for you. Your dad and I laughed and cried with joy and excitement as we painted and decorated your room. I always knew I wanted to be a mother, and I always knew that a baby would make me so happy.

But being a mother is much harder than I expected. No amount of reading could prepare me for taking care of you. As soon as I saw you, I knew I couldn't let you down. And yet, as hard as I tried to be the perfect mom, I just seemed to be having one failure after another, even with your dad helping me. I was constantly worried that you would die. I stayed awake three nights in a row to make sure you didn't smother or stop breathing. I became exhausted and soon was praying that God would let me die. Your poor dad would run from one end of the house to the other because you and I were usually getting pretty hysterical at the same time. He didn't know who to run to first.

Your grandma (Daddy's mom) insisted on coming and spending the night. I still couldn't sleep because I could still hear you crying across the house. I couldn't stop crying. I was terrified your dad and grandma would leave me alone with you and I would not be able to take good enough care of you. I am sorry, Joseph. I love you.

Day 7. *Dear Joseph,*

I went to see a counselor today who told me and my family I needed to go into the hospital. Even though you were well cared for by your dad and grandma, I felt I was depriving you. I just can't seem to bond with you; you don't feel like you're mine. I know it is not your fault. You are a wonderful baby boy. I am just not a good enough mother. I know in my head that this depression melts me down and isn't your fault. I can't help resenting you, though, but only because having you showed me how inadequate I am. I mean, you just aren't the bundle of joy I thought you would be. You are a bundle of joy, but I have a mothering defect, so there is no joy for me. You exposed the worst in me. The failure that I can't breast-feed or even function with a baby. My mothering light switch just won't turn on.

Day 8. *Dear Joseph,*

You've exposed that I am lazy and unreliable. You've exposed that I can't just forgive and forget ten years of my life as a child that were filled with rejection and loneliness. You've exposed that no matter how much I swore never to become like my mother, I still did. Underneath all the work I've done and the ways God has changed me and healed my heart, still my basic instincts are defective, because I was robbed of them. Without saying one single word, you have ripped off my happy mask. I liked my life before you came. I was happy, and my life was predictable. I had fun with friends and your dad. You changed all that. You did not ask to be born. Your dad and I wanted to have you. And I am sure that God wanted you to be born. You are a wonderful baby. You have not ruined my life. My mother defect has ruined my life, and bonding with you seems like such a remote possibility.

Day 9. *Dear Joseph,*

Dr. Paul Meier admitted me today to his day hospital in Richardson, Texas. He told me that most women get depressed when they have a baby, especially their first baby. He said my depression was pretty severe, wanting to die and all, but I promised him I would stay alive. He said everybody gets over depression with help if they cooperate. I hope he is not lying to me. I have a little bit of hope, though. People say he is an honest man and a good psychiatrist. He started me on an antidepressant to take every morning and a tranquilizer to help me sleep every night, since I was getting further and further behind in my sleep. He also gave me some vitamins to take every day, and he says when the chemicals in my brain build back up, I will be able to be a good mother and bond with you and even learn to like myself. I have never been able to do that.

Day 10. *It took me three hours just to fill out the psychological tests. Then I had to go to a lab and get blood drawn so Dr. Meier can see if I have any medical problems causing my depression, like thyroid hormones or my female hormones. Then I had to sit in front of five other strangers who are also patients at the hospital and share all our problems with each other. It was a hard day all around, but I will do whatever it takes to make this horrible pain go away. Dr. Meier said I will probably feel much better within* three weeks—almost for sure. If I don't, I may kill myself after I leave. I would drive my car in front of the train that comes near my house every day, so it would look like an accident.

Day 11. I went on the Internet today to read about train wrecks. I want to be sure that if I do it, I will die without killing anybody else. I know that the driver will feel bad, and I feel bad to do that to him. But hopefully I may not need to kill myself if I get better. The people in the group turned out to be really nice, educated, loving people, so I feel relieved about that. And the staff here is extremely loving and smart, and they dig stuff out of me that I never knew was there.

Day 12. Dr. Meier asked me if I had any dreams last night, and I told him the truth. In my dream my mother was driving a car and I was the age I am now, but somehow still living with her like a young child. I was in the backseat, and she was yelling at me and slapping me in the face. When she turned around to tell me how horrible I am and to slap me, she had a wreck and ran into a tree. Then I woke up in a panic attack, not knowing if either of us lived or died in the dream.

Dr. Meier said that my unconscious writes my dreams like writing a movie script, and that whatever I dream about I should talk about in therapy. He quoted a Bible verse that says God speaks to us in the night seasons, in our dreams.[1] He said he thinks the dream means that I am still basing my self-worth on lies my mom taught me. That is why I do not feel in control of my life. My mother is still in control of my life—driving the car that represents my life right now. I am only in the backseat in my life, with my mom's negative messages running through my head. I believe her negativity, and that is why I am depressed. He said I am a good mom but just think I am a bad one.

Day 13. Today my counselor made me put an empty chair in front of me during our private one-hour session. She made me pretend my mom was sitting in the chair. I had to look her straight in the face and tell her how

I feel about all the mean things she did and said to me all my life. I refused at first, but the counselor insisted. So I started to tell the counselor more about my mother, but she made me stop and look my mom in the eye in the empty chair and tell her, not the counselor, how I really felt. She told me to get out my emotions. I was shaking at first, but after a minute or two I burst out weeping and even screaming sometimes. I told her how furious I am that she has hurt me so bad and now it was hurting my own baby who I love. Then my counselor asked me to turn vengeance over to God and to release my mom from my life. Not to condone her, but to forgive her so she won't keep eating away at my joy all my life. I felt greatly relieved after I got my sadness and grief out in the open and wept and told my mom off, even though it was an empty chair.

Day 14. *I can tell Dr. Meier was not lying to me. I feel better already, and I don't know if it is from the meds, the sleep, the vitamins, the prayer, or the digging out of my root problems. My group therapist said it is from all of those things. He said that in James 5:16, the apostle James writes that if we admit our faults and problems to each other, we will be healed. And that is exactly what we do here seven hours a day, five days a week, for three weeks or so. We all share secrets we have never told anybody. It feels really good to know that other people have been through the same things and have felt the same way, and to see them recover too.*

Day 15. *I was able to hold Joseph in my arms tonight and feel deep love for him for the first time since he was born. Oh, I loved him even when depressed, but not anything like the awesome feeling I had tonight. Then Jose held me close and we had a family hug. Even our dog jumped into my lap and wanted to be in on it, licking Jose and me both in the face when we were kissing each other.*

Day 16. *I had a setback today. Mom called me and I took her call, and when she asked how I was doing, I told her I was feeling much better. When she asked how I was getting so much better at the Meier Clinics,*

I made the mistake of telling her that talking about all my anger toward her for yelling at me, and all my anger at myself for not being "good enough" to please her—that talking about all this and forgiving her was one of the main reasons I was doing better. She got so mad at me that she yelled that she was a perfect mom and that she had to hit me sometimes because I was such a bad little girl. Then she hung up on me. I got really depressed and felt like killing myself again for the first time in several days.

Day 17. *The people in the group all told me that I was still believing my mom. That I must still want her to change and become a good mom and love me, and that I think I need that to feel okay about myself. They reminded me that I do not really need my mom at all, any more than I needed their moms. Dr. Meier showed me a verse in Psalm 68 that says that God loves abandoned people and takes the lonely and places us in families.[2] He said that God wants me to love and be loved by new mothers and fathers and sisters and brothers from my church and my friends and siblings, not my mean mom. So today I gave up on my mom ever changing, and I felt relieved. If she ever does get better, that will be a bonus, but I do not need that anymore.*

Day 18. *Today Dr. Meier asked me to write something in my Bible or some other place where I won't lose it. I told him about my diary, and he said I could write it here—so here goes:*

Dear Roberta,

I am writing this letter to myself to promise myself that from this day forward I will be my own best friend. I will quit saying the horrible and nasty things I was saying about myself every day. I will never again say anything negative to myself that I would not tell my best friend or Jose if they did the same thing. What would I say to my best friend if she could not breast-feed, for example? Would I yell at her in rage and tell her she deserved to die in a train wreck for being such a horrible mother? Of course not. And yet that is what I have been doing to you, Roberta, and I promise to quit. I will be your best friend from now on and love you like God loves you. And I promise to build a nice support group of friends that I can share with the rest of my life like I have learned to share my innermost feelings here in group therapy at the Meier Clinics. Sincerely, me.

Day 19. *The day program staff had what they call "staffing" today. That means they sat around in a long meeting talking about me today, and about each of the clients here, to design a unique plan of attack for each of us depending on our needs and all. Then my counselor met with me this afternoon and told me what a good job I was doing of admitting my faults and talking about painful things and getting everything out in the open. They even decided I could go home a week early, after only two weeks, and just see the counselor once a week until I feel great two or three months in a row. I will see Dr. Meier for a medicine check in a month or so, and he says by then I should be feeling as good as I ever felt. If so, he will see me for fifteen minutes once every three months as long as I stay on meds. He said that if I am not feeling absolutely great, then he will adjust my meds or change something until we get it right, but that it will almost certainly do the trick this time.*

Day 20. *My counselor wants Jose to come in for a marital session before I leave the program. They said he seems like a wonderful husband, but that sometimes he can be a little too controlling or critical like my mother—but only a little bit compared to her. They want to be sure to talk to him about that. They want to help me to be stronger and to have boundaries to protect myself from not only my mother, but from anyone who tries to verbally abuse me or manipulate me through false guilt like Mom did.*

Day 21. *Jose and I met with the counselor together today. He is such an awesome husband. Totally nicer than my mom or my dad, too. When we pointed it out nicely to him, he saw that he was too controlling and critical sometimes, and he cried right in front of the counselor and apologized to me. That was very hard for him to do because he is a macho man and* *was embarrassed, but he said he loves me and little Joseph so much that he would do anything to give us a happy life together.*

Day 22. *Dear God,*

I was so mad at you. I thought you did not like me. I thought you could not possibly accept me. I thought you were off at a distance and did not really care about me except when you got mad at me. But now I realize that when I learned to pray as a little girl to my heavenly Father, I was thinking, Dear heavenly version of my earthly father and mother . . . I am so sorry for being so prejudiced against you. Now I am learning to see you as you really say you are in the Bible. You said in Psalm 139 that you designed me in my mother's womb, and did the same for Joseph. You said you think about me so many times every day that I cannot even count them. You said that you are always hugging me with one arm while bringing circumstances into my life and leading me with your other arm. Thank you for leading me to therapy to find out the truth about you and about myself. The truth has set me free from the pain of believing lies all my life about you and me. I love you more than I ever have, and I finally feel on the inside like you truly do love me unconditionally. I believe what you said in Romans 8:1 about there being no condemnation for me, so all the guilt that I carry around with me is either false guilt, or true guilt that has already been forgiven and forgotten by you. Thank you for giving me a son who is a miracle from you. Thank you that even though I will make many mistakes the rest of my life as a mother and otherwise, that is just part of being human. You will help me to learn from my mistakes and get better and better at being a mother and a wife and a friend. Amen.

Day 23. *I was discharged from the day program today after only two weeks instead of the usual three. Everyone in my group therapy went around the room and told me wonderful things that they saw in me. I cried and cried with joy, and also with sadness that I have to leave. I did not really want to come when I came, and I do not really want to leave now that I have tasted how awesome it is to share with other loving*

*human beings and to learn to love and be loved in spite of all my faults.
I knew Dr. Meier was writing a book on postpartum depression with Dr.
Clements and Nurse Lynne, so I gave him a copy of this diary and asked
him if he would put it in his book. He promised he would, but that he
would just change our names. I can hardly wait for his book to come out.
I hope and pray that the horrible pain I went through helps other postpartum women to get over their depressions and see that it is not only
possible, but also nearly certain that they will if they get the right kind
of help and cooperate.*

Sincerely, Roberta

2

Living in the Real World

Realistic Expectations for the Postpartum Period

Only a few things in life can bring a maximum of ecstatic and lingering joy:

1. The moment when you first feel peace with your creator and make a lifelong commitment to an intimate relationship with him.
2. The moment you say "I do" to a person you love more than you could possibly imagine, and he reciprocates that depth of love and eternal commitment.
3. The day you finally make peace with yourself, deciding once and for all to love and cherish yourself and to become your own best friend.
4. The day that flesh of your flesh and bone of your bones emerges from your womb, a new and eternal creation, totally dependent on you for survival—to raise, love, cherish, discipline, worry about, pray for, hope for, and fellowship with throughout eternity. A living soul whom you guide for eighteen or twenty short years and whom you prepare to survive independently without needing you to

think for her anymore, but who will always need your love, emotional support, and prayers.

Like anything, having or adopting a baby has its disadvantages—such as financial constraints, time constraints, periodic disappointments, potential rejections, illnesses, injuries, even the possibility of the child dying before you do. But for most people, the advantages will far outweigh the disadvantages.

Take another example. Most people will admit that marriage—even a strong marriage—has advantages and disadvantages. Even the best marriage means taking on new responsibilities and giving up some amount of self-centeredness because you can no longer think only about yourself. But that

very challenge is also the most significant benefit to marriage—
that you are no longer alone.

Even a relationship with God can have seeming disadvantages—like feeling guilty when you sin. But as we mature, we
come to realize that every sin we could possibly commit hurts
either ourselves or someone else. So given that, what advantage is it to be able to sin guiltlessly? We have learned, from the
experiences of thousands of clients, that sin always ends in pain.
By contrast, love and respect for our fellow man ends in joy and
a greater sense of self-worth. The point is that something that
seems confining can actually be phenomenally freeing.

The same principle holds true with having children. We
need to be realistic about what life with children is really like—
often confining—yet embrace the joy and freedom that can
result. Becoming a parent can free you from things that weren't
very good for you anyway, such as a life of self-focus, a preoccu-
pation with getting your own way, impatience, and pride. In its
place, you may find selflessness, service, patience, and humility.
Now that sounds like postpartum delight.

When the authors of this book use the term *postpartum
delight*, we mean a life of positive thinking but with realistic
expectations; a life of love; a life of responsible child rearing, with personal boundaries to protect your own needs and
desires; and a life of postpartum opportunities that outweigh
the inevitable postpartum disappointments.

Life with a Newborn

When you were a little girl, you probably played with dolls.
When you got tired of your little baby doll, you put her to sleep.
When you wanted her to wet, you squeezed. (I know because
I have two sisters.) When you wanted her to cry, you turned her
upside down or used some other gadget. But you played mommy

whenever you wanted to. When you were tired of playing with your doll baby, she conveniently always wanted to take a nap or settle down for the night, only to wake again when you wanted to play with her again.

Then adult life comes around, you get married, and you get pregnant, hopefully but not necessarily in that order. (Doing things not in that order adds its own stresses.) You get morning sickness (in most cases) and puke for anywhere from a few days early in the pregnancy to all throughout the pregnancy, sometimes so much that you require hospitalization to keep from dehydrating. You may experience anxiety about whether the pregnancy is going okay or if the baby will be healthy. If the pregnancy comes after infertility, you may have gone through a number of stressful and uncomfortable procedures.

You go to Lamaze classes and they tell you if you exercise, practice, breathe right, and have assistance, natural delivery won't hurt much. You attend LaLeche meetings and feel a lot of pressure to breast-feed your baby until much later than pediatricians usually recommend for the baby's health. Your parents want you to have a girl, but your in-laws want you to have a boy. Some friends tell you to not find out the sex of your baby until delivery, while others encourage you to find out when the sonogram tells your doctor what it is.

As a side note, it's probably best to know as soon as possible what gender the child will be. Why? Because you and your mate don't really know what you desire most on an unconscious level. So finding out as soon as possible enables you to rejoice with the parts of you that wanted that sex, and grieve now rather than at birth with the parts of you that may be disappointed in subtle or even obvious ways. Then you're left with realistic expectations.

When you played with baby dolls growing up, you did not gain weight before or after the "birth" of your newborn. Then real life comes along, especially with the birth of that first baby. After gaining forty pounds instead of the twenty-five your doctor has encouraged you to limit it to, your water breaks, you go into labor, your husband debates what to wear to the hospital before rushing you there, and labor really hurts in spite of all the breathing techniques, just like the book of Genesis says it will. After eighteen hours of labor instead of the two you were expecting, the baby comes, perhaps with some complications. You change your mind and beg for a spinal injection to end your pain, but the doctor tells you it is too late. The doctor has to do an episiotomy (cut your vaginal wall to let the baby out). You lose 500 cc of blood during the delivery, causing anemia for a week or so, with resultant tiredness and some mild depression just from that alone.

Then the baby comes, and it is not at all like the baby dolls you played with. It looks funny, but neither you nor your relatives discuss it, because nearly all babies look funny at first. (You would too if you were an eight-pound bunch of cells squished through a tube a few inches in diameter.)

You can't put the baby to sleep when you want to, even when you want to go to sleep yourself. He has wax in his ears, crud in his belly button, tears coming out of his eyes, urine squirting in your face, and vomit landing on your shirt—basically, everywhere there is a hole, something is coming out of it! Your husband does not help change the diapers like he promised he would. Your mother-in-law is at your home to help you, but she rearranges all your furniture in a way you just hate.

Let's just say reality, especially with the first baby, can be quite a shock. Is it any surprise that so many women have some degree of postpartum "blahs" after any delivery of a baby?

When you are in your nineties, on your deathbed, and surrounded with loving support from your kids, grandkids, and great-grandkids, you realize how much it was worth all the hassle and pain. And far sooner than that—when your baby beams his or her first smile, when you hear "Mama" for the first time, or when you see your husband transformed by fatherly love—you will experience joy and fulfillment. The Bible teaches us that children are a blessing from the Lord, and a blessed person has her quiver full of them (see Psalm 127).

Dealing with Postpartum Blahs

For those of you who are normal human beings and do experience some degree of postpartum blues or at least postpartum blahs, we have the following suggestions to lessen your pain and reverse the course. Keep in mind that these suggestions are focused on mild cases that have mainly circumstantial causes. In later chapters we'll talk about risk factors, symptoms, and treatment for more severe cases.

1. You can take control of your life and prevent some postpartum depression by knowing ahead of time how common it is. Consider tapping into the help of God, a good ob-gyn doctor, a support group, proper nutrition, prenatal vitamins, a reasonable lifestyle, and realistic expectations.

2. Realize that with the loss of blood at delivery, you will have a mild anemia that will correct itself within a week or two. During that rebuilding of your blood supply, you may be mildly sluggish or feel sadder than circumstances would otherwise warrant. Encourage yourself that this will get better as your body recovers from the stress of childbirth. Your physician should run a postpartum blood test to check especially your thyroid function, hormone levels, and iron level, all of which can contribute to postpartum depression. If any of these are not what they should be, your doctor may prescribe medication or ask you to increase your consumption of iron-rich foods.

3. If this is your first baby, expect some degree of sadness and self-pity, but know that it will get better. Have you ever noticed how mothers who are delivering their sixth or eighth babies tend to take it in stride, like another "day at the office"? Experience has given them realistic expectations of the refreshment and joy right on the horizon as their bodies recover. Their memories of all the previous recoveries have now made them strong, and they know they will recover again and just need to be a little patient.

4. Go ahead and cry whenever you feel like it, without being embarrassed. If you don't let your anger and sadness out, these negative emotions will deplete serotonin in your brain and lead to a more severe clinical depression. Jesus said that those who cry (mourn) are truly blessed—because they will certainly be comforted (see Matthew 5:4). When a wave of sadness hits you over the surprising setbacks, don't fight it. Go with it. Cry.

5. Find an understanding friend who will cry with you and listen to your ambivalent feelings without condemning you or laying a guilt trip on you. Remember, the Bible says that there is no condemnation to those who belong to him (see Romans 8:1). Stay away from negative people who are critical or condemning. Hang out with a positive support group of people who admire you and empathize with the miraculous and stressful experience you have just been a part of. If this means dismissing your mother or mother-in-law prematurely, creating some family tension, then so be it. Protect yourself like you would want to protect your own best friend if she were in similar circumstances.

6. Breast-feed if you can, and don't feel guilty if you can't. When you breast-feed, your body produces prolactin, which makes the milk come to your breasts and release to your

baby. It also gives the baby antibodies that protect her from infections for the next eighteen months—even if you breast-feed for only one or two days.

If you plan to breast-feed but then find you are unable to, provide excellent replacements and do not allow yourself to have any false guilt about it. Some women can and some women cannot breast-feed. If you have to bottle-feed your baby, the world will not come to an end over it. He will do just fine, and so will you. Breast-feeding is a good choice, but it is still a choice, not a mandate.

7. Since stress is a major cause of postpartum depression, take charge of your life and eliminate as much stress as possible. Don't be afraid to ask for help from your church, friends, or one of a number of charitable organizations that are available to meet needs. If you need to, see a professional counselor to bring life's stressors into perspective. Make decisions you will be proud of thirty years later.

8. Hormonal factors can play into postpartum depression. A good ob-gyn can eliminate these by adjusting your hormone levels if needed. Don't let chemical changes in your brain or body ruin your life or even your pregnancy. There are always solutions.

9. Talk openly about your normal ambivalent feelings during pregnancy. By doing this, you will be less likely to have postpartum depression. So talk about your fears—perhaps fear of labor, worries about new demands on your time, concerns about the baby's health—as well as the joys. The emotions and fears you keep locked up inside will show up in nightmares and anxiety and depression. The emotions and fears you share with a support group will dissipate, like letting the air out of a balloon. A shared burden is half a burden.

10. Pray about your worries and ask for God's wisdom in what-

ever situations you face. The Bible promises peace to those who bring their anxieties to God in prayer (see Philippians 4:6-7).

11. Follow a healthy diet before and after you give birth. This is especially important if you are breast-feeding, since you are now feeding two people.

12. Take prenatal and postpartum vitamins and essential amino acids. These help build the chemicals in your body and brain that make you healthy and happy. (We will discuss nutrition and vitamins in greater detail in chapter 4.)

Ellen: PPD after placing a baby for adoption

Ellen was a wonderful teenager who nevertheless messed up and got pregnant without intending to. She wanted to do the right thing—something she could be proud of for the rest of her life—so she decided to place the baby for adoption. (Much like another Ellen—Ellen Page, the actress in the phenomenal movie *Juno*, in which a teen does this very thing.) She received excellent counseling at a pro-life center in Dallas and dealt with her pregnancy quite well. She had a normal delivery and chose not to see the baby after the birth because she knew how hard it would be not to get attached if she did. Objectively she felt certain that it would be best to give the baby to a Christian couple she had preapproved, a couple who were mature and had longed for years to have a baby of their own.

After the baby was born, Ellen had the usual stresses to recover from. In addition, she did not have her support group around her to praise her for the beautiful baby she had helped God create. She had a family history that included an alcoholic father and a bipolar maternal grandmother. She became unexpectedly depressed and even developed some suicidal thoughts, thinking of several possible methods of killing herself even though she assumed she would never really do it. Fortunately she shared these feelings and thoughts with the loving counselor at the pro-life center who had been such a support to her during the pregnancy. The counselor referred Ellen to Dr. Clements and me, and we had her come into our day program seven hours a day, five days a week, for three weeks.

Through intensive counseling that dealt with her entire life of stresses, Ellen grew tremendously. We also gave her medication for six months to restore her happiness and make sure she did not lose touch with reality. She learned so much about herself and about God during her stay that she decided to become a counselor herself. Seven years have gone by, and she is now happily married to a wonderful man, has a child of her own, works part-time as a professional therapist, and volunteers two hours a week at the pro-life center that turned her life around.

3

Evaluating Your Chances

Risk Factors for Postpartum Depression

Postpartum depression can strike any new mother. It finds first-time mothers, experienced mothers, middle-aged mothers, young mothers, poor mothers, wealthy mothers, white mothers, black mothers, Hispanic mothers, Asian mothers, and many more. Postpartum depression is no respecter of race, age, or social status. Totally preventing any person from developing depression at any stage in life is not yet possible.

We understand that the idea of postpartum depression can be scary, but we firmly believe that it's better to be informed than to be surprised later on. When you know about postpartum depression, you know what to expect, you have some tools for dealing with mild cases, and you know what symptoms will occur if the depression is becoming more serious. You'll know when and how to get treatment. Part of being prepared is knowing if genetics or other factors make you more susceptible to postpartum depression. That's what we'll cover in this chapter.

We are psychiatrists (and a psychiatric nurse), not mind readers. Only God is omniscient! So we can't accurately predict who will and who will not develop postpartum depression.

Think about cancer as a similar example. Millions of people who exercise regularly, eat healthily, and abstain from smoking and drinking alcohol develop cancer each year, while millions of out-of-shape chain-smoking alcoholics manage to escape cancer's deadly grip.

So predicting who will develop postpartum depression may seem akin to playing Russian roulette. However, we do have the ability to identify those women who are substantially more vulnerable. Genetics play a large role in many psychiatric disorders—especially depression and bipolar disorder. (Our [Dr. Clements's and Dr. Meier's] recent best seller, *Blue Genes*, thoroughly explains the influence genetic factors exert in common mental problems, including postpartum depression.)

This knowledge is significant because it enables family members to remain more aware of the potentially dangerous situation at hand. They can watch for signs of depression and even psychotic behavior more vigilantly. The earlier a serious depression is caught and treated, the better.

Risk Factors

Here are some of the identified factors that lead to an increased likelihood of developing postpartum depression. We hope that understanding these will help you develop a game plan for preventing it or lessening its effects. Many of these risk factors are physical or circumstantial in nature; some are emotional.

Physical or circumstantial factors

History of moderate to severe premenstrual syndrome (PMS), or, using today's politically correct term, premenstrual dysphoric disorder (PMDD). PMS generally falls into one of two main patterns and usually occurs one to two weeks prior to the onset of a woman's menstrual period. The first pattern we refer to as the "mad" woman syndrome, as the symptoms are more outwardly expressed. Increased irritability, anger, hostility, and expressed negative emotion dominate the female's demeanor. The second pattern we call the "sad" woman, as the predominant symptoms are sadness, emotional withdrawal, increased anxiety, repetitive negative thoughts, and repressed negative emotions. When these women do express any negative emotion, it is often in the form of nagging.

Why some women suffer horribly with PMS while others never notice it is not yet clearly understood, but it is believed to be linked to hormone imbalances. Later we will explain the role fluctuating hormones play in postpartum depression. It makes sense that women who already suffer depressive symptoms from monthly hormone imbalances would be more prone to severe fluctuations following a delivery, with its major hormonal shifts.

Poor support from partner. Lack of support from a spouse adds emotional and physical stress to any new mother. In fact, marital dissatisfaction is a high predictor of postpartum depression. Women in unstable or abusive marriages are often ambivalent about their pregnancies. They may want a baby but be conflicted about bringing such a helpless and impressionable infant into a family situation filled with strife. These women sometimes wait for weeks before telling anyone, including the fathers, about their pregnancies. During this time they often struggle with urges to get an abortion, especially if they are actively being abused or have a partner addicted to drugs. Considering abortion, even if the woman is unlikely to actually have one, is extremely stressful and brings considerable guilt— particularly for a Christian mother.

I urge any readers in an abusive marriage to do what you would advise your best friend or your own daughter to do under similar circumstances: Protect yourself from all sorts of abuse.

Do not stay in an abusive relationship for financial reasons. Separate from an abusive partner. Insist on marriage counseling, and if this does not work (it won't work if he won't work!), then protect God's daughter—you.

Some troubled couples think having a baby will stabilize their relationship. We have three words of wisdom for them: Don't do it! This is a dangerous myth! Babies—no matter how wonderful and loving—add stress to a marriage relationship. Some religious communities even promote having a baby to strengthen a weak marriage. This thinking has led to unhappy, chaotic home lives; unwanted depression; increased divorces; senseless suicides; and messed-up kids. In these situations the rate of depression and unhappiness is high for both the husband and the wife.

Studies show that having a baby in the first two years of marriage actually results in an increased divorce rate. After two years of marriage, childbirth can motivate some parents to grow up and develop a healthier relationship.

Poor support from family and friends. We're not trying to insult your intelligence, as this statement is about as surprising as Dolly Parton's admitting to plastic surgery. But we put it here to motivate you to do all you can to build a support group around you. That is the purpose of the church. All through the Epistles, we are encouraged to love one another, encourage one another, exhort one another, speak the truth in love to one another, and on and on. (See Colossians 3:12-14 for one example.) Great support in the postpartum period means people who will bring you meals, who can help with household chores while you are recovering from childbirth, who can give you a break on days when the baby is fussy, or who will take care of your older children when needed. You will benefit from cultivating that kind of support.

Post-abortion depression

Pregnant women who choose to abort a baby generally have much more severe depression afterwards, often lasting a lifetime unless they get counseling to finish grieving their choice. In fact, as we write this, the news is breaking about a thirty-year-old well-known British artist who committed suicide after aborting twins. In her suicide note she told how the decision to get an abortion was a mistake and she felt like she died when her babies died. Sadly, she decided to end her life to be with them.

Often, the post-abortion depression lies under the surface, and the woman does not even know why she is depressed. Also, having a secret or even not-secret abortion in the past often brings lingering unconscious grief and other buried emotions that complicate future deliveries. We call this postpartum depression with complicated post-abortion syndrome.

The good news is that women recover from depression no matter what its source, given proper treatment.

Jennifer's story

Jennifer was a young professional woman in her late twenties who came to the Meier Clinics day program because of a severe depression that had hit her every August for seven straight years. When I (Dr. Meier) evaluated her, I asked her a host of questions to rule out all the possibilities I could think of. It turns out she had had a quite normal and happy childhood and had never been depressed before these seven consecutive depressions that lasted a month or two each. I asked Jennifer if anything had happened in August seven years earlier. Often, a person suffers what we call an "anniversary illness" on or around the time of a death in the family or other significant loss. But Jennifer couldn't think of any such occurrence in her life.

Our staff probed for several days and could find no root problem and no genetic or medical reasons for her depression.

We are seldom stuck, but we were with Jennifer. So I asked her if we could pray together for God to reveal to us the root cause of her annual suicidal depression. During my prayer, I asked God to help us find the problem and maybe even give Jennifer a dream to show us what we were looking for.

The next day, I asked Jennifer if she had had a dream, and she was obviously disappointed that God had not given her one. Then I told her that *I* had had a dream. I admitted that while the dream may have come from God, it could also have come from the jalapeños I had eaten at a Mexican restaurant the night before. In the dream, Jesus told me to ask Jennifer a very personal question.

"Jennifer," I gently asked, "did you have an abortion in the past? You told me the first day that we met that you had not had one, but were you telling me the truth?"

"Well, Dr. Meier, I *did* have one," Jennifer admitted. "But I didn't tell you about it because it did not affect me in the least."

"When did you have it, Jennifer?" I asked.

"Let me think," she replied, and then thought for a while. I could see her begin to blush as she remembered the date—August, seven years earlier.

"But it can't be that, Dr. Meier," she said. "It never bothered me. I knew it was the right decision at the time. It must be a coincidence that it happened that month of that year."

"Well, Jennifer," I replied, "there is a simple way to find out."

I asked her to guess whether the unborn baby was a boy or a girl, and then give him or her a name. I told her to think of her baby up in heaven having a good time with God and waiting to get to know her someday in the future, and then I asked her to write her child a letter expressing her feelings about him or her, and about her decision.

"No problem," Jennifer replied nonchalantly.

That night, Jennifer wrote the letter, and halfway through writing it she began weeping profusely. All of her buried feelings of guilt and remorse came bursting out like a geyser. She wept off and on for several days, and dealt with all her unresolved post-abortion issues with a counselor. Our goal was not to lay a guilt trip on Jennifer or to convince her of our own pro-life position, but rather to take her to Jesus, where she could pray for forgiveness for the guilt feelings she was now aware of, and develop a closer walk with him. We even had a burial service for her unborn baby, symbolizing the loss of her child while at the same time reminding her of the joy she will experience in meeting that child in eternity. Needless to say, Jennifer's post-abortion depression left her within a week of grieving the truth, and has never returned in the years that have passed since I saw her in our day program.

Being young and alone with limited resources. The "treacherous triad" is (1) living alone, (2) getting pregnant at a young age, and (3) having limited finances. Each situation alone is a significant stressor, but combining the three together predicts high rates of depression for a new mother.

Young age at pregnancy: The age at which women have their first child has been rising each decade. Much of this may stem from women listening to their mothers and grandmothers who said, "I wish I would have waited until I was older to have children." Many women think they would have been better parents if they had waited until they were more mature.

The trend for many women today is waiting until they attain a bachelor's and sometimes graduate degree, start a career, or develop a stable financial situation. These accomplishments can boost self-confidence, and the end result of a career is that the woman is not totally dependent on a man for support, which in turn gives freedom from being "stuck" in an abusive relationship. (Of course, the downside to this is that women who wait too long to have children may experience more infertility problems when they do decide it's time to start a family.) Younger mothers also typically have less experience and less confidence than their older counterparts.

Living alone: A new mother who lives alone is also usually a single mother with limited support. (Although in this era of increased military deployments, a wife with a deployed husband may function as a single mother for a year or more, with the added stresses of worrying about her husband's safety.) Caring for a newborn is a full-time job (at the least). Adding household chores to the mix—and the fact that there are no reinforcements to take over when you're spent physically, emotionally, and mentally—can be a recipe for nervous breakdown.

In the book of Ecclesiastes, King Solomon explains how two are better than one:

> Two are better than one, because they have a good return for their work: If one falls down, his friend can help him up. But pity the man who falls and has no one to help him up! Also, if two lie down together, they will keep warm. But how can one keep warm alone? Though one may be overpowered, two can defend themselves. A cord of three strands is not quickly broken.   (Ecclesiastes 4:9-12, NIV)

Certainly many women and some men have successfully raised children on their own—and most will tell you it was extremely stressful. God planned for there to be both a mother and a father for a reason. But Psalm 68 promises that our loving God takes the lonely and places them in families (see verse 6). So if you find yourself in a single parenting situation, God will help you to find substitute mothers and fathers and sisters and brothers. Do not underestimate the importance of this.

Limited finances: Wealthy mothers are by no means immune to postpartum depression, but limited finances is one stressor they can skip. For others, money can be quite anxiety provoking. Prenatal physician visits cost money, and hospital bills, especially for the uninsured, are outrageous (unless you think $15 for a toothbrush is reasonable). The cost of formula, if you use it, and diapers can add up as well. The latest consensus is that designer baby clothes might be a rip-off too. (For some reason infants don't seem to appreciate them any more than discount store brands.) Having limited finances can lead to fewer choices about work and child care as well as fewer activity options for getting out of the house.

Ambivalence about the pregnancy. Nearly every pregnant woman will have at least a few ambivalent feelings about having a baby. This is perfectly normal. Of course, the greater the ambivalence, the greater the odds are for pre- or postpartum depression. Sharing your ambivalent feelings with trusted loved ones or a counselor can help ease or even prevent such depression. Ambivalence can occur even in stable marriages. An unexpected pregnancy—especially with women over forty years old—often leads to mixed feelings. Having twins, triplets, or quadruplets can be an unexpected twist. In fact, multiple births are becoming much more common today with new fertility drugs and egg implantation methods.

Health problems identified in the fetus during pregnancy can also lead to ambivalent feelings. Today's technology enables physicians to recognize numerous physical and genetic defects while a fetus is still in the womb. Extra-sensitive ultrasound machines can expose physical malformations in a fetus, such as deformed or missing body parts or abnormal organs, as early as the middle stages of pregnancy.

Hundreds of genetic malformations (such as Down syndrome, muscular dystrophy, or fragile X) can be confirmed early in pregnancy. Think of how distressing it is for parents to know the painful future their child will face—before he or she is even born. And yet couples we've spoken to who have chosen to give birth to babies with known severe birth defects nearly unanimously share with us the enormous growth that took place in their lives for having gone through it. Their humility and maturity grew as they realized they would someday spend eternity with that same child as a totally healthy person. We will revisit this subject later, but for now, we acknowledge that concerns about what the baby will be like, about having a child who is "different" and doesn't fit your ideal, and about potential difficulties in caring for him or her can all cause ambivalence.

Before moving on we must mention this—sometimes the grim predictions can be wrong. A patient of Dr. Clements's had been told her baby would be born both blind and deaf and probably with severe mental retardation. She and her husband were urged to abort the fetus. Thankfully they were strong Christians who decided they would have and care for this child no matter what the circumstances. Imagine their pleasant surprise when the woman gave birth to a perfectly healthy baby boy, who could both see and hear just fine!

More children. Marie Osmond, the famous singer and actress, wrote the book *Behind the Smile* detailing her struggles with postpartum depression. She is a common example of mothers who experience a worsening of depression after each successive pregnancy. We appreciate her vulnerability in showing how often this really does occur.

For most moms, the first baby is the most likely to cause postpartum depression, although for some, the depression gets worse with each subsequent birth. Researchers aren't sure why this occurs.

Emotional factors

Prior history of depression. Anyone who experiences just one episode of major depression (symptoms lasting two weeks or longer) has a 50 percent chance of having another bout of major depression if he or she is not in treatment. With a history of two episodes of depression the likelihood of recurrence jumps to 70 percent. Those of us who have had three or more episodes of depression in our lifetimes have the odds stacked against us, as depression returns more than 90 percent of the time.[1] As a result, everyone with recurrent depressions is advised to continue lifelong antidepressant medications and periodic counseling even after starting to feel better.

Bipolar disorder. Women with bipolar disorder types I and II are at high risk for postpartum depression. Recurrent depression is actually a part of bipolar disorder. We will explore the recommendations for treatment during and after pregnancy in women with bipolar disorder in an upcoming chapter. Dr. Clements and I have treated many bipolar women successfully right through pregnancy, some through several births.

Family history of depression. Genetics do play a factor in mood disorders, although usually it takes a stressful event to activate the symptoms of the mood disorder. Dealing with the stresses of a newborn can definitely pull the trigger on depression in someone with underlying tendencies. Decreasing stress makes it less likely a genetic predisposition will be triggered. Also, taking medications for the genetic predisposition will make it less likely that postpartum depression will show up, regardless of stress level.

Depression during pregnancy. This seems like a no-brainer, but depression in pregnancy is often overlooked as a risk factor for postpartum depression. Some physicians refuse to treat depression during pregnancy because they are afraid that if the baby is born with birth defects, the medication will be blamed (even though the risk of an antidepressant contributing to a birth defect is quite minimal). Depressed pregnant women on antidepressants actually have healthier babies than depressed pregnant women who do not take an antidepressant.[2] There is also a myth that being pregnant protects a female from depression, but that's certainly not true.

High Risk

We can now even identify the group that's "extremely high risk" for postpartum depression, which raises another dilemma. In addition to receiving keen observation and emotional support, should these women go ahead and start medical treatment before the baby's birth? In medical jargon this is known as prophylactic treatment.

The debate concerning prophylactic treatment continues to become more prevalent in numerous medical diseases, as we gain a better understanding of the powerful effect genetics exert on an individual's health and even personality. Many adult children of parents who suffered from Alzheimer's disease are beginning prophylactic treatment with Alzheimer's medications in their thirties and forties. The hope is this might prevent or at least delay their own development of dementia symptoms. Also, the psychiatric community is currently debating whether or not children of schizophrenic parents should start taking antipsychotic medication, even before symptoms appear.

So if you are pregnant and have genetic relatives with a history of mental chemical imbalances, discuss this with your doctor or a psychiatrist. Do all you can ahead of time to prevent a postpartum depression or even worse. If you start getting some of the symptoms listed in the chapter on postpartum psychosis, taking a dopamine medicine would be a wise choice, as that would likely prevent a full-blown psychotic breakdown.

If you have multiple risk factors, we encourage you to be proactive. Consider seeing a doctor or psychiatrist while you're still pregnant. Be especially vigilant about taking care of yourself after the birth, and ask your spouse or other loved ones to carefully observe you and note if you are exhibiting any concerning symptoms. If you start to feel down, apathetic, or out of control, see a counselor or psychiatrist right away.

Tools for Prevention

As we have said, our goal in discussing these risk factors is not to cause fear, but rather to offer hope and help. Postpartum depression is never inevitable, and it can be cured. In the last chapter we provided suggestions for handling a mild case of postpartum depression. Here we offer ideas if you have multiple risk factors or if you develop a more serious case. We hope these will be helpful for you and give you proactive steps to take.

1. Postpartum depression can be due to genetic factors, as mentioned above. So if you have inherited depression, obsessive-compulsive disorder, bipolar disorder, or any other variety of "baby blue-genes," see a competent psychiatrist who can find you the minimum of necessary medications

that will not only prevent depression but also be safe for your baby.

2. If you do have postpartum depression, don't be ashamed to tell your doctor or to see a psychiatrist or counselor. Counseling and stress reduction are often sufficient to overcome postpartum blues. The best counseling you can get is good insight-oriented therapy.

3. For severe postpartum depression, you might want to consider more intensive therapy like we offer in our day programs. You may also need to have psychiatric medications added, deleted, or adjusted.

4. Sometimes antidepressants are needed to get you through the baby blues, and sometimes antipsychotic medication is prescribed. These are both quite normal. If your brain tank is out of gas, don't be too proud to fill the tank with nutrition and medications if necessary. If your depression results in wishes that God would let you die, or even suicidal or homicidal thoughts, go see a psychiatrist and get on a good antidepressant like Cymbalta, Effexor XR, Lexapro, Zoloft, Fluoxetine, or Wellbutrin XL. These antidepressants usually do not cause weight gain. (Some of the other antidepressants can cause a twenty- to thirty-pound weight gain, which would make most women more depressed.) If the antidepressant blocks your ability to enjoy sex with your husband, preferably at least six weeks after the baby is born, then either switch to a different one or add Wellbutrin XL to your current antidepressant and the problem will usually go away. If you do not have a history of prior depressions, you will almost certainly be able to quit the antidepressant within six or eight months, under the supervision of a physician. You may never need an antidepressant again unless you have further postpartum dips.

5. In about 3 percent of postpartum depressions, the brain chemicals get so out of whack, due to either too much stress or a genetic predisposition, that you become psychotic. This means that you become more paranoid and even delusional. We'll talk more about this in chapter 7, but rest assured that a psychotic breakdown is extremely serious, and you need to get psychiatric help immediately.

6. Remember that recovery from postpartum depression is gradual and uneven. You may feel a lot better several days in a row, then have one bad day and overreact, even thinking, *All is lost. I am hopelessly depressed and will never recover. I might as well commit suicide.* You would be surprised at how often I hear this in my psychiatric office. I reassure these patients that postpartum depression can be helped nearly 100 percent of the time with medications, counseling, or both.

Remember that Satan is the accuser, and he would love to destroy you and make you believe negative lies. Be patient. First Peter 5:8-9 warns us to watch out for the devil, who is looking for victims to devour. In verse 10, God promises that "after you have suffered a little while, he will restore, support, and strengthen you, and he will place you on a firm foundation." Rest on that promise!

Barbara and Steve: PPD with a history of depression

Barbara and Steve had been married for nine years when they decided it was time to start a family. After three years of trying to get pregnant, Barbara followed her doctor's recommendation for fertility drugs, and a month later she was pregnant. But two months into her pregnancy she recognized the signs of depression, which were all too familiar to her, having experienced it before and having seen it in her family members growing up. She was tearful, couldn't sleep, and had no energy. Barbara knew that without treatment her symptoms would begin to include difficulty making decisions, anxiety, and suicidal thoughts.

She did the responsible thing by admitting her depression to her doctor. He wisely started her on an antidepressant, which she continued throughout her pregnancy. She gave birth to a healthy son and continued to do well with minor adjustments to her medications.

Four years later, after once again taking fertility drugs, she was pregnant again. It was a shock when she and Steve were told to expect not one but four babies. They were told the risks of multiple births and were encouraged to terminate two of the babies. Barbara was devastated. She cried for a week and struggled with her choice. Eventually she and Steve saw another doctor for a second opinion, and they were relieved when he did not recommend terminating any of the babies. The question was settled, and they made a decision they could live with and have peace about.

When she initially found out about the quadruplets, Barbara went through the stages of grief, shock, and anger. She asked, "God, do you know what you are doing?" She wished it were all a mistake, hoping that when she saw the sonogram she would see one heartbeat instead of four. It wasn't a mistake, and she felt overwhelmed by what lay ahead. Even with these circumstances, she managed to prevent depression with counseling and nutrition and by sharing her concerns with God, family, friends, and a therapist. She spent the last five weeks of her pregnancy in bed at the hospital to protect the babies. Eight weeks before her due date a C-section became necessary. Three girls and one boy were born, and after four weeks they were healthy enough to come home.

Even with family and friends taking shifts to help with the babies' care, Barbara began having trouble sleeping. With all the stress and insomnia, she began having anxiety and panic attacks. When she developed thoughts of putting a gun to her head, her husband brought her to the Meier Clinics day program. She was started on medication and began dealing with her anxiety and fear of the future.

She told me, "The change to our lives was huge, Dr. Meier, and I needed to learn how to adjust and make it work." The logistics of four babies meant there was no going to the mall or to church. The only outings were to the doctor's office. Barbara struggled to bond with her babies because of all the time and energy it took just to care for their needs. She felt disconnected. But after three weeks in the program she developed positive hopes about her future and realized that God had called her to a very special life. She returned home to supportive family and friends better able to handle the stress of being a mother of quadruplets. She found postpartum delight. She realized that raising quadruplets would have to be a team effort, and she had to rely more on family and church friends to help her out with chores, emotional support, and even babysitting to give her time away from the quads. She began to realize the uniqueness of her situation in life. She also began to take antidepressant meds and scheduled regular appointments with a counselor.

Of course, few women will ever face the news that they are carrying quadruplets! But most women are surprised by some aspect of their pregnancies or of motherhood. Barbara's example shows how valuable it can be to know your own tendencies or risk factors (in her case, a tendency toward postpartum depression), to pay attention to early symptoms, and to get help when needed.

4

Nutrition or Medication?

Restoring the Body's Chemistry

The brain is one of God's most incredible creations. It's capable of extreme creativity, intense feeling, and logical analysis. It's the means by which we understand the world. But as incredible as it is, it can also be fragile. The brain is affected by many different factors. Without the necessary brain amines (chemicals) and nutrients, we will not function correctly.

In this chapter we'll look at critical nutrients our brains need and the best ways to get them.

Creating Critical Brain Amines

First we'll look at the most important brain amines and what they do.

Serotonin is to the brain like gasoline is to our cars. It is the most important chemical in the entire body.

I (Dr. Meier) published some of the original research on serotonin while in graduate school at Michigan State University in 1967–68, so this is a subject near to my heart. Serotonin is the main brain amine that helps us experience peace and joy. It is essential for many emotions, including love, and even

for dreaming and sleeping. Serotonin is built from the essential amino acid tryptophan. Tryptophan is highest in bananas,
turkey meat, beef, and peanuts.

Bananas are probably the best all-around food we can eat
for our happiness and mental health. Have you ever seen a
depressed monkey? I haven't. They are always running around
hugging each other and playing, and I think eating bananas
must be part of the reason!

Norepinephrine is another "happy" brain amine, one
that helps us experience not only joy, but also motivation,
focus, concentration, and enhanced sexual enjoyment.
Norepinephrine is built in our brains primarily from the
essential amino acid phenylalanine in our diets. And phenylalanine is highest in vegetables, juices, yogurt, and—believe
it or not—certain artificial sweeteners like aspartame, which
is given a bad rap by some.

Dopamine is the brain amine necessary for sanity, but it also
brings us peace and a feeling of well-being, as well as sexual
enjoyment. Incidentally, ADHD (attention deficit/hyperactivity
disorder) is helped also by norepinephrine and dopamine.
Dopamine, the sanity and pleasure chemical in our brains—
and the one that prevents psychosis—is built primarily out of
the essential amino acid phenylalanine, as is norepinephrine.
Choline and tyrosine are also helpful essential amino acids that
contribute to the brain's construction of these vital brain amines.

If your serotonin and/or norepinephrine levels become
lower than normal, you become increasingly depressed and
unmotivated and anxious. If dopamine activity varies out of the
normal range, either too fast or too slow, various brain functions
are affected, and the result can be psychosis (becoming delusional or paranoid, hearing voices that are not there), or symptoms of Parkinson's disease, such as tremors, rigid muscles, and

difficulty with body movements. These dopamine mechanisms are not totally understood yet and are still being researched as this book is written, but we hope they will be more fully understood within a few years of scientific research.

Medication and Pregnancy

Choosing to take medication during pregnancy and while nursing can be a difficult decision for women.

All psychotropic medications cross the placenta and are present in the amniotic fluid. This has always caused concerns for the physician, the woman, and her family, regarding the woman's safety. In a Canadian survey of family physicians, 23 percent said they would advise a patient to discontinue antidepressant medication if she became pregnant, and 51 percent said they lacked the confidence to prescribe antidepressants to a pregnant woman even though 38 percent said they considered SSRIs (selective serotonin reuptake inhibitor—a type of antidepressant) to be safe during pregnancy.[1] Despite the increasing evidence of the safety of antidepressant therapy in pregnancy and the known negative effects of depression on pregnancy, there remains a general perception that medications are not safe to use during pregnancy and postpartum while nursing.

Unfortunately this misinformation can result in women forgoing treatment or abruptly discontinuing their medication. As a result there can be physical and psychological effects for both the mother and baby. Some medications can produce symptoms of withdrawal if stopped suddenly. Symptoms of anxiety, depression, and thoughts of suicide may return. Experience shows that women who are depressed during pregnancy are at a greater risk for poor nutrition, are less likely to follow through with prenatal care, and are more prone to medicating with alcohol or other substances.

There is some evidence to support the idea that depression affects babies even before they are born. Elevated cortisol and norepinephrine levels and reduced dopamine levels have been detected in babies whose mothers were depressed. Some behaviors seen in these babies prior to mother-infant interactions were excessive crying, lower orientation scores, inferior excitability, and more abnormal reflexes.[2]

These children tend to have delayed cognitive, psychological, neurological, and motor development. Compared to non-depressed mothers, those who struggle with depression have three times the risk of serious emotional problems in their children and ten times the risk of having poor mother-child relations. When a woman is depressed she tends to be withdrawn, more unresponsive, and negative in terms of behavior. This seems to result in infants who are fussier, make fewer positive facial expressions, and vocalize less. These behaviors may continue through age four to eight. The good news is that when Mom is no longer depressed, the child's behavior improves.[3]

Untreated depression can also affect the outcome of the pregnancy. Anxiety disorders have been associated with an increased risk for forceps delivery, prolonged labor, fetal distress, and preterm delivery.[4] Depression can increase the risk for low birth weight, miscarriage, bleeding during pregnancy, and C-sections.[5]

Because the consequences of prenatal and postpartum depression can potentially be serious for both the mom and the baby, it is important to encourage diagnosis, education, and treatment, which may include medication. To address the concerns of prescribing medications safely, the American College of Obstetricians and Gynecologists issued guidelines to assist physicians in providing the best options for treatment.

Getting Necessary Vitamins

Psychiatric medications do an excellent job of preventing brain amines from being depleted, allowing them to accumulate in the brain to bring about cure. However, many psychiatrists overlook the fact that the only way to *create* these brain amines is with proper nutrition.

A big problem we have as humans is that when we do eat the essential amino acids in nutritious foods like bananas, meats, dairy products, and vegetables, these essential amino acids cannot get directly into our brains to produce the necessary brain amines. What is known as a "blood-brain barrier" prevents this. The only way for these essential amino acids to get into our brains is to be transported there by vitamin B_6, probably the most important vitamin in our diets.

Vitamin B_6 is a water-soluble vitamin rather than a fat-soluble vitamin. Fat-soluble vitamins can be stored in the body, but water-soluble vitamins cannot be stored and have to be eaten in adequate supplies daily. So to stay sane and happy, we all need to eat an adequate supply of vitamin B_6 each day, a fact which very few people realize.

Vitamin B_6 is highest in pomegranates, prunes, figs, dates, and raisins—all foods that are prevalent in the Middle East but are not so common in American diets. So let us ask you for an honest answer. How many of these foods do you eat daily? Us either! Fortunately, B_6 is also present in meats, bananas, and potatoes.

Americans eat a large quantity of junk food, and it's likely that poor nutrition is a factor in increased rates of suicide and depression. Of course, the major causes of that increase are probably the demise of morals in our culture, and the breakdown of the family. But worsening nutrition could also be a factor.

Even healthy foods we eat do not have as many nutrients in them as they did in the past because our soil is more contaminated. That is why farm animals that did not need nutritional supplements in the past need them now if the ranchers want to make a profit and produce healthy animals.

To get around this dilemma, our clients take an ounce or two a day of To Your Health or another liquid vitamin supplement. (I, Dr. Meier, take this supplement daily as well.) To Your Health liquid vitamins are so powerful, in fact, that when a medical school did a two-month scientific trial on just two of its ingredients, tryptophan and B_6, comparing them in double-blind studies on depressed patients in Kansas, those on tryptophan and B_6 had higher recovery rates than those on a known antidepressant. Liquid vitamins are 98 percent absorbed, in comparison to pills or tablets, which may or may not be adequately absorbed, depending on their dissolvability.[6] To enhance brain function, mental alertness, and clearer thoughts, and to delay the aging process on the brain, we also start our clients on a more recently developed supplement called BriteAge brain nutrients.

The vast majority of our patients do not need medications at all—just better nutrition and the proper, insight-oriented therapy. But in cases of postpartum psychosis or severe postpartum depression, medications are a must in addition to the natural products.

It takes time for the brain to restore amines to their normal levels, even with the best of medications and the best nutrition. Antidepressant medications speed this recovery of brain amines, but it still takes five to ten weeks even with proper nutrition and the best medications. Antipsychotic medication takes even less time to be effective. Anxiety is the easiest symptom for a psychiatrist to relieve, with medications that begin to work within four minutes of taking them.

Postpartum psychosis is a totally curable disorder if treated properly. If untreated, or if treated improperly, it can have effects that linger for a lifetime, or even result in lifelong psychosis. Medications are an absolute must for this disorder.

Medications and Nutrition during Pregnancy and Breast-feeding

We always recommend taking prenatal vitamins during pregnancy, to help the baby have maximal potential physically and mentally. I suggest that pregnant women follow this, after delivery, with To Your Health liquid vitamins. Again, this regimen includes nearly two hundred natural vitamins, minerals, and antioxidants, including "brain food"—essential amino acids that, along with vitamin B_6, go directly to the brain to form serotonin, dopamine, and the other key brain chemicals that keep us happy, worry free, mentally sharp, and in touch with reality.

Samantha: Poor nutrition and PPD

Samantha was an attractive thirty-three-year-old physician. She had grown up dreaming of what she considered the ultimate career: being a doctor. Being a perfectionist served her well during her training. She was driven to succeed, and succeed she did, graduating near the top of her medical class.

During medical school, Samantha also developed a growing relationship with a classmate, Matt, who became the love of her life. Both had their lives all mapped out.

Samantha finished school first and went into practice as a general practitioner, while her newlywed husband, Matt, did his residency in neurology. Both felt it was time to start a family, also planned and scheduled.

Postpartum depression was the farthest thing from Samantha's mind. She continued to work her very busy schedule throughout her pregnancy. In spite of knowing better as a physician, Samantha was often in such a hurry that she ate junk food from the vending machines in the halls or wherever she could find a quick bite. She gained more weight than she intended, and even developed gestational diabetes, which can often result in large babies.

Samantha was concerned that her labor could be difficult due to the large size of her baby's head. When she began labor on October 30, she received medication, but she wasn't progressing. She was given the choice to go home and progress or have a C-section. She did not want her baby to be born on Halloween, so she opted for the C-section, which led to a longer stay in the hospital.

Once she was home, her husband, Matt, resumed his busy schedule, leaving her home alone. She wished the baby had come with instructions. She didn't know what he was trying to communicate through his crying, and she felt like a bad mother, because she had no energy to keep up with activities around the house.

She continued to eat poorly—whatever she could fix quickly. She had taken some prenatal vitamins before the baby's birth but was no longer taking any vitamins. She decided it was time to see a doctor and was started on an antidepressant. She and the baby both began sleeping, and soon life was at least improved enough for her to go back to her regular schedule. Samantha had gained sixty pounds during her pregnancy, so she began to self-medicate to lose weight and increase her energy.

Returning to work caused conflicting emotions. Samantha wanted to maintain the career she had worked so hard for, yet it was difficult to leave her son in the care of someone else. Working full-time, she continued to self-medicate with pain killers while continuing to eat poorly. She worked out on her lunch break. Eventually she began having mood swings, staying up late working on projects, and needing little sleep. She felt driven but then would crash and sleep all weekend. Her irritability began to affect her marriage.

A few years later she became pregnant again. One month before the birth of her daughter, her grandfather died. She was grieving when she felt those first contractions. She begged for medications to ease her anxiety at the time of delivery and was angry and agitated when she did not get the medication she requested. After all, she was a physician and felt entitled to have her medication wishes honored.

When her baby was born she panicked because she heard no crying and felt it was her fault from having taken the narcotic pain medications during pregnancy. Her baby was healthy, but Samantha struggled with shame and guilt. The mood swings continued in spite of seeing two doctors and starting medication.

She vacillated from depression and fatigue to irritability, impulsive spending, and insomnia. Her depression and irritability escalated, and in one fit of rage she threatened the life of her mother, husband, and father. She was horrified by her behavior, and she was admitted to the hospital with suicidal thoughts. She felt out of control.

Once she was home, she was desperate to get the help she needed. While attending church, she and her husband picked up our book *Blue Genes*. After reading it she realized that she had a genetic disorder known as bipolar II. She also read the nutrition chapter in that book and realized she had sabotaged herself by not eating correctly and by not taking any nutritional supplements.

Samantha and Matt called Focus on the Family, who referred them to the Meier Clinics, where she was admitted to our day program. Her postpartum depression was complicated by her mood swings, which were diagnosed as bipolar disorder. We gave her a mood stabilizer and an antidepressant to deal with the bipolar disorder. We also persuaded her to take To Your Health liquid vitamins daily, along with BriteAge brain nutritional supplements.

Once Samantha's mood was stabilized, her therapist helped her deal with her spiritual and emotional issues, such as bitterness toward her shaming and controlling mother. She also began working on her false beliefs, including feeling as though she could never meet the standards of other mothers. She especially could never satisfy her own mother, so she gave up on ever doing that. Her perfectionism, which had served her well in medical school, had also kept her from seeing her life realistically.

When she was discharged from the program, Samantha felt hopeful about her future. She has put into practice the spiritual and emotional attitudes and actions she learned in therapy. She also remains on her medication and vitamins, and realizes these are necessary for the rest of her life. They have become a lifelong routine and commitment. The vitamins with built-in essential amino acids not only helped her health, but also vastly improved her mental state of mind.

5

Physical Factors

Medical and Hormonal Problems That Can
Hinder Pre- and Postpartum Delight

As we've discussed, postpartum depression has many root factors, ranging from the spiritual to the mental to the physical. For best results, each needs to be considered and treated individually, although of course not in a vacuum. In this chapter we'll look at some medical and hormonal problems that can be significant hindrances to postpartum delight. We'll discuss symptoms you may recognize as well as possible treatments.

Infertility

Infertility affects 7.3 million Americans, which is about 12 percent out of couples who desire to have a baby.[1] Infertility is technically defined as not being able to get pregnant despite trying for one year. We also see women in our practice who can get pregnant but are unable to carry a pregnancy to term.

Infertility can bring plenty of depression. It can stress marriage relationships—in fact, we've even seen it lead to separation or divorce. It can also lead to feelings of worthlessness, questioning of God, and, in some very sad cases, suicide.

Wise King Solomon teaches us that hope that is deferred

brings pain, but when hope is finally fulfilled, we are rejuvenated, like a tree of life (see Proverbs 13:12). When an infertile couple finally becomes pregnant and has a healthy child, it can be a wonderful, awe-inspiring experience. But previously infertile women can still be prone to postpartum depression.

Why? For one thing, fertility treatments are often effective, but they are quite expensive. Unfortunately insurance companies rarely pay for infertility treatments. By the time a couple has all the medical tests to find out what's causing the infertility, pays for the fertility medications or the in vitro fertilization, and pays the physician bills, it's not unusual for the cost to be over fifty thousand dollars out of pocket.

We find infertile women are often racked with guilt that they and their husbands had to spend so much money to have a child. We also find some insensitive husbands who constantly remind their wives how much money the pregnancy cost them. Yes, fifty thousand dollars could buy a nice car, but how much more joy is a child than a car that won't be worth twenty thousand dollars after a few years?

Going through infertility and the treatment for it can also be highly stressful, and that stress and anxiety can continue through the pregnancy and contribute to depression. A high-risk pregnancy can also be a factor.

Unrealistic expectations may be an issue as well. If you have begged, prayed, and hoped for a child for multiple years, you may assume that once you have one, everything in your life will be perfect. That may clash with reality once the baby is born and you discover that he or she is a lot of work! Some previously infertile women may also feel guilty about having any negative thoughts about pregnancy or parenting, since they wanted it so badly.

Many couples who cannot get pregnant pursue adoption,

which is a wonderful possibility. Today more than 100,000 children in America are in foster care, waiting to be adopted.[2] These innocent children are longing to feel loved and be a part of a family. What better way to show God's love than by adopting and caring for a child? It is, however, necessary to grieve the real losses of infertility so you can be ready to embrace the new reality of adoption as the blessing from God that it is.

Every baby in the world, whether the biological offspring of his or her parents or adopted, was designed by God even before the foundation of the world (Psalm 139).

Momnesia

Momnesia is a brand-new term that best describes the forgetfulness (mild amnesia) that is so common in postpartum moms. It is nearly always simply a result of postpartum depression and resultant serotonin depletion. You need adequate serotonin and norepinephrine in the brain to have good memory and concentration abilities. As discussed earlier, these chemicals can be restored by a combination of practicing forgiveness, particularly if you have a difficult past; reducing stress; getting nutrition with "brain food"; and taking antidepressant medications if necessary.

Matigue

We might as well coin a new word for postpartum fatigue, so I guess *matigue*—representing maternal fatigue—is as good a word as any. Suffice it to say that matigue is a common occurrence postpartum for a whole bunch of reasons.

A common question asked by many new mothers is this: "It has been weeks since I had my baby, and I am still tired all the time. When will I feel rested again?"

Not only has the body undergone the physical and emotional challenge of childbirth, but there are also many new challenges in caring for a newborn. For most women the feeling of fatigue and exhaustion lasts from weeks to several months.

Fatigue is an immense problem in postpartum women, again for a variety of reasons including anemia, hormone shifts, thyroid shifts, interrupted sleep for breast-feeding, and depression itself, which causes fatigue. Most women experience a post-partum period of fatigue whether or not they get depressed, but depression makes it much worse.

Men usually will not have significant fatigue problems unless they are depressed. Low serotonin from all the stress, repressed anger over a variety of pregnancy-related concerns, guilt, alcohol abuse—all these things are causes of serotonin dumping and thus resultant postpartum depression in men.

Sleep and Depression

Poor sleep and depression have been linked for several decades. There remains controversy over which is the chicken and which the egg. Does poor sleep result in depression, or does depression result in poor sleep? After years of study, thousands of volunteer patient hours, and millions of research dollars, we still don't know. The best answer we can give you today is *both*!

Newborn babies, no matter how beautiful and cuddly, wreak havoc on their mothers' sleep schedules. For some reason babies will not comply with our American schedule of eating three meals per day or sleeping eight hours continuously. They want to eat every few hours and then take a quick nap between meals—and they expect their mothers to convert to their schedules.

Anyone who has been around a newborn for any length of time knows that the number of hours of sleep deprivation mothers endure is astronomical! Some people (including, sadly, some physicians) believe that mothers are genetically programmed by natural mothering instincts during the post-partum period and therefore require less sleep. We believe that parents of newborns (both mothers and fathers) rise to the occasion when it comes to caring for their babies. Devoted parents modify their lifestyles to best meet the demands of raising their infants. But even so, sleep deprivation takes its toll on everyone affected.

Normal sleep

Sleep occurs in approximately ninety-minute cycles. We start off in a very light sleep (stage 1) and then progress through stage 2 into the deep sleep stages (3 and 4). We also go through a stage called REM (rapid eye movement), in which most of our dreaming occurs. The deep sleep stages physically refresh us and the REM stage helps to mentally refresh us.

When a mother awakens every few hours during the night to feed or care for her infant, she must restart her interrupted sleep cycle from the beginning. So she not only has diminished overall time sleeping, but she may also have an improper amount of time spent in the different sleep stages. Someone who wakes up a lot will be deficient in both the deep stages and REM sleep.

Poor sleep impairs us both physically and mentally. Enough sleep deprivation can also lead to psychotic thinking, even in patients with no history of mental illness. We've seen patients who have become paranoid or delusional or experienced hallucinations after as little as one night of sleep deprivation. It is not uncommon for college students (or grad students) to experience psychotic thinking after staying up studying for tests. This is especially true if large amounts of caffeine or other stimulants are used to keep them awake.

A few years ago we admitted Tim, a young professional

businessman, to our day hospital after he told his friends their TV was talking to him. Another psychiatrist told Tim and his family that he probably had schizophrenia. The whole family was distraught, needless to say, when they first brought Tim in. Tim's father ran a very successful corporation and had been grooming Tim to take over the business for him. These plans were now up in the air as the family worried over Tim's future. They had secretly begun talking about moving Tim back in with his parents to live out his life.

Thankfully Tim did not have any type of mental illness—just March Madness. The whole "talking TV" ordeal came about after he had stayed up for several days watching the NCAA basketball tournament. He averaged two hours of sleep a night over a four-day period. A few full nights of sleep brought him back to the old Tim. His family was quite relieved.

Tim also admitted that he had taken "buzz beans" (slang for chocolate-covered espresso beans) in order to stay alert. Stimulants like caffeine, diet medications, over-the-counter cold medications (pseudoephedrine hydrochloride), and prescription stimulants like Ritalin all saturate our society today. These substances not only interfere with our body's natural sleep and wake cycle (circadian rhythm), but also make our brains more susceptible to paranoia, delusional thinking, and hallucinations. They can also cause or worsen depression in some people.

Sleep deprivation plays a large role in postpartum psychosis. Lack of sleep adds to the brain chemical imbalance that culminates in a psychotic episode. Sleep deprivation can also trigger a manic episode in a bipolar patient. The first key to correcting both of these conditions is restoring sleep—the faster, the better.

Sleep management 101

Former Pennsylvania senator Rick Santorum wrote a book titled *It Takes a Family*. That premise has never been more true than when it comes to making sure momma gets her sleep—cause "if momma ain't happy—ain't nobody happy!" Here are the areas of sleep management we address at the Meier Clinics:

Tips for Mom

- Have a comfortable bed.
- Have a dark and quiet bedroom. (Even night-lights can impede our brains' production of melatonin, a sleep-promoting hormone.)
- If you need a night-light, use a red one. Melatonin does not respond to red light.
- Don't exercise for at least four hours prior to bedtime.
- Turn off all TVs, radios, cell phones, and other noise-makers. (Leave the smoke alarm on, though.)
- Use the bedroom for sleep and sex only—though it's probably mostly sleep nowadays. (Don't use it for the headquarters of your scrapbooking spread of baby.)
- Catnaps during the day are fine—just keep them short so they don't interfere with nighttime rest.

Tips for Dad

- In addition to following the points we gave Mom, try to take nightly shifts feeding the baby. (One night on, one night off is optimal to give both of you longer unbroken periods of sleep. Having the partner with the night off sleep in a separate room during this time period may ensure that he or she doesn't get awakened every time the young prince calls for one of his subjects.)
- If Mom breast-feeds, encourage her to pump during the day so you can take a night feeding.

Ace in the hole

Video this grueling after-hours work that you as parents are lavishly bestowing on your infant. Hopefully when you're old and it's time for junior to cast you into a nursing home, you can show him or her this heart-tugging video and he or she will put you up in a pretty snazzy pad. (Assuming you will be able to find some relevant technology in that day that can play the outdated video recording.)

Sleep and alcohol

Alcohol is often thought to be a sleep promoter—after all, having a few drinks usually makes you sleepy. Alcohol does help you fall asleep initially, but when the liver starts metabolizing it (breaking it down), the alcohol activates you, causing fragmented sleep—particularly in the second half of the night. Alcohol also passes through breast milk into the baby's mouth and body, which is very dangerous. It can trigger seizures, which can result in death. Alcohol can also destroy the frail developing digestive system and brain of a newborn.

Alcohol can cause adults to experience a deep, comalike sleep during the first part of the night. They might not be able to hear or awaken to a crying or distressed baby. Even small amounts of alcohol can interfere with balance, increasing the chances of dropping or falling on a baby.

We call this to your attention not to preach, but just as a reminder, as we have known of a few cases in which a parent accidentally injured a child when alcohol was involved. These adults were racked with guilt and remorse for years. Also, when something like this happens (or is even suspected of happening), the state can investigate and remove any children from parents they deem an endangerment.

Treating sleep problems

If improved sleep hygiene does not remedy your sleep problems, then we recommend using a sleep aid on a short-term basis. Some mothers are scared these medications may put them in such a deep state of sleep that they won't be able to awaken if the baby is crying, nor will they be able to get out of bed the next morning. This is rarely the case. Sleep medications can and do have side effects, but when they are used on a short-term basis, these effects are mild compared to the effects of not sleeping.

We often prescribe the sleep medication Rozerem if a patient has to use one. It is not addicting, doesn't interfere with a person's sleep stages, and rarely interferes with any other medications or treatment that Mom is taking. It can increase prolactin levels, which can increase moodiness, irritability, and headaches, and interfere with the ability to start menstruating again, so we will usually keep a close watch on those.

Good sleep helps women avoid postpartum depression, and it speeds the recovery from postpartum depression in those who already have it.

Miscarriages

Postpartum delight can involve recovery from the grief of a miscarriage, which happens in approximately one-third of pregnancies. If you want six children, plan on an average of nine pregnancies with three miscarriages, some so early you may not even notice them.

Recovery includes weeping over the loss, finding someone with enough Christlikeness to weep with you, and realizing that the miscarried child is in heaven (see 2 Samuel 12:23). He or she is waiting to spend eternity with you someday and is getting the bliss of heaven without going through the trials of earth first. Grieve this significant loss even as you rest in the hope of heaven.

Preeclampsia

Rarely, a pregnant woman's blood pressure will rise and continue to rise until it reaches dangerous levels. This can even result in death if untreated. Genetic predisposition may be an important factor in preeclampsia, and stress has also been implicated. But no matter what may cause it, be sure to see a good ob-gyn doctor regularly during pregnancy and have your blood pressure monitored. Preeclampsia can be treated, and the baby may even need to be delivered somewhat early if this condition persists. Like any stressful situation, preeclampsia or other pregnancy complications can be a factor in depression.

Placenta Abrupta

In about 1 percent of pregnancies, the placenta will tear loose from the womb early, causing bleeding.[3] If this happens, we encourage women to go immediately to the nearest emergency room because if the abruption is severe or complete, the lives of the mother and the unborn child are in danger. If the condition is caught in time, an emergency C-section can often save the lives of both.

Babies with Birth Defects

We have known some godly couples who adopted one or more babies with birth defects. They wanted to accept the challenge of helping those babies become as independent and productive as possible, and to grow themselves. However, very few couples who are pregnant pray for a disabled baby so God can use the situation to bring about strength and humility in their lives. The divorce rate goes up slightly for couples who have a baby born with significant birth defects,[4] because of the stress and because human nature is such that each parent may blame the genes of the other.

There is nothing wrong with praying for a healthy baby and delivery, as long as you also pray that God will help you love the baby no matter what. In reality, there is no such thing as a baby with no birth defects. We all have strengths and weaknesses, and we were designed by God even before we were conceived, according to Psalm 139. I (Dr. Meier) have significant ADHD, a genetic tendency toward mild seasonal mood swings regardless of circumstances, and a directional IQ that may actually be a negative number! But I can love and be loved, and I can do productive work, including writing a novel in a week or two.

About 3 percent of babies have significant birth defects.[5] When the surprise of having a baby with a birth defect comes, grieving the disappointment of what you had been hoping and praying for is totally normal and proper. Get support from family and friends who can grieve with you. Then make an effort to move on. Ideally, you love the baby anyway, make the best of the situation, and become a better person than you would have ever become with a healthier baby.

Stress

In our book *Blue Genes*, we describe how combining genetic tendencies for a mood disorder with extra stress results in an unstable mood.

We know that stress plays a huge role in the development of postpartum depression (and all other depressions as well). Stress is physical, mental, emotional, or spiritual strain. We face some degree of stress every day. Stress can lead anyone into depression, mood swings, anxiety, panic, or even a psychotic breakdown—and those of us with genetic tendencies are particularly sensitive to stress.

The combination of carrying a pregnancy, going through delivery, and then caring for a newborn is extremely stressful—physically, mentally, emotionally, and spiritually! New mothers face hormonal fluctuations, sleep changes, and diet changes starting in pregnancy. Medical research shows that just one of these factors causes enough stress on the body to lead to depression, so imagine the power of all three combined.

About one out of three births in the United States is by cesarean section.[6] These mothers have the added task of recovering from major surgery, while tending a baby and withstanding wild hormone swings.

We encourage you to get help from family and friends in the first weeks after delivery. If the stress is still too great, consider talking through some of the significant issues with a reputable counselor.

Hormonal Factors

Although a psychiatrist can treat depression, he or she will often refer a woman to her obstetrician if hormonal imbalances are suspected. These imbalances can occur in a number of areas.

Estrogen and progesterone

The reproductive hormones estrogen and progesterone increase dramatically during pregnancy—they have to for a woman's body to sustain the developing baby. Progesterone helps increase pain tolerance and works as a natural antianxiety supplement in the pregnant female (a handy painkiller, even before the invention of epidurals). Once the baby is born, though, the levels of estrogen and progesterone both start plummeting within forty-eight hours. Many physicians feel that these rapid fluctuations are what puts some women over the edge.

In some studies, researchers have given women medication

that decreases levels of both estrogen and progesterone. Some of the women developed depression from this, but others didn't. On further investigation the researchers found that women with a history of past depressions were much more likely to experience depression in the study.

In other studies, researchers have created depression in women by giving them drugs that make just their estrogen levels drop rapidly. And still other studies have shown depression in both men and women when their levels of progesterone were increased—without affecting estrogen (yes, men do have small amounts of estrogen).

This evidence shows us that what's very important, especially when it comes to mental health, is the balance of estrogen and progesterone. This is often referred to as the estrogen/progesterone ratio (E:P ratio).

Prementrual syndrome (PMS), which millions of women experience monthly, causing sadness, irritability, social withdrawal, anger, crying spells, severe fatigue, poor sleep, increased sensitivity to pain, and even suicidal ideation, is thought to be spurred on by rapidly dropping estrogen levels.

Cortisol

Cortisol is known as our "stress hormone." It is made in the adrenal glands, which sit on top of our kidneys. They release more cortisol during stressful times.

Cortisol activates certain areas of the brain to help us handle a present or upcoming stressful event. A sustained high level of cortisol, which might happen in a time of chronic stress, takes its toll on our minds and bodies. Sustained overactivity in the limbic system of our brain (the emotional center) increases anxiety, irritability, and negative moods. Overstimulation in this area also interrupts sleeping patterns and appetite.

Chronic high levels of cortisol lead to decreased functioning of our immune systems. This ushers in more colds and sickness. It can also worsen autoimmune disorders, such as psoriasis, fibromyalgia, chronic fatigue, and arthritis. Females with increased levels of cortisol are also very prone to gaining weight.

Cushing's disease is a medical condition in which the adrenal glands overproduce cortisol. Depression, psychosis, and suicide rates are very high in people with this condition. This has led researchers to look for new treatments that target the overproduction of cortisol. These may be the antidepressants of tomorrow.

We don't treat cortisol levels that much today, but as fast as medical knowledge is advancing, we may be by the time this book is out. One reason is that cortisol levels can be tricky to measure. Your adrenal glands release it in pulses and in response to stress, so the measurement can vary from hour to hour. Blood and saliva tests reveal the level only at that moment. The most accurate way to measure the cortisol level is a twenty-four-hour urine collection. Doing this requires you to pee in a big plastic pitcher for a whole day and keep it in the refrigerator. This test can be a hassle, but it is accurate.

One troubling trend we see today among patients seeing herbalists and naturopaths is the treating of "adrenal fatigue." Patients are told their adrenal glands are worn out from stress and are not producing enough cortisol. We've seen many patients who've been given this diagnosis and then put on cortisol replacement treatment after only a saliva test. We've seen these patients develop depression, anxiety, insomnia, memory problems, and weight gain after starting these treatments.

Adrenal fatigue is quite rare, but it's a serious medical condition that can lead to death. If any health care provider suspects you have adrenal fatigue, we encourage you to see an endocrinologist, who is a medical specialist with years of training in this particular area.

Testosterone

Yes, women do have testosterone, just as men have estrogen. Female testosterone levels are about 1 percent that of males. This amount, though small, plays a huge role in the functioning of the female brain and body. Sufficient testosterone is needed for energy, sexual desire, maintaining muscle development, and improving mood.

Low testosterone levels result in fatigue, decreased sex drive, poor memory (specifically short-term memory), and weakness (breaking down of muscle mass). Testosterone improves your body's ability to burn off fat—which is definitely an advantage in the postpartum state. Contrary to popular belief, replacing testosterone will not beef you up like Arnold Schwarzenegger.

Testosterone needs to be in the normal range. When a female's testosterone levels are too high, they stimulate the growth of thick dark hairs on the body and face. Excess testosterone also causes acne and a deepening of the voice. However, low testosterone is much more common than high testosterone.

Women tend to feel their best somewhere in the top 33 percent of the normal testosterone range. Exercise boosts testosterone production. Creams and gels to help replace testosterone are also available. A testosterone patch specifically for women is supposed to be on the market soon.

Glucose and Insulin

During pregnancy your body changes the way it processes glucose (blood sugar). Much of this is brought about by the weight gain associated with pregnancy. Our bodies break down the food we eat into proteins, carbohydrates, and fats, and then absorb each of these into the bloodstream. Carbohydrates are further broken down into simple sugar—glucose. Glucose levels increase in the bloodstream during the first few hours following a meal.

Rising blood sugar levels stimulate our pancreases to release insulin. Insulin allows our organs and muscle cells to absorb glucose from the bloodstream. (I picture it working by unlocking the front door of the cell and then letting in the right amount.) Cells need glucose to have energy to function. Since insulin is sending glucose out of the blood vessels and into the cells, it *reduces* the blood sugar level. If your body doesn't produce enough insulin, or the insulin doesn't work right, your blood sugar levels become abnormally high. This is diabetes.

Each year millions of pregnant females develop diabetes during their pregnancies, a condition is called gestational diabetes. It's almost always due to insulin not working right. Most of the time it resolves in the weeks following childbirth, but 19 percent of women will develop type 2 diabetes after pregnancy.[7] This is one reason that good prenatal care is so important.

Your doctor should regularly check your blood sugar levels during pregnancy. Doctors will usually have you fast (not eat for at least eight hours) and then measure glucose levels. If that test is abnormal, they may have you go to the lab early in the morning (while fasting) and drink a sugary drink. Your glucose levels will then be measured several times in the next few hours. This is a very accurate test, but you do leave feeling like a pincushion!

Managing diabetes consists of following a strict low-carbohydrate diet, participating in a proper exercise program, and using medications if your doctor thinks it necessary.

If your insulin works too hard or you're not eating frequently enough, your blood sugar level can drop below normal. This is called hypoglycemia, and it happens most often several hours after a meal. Hypoglycemia can cause sweating, shakiness, sensations of hunger, rapid heartbeat (which can be irregular), and severe anxiety or irritability. It can also cause headaches, blurry vision, sudden fatigue, and confusion. Hypoglycemia also substantially increases your risk of fainting.

Hypoglycemia is usually treated by revamping your diet—learning to eat smaller and more frequent meals. Balancing the proteins and carbohydrates in your diet also stabilizes your blood sugar. Experiencing hypoglycemia while caring for a newborn can be dangerous. Episodes of confusion, vision changes, and loss of consciousness are not good, especially if you're home alone with your infant.

Hypoglycemia can affect every area of a person's life. Continued hypoglycemic symptoms can render someone fearful to leave her house. She may be terrified by the thought of having an "episode" in public. One particular patient of ours started feeling light headed while buying diapers at Wal-Mart. She ran over to the candy section and ate a chocolate bar immediately. Luckily the security guard who was monitoring the store cameras that day knew her—so she wasn't arrested for shoplifting.

We send every patient with hypoglycemia to a nutritionist who specializes in this area and can teach patients how to eat a proper diet to avoid episodes.

Postpartum Thyroiditis (PPT)

The thyroid is a small gland located in the neck right under the Adam's apple. Even though you can rarely see or feel this gland, don't think it's insignificant. It has been compared to the gas pedal on a car! Thyroid hormone sets your body's metabolism—the rate of calories you burn while sitting still. The higher your thyroid hormone levels, the faster you burn calories. When thyroid levels are low, your body goes into more of a hibernation mode.

For some postpartum women, fatigue may be due to an underlying medical condition called postpartum thyroiditis (PPT).

The most common cause of PPT is an autoimmune disease. The body produces antibodies against its own thyroid cells, either causing an excess of thyroid hormone (hyperthyroidism) or destroying so much thyroid tissue that the thyroid cannot produce enough thyroid hormone (hypothyroidism).

Thyroid hormone levels play a huge role in determining your mood, energy level, weight (including the ability to lose weight after delivery), amount of sleep needed, sexual desire, and ability to stay warm. Both hyperthyroidism and hypothyroidism can cause severe mental problems if left untreated, even psychotic depression or mania.

Millions of Americans suffer from hypothyroidism, and females are more likely to be afflicted with it than men. Many women develop it during pregnancy, so it is extremely important for your doctor to check your thyroid hormone levels routinely. It's not uncommon for us to see women at our clinic who have been suffering with severe depression for years yet have never had their thyroid checked. Thyroid levels can be checked with a blood or saliva test.

The thyroid gland's function is to take the iodine found in many foods, such as bread, seafood, and salt, and convert it into thyroid hormones. The thyroid hormones thyroxine (T4) and triiodothyronine (T3) are produced when the gland's cells combine iodine and the amino acid tyrosine. These hormones are released into the bloodstream and carried throughout the body. Their main function is to control metabolism (conversion of oxygen and calories to energy), and every cell in the body is dependent upon the thyroid hormones for metabolism regulation.

Diagnosis and treatment

Thyroiditis refers to "inflammation of the thyroid gland" and is thought to be an autoimmune disease. It has been shown to follow three stages. The first is hyperthyroidism, which seems to happen one to three months after delivery. The thyroid gland produces an excess of thyroid hormones. This causes symptoms such as increased heart rate, restlessness, anxiety, insomnia, and weight loss.

Stage two usually happens three to six months after birth and is called hypothyroidism. A lack of hormone production results in symptoms of fatigue, weight gain, hair loss, temperature changes, constipation, and depression. Women with hypothyroidism may also have trouble with memory and concentration. (See the appendixes at the end of this book for additional symptoms).

Many postpartum women move into stage three, which is recovery, and the body returns to a normal thyroid state without treatment. During the period between the hyperthyroid and hypothyroid state the levels can be within normal range, which can make diagnosis difficult if the tests are done during this period.

Hypothyroidism is treated by taking thyroid hormone, which can be made synthetically and comes in a tablet form. Your doctor can start you on a low dose and work it up, checking your levels along the way. There is also a natural brand called Armour Thyroid, which is derived from the thyroid hormone of pigs.

Some doctors may be too rigid. If your thyroid hormones are at the low side of the normal range, your doctor may refuse to treat you even though you have obvious symptoms. When you have symptoms from thyroid hormone levels that are within the normal levels on the charts but low for you, it's called sub-clinical hypothroidism. If your doctor will not treat this, see an endocrinologist, who specializes in hormonal issues.

You are at a greater risk for developing PPT if you have any of the following risk factors:

1. The presence of insulin-dependent diabetes.
2. Family history of thyroid disease.
3. A goiter and thyroid antibodies, which are detected through a blood test.
4. Previous occurrence of PPT.

Studies indicate that 50 percent of women who experience PPT develop permanent hypothyroidism within five years of their pregnancies. There is a recurrence of 70 percent with subsequent pregnancies, and one-third develop hypothyroidism within two to four years.[8]

Because some of the thyroid symptoms include fatigue, insomnia, and depression, they can be easily overlooked or seen as normal for the new mother. (See appendixes 1 and 2 at the back of this book for a more extensive list of symptoms.) Recognizing the symptoms of thyroid dysfunction in yourself can be the first step in getting help. The proper treatment can dramatically affect your future physical and mental health. If you identify with thyroid dysfunction symptoms, seek treatment from your ob-gyn, primary care physician, or an endocrinologist.

Carey: Postpartum thyroiditis

I had just given birth to a beautiful eight-pound, two-ounce baby boy named Alexander. I was seventeen at the time, three weeks away from my eighteenth birthday. In spite of my being a single mom, the unconditional love of my parents and friends made it easier for me to forgive myself for having gotten pregnant in the first place. After weighing the options, I decided to parent my baby, and I continue to believe that it was the right decision for me.

Life seemed to begin for me soon after delivery, as I experienced an overpowering love I had never known before. This love started as an outpouring from my heart into my son's life but soon became an inpouring into my life from God.

As I relished those first months of diaper changing, feeding, and first everythings for my son and me, my body was going through rapid changes that would begin to impact my life permanently. Unbeknownst to me, my thyroid gland began to speed up rapidly, producing more thyroid hormone than my body needed. This caused my heart to beat faster, my hair to thin, and sleep to elude me. Ah, the joys of new motherhood, I thought to myself, figuring it was all a part of postpregnancy adjustments.

When my son was six months old, I went in for a physical. My doctor at the time gave thyroid blood tests routinely along with several other examinations. After my test came back, the doctor sat me down and explained how I most likely had a hyperthyroid condition. My thyroid gland was producing too much thyroid and would probably need to be removed through nuclear radiation. But I didn't need to worry, he said, because people like George H. W. Bush had had this done and lived perfectly normal lives. I was stunned, surprised, and a little scared, to say the least. In order to move forward with my treatment, I had to make an appointment with a specialist, called an endocrinologist.

It took almost two months to get a new patient appointment with the doctor I chose. When the time finally came for my appointment, the doctor had me get thyroid blood tests again. We were sitting in a normal patient exam room. I was on the patient bed, with the white translucent paper crinkling with every nervous wiggle. My mom was standing next to me.

The doctor entered the room, flipped open the chart, and read me my blood results. My body had gone into hypothyroid mode, and my levels were now so low the doctor didn't even think my test results were real. He told us that there must be a mistake; if my levels were this low, how could I even walk around? I was retested and the results came out the same. So that's why I was so tired and depressed! I thought it was because I was still adjusting to being a new mom. What did I know? I was just a kid with a kid.

Based on the fact that my thyroid levels had gone up and then down, my endocrinologist diagnosed me with Hashimoto's thyroiditis. I wouldn't learn until later that this is an autoimmune disorder where a person's immune system attacks any cell that produces thyroid. Basically, the thyroid gland is seen as a giant virus and attacked by the body until it is destroyed.

While my body was going to war with itself, the doctor prescribed me a standard synthetic thyroid pill to give my body what it was lacking. I started to feel better even though I didn't know I had been feeling worse. My hair thickened. I lost weight, and I even had enough energy to enroll full-time in a community college while raising a ten-month-old little boy.

As my body seemed to normalize, so did my life—until one day, my gynecologist decided that the brand of synthetic thyroid I was taking wasn't the best for me and that maybe I could do with a lower dose. By this time I wasn't consistently seeing my endocrinologist, since I had moved, so I took her advice as my leading care provider.

Strangely enough, I started feeling depressed, losing my hair, and gaining weight. I thought it was because I had just broken up with my boyfriend, and I didn't realize that my thyroid might have something to do with it. After a year of struggle, I began to suspect something more than a breakup was at work.

I went in and was retested by my doctor. "Nope, your blood work is fine. It must be something else." That was always the response.

"But I still don't feel well." I kept thinking that I would feel better soon. I tried a different doctor, who was a general care provider. He switched my medicine to a natural thyroid dose made from pig thyroid. It sounded great to me, but what I didn't realize was that this type of thyroid's dosage was difficult to regulate. While the label said I was getting a certain dosage each time, that might not be exactly true.

My struggles continued. Finally I decided that this condition might be serious enough to see a specialist. By the time I made an appointment with an endocrinologist, I had gained over forty pounds and was very depressed. Having a low thyroid is like trying to run uphill. It just makes life harder.

After I met with this doctor and had extensive blood work done, she decided to put me on the synthetic thyroid I had started on years ago. After a couple of adjustments I was feeling much better. Thankfully this doctor looked at not only my blood work, but also my symptoms, when making a medicine adjustment. I now feel much better and my symptoms of depression, rapid weight gain, and hair loss have all greatly decreased.

Through this whole process, I realized how important my thyroid issue was. It was important enough that I had to go to the trouble of finding a good specialist and sticking with her. Important enough that I had to be consistent in taking my medicine every morning, making and keeping doctor's appointments, and keeping my prescription filled. It also means taking care of my body in other ways not directly related to the thyroid, like eating healthy foods and exercising. Overall, consistency in good self-care is the key to living with this disease.

My body gave me unexplained and persistent postpartum depression. Taking care of myself, seeking the best doctors I could find, and following their advice for medications eventually got me to what I believe to be a permanent postpartum delight. My joy and my spontaneity returned. Soon I was dating again and found an awesome husband who totally accepted both my son and me. (He thinks he found me, but we women know how that works!)

6

Finding God in the Midst of Pain

The Spiritual Side of Postpartum Depression

Then God blessed Noah and his sons, saying to them, "Be fruitful and increase in number and fill the earth." (Genesis 9:1, NIV)

God instructed first Adam and Eve and then Noah to be fruitful and multiply. He has yet to rescind that order! So why would a blessing by him—bringing a beautiful child into the world—be followed by misery and sadness in millions of women throughout the world? (Postpartum depression is reported in all cultures, not just the United States.) Does the Bible address this issue? Can the Bible shed any help or instruction in preventing or overcoming postpartum depression?

These are important questions, and we'll do our best to address them below. But a more basic question comes from many of our patients. They ask, "Is the Bible, a book written thousands of years ago in a vastly different society, even relevant to my life in the twenty-first century?" We, as Christians first and physicians second, do believe the Bible is relevant in the lives of all generations and in every human society. We like this mnemonic device that defines what the Bible is for us:

Basic
Instruction
Before
Leaving
Earth

Because we believe the Bible is supremely relevant, we'll take a story from the Old Testament to illustrate how God helped someone who experienced depression.

A Depressed Prophet

Chapters 18 and 19 of the book of 1 Kings recall the literal mountaintop experience of Elijah, one of God's most faithful prophets. At the top of Mount Carmel, Elijah challenged 450 prophets of the false deity Baal to call their god to set fire to a bull prepared for sacrifice. The prophets jumped, screamed, danced, and yelled most of the day, but not surprisingly, they were unsuccessful at eliciting any response. When they gave up, Elijah had all the people who had gathered to watch this spectacle pour jars of water over the bull and the wood prepared for the sacrifice. He wanted to make the contest even more challenging! Elijah called on the Lord, who immediately sent a blaze of fire straight from heaven. It disintegrated the bull, the wood, and all the water! The people, gasping in amazement, bowed down and praised the Lord. They also rounded up the prophets of Baal and slaughtered all 450 of them. In those days, when they had a contest, they didn't fool around—there was no rematch for the loser.

But after this stunning defeat of 450 men, Elijah almost immediately fled from one woman—Queen Jezebel. This is hard even for psychiatrists like us to understand. Did Elijah grow up with a really abusive mother who taught him to panic at any woman's wrath? The Bible doesn't say why this rather strange turn of events happened, just how.

Jezebel, an avid worshiper of Baal, was incensed that Elijah had won the contest and killed the false prophets. She vowed to have Elijah killed immediately. So rather than celebrate the Lord's victory, Elijah found himself fleeing for his life. The next day we find Elijah sitting under a tree praying for God to let him die. His words are telling: "'I have had enough, LORD,' he said. 'Take my life, for I am no better than my ancestors who have already died'" (19:4). Despondent and discouraged, he was convinced that he alone in the whole country loved the Lord—and that his faithful service was about to be rewarded with execution. His whole adult life had been spent in zealous service for the Lord, yet the people were stubborn in their idol worship and he felt all his work had been in vain. He was ready to give up.

It is interesting to see how God chose to cure Elijah's bout of suicidal depression on this occasion. His first action was to cause Elijah to sleep. His second action was to send an angel to feed Elijah. They didn't have liquid vitamins back then, so they must have fed him bananas or something to get tryptophan into his system, maybe mixed with a pomegranate or two and a little bit of "angel food cake."

We are joking, of course. God may have used tryptophan and all that, but God is God and could use whatever he wanted to cure Elijah—or you—from "the pits." God may have used brain amines, or he may simply have encouraged Elijah with the kind act of feeding him. Only God knows.

Knowing modern-day psychiatry research, both of these first steps are extremely helpful. When people come to Dallas from around the world to be treated by us, we give them proper nutrition and do our very best to be sure they get a good night's sleep every night, even using nonaddictive sleeping pills if necessary. When you sleep, serotonin actually rebuilds in your brain, restoring more joy in the morning.

God used an angel to give Elijah nutrients and a good night's sleep. At that point, Elijah was finally ready to receive encouraging therapy from the words of the angel. Elijah had become paranoid—he felt he was the only man left on earth who was still serving God, undergoing persecution, and refusing to worship Baal. But then the Lord appeared to Elijah in a "gentle whisper" (19:12). He gave Elijah a little reality check and told him there were actually seven thousand others who were serving him and had not bowed their knees to Baal. Elijah was not alone, by far.

So what does this story mean to our discussion of postpartum depression?

It's clear that Elijah's depression was aggravated by circumstances, stress, negative thinking, lack of rest, and probably out-of-kilter brain amines. God didn't cause it, but it happened in this fallen world we live in.

Postpartum depression was never in God's plan. In fact, Psalm 127:3 says, "Children are a gift from the LORD; they are a reward from him." But in our world full of sinfulness and sickness, some things have become twisted. Our brains and bodies don't always work the way they should, and medical and psychological issues result.

We don't always know why this happens. But we do know some things about how God responds.

First, we can be encouraged by God's tender care for Elijah. He didn't dismiss Elijah's feelings or tell him to get back to work; he cared for him physically, emotionally, and spiritually. He will do the same for us. First Peter 5:7 directs us, "Give all your worries and cares to God, for he cares about you."

Second, we can be renewed by what God says is true about us.

When we believe lies, like Elijah did, we often feel unworthy, isolated, and paranoid. But when we remember the truth—that God has created us in his image, that he loves us as we are, and that he extends grace to us—our sense of reality is recalibrated. After all, this is a God who refers to us as "dearly loved children" (Ephesians 5:1, NIV).

Third, we can be assured that when we're depressed, God doesn't dismiss us as somehow less spiritual. If Elijah—lauded throughout Scripture as the most significant prophet after Moses, and so close to God that God took him directly to heaven rather than having him suffer death—could experience depression, anyone can. Depression's causes can include spiritual factors, but depression doesn't signify particular sin or distance from God.

Finally, we can be reminded that just like Elijah, we aren't self-sufficient. In Proverbs 3 we read over and over how important it is to realize we don't know all the answers. We must seek wisdom and new insights about ourselves and about life from God and God's Word. Solomon writes, "Don't lose sight of common sense and discernment. Hang on to them, for they will refresh your soul. . . . They keep you safe on your way, and your feet will not stumble. You can go to bed without fear; you will lie down and sleep soundly" (verses 21-24). When we're depressed, we need to be open to hearing from God and from others who love us.

The authors of this book always encourage patients to address spiritual factors as they undergo therapy. Confessing sin and not trying to hide from God can be healing. So can reframing our view of God, if it has been distorted by our own experiences. Understanding who he made us to be and how much he loves us is critical to spiritual health.

In the rest of the chapter we'll look at specific situations—

spiritual guilt, judgment from other Christians, and an abusive past—that can contribute to the spiritual factors involved in postpartum depression.

Dealing with Spiritual Guilt

Depression during or after pregnancy is extremely difficult to talk about with your mate, family, or close friends. Many times they try to help you feel better by reminding you of all the things you have to be joyful and thankful for, such as your baby's health, your physical health, your supportive family, and your blessings from God. Deep inside you already know this and have thought about it a hundred times, and you feel awful because you are blessed but still depressed.

You may feel even worse because you think your ingratitude is sinful. In all likelihood, your depression probably does not involve any sin at all—just hormone shifts, stress, lack of sleep from feeding the baby, anemia, etc.—none of which are your fault. You can be deeply spiritual and totally grateful for all the Lord has done for you and still feel suicidal or even go psychotic when you have a chemical imbalance, as you can see from all of our case studies.

We mentioned earlier that the best way for fellow believers to respond to you when you're depressed is to mourn with you. If those around you don't do that, remember that God himself is coming alongside you—not to chastise you for your attitude, but to help ease the load. Psalm 68:19 says, "Praise the Lord; praise God our savior! For each day he carries us in his arms." And Jesus offered similar encouragement and support: "Come to me, all of you who are weary and carry heavy burdens, and I will give you rest" (Matthew 11:28). Please don't feel guilty because of your depression, and please don't hide from God because you're ashamed. Rather, run to him! He will comfort you.

Dealing with Spiritual Judgment

It's an unfortunate reality that even in the twenty-first century, women still encounter unfair treatment—sometimes from family members, employers, physicians, or even their own church or fellow believers! As psychiatrists and a psychiatric nurse, the three of us have treated hundreds of cases of postpartum depression that were caused primarily by the anger and bitterness that built up when a woman experienced the judgment and unexpected hypocrisy of other Christians. In this section we'll talk about how this sense of marginalization can contribute to postpartum depression.

Many women feel like second-class citizens within the church. Certainly over the generations women were often told—directly and indirectly—that they were not as significant as men and had far fewer choices. Some women have been discouraged from careers at which they could excel, from ministry through which they could bless others, from education that would enrich their lives, or even from expressing their opinions. This is inevitably discouraging.

In addition, we have observed a significant double standard in the way some Christians treat women who have been involved in sexual sin. For example, in some Christian colleges and Bible schools throughout the United States, if a female student gets pregnant, she bears full responsibility for the situation. She may be expelled, but the man may not be disciplined whatsoever or else will get a minimal "hand slap."

I (Dr. Meier) treated a sweet college cheerleader at one of our nation's largest universities who was date-raped three times, twice with a drug in her Coca-Cola, by college males she was not even on dates with—just friends of friends. She had suicidal postpartum depression for two straight years after getting her second abortion at the urging of her parents and Christian friends. Only God could help any reasonable woman not to get depressed under unfair rejection like that.

By contrast, consider the famous passage in John 8. When a crowd of men of all ages, holding rocks in their hands, brought to Jesus a woman they had caught in adultery, they asked Jesus if she should be killed as the law of Moses dictated. Jesus wisely answered the men, "Let the one who has never sinned throw the first stone" (verse 7). One by one, these men walked away. The first to leave were the oldest men. While the Bible doesn't tell us why, I like to imagine that they were more humble than the younger men and more willing to admit that they had also sinned in their lives. Eventually the younger males also left, rocks still in hand. Jesus then turned to the woman and asked, "Woman, where are they? Has no one condemned you? . . . Then neither do I condemn you. . . . Go now and leave your life of sin" (John 8:10-11, NIV).

Too often Christians are overly critical of women. But Jesus extended grace and forgiveness when others gave only judgment. The authors of this book want to follow his example. We feel a special love for these women, as Jesus did.

Far from considering women second-class citizens, Jesus honored them. In fact, he honored women so much that some of the last people at his side when he died and the first humans at the tomb when he arose were Mary Magdalene and "the other Mary"—probably Jesus' mother. Matthew 28 says that even before Jesus came and spoke to them, an angel from God was at the tomb to address them, instructing them to tell the other disciples that Jesus had arisen and would meet them all in Galilee.

Throughout the Old and New Testaments, God talks over and over again about the importance of loving, respecting, and caring for widows and orphans. One of the strongest statements comes in Deuteronomy, where the Levites read the law to the Israelites: "Cursed is the man who withholds justice from the alien, the fatherless or the widow (27:19, NIV). Divorced women qualify as "widows" too, in our opinion—as do many married women who are in a sense "psychological widows" because they have been emotionally abandoned by their husbands, whether the husbands live with them or not.

In Psalm 68, God refers to himself as "father to the fatherless, defender of widows" (verse 5, NIV). Verse 6 says he takes the lonely and places them into families. He wants you, no matter who you are, to be fathered and mothered and brothered and sistered.

So be encouraged. No matter how marginalized or judged you may feel by other humans, know that in God's view you are valuable, loved, cherished, and cared for.

Dealing with the Spiritual Ramifications of Childhood Abuse

Childhood abuse can affect every aspect of your life, from your self-image to your marriage, your parenting, and particularly your view of God.

Whenever people say they are angry at God, it often means they are angry at their fathers. When we were kids learning to say our good-night prayers, research shows that we were thinking, *Dear heavenly version of my earthly father.*

If your father was abusive, you likely spent a great deal of time trying to convince yourself that he was not really as bad as he truly was. We tend to put parents on a pedestal because we crave their approval so badly. But if they were abusive in any way, we have a lot of anger, and we have to explain to our confused brains what all that anger is doing floating around in our unconscious. So we look around for the sweet mom or someone else who won't reject us, and we convince ourselves that person is the "bad guy."

We displace our anger to whoever won't reject us. It is not fair, but it is extremely common. And more often than not, we blame our heavenly Father for whatever we are angry at our earthly fathers for and are afraid to admit it. I encourage you to work through your anger toward your parents or whoever abused you. The spiritual benefits are great. When our patients talk out their repressed anger toward Dad or Mom, their relationship with their heavenly Father seems to become intimate quite quickly.

A young child who is repeatedly abused thinks to herself, *I am getting abused because I am such a bad little girl. I am trash. I deserve to be abused. My dad (or abuser) hates me and he knows me best, so I hate me too. I am disgusting.* The abused child has false guilt that is extremely difficult to overcome.

Childhood abuse is never your fault. Never, ever! Ephesians 4:26-27 teaches us that getting angry is not a sin. But hanging on to the anger past midnight—letting the sun go down on your wrath—is a sin. And it gives Satan a foothold in your life that may lead, among other things, to repressed anger and then to depression. Instead of stuffing anger, go ahead and get angry. Verbalize it. Then forgive (whether or not the person repents), protect yourself from future harm from that person, turn vengeance over to God, and let God take the night shift. Let it go.

Maggie: Dealing with childhood abuse

Maggie got pregnant on her honeymoon. From that day forward her husband, Connor, had to tread lightly around her to see if it was safe to be near her. He never knew if he would eat dinner or be wearing it. Maggie stopped her antidepressant when she learned she was pregnant, so it was nine months of mood swings and irritability.

After twenty-five hours of labor, her daughter, who weighed 10 pounds, 4 ounces, was born by C-section. Maggie's first thoughts were, *Put her back! What do I know about taking care of a baby?* She and her husband had moved recently, leaving behind their support system of family and friends. Even though the house was filled with boxes that needed to be unpacked, Maggie wandered aimlessly from room to room.

She felt fat and unattractive after gaining sixty-five pounds during pregnancy, and her main source of support and affirmation ended when she quit her job as a hair stylist.

Maggie's mother had died of cancer when Maggie was only four. Her last memory before her mother died was of her cat jumping on her mother's head, pulling off her mother's wig, and exposing her bald head. The image terrified Maggie. Soon afterward, trying to escape from an abusive father resulted in transferring from foster home to foster home.

As an adult she struggled with depression, and self-medicated with alcohol. She used men as a meal ticket, not really connecting emotionally until she met a good friend at work. That friend helped Maggie look at her anger in relationship to her past. She also introduced Maggie to the man who won her heart.

Although Maggie became a Christian through her friendship, she stayed angry at God for allowing her past abuse and lonely childhood. Now as she held her newborn, memories of childhood flooded her mind, and she felt inadequate to be a mother. She began having trouble sleeping, and she had no energy to care for her baby. The anxiety made her feel restless and unable to eat or concentrate.

It was time to get help and restart her medication, so she was admitted to the Meier Clinics day program. In Maggie's case, her postpartum depression was not due primarily to any genetic predisposition or even to major hormone shifts. She did have symptoms of a serotonin depletion—waking up in the middle of every night, sad and painful thinking, death wishes, lack of motivation, worsening of concentration and memory, increased perfectionism, and irritability. But we determined that the real problem was not genetic, but repressed anger because of her abusive past. Maggie was counseled to face her anger toward her father and God.

Digging up Maggie's childhood and getting her in touch with buried emotions and root problems led us straight to her father. She had displaced anger toward God, toward her husband, Conner, toward herself to the extreme, and now toward the newborn baby. The unconscious sin of bitterness in all these forms was causing her postpartum depression.

Becoming aware of this and grieving and forgiving all of the above resulted in the cleansing of Maggie's soul. It also brought relief from her depression and even from panic attacks. That's because anxiety is a fear of finding out the truth about our own thoughts, feelings, and motives. These things can be difficult to face. But in Maggie's case, when the truth was discovered and dealt with appropriately, the anxiety disappeared without the need for medications. Maggie's spiritual and mental healing was a process and took several weeks. She grieved her past, grew in intimacy with God, and gained confidence about being a new mother.

Conner loves us! The dinner is always on his plate now, and never on his face.

Finding Joy

If you find that your joy in life is being stolen due to spiritual factors, here are a few additional thoughts to help you develop a stronger connection with God:

1. Pray to improve intimacy with the real heavenly Father, not the imagined one.
2. Meditate daily on Scripture, especially on passages about the true nature of God and his desire to have a relationship

with you. Try reading Psalm 68, Psalm 103, Psalm 139 (the very best in our opinion), John 3, John 10, Romans 8, or Romans 12.

3. Realize that Jesus promised an easy yoke and a light burden (see Matthew 11:30). Living a life in relationship with God is not supposed to be hard! Get wise counsel from friends, teachers, pastors, and professional counselors as to how you can use your particular talents to carry out the easy tasks and light burdens that Jesus has chosen for you. (Read the Beatitudes in Matthew 5 to help you get started.)

We want to end this chapter with an additional case study. This one, about a narcissistic patient, may be harder to relate to in some ways. But we include it because it shows God's amazing power to transform lives. Sometimes, when we get our spiritual lives in order, everything else falls into place. Don't get us wrong—Julia still needed medication to control the physical factors contributing to her depression, and counseling to deal with the emotional factors. But coming face-to-face with a God who wanted the best for her was the first step that changed everything. We hope this story encourages you as you think about what God wants to do in your own life.

Julia: Transformed by Jesus

I (Dr. Meier) met Julia a month after she had given birth to her first child, a daughter. Julia was a narcissist first class, with borderline personality disorder on top of that. She had almost no conscience. She acted as though the world revolved around her. Having a baby definitely sent her into a humbling tailspin—and she had no intention of ever being humbled, thank you! She became suicidal and even bordered on psychosis in brief waves, toying with the idea of killing her baby by smothering it and making it look like SIDS.

She had a great husband. Sean was a good leader everywhere but at home. He was totally dominated by Julia, as he had been by his mother all his life prior to marriage.

Julia was carrying on one affair after another, seeking pleasure wherever she could. She had a well-paying job in a sales environment where she could travel with whomever she was interested in at the time. She had sex, power, money, freedom, and prestige at work for being a top salesperson, but she was still always on the verge of being suicidal and could never figure out why. She was lonely. No one knew the real her, not even Sean, who never even suspected her double life.

Having the baby, especially a girl who began immediately to remind her of her miserable self, really upset the applecart. Julia had to miss work for six weeks or so. She had all the normal hormone shifts, but mostly she was furious all the time because she resented every time she needed to change a diaper, feed the baby, check the baby when she cried, and any other minor disruption in her life.

Julia became suicidal, so she came to our day program. She had no interest in its Christian orientation; she came simply because her ob-gyn and her pediatrician both told her it was the best place to get rapid care. She came basically expecting to run our day program while she was there, as she felt entitled to do.

Like nearly all of our narcissistic patients, she immediately griped about our strict rules about showing up to all classes and group therapy sessions on time. She also pitted staff against staff. She called me Paul the first time she met me, instead of the usual "Hi, Dr. Meier. Nice to meet you." She was flirtatious, even when suicidally depressed. She used the staff bathroom rather than walk down the hall to the bathroom for the general public, and became miffed when we asked her not to. She told me (untruthfully) that the nurses had said bad things about me, and she told the nurses (untruthfully) that I had said bad things about them. Fortunately our staff is close knit and loving, like a family, and we have worked together delightfully for many years.

We confronted Julia and told her she would have to shape up or be expelled. She was so insulted she almost left. But I asked to have a little chat with her.

"Julia, isn't it right that you have been depressed your entire life, basically?"

"Well, yes, Paul."

"And isn't it true that for the past month since your daughter came you have been both homicidal and suicidal by your own admission?"

"Well, yes, Paul."

"Your psychological testing showed you to have not only suicidal depression, but also narcissistic and borderline personality disorders, and we explained that to you as soon as the results came in, correct?"

"Well, yes, Paul."

"Julia, I am going to really surprise you right now by asking you to do the most selfish thing you could ever possibly do."

"Really, Paul?" she exclaimed, excited to hear some new sins to replace the ones she was getting bored of.

"Yes," I replied matter-of-factly. "I would like you to consider totally dedicating your life to God and to serving others, while falling deeply in love with the real you at the same time."

"That doesn't sound like very much fun, Paul."

"But Julia, listen to my reasoning. The only truly happy and fulfilled people on planet Earth, according to all the psychiatry research on millions of people throughout the world, are people who take the time to deeply love and be loved. Happy people take responsibility for their own needs instead of manipulating others to do everything for them. Happy people are humble, godly, loving people who put the needs of others even before their own, but not in a masochistic sense. They have friends who know all their faults but love them anyway.

"Your life has been miserable and still is. You have tried to enjoy life and give it meaning through sex, power, money, prestige, and deceit. You live a double life. And even at home you are selfish and bossy and resent having to give of yourself in mothering just like your mother resented having you. Do you really want to be your mother? Or do you want to totally give your life to developing a relationship with God so he can lovingly help you learn how the happy people live and think and behave?

"Doing this is actually the most selfish thing you could ever do, because it is absolutely the best thing you could do for yourself. Believe me, Julia, the most painful experience anyone should fear in life is dying all alone, with no one at your bedside who will actually miss you when you are gone. And that is where you are headed."

I have given this same speech to hundreds of borderline patients in my career. And a majority of the time it works, as it did this time. Julia wept openly, feeling deep remorse. She felt exposed but loved at the same time. She grieved over the effect she had allowed her mother to have on her. Then she asked to pray with me, right on the spot, to ask God to forgive her for all the people she had hurt. She asked him to become her friend and help her become more like him. She wanted to try out this new life of loving and being loved instead of manipulating, lying, using, abusing, and experiencing utter loneliness and despair.

Don't get me wrong. Julia did not change from being Julia to being Jesus overnight. The Bible teaches us that when we give God our lives, we are in the process of "becoming" new creations—it doesn't happen all at once (see 2 Corinthians 3:18). But she was headed in the right direction. When we pointed out selfish things she was doing in the day program, now she had insight into them and learned how each of them was actually self-destructive. She wanted to quit doing them.

Julia grew tremendously in the day program, and then in outpatient counseling once a week for about a year thereafter. It has now been about sixteen years since we treated her in the day program, and I continue to see her every three months to give her the medications she needs for some genetic problems, like ADD and a little OCD. I saw her a few days ago with her happy teenage daughter, who was bragging about her mom buying her first car on her sixteenth birthday.

"Lots of changes in your life since you came here when she was a baby, Julia, right?"

"Oh yes, Dr. Meier," she said. "And I have been very happy ever since I asked God to come into my life right here in your office."

By the grace of God, people can change!

7

Confronting the Worst-Case Scenario

Postpartum Psychosis

The rarest and most serious form of postpartum depression is postpartum psychosis, which involves dangerous delusions and often violent behavior. It occurs when the serotonin in a woman's brain becomes depleted and her dopamine levels are severely off. Although postpartum psychosis is rare, it is extremely serious and needs to be treated immediately with psychiatric medications to correct the chemical imbalances in the brain.

This is scary—no doubt about it. Many people have never observed a psychotic breakdown, and the idea of it happening to them or their spouse is terrifying. We encourage you to read this chapter even though it may make you feel uncomfortable. Keep in mind that the odds are it will not happen to you. (In fact, research says there are only one to two cases of postpartum psychosis per one thousand births.[1]) But if it does, you and your family need to know the signs to look for so you can get immediate help. And the good news is that postpartum psychosis is treatable. With the correct medications, nutrition, and therapy, a patient can often be restored to her normal self within several weeks.

There is nothing shameful about postpartum psychosis—or any postpartum depression, for that matter. It is a medical problem that can and should be treated by medical professionals. If you are concerned about yourself (or, dads, if you're concerned about your wife), please seek treatment right away.

We'll start the chapter with the story of Brittney, a young woman whose third pregnancy resulted in a dramatic case of postpartum psychosis.

Brittney: A frightening descent

"What are you doing?" Brad yelled as he awakened abruptly at 3 a.m., deflecting the butcher knife lunging at him. The knife tore into the side of his chest. He wrestled with the surprise intruder, only to be amazed that it was his dear, sweet wife.

"I will kill you, Satan!" Brittney screamed back, pulling her hand away from his grip to stab him again.

Brad was a foot taller than Brittney and outweighed her by eighty pounds, but it took all of his power to pin her down and prevent a second stab. They had had an intimate marriage for over a decade now, so Brad was totally stunned by this near-death experience.

"Brittney, I'm your husband, Brad," he cried out to her, panting from pinning her to the ground faceup. "Wake up! What's happening to you?"

"You are not Brad," she screamed back at the top of her lungs. "You are Satan, and I am an angel of God, sent here to slay you. I hear his voice right now commanding me to slay you, and he will give me the strength to do so."

By now, one-week-old Justin was screaming from his make-shift crib a few feet away. Their six-year-old son and three-year-old daughter had been awakened by all the havoc and were trying to help their sweet mother from being pinned down by Dad. But Brad managed to persuade them to back off because he was trying to help Mommy.

His pants hung over a nearby bedroom chair, so he quickly pulled the belt out of them and managed to tie Brittney's hands behind her back. Brittney and Brad were missionaries at an orphanage in Africa, so there was no 9-1-1 to call. Instead, Brad called their closest friends and associates, Ashley and Josh, who fortunately lived just a few houses away. The word *houses* is an overstatement. They were more like shacks. The four friends were living at poverty level to fulfill their dream of helping kids whose parents had died of AIDS. Just five days earlier, the kitchen floor at Brad and Brittney's house had even caved in, adding additional stress to Brittney, who had delivered her newborn son, Justin, eight days earlier.

Ashley and Josh, still dressed in pajamas and robes, arrived within four or five minutes. It seemed like an eternity to Brad, who continued to hold Brittney down to protect her and their family, while trying to make sense out of the whole bizarre incident. Brittney kept answering the voices she thought she heard and looking around to see where they were coming from.

Living in a remote area in Africa, their choices for help in such a bizarre situation were few. The four of them had read numerous counseling books and self-help books by me (Dr. Meier) as part of their training, so they called the number for the Meier Clinics on the back of one of the books. They told the phone counselor that it was a life-and-death emergency and that they needed to speak to me right away—from Africa. The phone counselor transferred the call to me directly, and I talked to Ashley.

"The care in that remote area will probably be quite

primitive," I told Ashley, nearly in tears myself when I heard what had happened. I had heard stories like this one scores of times in my career—some after it was too late. But true stories like this one always break my heart. "I want to treat Brittney myself," I continued. "If you can get her under relative control and get her here to my Dallas day program, then we can almost for sure get her back to normal in about three weeks. Don't worry about the cost if you can get her a flight here. Your mission board is good about helping its missionaries, and we will give a discount to cover the rest."

"I am positive the mission board will do all it can to get her to you, Dr. Meier. But she is a wild woman right now, so how can we possibly get her on a plane?"

"Well," I replied, "it is highly unlikely that there will be any of the really good new antipsychotic medications there where you live. So as soon as you and I finish going over these instructions, the three of you need to take her directly to the nearest safe mental hospital, if there is one, and ask them to put her on Haldol, an old medicine that they will almost certainly have."

"There isn't any hospital anywhere near here where she could be locked up or strapped down," Ashley protested. "And there are no doctors for miles, either."

"Okay," I said, thinking quickly. "Let's go to plan B. Go to the nearest pharmacy and tell them you need about forty 5-milligram tablets of Haldol. If they won't give these to you, have them call me, and I will do a phone prescription for them. Write down my mobile number and keep in touch with me, and I will tell you what doses to use, depending on Brittany's side effects. Go ahead and ask for some one-milligram tablets of Benztropine as well. We need to block the side effects of the Haldol, if there are any.

"Give her the best multivitamin you can get your hands on, and give her plenty of bananas and meats, especially turkey meat, vegetables of all kinds, and even peanuts.

"Be sure she swallows her medications every night, even if she has to open her mouth to prove to you that she is taking them. No natural products that can cure a psychosis have been discovered yet—only powerful medications can do that—so don't risk her missing any doses of the meds.

"You and Josh and Brad will have to take turns staying awake with her around the clock to be sure she does not have another violent episode. Don't be fooled by her previous sweet nature. She has had a postpartum psychotic breakdown with reality, and she has no idea of right and wrong right now. In fact, she believes from the bottom of her heart that killing all of you would be the right thing to do, in obedience to the 'voice of God' that she thinks she is hearing.

"She has gotten so depressed that not only is her serotonin—the happiness chemical in the brain—depleted, but her dopamine has also gotten out of whack. That causes her to lose touch with reality and to think she hears voices, which in turn causes her to believe paranoid delusions of persecution or grandiosity. The Haldol should quiet her down quite a bit either within an hour or within a day or two at most."

Ashley was now crying on the phone to me. "It's hard to see how a simple chemical imbalance could cause a sweet friend like Brittney to turn into a cold-blooded murderer, bent on killing her entire family."

I responded, "If any scientist injected you or me or anyone else with a chemical that would mess up our dopamine level, we would probably be thinking and doing very similar things. It's just as if your computer got short-circuited and could no longer process information correctly but kept trying to do so erroneously. Explain to the kids as soon as possible that Brittney does not know what she is saying or doing, or it will be even more traumatic for them than it already is. In fact, get them to go to a nearby room with the door open so you can see them but where they won't hear their mother."

Ashley complied with my wishes, and then came back to the phone. "Okay, Dr. Meier, I go to the pharmacy as soon as it opens and get the Haldol. Then what?"

"Have her take some of the Haldol, and as soon as she becomes improved enough to be cooperative, get tickets to Dallas for all of you. Surround her even in the airplane, with one adult always on either side of her. Follow her to the toilet and stand outside the door. When she gets to Dallas, we will have hotel rooms available for your two families a block or so away from my clinic. I will put her on modern, powerful medicines that will pull her back to reality and will help her postpartum depression at the same time. As she regains reality, we will also do seven hours a day of counseling with her to help her recover. She will be so shocked and feel falsely guilty when she finally realizes what she almost did to herself and the people she loves most."

Brittney's husband and friends did exactly as they were told, calling me once a day to give me an update. Three days later she was able to fly to Dallas with her entire family and Ashley's family too.

I did a thorough evaluation of Brittney when she arrived at my office in Dallas. I asked her questions to rule out every other diagnosis I could think of, and ran lab tests on her blood to be sure the delusions were not caused by hypothyroidism or some other physical disease, which they easily could have been. We did psychological testing and confirmed the diagnosis of postpartum psychosis.

After our assessment of Brittney, I started her on the best and latest dopamine medications available (called atypical antipsychotics). I knew that within a week or two on these, Brittney would no longer have delusions or hear voices. Her sanity would almost certainly be restored.

I also started her on the best antidepressant available, one that allowed serotonin and norepinephrine to accumulate to levels sufficient in order to cure her depression. The anti-depressant takes about five weeks to have a total effect, but I knew that if she stayed at the clinic three weeks, as anticipated, she would be not only sane again, but well on her way back to a fully joyful life with the likelihood of becoming even happier in the next two weeks.

I gave her strong sleeping pills not only to help her brain recover during sleep, but also to assure her husband and friends some sleep, since up to this point, they had had to take turns staying awake with her. Within a couple of days on the new meds, Brittney was well enough to participate in our group therapy sessions, and well enough not to need her family to stay awake with her any longer. By the seventh day, she was totally normal and dealing with the post-traumatic stress of realizing what she had almost done, including actually stabbing her hus-band once, and with the depression that triggered all this in the first place.

I asked Brittney all about her childhood, all her past relation-ships, and all her current relationships. She was about as normal as any human could be. She came from a healthy family and had an outstanding marriage. Her lifestyle was very stressful, however, living in such primitive conditions. She also had some obvious genetic predisposition to depressions, especially postpartum. Many of her female relatives had gone through similar experiences. In fact, after Brittney's first pregnancy six years earlier, she had gotten moderate postpartum depression but had pulled out of it in a month or two on her own. After her second pregnancy three years later, she had become suicidal and depressed. She was put on an antidepressant in Africa and it pulled her out of that depression in spite of being one of the older, less-efficient antidepressants. So each pregnancy resulted in a worse depression, the third leading to psychosis.

After a total recovery, Brad and Brittney decided, and I think correctly, that as awesome as their ministry had been to the orphans in Africa, it was just too much stress for Brittney to handle. Instead, they took a job in the Chicago headquarters for their mission board, where they continue to make a major contribution to world missions.

After Brittney's recovery, I encouraged her to stay on the antidepressant the rest of her life, just to be sure the depression never returns. I told her she could wean off the antipsychotic medicine gradually. Brad was nervous about this, so together we decided to leave her on it an extra six months, then to wean her off it gradually to see if any of the voices or delusions started to come back. They didn't.

Brad and Brittney continue to this day to see one of our psychiatrists at our Wheaton clinic (in a suburb of Chicago). They keep in touch with postcards and visited me just recently when they were in the Dallas area on business.

Brittney had her tubes tied so she would never get pregnant again. If she had wanted to have more babies, though, she could have, if guided by a competent psychiatrist, taking whatever meds would be safe and appropriate for her situation at the time. The correct medication would prevent future depressions or psychoses.

Watching for Symptoms

Postpartum psychosis affects about one out of a thousand women. In addition to the symptoms associated with postpartum depression, these women may also experience:

- feeling detached
- auditory hallucinations—voices talking to them that are usually derogatory or violent (e.g., "Kill your baby.")
- hallucinations, which may be visual, olfactory (smell), or tactile (touch)
- delusions—thoughts based in unreality (e.g., "My baby is the Antichrist.")
- bizarre behavior
- elated manic mood
- strong urges to kill themselves, the infant, or others

Postpartum psychosis usually develops abruptly, sometimes in as little as forty-eight to seventy-two hours after giving birth. This condition is a medical emergency requiring immediate hospitalization of the mother so she can receive treatment and the child can be protected.

Five common symptoms often occur a day or more before the psychotic breakdown, and they all start with the letter A. Watch for these in anyone that you suspect may be on the verge of a psychotic breakdown (*nervous breakdown* in the old terminology). Because it's difficult if not impossible to identify these symptoms in yourself, I address this section to husbands and others close to the postpartum woman.

Affective disorder. "Affect" means "mood." Before a psychotic breakdown, the person usually develops what is known as flat affect, or a blank stare. However, on rare occasions, the person could exhibit inappropriate emotions, such as laughter at sad moments or tears during a joke. Of course, my (Dr. Meier's) jokes are so bad that they do bring tears to people's eyes, so I cannot use that as a diagnostic test.

Ambivalence disorder. All humans get irritated from time to time, but before a break, the moods swing much more dramatically. The slightest thing may trigger emotional outbursts of disproportionate rage. One client came to my office on the verge of a break with reality, and she was nice to me one minute, then throwing a vase at me a minute later for no reason at all.

Associative disorder. The conversation of a woman on the brink of a break will not make as much sense as it normally would. She will have loose associations, meaning that the topics will wander back and forth to different topics that are only loosely associated with each other, if at all. She may ask you about your new purse, and then discuss the weather before you even have a chance to answer her. She will also have tangential thinking, meaning that her conversation may wander off onto unrelated tangents. She may even exhibit thought blocking when, in the middle of a conversation, she forgets what she was taking about. We all do this once in a while, but a psychotic or borderline psychotic person will do this to the extreme.

Anhedonia disorder. "Anhedonia" means she loses her ability to laugh or have fun. If she watches a funny movie with you, she will stare at the screen and not laugh. She may go into a prolonged state of sadness and withdrawal. Remember that nearly all depressed people have this symptom too, as well as very normal people who are going through a normal grief reaction for a short period of time.

Autistic disorder. People who exhibit this symptom become similar to someone with childhood autism in the sense that they become so woven into themselves that they may not even hear others who stand near them and call their names. They are "spaced out" in a world of their own.

A postpartum mother may exhibit two or three of these five A's for a day or two, and then suddenly take the plunge down the volcanic crater into a full-blown psychosis, leading to all sorts of pain and havoc in her life and the lives of those around her. Delusions or hallucinations occur only after a break. The delusions nearly always make the person feel important. She might think she is Jesus or Mother Teresa, or simply herself with supernatural powers and omniscience. The delusions can be grandiose, such as believing that the TV commentator is talking to her through sign language during the newscast. Or the delusions can be persecutory, such as thinking that the FBI is following her wherever she goes, hidden video cameras are everywhere, or her phone is bugged by the CIA.

Most people who become psychotic do not have the foggiest idea they are becoming psychotic. They strongly believe their own delusions.

Many years ago, for example, I (Dr. Meier) had a patient who came into our psychiatry unit completely delusional and hearing imaginary voices. He was an airline pilot of a major airline. At that time I had a pastor who believed he could cure anything just using the Bible, and that psych meds were unnecessary.

So I challenged him to come and persuade my psychotic airline pilot to give up his delusions, all of which contradicted biblical principles even though this pilot was a committed Christian. After ninety minutes of the pastor showing this pilot how his delusions and voices contradicted the Bible, the pilot waved his head slowly back and forth, scratched his chin, and said sincerely to my pastor, "And to think that all these years I thought the Bible was true. You have proven to me that it can't be." In his psychotic state, he was willing to give up his belief in the Bible rather than his own delusions.

By the way, that pastor resigned as pastor, went back to grad school, and became a Christian therapist. He now runs his own successful clinic in Virginia and devotes a lot of time to educating and training missionaries and helping the poor around the world. He also remains my close friend.

Hallucinations can be visual (thinking they see an angel), olfactory (sensing smells that do not exist), or tactile (thinking people are touching them when they are not), but this last category is very rare unless the person is withdrawing from addictions to drugs or alcohol. Psychotic hallucinations are nearly always audible voices, usually saying derogatory things.

If a person is religious, she will usually have delusions and hallucinations that coincide with that religion, such as a Christian hearing voices she thinks are demons. But I know these voices are not demons because every time I give a psychotic patient a dopamine medicine, like Abilify or Risperdal, the voices go away. So it could only be demons if all demons are allergic to Risperdal and flee from its presence! I don't mean to make light of this or imply that a spirit world does not exist. But this reaction does mean that these voices, if they come, are a chemical reaction only, and are easily corrected by replacing the right chemical in the brain.

Nearly all psychotic people also become more paranoid. Some people are paranoid all their lives, sometimes genetically and sometimes from abusive childhoods. Paranoid people are:

- Self-righteous—they are always right and you are wrong in every argument.
- Condescending—they look down on you as though you were less important.
- Critical—criticizing you for things that are relatively insignificant.
- Controlling—they have trouble delegating and have to be in control.
- Projecting, or ascribing evil motives to others as a method of self-defense. So if the paranoid person has a lust problem, he accuses his wife of running around on him. If a paranoid woman is angry, she sees anger in your face when it is not even there.
- Hostile. If a sweet little newborn puppy was owned by an abusive sociopath who kicked it across the room all the time, the puppy would become so angry that it would become a paranoid dog, thinking all humans were out to get it. If a kind human walked in the room and reached down to pet that dog after a year of abuse, the dog would almost certainly bite the hand of the kind person.

There are basically three ways a person could become paranoid:

- Grow up in a very abusive home where enough anger accumulates to make her paranoid.
- Inherit paranoia, in which case she would probably but not necessarily be paranoid all her life.
- Have a temporary chemical imbalance in the brain affecting dopamine, due to postpartum depression, some other depression, hypothyroidism, parkinsonism, a brain tumor, excessive alcohol abuse or abuse of a host of other drugs, steroid use, or anything else that messes up the

brain chemistry—even a diet that does not have enough phenylalanine or vitamin B_6 in it.

Getting Treatment

What's particularly troubling about women with postpartum psychiatric problems is their reluctance to come forward. The media's over-sensationalization of rare cases like Andrea Yates, a Texas woman who killed her five children after a recurrence of postpartum psychosis, have women terrified.

As psychiatrists and a nurse, we get so angry when cases like this hit the news and we hear people self-righteously yelling, "Any mother who does something like that should be fried in the electric chair." Perhaps a mother who would do these things out of sin and selfishness should, but people don't realize how postpartum depression can result in chemical imbalances that render the mother totally out of control of herself and with no clue about reality.

Women have an unspoken fear of being deemed "crazy." This is compounded by the horrifying notion that the state could seize custody of your children if you dare tell anyone the frightening thoughts torturing your mind. It's actually the other way around; it's the people who continue to refuse help who end up losing their children. The reality of the Andrea Yates case is that her tragedy could have been prevented by correct attention and treatment.

Again, we include all of this information not to scare you but to inform you. If you suspect that you or your spouse is on the verge of a break, please make your safety and that of your baby your first priority. Don't waste time feeling embarrassed or ashamed. Instead, get to a psychiatric facility immediately where you or she can get medication, nutrition, and counseling until back to normal.

Rest assured that after this is over and the cloud lifts off of you, you will be able to smile again! You will be able to bond with your baby and resume normal family life. Have the courage to seek treatment. It can only get better from there.

Not Just for Women

When Dads Become Depressed

This book is primarily written for women, as you are the ones who primarily deal with postpartum depression—for obvious reasons! Women are the ones whose bodies change through the forty or so weeks of pregnancy. You alone experience the hormonal surges after delivery, and if you're breast-feeding, you bear most of the burden for feeding the baby in those mind-numbing early weeks. While many husbands are active participants in labor and delivery, there's no changing the fundamental fact that it's your body undergoing the contractions—and your body recovering afterward, whether from a vaginal delivery or a cesarean section.

We don't deny or downplay any of this, of course. As we've said throughout the book, there are reasons—physical, mental, and spiritual—why many women undergo a degree of postpartum depression. Yet at the same time, studies show that many new dads experience some form of postpartum depression as well. Why? Well, men may not have the hormonal changes, but they certainly experience the life changes that come with a newborn. Just as with new moms, new dads can experience sleep deprivation, poor nutrition, additional stress, and additional responsibility. And a new dad also often sees his relationship with his wife changing and sometimes struggles to figure out his new role.

It's important for us to address this in our book because postpartum depression—whether in the wife, the husband, or both—affects the whole family. It's a family problem. We want to see families where every member together experiences postpartum delight. So in this chapter we'll often talk directly to dads.

Men and Depression

More women get treated for depression than men, but this doesn't mean that more women suffer from depression. Rather, it would seem that more women than men are willing to admit that they are depressed and get help.

An interesting observation, from our experience and research, is that single women have only about 2 percent more depression than married women of equal educational and socioeconomic status. In contrast, single men have significantly more depression and major physical illnesses than married men of equal socioeconomic status and education.

Men apparently need women much more than women need men. These findings were a little humbling for Drs. Clements and Meier, but Nurse Lynne Johnson tried not to rub it in too much—just a little bit. Men may be the stronger "vessel" physically, but most women are stronger emotionally. Maybe that is why the Bible says that a man who finds a wife finds a good thing and obtains favor from the Lord (see Proverbs 18:22).

Other gender differences include how the depression is expressed. When a new father is depressed, more verbal—and even occasionally physical—fights occur between him and his wife. By contrast, moms who are depressed are less likely to fight and more likely to withdraw and stay relatively nonfunctional.

Oftentimes the subtle sad feelings that many men have when becoming a father will press a dad to start overworking, perhaps begin drinking, or even have an affair. These are all ways of avoiding the truth, instead of being a man and facing his emotional pains, fears, insecurities, and ambivalent feelings.

Male postpartum depression can result in conflicts, hostility, alienation, and even divorce, which is very unfortunate because the depressed person is not really himself. It is regrettable that a temporary chemical depletion of serotonin could end a marriage or even a life.

Causes of Male Postpartum Depression

Again, men don't have the blood loss, the hormone changes, and the other physical contributors to postpartum depression that women do, but they often experience blues and depression after the pregnancy as well. Some men even experience weight gain and have strange cravings during the pregnancy, whether depressed or not. I (Dr. Meier) am so empathetic that I had as much morning sickness as my wife did during each pregnancy. Even before marriage, in medical school, when I saw people vomit I would empathetically vomit too. When I had to let patients know that their test results just revealed that they had cancer, I would cry so much they had to comfort me!

Just as mothers have anxieties about being new moms, fathers share the same anxieties about being new dads. They often worry about a host of things related to the pregnancy, including family finances, their wives' health, and new responsibilities. New dads can also have sleeping and eating problems, especially poor nutrition in this junk-food world.

Having a baby causes a lot of commotion, with many highs as well as lows. For men, it can lead to more worry as well as more pleasure, probably more than anything else that happens in their lives.

One large adjustment for both the mom and the dad when that first baby arrives is coming to grips with the legitimate fact that many of their needs that were readily met before may go unmet now that the baby is the number one priority of their lives. Although women have a hard time trying to readjust to all the pressures of a new baby, men, it seems, have the hardest time coming to grips with their needs not being responded to.

Men seem to have more trouble letting go of their freedoms, including their routines and perhaps even their self-imposed duties. Remember that not liking to give up some of their old ways and old freedoms doesn't mean they don't love their babies. Some ambivalent feelings are natural.

Having a newborn involves some legitimate losses. Unresolved grief about any of the losses results in stuffed anger, serotonin depletion in the brain, and depression. If you find yourself going down that slippery slope into depression and despair, let us warn you that it can get more painful than any broken bone or broken relationship you have ever experienced. When you find yourself getting more irritable (a common symptom in men), or waking up at 3 a.m. every morning and taking a half hour or more to get back to sleep, feeling fatigued all day, withdrawing from others, and experiencing lingering sadness, go get help.

The most sure cure for depression for men, just as for women, involves first of all a thorough evaluation by a professional therapist or psychiatrist to determine the type and degree of depression. If it is purely genetic, medicine will cure it within five to ten weeks. But even if it is primarily circumstantial (for example, there's a genetic predisposition, but adding a baby tips it over the top), meds may still be necessary if the depression is severe enough that you miss work or even feel like dying.

Getting professional counseling or meeting with your pastor can help you address any spiritual causes that need to be dealt with. Resolving emotional conflicts, which may involve current events that trigger emotional responses because of childhood experiences, takes the insight of a professional counselor.

When you get help for depression, you help yourself prevent it for the rest of your life, and you learn how to protect your family from it the rest of their lives as well. What is that worth? For various educational helps to prevent or cure depression, go to http://www.meierclinics.org.

Connor: Circumstantial depression

In chapter 6, we talked about Maggie, who became pregnant on her honeymoon and dealt with mood swings for her entire pregnancy. Her husband, Connor, became so wary of her moods that he would poke his head in the door to see if it was safe to come in. Maggie had a huge amount of anger toward her abusive father that she had never dealt with, and she took it all out on Connor.

Connor, who was a wonderful man from a functional family, found himself the scapegoat of a life of displaced anger buried within Maggie. The men in her life had let her down and hurt her. She loved Connor but would only let him get partway toward emotional intimacy. And after the birth of their daughter, things were even worse due to her postpartum depression.

Connor began to become affected as well. He started waking up in the middle of the night and having trouble falling back asleep. Soon he became more forgetful and less productive at work. He became so fatigued keeping the family functioning that he felt like throwing up his hands and giving up. He loved Maggie and wanted to help relieve her depression, but now he felt like they were both drowning in the ocean, begging for someone to throw them a life preserver.

When they decided it was time to get help for Maggie and restart the antidepressant medication that had helped her so much in the past, Connor came with her. Since Maggie was having some suicidal ideation and was more depressed than Connor, she was admitted to the Meier Clinics day program. She was counseled to face her anger at her father and God. It was a process that took several weeks. She grieved her past and gained confidence about being a new mother.

But she also received marital therapy with Connor, and together they learned new communication skills to help each other. Connor saw a therapist of his own and recovered without medication, just receiving insight-oriented individual therapy, marital therapy, and nutritional supplements. Through these things he received the tools he needed to deal with his own depression and to work through his wife's issues as well.

A Dad's Adjustments to Parenthood

We've talked quite a bit about adjustments women need to make when newborns join the family. Let's take a minute to look at some specific ways fathers need to adjust to their new roles. Struggles in adapting can sometimes be a cause of depression.

Father as protector

Fathers generally want to protect their families in multiple ways. They want to protect their families from physical harm, and also from going without necessities because of insufficient finances. New dads in particular worry about whether they will be able to earn enough money for adequate care of that child as she grows up—"How are we going to afford raising her, then college, and then a wedding?" Lots of dads obsess about these things. And finances often change during and after a pregnancy, depending on the wife's health and plans for working after the baby is born. Some men have to take extra jobs and work overtime when their wives become pregnant or when the child is born, which is an extra stress. During this period there's often a fear of the unknown.

Many new dads also report that they start feeling very left out during pregnancy and even after the birth of the child. The future dad sees his wife having the baby showers and people oohing and aahing over her expanded belly, but he may feel ignored or unimportant. Also, men just don't seem to have that physical connection to an unborn child that the mother does. The man is not the one feeling the baby kick and experiencing changes to his body. Men tend to start feeling very excluded early in the pregnancy, and that can get worse as the pregnancy progresses and even after the child is born. This "left-out" feeling can make pregnancy and fatherhood frustrating.

A lot of this can happen just because of the traditional social forces that influence men in our current but ever-changing culture. Husbands are often taught to be "the man" and that they are not supposed to have feelings like loneliness, fear of rejection, sadness, or even deep love. So when men are experiencing lots of anxiety, worry, and maybe even jealousy, they are usually reluctant to tell their wives. They may even feel as if their issues are trivial compared to their wives being sick all day long or struggling with the physical effects of childbirth. Loving husbands have a great deal of empathetic compassion for their wives. Their natural inclination to love and protect their wives—which they may define as not expressing negative emotions to her—will usually win out.

But being the family protector does not mean the new dad is immune to many of the problems and difficult adjustments his wife must face. We urge men not to dismiss their concerns throughout that nine-month transition in their lives from husband to father. We encourage men to be honest with their wives about their emotions, admitting their fears and concerns. They also need to be good listeners, eager to hear their wives' feelings, concerns, hopes, and fears. We urge both of you to balance any fears with positive hopes and dreams.

Finding adequate support

Women usually have quite a bit of support from relatives, friends, classes, and even regular ob-gyn visits. But there's very little support for men. Even most childbirth classes are more geared toward mothers and offer little for fathers emotionally—about what they'll be going through before, during, and after the baby is born.

But your role is just as important as your wife's in this transition. God designed it that way. You need each other. And your baby needs both of you.

In our Western culture, men have typically lost an emotional intimacy that men used to have with other men. Women often have one or more close friends with whom they can share everything, whether they're happy, sad, or angry. But today's typical young dad looks to his wife to get his understanding and his comforts met. This is awesome, but it's often not enough. Ideally, he should also have a male support group.

We strongly recommend that every man and woman have a long-term prayer partner of the same sex. It should be someone you can trust not to gossip, someone you can confess to and who will confess his or her sins right back to you. Preferably this person will also be a parent who can relate to your postpartum adjustment.

Since the only people on earth who have true happiness and meaning in life are people who have emotional intimacy with one or more other humans, it is important to have this kind of support not only to prevent depression, but also to recover if a depression does come.

Being an active parent

After the baby is born, men often think of themselves as the "backup parent" or "second-degree parent." A lot of fathers have that perception because they feel somewhat inept at parenting—and they may be to some extent because they have never done it before. While many women have previous experience babysitting or caring for young children in a church or other setting, the average man may not.

It is important that men do not surrender their position as fathers, and that they do stay active and involved, whether that means accompanying their wives to some prenatal appointments or learning how to bathe the new baby. Dads may feel a little bit awkward at first, but they need to stay connected to both their children and their wives.

We encourage dads to go with the flow and enjoy their new role, like they would a promotion at work, rather than giving in to their fears about being a father by hanging back and letting their wives do everything. If they do abdicate their promotion to fatherhood, they're going to feel more like a babysitter than a parent. Parenting is meant to be a partnership between husband and wife.

Some men also have a strong impulse to be at home and care for their wives and babies instead of going back to work. In some cases, due to a variety of circumstances, the husband may be best suited to be the stay-at-home parent with the wife perhaps better suited to work full-time. This is a matter for discussion and prayer. God certainly created women, on the whole, to have a natural nurturing instinct, but men can be excellent caregivers as well. The Bible has far fewer hard-and-fast rules for God's children than many people impose on us.

Travis and Monica: Father as protector

Monica was a thirty-year-old stay-at-home mom. Her husband, Travis, was thirty-two years old and a very successful salesman. He was fun loving and laid back, but was determined to be a fantastic dad and husband. Monica was a lifelong perfectionist, partially as a result of the conditional acceptance she felt growing up, and partially because of a genetic trait that ran in her family.

Monica was the oldest child in her family and the only daughter. Her mom was stricter and had more unrealistic expectations of Monica than she did of her other three children. Monica was always a compliant child, craving her mother's acceptance.

After the birth of her second child, Amy, Monica began to have crying spells and irritability, and she gradually withdrew from her family and friends. Sleep became a problem as she lay in bed, her mind racing. When anyone becomes depressed, he or she becomes more angry and irritable just from the serotonin depletion. The irritability seems like it must have some external cause, but it usually doesn't.

Monica's subconscious reasoning became something like, *Well, I am feeling more sad and angry and really irritable, so Travis must be doing things that are irritating me. What can they possibly be?* He became the scapegoat of her biochemical irritability.

Travis rolled with it all at first, but eventually he began to feel rejected, looked down on, crushed—almost destroyed by the sudden rejection from the woman who had loved him for so many years. Travis also became depressed. He had to adjust to having a baby like every other father, but he also had financial worries. He was helping Monica by changing diapers, but he was also trying to be her counselor and failing at it.

Monica's depressive symptoms were familiar to her because she had experienced them with the birth of her first child four years before and had come to our clinic. This time, the changes were gradual over several weeks. She was afraid to tell anyone, because Andrea Yates was in the news and Monica did not want the postpartum depression label. But she knew she was sinking fast.

Travis became alarmed when she said she was so miserable she wanted to die. Travis was depressed too but did not have death wishes. Travis finally persuaded Monica to come see me (Dr. Meier), but this time they would come together, for both of their depressions. Monica relented and they came for back-to-back one-hour evaluation sessions. After getting a thorough history of Monica's current symptoms, I told her what she did not want to hear: she needed medication and would have to stop nursing her baby after only eight months. Many women consider this a reasonable time to stop anyway, but being a perfectionist, Monica felt she needed to breast-feed at least another year.

The next day she woke up with a debilitating panic attack. Panic attacks come when the truth is threatening to emerge into conscious awareness, and the brain is fighting with all its strength to keep the truth buried. We do this in an attempt to protect ourselves from having to admit weakness, ignorance, or the degree of our rage. In our session I had showed Monica how her anger was just a biochemical phenomenon, and that Travis was her convenient scapegoat. When she could not think of anything he was doing that warranted her hostility, it dawned on her that I might be correct. But it's hard for anybody to grasp that we could be so out of control of our own thinking processes and have so little clue into the truth.

The guilt over no longer being able to nurse her baby had consumed Monica to the point where she found it difficult even to look at her daughter. She felt she had lost the connection with her baby and no longer knew how to meet her needs. She feared her daughter would think she no longer loved her.

She confessed that what she really felt most guilty about was not wanting to be induced. As a perfectionist, she had a vision for how she wanted childbirth and parenting to be. It included things such as a natural childbirth with no inductions or interventions, delivering in her own home with only a midwife present, recovering without medications, especially psychiatric medications, breast-feeding for two or three years or even longer, and then homeschooling her children.

Some of these things can be wonderful in moderation. But birthing at home without a doctor is statistically threatening to the life of the newborn child, since complications often arise.

As a result of Monica's perfectionistic pride, her brain fooled her into thinking that she was "trusting God," when in reality she was not using the brain God gave her with the instructions that "in a multitude of counselors there is safety" (Proverbs 24:6, NKJV). So when she refused her doctor's advice to be induced at term, her baby was born two weeks late and weighed more than ten pounds, threatening the life of the baby as well as her own life. Amy had to be delivered with forceps. She would have certainly died without the forceps delivery by a trained obstetrician, and Monica almost certainly would have as well.

There was neurological damage to Amy's right side, which required physical therapy. Monica couldn't come right out and ask her doctor, "Was it my fault?" because he might confirm what she already believed: the neurological damage to her baby occurred because of Amy's size and could have been prevented by Monica's being induced earlier. But Travis did ask, privately, and was told the truth by the doctor.

Travis had argued with Monica about every one of her decisions to "lean on her own understanding" when Proverbs 3:5-6 clearly warns us not to. But he had reluctantly given in on most of them, and now he also felt guilty for not protecting Amy more from the prideful decisions of her mother.

Divorce is not uncommon when things like this happen, or even when a baby is born with a genetic disorder that could not have been prevented. But Travis knew that in spite of her pride, Monica had many wonderful assets. He was determined to love her unconditionally, no matter what. He was careful not to accuse her. He decided to let God do the convicting, and then to help her forgive herself when the truth did dawn on her.

But now the truth was so close to coming to Monica's conscious awareness that her anxiety was almost debilitating. Medication began to help. Friends and family helped her by taking her to her doctor's appointments, sharing their stories of postpartum depression over lunch, or calling in the middle of a hard day and just listening.

Travis helped her make a list of all the positive aspects of not nursing, including sleeping through the night, wearing a normal bra, the kids having a happier mom—and the list got longer and longer. And with therapy in addition to antidepressant meds, Monica eventually could look at the truth and ask God's forgiveness for her pride.

Monica eventually forgave herself, and then had to forgive those who had persuaded her to make these decisions that ended up permanently harming her baby, Amy. Thankful for the support of her family and friends, she has fully recovered from her depression and enjoys the time spent with her husband and children.

Travis also received outpatient counseling twice a week for several months to help him forgive Monica, forgive himself for not being stronger, and forgive those who had misled Monica in the first place. He realized more than ever that every father's role includes being a protector for his own family.

9

A Dad's Role

Supporting Your Wife through the Postpartum Period

One of the best supports a woman can have during the postpartum period is a loving, involved husband. Dads, in this chapter we'll address a few practical things you can do to help your wives thrive after a newborn joins the family.

Offering Support and Encouragement

Realize that it's hard for a new mom, depressed or delighted, to get everything done now that she has added responsibilities with the baby. Together, discuss and agree on how to reshuffle the household chores.

Also, consider taking over the middle-of-the-night routines sometimes so that she can get a full night's sleep and get her sleep rhythm restored. This can make a big difference, because a lot of serotonin—the happy chemical—is restored in the brain while we sleep and dream.

Be as patient as you possibly can. Give your wife examples of the things she's doing well—even little things, such as noticing her smiling at the baby and telling her she is a good mom. If you tell a woman she is beautiful, she may not believe you.

But if you tell her she has beautiful eyes (or whatever specific honest compliment you can think of) and how much you love to look in her eyes to see the love in them, she will believe you and be encouraged.

As a new dad, you can restore a positive outlook when your wife doesn't feel like a good mom. You can say you understand that she may be feeling that way and that you're sorry for those feelings, but then you can praise specific mothering acts that are loving and kind and correct.

Probably the greatest thing you can do during this period is just be patient and tolerant. And of course, the Bible tells us that the greatest of all these things is love (see 1 Corinthians 13)—so just love her. The authors of this book celebrate every new dad who is reading this sentence right now, because we want both you and your wife to experience postpartum delight.

Watching for Depression

Since 80 percent of women have some degree of postpartum depression, husbands would be wise to observe their wives daily for signs of depression and catch it early if it occurs. Even if she insists she's fine, you may still notice things that she may be denying, like sluggishness, fatigue, frequent bursting into tears, increased irritability, withdrawal from friends (or even from you), and insomnia even when she has time to sleep.

Wives can think they are feeling normal after childbirth, in spite of not experiencing joy and elation. So look for fatigue and sadness, but also hopelessness, depression, appetite changes, poor concentration and confusion, memory loss, overanxiety for the baby, uncontrollable crying, a blank stare, irritability, and unrealistically negative statements. These negative statements often include such things as "I'm not a good mother; I'm inadequate."

Other signals include excessive guilt feelings, lack of interest in the baby, fear of harming the baby or herself, fear of losing control and going crazy, exaggerated highs or lows, lack of interest in hugs, and intrusive, repetitive thoughts. New moms with underlying perfectionism, either from their genetics or because of the way they were raised, often become more obsessive-compulsive from the stress and hormone changes of pregnancy.

If her depression worsens, you may notice intense anxiety with panic attacks that often include rapid breathing, rapid pulse, hot or cold flashes, a sense of doom, chest pains, dizziness, shaking, and a feeling of wanting to run away. A fear of dying or of "going crazy" are common during a full-blown panic attack. These fears are unfounded, but occasionally the fear of going crazy is insight into the fact that she is losing touch with reality.

Dads, you play an important role because oftentimes you are the first ones to realize there is something wrong. You are the ones usually required to intervene in an emergency. You're also in the best position to monitor how the moms are doing on a daily basis, and you will likely assume more responsibility for the well-being of your families.

Be as educated as you possibly can on postpartum depression. It is important that you understand the things that you need to look for, when to seek further help (especially if the depression gets into psychosis), and how to get plugged in to a doctor who is trained in postpartum depression.

If Depression Comes

If your wife is going through postpartum depression, it's important not to take it personally. It has everything to do with circumstances, hormones, lack of sleep, and possibly genetics—but little to do with you.

Women suffering from postpartum depression can be confused about how they feel at what is supposed to be one of the happiest times of their lives. It might be the equivalent of winning the Super Bowl and being voted the MVP, but then feeling too sad to go to the after party. This ushers in a huge black cloud of guilt, which worsens the already-present despair.

The depression is not her fault, and it certainly is not your fault. A lot of fathers get frustrated because men have the "fix it" mentality. Husbands can help, and they can support, but they're not going to be able to fix it, and there are no quick fix solutions. Get the support needed, dads, so you can be there for her. Sometimes the father gets so overwhelmed with what he needs to do for the family that he doesn't offer the support his wife needs to get through this time.

Be supportive, but don't allow your wife to verbally abuse you, which she may be tempted to do just because of the irritability that comes with depression. She may say hurtful things, but if you do not feel that you deserved being snapped at, you can explain that to her calmly.

A postpartum depression, psychotic or not, can last anywhere from a few weeks to many years. But in most cases we can get even the psychotic type most of the way toward recovery within three weeks of day program care. Medical knowledge doubles every five years, and most of the wonder medications we use today to bring about rapid recovery did not even exist five years ago.

Dads, it's wise for you to attend as many doctors' appointments with your wife as you possibly can. This demonstrates to your wife how much you care about her, and it also gives you a chance to ask the doctor questions and to hear his or her instructions.

If your wife is undergoing treatment, it is important to

continue even if she starts to feel better, because discontinuing treatment can be dangerous and the relapse can be even harder.

Something else that the dad may have to look at is how to rebuild the family. Of course, building trust between the married couple is really important, especially if the postpartum depression became severe. Trust—even the trust to leave your child alone with your wife—can be built again over time. Follow the guidance of a trained psychiatrist, not only your own judgment.

Postpartum depression can be scary. But be encouraged. When your wife's brain chemicals return to normal, things will change again and you will both be happier and wiser than ever before.

10

Becoming a Family

Postpartum Changes in the Husband-Wife Relationship

A healthy marriage can be one of the most significant assets to postpartum delight. The unconditional love, steady support, and partnership of a committed spouse can be a rock in a time of significant change. Husbands and wives can encourage one another, and that support and encouragement can lessen the effects of postpartum depression. Loving grandparents can also be a tremendous support in a host of ways, including babysitting and giving Mom and Dad some breaks from child rearing.

But there's no doubt that the postpartum period can challenge even the strongest relationship. Moms typically are the first ones to experience a drop in relationship satisfaction, but eventually many dads do too. New moms often feel overwhelmed by their new responsibilities and may resent that their husbands don't help as much as they think a husband should. A typical new dad will tend to worry about how his relationship with his wife is going to change in every aspect.

Having that first baby is a profound transition in the lives of a couple. That's why we're taking a chapter to discuss communication and romance during that transition. How can couples keep these areas of their relationship strong? Healthy families have a positive environment. The most important thing parents can do for their newborn baby and any future children is to love each other well.

Do you remember the adjustments you made in your first year of marriage? As psychiatrists, we seldom hear someone tell us, "Wow, adjusting to marriage was a lot easier than I thought, and my mate turned out to be a lot more loving and awesome than I could have ever anticipated." Oh, it does happen once in a while, on rare occasions. But the rest of us tend to idealize what marriage will be like and have to adjust to some of the pains of reality.

Having your first child is the same thing all over again. Almost 100 percent of parents who do not yet have a child expect too much of themselves and that child when he or she comes.

Postpartum Challenges
Sex

Most new dads probably worry that their sexual relationship with their wives may change negatively after having a baby. The truth is that for most couples, lovemaking does decline in the early months of parenthood—in part because the wife may be physically uncomfortable with sex due to childbirth and hormone changes, and in part because of the exhaustion and new responsibilities that often accompany a new baby. And if either partner experiences depression, intimacy will likely decrease more because of pessimism and the desire to withdraw.

To prevent resentment, it is vital for the mom and dad to keep an open dialogue about their needs and how they feel about their sexual relationship. A lot of couples seem to have a hard time doing this because they are afraid of hurting their partner with their openness.

Some men have a difficult time adjusting to the changes in their wives' bodies after the birth of a baby, or maybe even during pregnancy. A pregnant woman or a postpartum woman who is breast-feeding are both awesome illustrations of love in action. A pregnant wife is gorgeous to a husband who has a mature perspective of the miracle of a new baby.

Some men and women, unfortunately, fall into the trap of what the advertising media says about how a woman's body should look, basically half starved. This can create all kinds of problems for men as well as their wives. These unrealistic expectations are probably part of the reason for the vast multibillion-dollar epidemic of cyber pornography. Porn is often used as a substitute for emotional or sexual intimacy and leads to depression and loneliness. A temporary high causes a long-term low.

So it's important that fathers free themselves not only from porn, but also from having ridiculous fantasies and expectations from the unfortunate commercialism of a woman's body. If he is wise, he will appreciate who his wife is as well as how she looks.

Most couples can enjoy physical intimacy almost until the delivery date, and again after the wife recovers from the delivery, which can take several weeks. But during that hiatus, it is important to still cuddle and enjoy each other not only emotionally but also physically. Our best advice for resuming a sexual relationship is to take it slow. Wives, recognize that your body may respond differently because of postpartum hormones and breast-feeding. You may find yourself needing lubricant even if you've never needed it before. Your breasts may leak milk at inopportune times. Be patient! Your body will get back to normal. In the meantime, try to be able to laugh together and be patient. Keep the focus on resuming connection between the two of you.

Husbands who buy into our culture's view of a physically ideal woman end up getting angry at their wives for being normal, and holding in anger is the primary cause of depression. The ignored or irrationally criticized wife will likely also become appropriately angry, which is fine unless she also holds on to it—in which case she will get depressed too.

As the apostle Paul taught us so correctly two thousand years ago, getting angry is normal and not a sin, but hanging on to it past bedtime is unhealthy (see Ephesians 4:26). He was scientifically correct two millennia before serotonin was even discovered.

Romance

Remember that you are partners. As psychiatrists, we have seen male-dominated marriages where the husband is more like a dictator than a mate. And we have seen female-dominated marriages where the wife hands the husband a to-do list every morning, like she is the president of the corporation called "family" and the husband is relegated to a gofer and a handyman. When either of these happens, the marriage dies.

For romance to remain in any marriage, husband and wife need to remain equals. The words *should* and *shouldn't* are acceptable in teacher-pupil relationships, boss-employee relationships, and parent-child relationships, but never in a marriage. Whenever a husband or wife hears the other saying to them, "You should burp the baby this way" or "You shouldn't call me at work," or giving orders in other forms, it kills romance, because those are parent-child messages.

Instead, both husband and wife need to tell each other "I feel" messages. For example, "I feel sad and anxious when you come home late from work by two hours and don't call to let me know you are coming home late." Or, "I feel frustrated when you correct the way I'm holding the baby, because I feel like the babysitter instead of the parent." You're leaving your spouse with the decision about whether or not to change the behavior, but you're letting him or her know how his or her actions make you feel. This kind of humility will probably result in the spouse wanting to change to stay connected to you. But "should" and "shouldn't" messages almost certainly will be met with resistance, rebellion, and the death of romance.

Let's say the wife is more of a perfectionist than her husband, for example. So she makes a list of thirty things that she thinks need to be done to make the home "perfect." But instead of dictating to her hang-loose husband, she could show him her "wish list." After he looks it over, he may say, "I certainly don't want item number 38 on your list here, honey—changing our two-car garage into a one-car garage and a garden room! But the rest of these are fine with me, even though I don't think half of them are necessary. But if they are important to you, and we can afford them, these are up to you whenever you can hire someone to do them. And these eight items here I totally agree are necessary, especially in time for our baby to arrive, so I will help you all I can to do these ourselves."

Fostering romance takes time and effort. Work on your relationship. Think about it in your spare time. Share feelings, listen to feelings, keep going on dates, and think of small acts of kindness or service you can do for each other. Maybe it's bringing home a single rose with a love note, or making an effort to call during the day to say "I love you" and express appreciation. Have postpartum delight as a major goal.

What *not* to say when your wife has a baby, especially if she is struggling with depression:

- "Snap out of it." If she could snap out of it, she would. And this comment can actually create more anxiety, anger, and irritability for her, as well as false guilt and shame.
- "Think about the good things we have going for us and the depression will go away." It's true that thinking about the good things would be helpful, and might even contribute to the recovery. But postpartum depression is usually a complex disorder, involving much more than just a negative attitude.
- "Quit feeling sorry for yourself." You—the husband—will feel very sorry for yourself after she reacts to that condescending statement!
- "Can we have sex yet?" No comment!
- "How come your stomach is still protruding even though the baby is out of it?" It takes weeks or even a couple of months for the woman's body to readjust after delivery. Carry a watermelon around in your own stomach, Dad, and see how long it takes your stomach to unstretch!
- "I love you no matter how you look." You mean well, but this is telling her she looks ugly.
- "How come my dinner isn't ready yet?" You should be fixing it yourself for a while or purchasing healthy foods to bring home to her much of the time.
- "My mom did just fine when she had us, so why are you having such a tough time of it?" She is not your mother, thank the Lord! Her chemicals are different than your mother's, and that is probably what is making her more depressed than your mother may have become after her first baby.

Communication

Healthy communication is one of the building blocks of a marriage. If you can talk through things together, you can get through things together.

Moms and dads who hold in their feelings suffer more depression and more illnesses. So remember the biblical injunction to "speak the truth in love" over and over again (see Ephesians 4:15). Verbalize your emotions but always in a respectful, constructive way—not to get personal vengeance. Speaking the truth in love, even about anger, produces more intimacy, not less. Anything short of that produces animosity and division. You and your spouse are on the same team.

Also, verbalizing feelings tactfully will prevent you from acting out those same feelings physically or even with verbal abuse. By contrast, holding your anger in reduces serotonin and causes depression.

Following are some basic helps for honest communication:

1. Agree to listen to your spouse's feelings, even if you disagree with the appropriateness of those feelings.
2. Commit to being honest with yourself and your spouse, using discretion on what to share with whom.

   When I (Dr. Meier) started a national, live talk radio show in 1985, heard by about a million people a day, some of my friends thought I shouldn't do it because I am too honest. I speak whatever I am thinking first, then listen to what I already said to decide whether or not I should have said it! If I lusted after a jogger in my neighborhood on the way to work, I shared it on the radio at noon. (My wife never listens to my programs for that reason.) A few Christian stations kicked me off the air in their cities because of it, but I decided to be honest and let the chips fall wherever they fell. Most Christians appreciated it and felt more able to be honest themselves. But use your judgment about what is appropriate to share with your spouse and what is not.

3. Consider all the factors in any conflict. Is your spouse more irritable because of a recent loss? Do past experiences or abuse make him or her untrusting? Are hormonal changes a factor? Did you offend your spouse when you were being selfish or controlling?

4. During any confrontation, keep a secret second conversation going on with Jesus. Ask him for insight into the situation, love for the other person, and forgiveness for your own sins in the matter.

5. Don't make "you always . . ." or "you never . . ." statements. Keep the conversation focused on whatever current event most recently offended you.

6. If your spouse asks you to change something, don't say "I'll try." Since as humans we are all depraved, "I'll try" usually ends up meaning "I'll make a halfhearted effort but I won't quite succeed." Instead say "I will" or "I won't." It's more honest.

7. As we mentioned earlier, avoid "you should . . ." or "you shouldn't . . ." statements with your spouse. Let God speak those absolutes. Instead, tell your spouse how you feel about his or her actions. Giving orders sounds condescending and will make the person want to do the opposite. But most people will listen to your honest feelings and your love.

8. Always speak the truth in love. Yelling and being sarcastic won't change things for very long. Loving confrontation has a chance to.

9. Make your goal conflict resolution, not a "win" for yourself. When a conflict resolves, you, the other person, and God all win.

10. If your spouse is trying to confront you lovingly with the truth, consider him or her as an instrument of God. God uses other people to help us become more like his loving, honest nature. Proverbs 9 tells us to share the truth with wise people, and they will love us for being honest with them, even if we are correcting them (see verses 8-9). This is tough for many of us, but we can strive to be teachable.

Finding support

Both spouses need settings where they can share about their feelings and their family situations. The transition of becoming new parents can actually generate more distance between spouses, so it's really important that couples learn to rebalance their relationship.

Men in our society seem to be, overall, far inferior to women at building a support group. But all humans need that kind of support. We each need at least a couple of friends who know our secrets and love us just the way we are.

Seek out people like that. Some organizations have support groups and counseling, like Celebrate Recovery for personal growth and help overcoming various addictions, or MOPS (Mothers of Preschoolers) for support for moms of young children.

No marriage is perfect, because no person is perfect! As you go through the postpartum period, you'll find that accepting the fact that we all make mistakes will contribute toward postpartum delight. We urge new parents to remember that mistakes are just a normal part of being a spouse and becoming a parent. It's possible to learn from our mistakes and beat the blues. We want you to succeed at becoming a "delightful" mom and dad and a unified couple.

Erin and Tom: How good marital communication can save lives
Tom and Erin Franklin entered the Meier Clinics in Dallas,
Texas, the Monday after Thanksgiving. The couple's pastor had
urged Tom to bring Erin for an evaluation. Erin appeared very
nervous as she began telling her story to the day hospital staff.
In fact, she broke down crying after the first few sentences, so
Tom took over.

The couple had delivered their first baby six weeks earlier—
a healthy eight-pound baby boy named Austin. Tom and Erin,
both in their midthirties, had been trying several years for children. Needless to say they were both overjoyed when the news
came that Erin was finally pregnant. They both wished for a boy,
but their main concern was that the child would be healthy.
Both requests were fulfilled, as Austin was indeed healthy.

Tom and Erin were both devout Christians when they met in
college and married two years later. Both of them were reared in
Christian families, whom they continued to have great relationships with, and the extended families were very excited about
Austin's birth. The labor and delivery progressed smoothly,
and Tom and Erin left the hospital, headed for home with little
Austin in their arms, less than seventy-two hours after checking
in. Tom remembered feeling that day that God had perfectly
answered their prayers.

A week after arriving home, Erin noticed that she felt utterly
exhausted and irritable, sometimes to the point that she would
lie on her bed and cry during the day. The doctor assured Tom
that this was normal as most women are "emotionally spent"
after nine months of pregnancy and then delivery. His order
was more rest for Erin. Tom took over most of the housework to
give Erin a break. Erin also started pumping some breast milk
during the day in order for Tom to administer Austin's night
feedings, allowing her to sleep.

What *to* say to your wife after she has a baby

- "We're going to get through this together." Constantly remind her that you are there for her, and that nothing's going to change that. You still love her, and you're in this thing together.
- "What can I do for you?" Consider doing some simple things, like running a bath for her, or pampering her in a way that makes her feel secure and loved.
- "Maybe I don't understand exactly how you're feeling, but I'm sorry you feel that way."
- "I love you, and the baby will grow to love you very much too."
- "You're going to recover and feel like yourself again."

Two weeks later Erin felt even worse. The crying had now become daily. Erin dreaded the thought of just having to get up in the mornings. She felt overwhelmed and fearful. Erin started begging Tom to stay home with her instead of going to work and leaving her all alone. Tom, with his boss's permission, started working from home, but even then he couldn't concentrate on his work for continually worrying about Erin.

Tom's concern increased when Erin started making statements such as "I'm a horrible mother." Tom tried to console her, saying, "You're going to learn everything you need to know and be fine."

Most concerning to Tom was the fact that Erin seemed disinterested in spending time with Austin. She would feed and change him but then immediately hand him off to Tom or put him in his crib. Tom could see Erin going downhill, but the doctor again reassured him that Erin would be fine; she just needed some time to adjust to the demands of motherhood.

As Thanksgiving approached, Tom wondered if Erin could

pull herself together enough to handle the day with their families. Neither one of them had told their families what was happening with Erin; Tom didn't want to scare them.

Erin managed to dress up and put a smile on her face as they traveled to her parents' house Thanksgiving Day. Everything started off well until Erin joined a group of women conversing in the den. She shared with them that she had been very tired and sometimes wondered if she was really cut out to be a mother. Erin's mother, Susan, scolded her immediately, saying, "All of us prayed for years that you would get pregnant and have a healthy baby, which the Lord has finally given you. Austin was clearly an answer to prayer. How in the world can you question God?"

Tom's mother, Jane, then added fuel to the fire by telling a story about a young lady in her church who had recently had a baby with numerous mental and physical problems. Jane bragged about how resilient this young mother was and told how she brought that baby to church every Sunday, showing him off to people with as much pride as if he had been perfect. This could be an encouraging story in the proper setting, but in this setting, it just heaped more shame and false guilt on Erin.

Erin could feel herself becoming more and more anxious. She was afraid to consciously acknowledge her own rage toward her mom for being so condemning, toward Tom's mom for exacerbating the situation, and toward herself for not being perfect enough to please either mother. Her heart raced, her palms became sweaty, she started trembling, and she felt a wave of nausea deep in her belly. The room started spinning as Erin's mind started racing, thinking, *I have to get out of here or I will smother!* She jumped up and ran out of the house into the first safe spot she could find—her car.

Tom heard the commotion from the kitchen and ran into

the den searching for Erin. "What did you do to her?" Tom asked Susan.

"Nothing," Susan replied. "I was just trying to make her feel better by reminding her how Austin was an answered prayer from God and that some other people aren't so lucky."

Tom found Erin in the car, where she begged him to get Austin and take her home because she was too embarrassed to go back in. Reluctantly Tom followed her wishes. On the drive home he didn't know which emotion to feel. He felt sympathy for Erin and knew she hadn't been feeling well, but the other side of him could not understand her thinking process. She now had the beautiful baby boy that they had long dreamed of. Other areas of their life together were going well also. Why was his wife continuing to get worse instead of better like the doctor suggested she would? Was she just feeling sorry for herself? Was it that motherhood was overwhelming and she was being a baby about it? Or was there really something seriously wrong with her?

"Something's got to give, Erin," Tom told her. "You can't keep going on like this. What can I do to help you? I don't know what you're thinking. I don't know what you're feeling. And I don't know what I need to do from here."

Erin broke down, admitting that she didn't understand what was happening to her either. "I know God has blessed us with the son we have always prayed for," she said. "I know your mom was trying to make me feel better, but I felt so guilty as she talked about the mother with the brain-damaged baby.

"Please don't freak out on me if I tell you this, Tom, but I think you and Austin would be better off if I were not around. I know you could find another wife who would be the mother Austin needs. Two days ago when I was driving to town I thought seriously about turning the steering wheel and driving off of the bridge.

"What scares me most is that I've even had thoughts pop into my head about hurting Austin, though I know I'd never do it. When he cries, or when I'm upset, these thoughts come over me from out of nowhere. If I were dead you would not have to be dealing with all of this craziness right now.

"I feel like the most horrible person in the world for thinking this, but I can't stop these thoughts from happening. I also think about Andrea Yates, the lady in Houston who killed her five children, and worry if I could possibly lose it enough to do something like that. I haven't told you, but that's why I don't want to be at home by myself with Austin. If you're there and I go insane, you could stop me.

"I want this child as much as you do. I know deep in my heart how joyful I am and how much I love him, but I can't explain why I'm acting this way. I've read about other women who were like this after having a baby, so I know I'm not the only person in the world feeling this way.

"I also saw Marie Osmond tell Oprah Winfrey that she thought about driving off a bridge after the birth of one of her children. She got help and went public about it, even against her family's wishes. I know I need some help, but I don't know what to do either. The doctor keeps telling me I'll get better, but I can't take this much longer."

That night their pastor suggested that Erin had postpartum depression and that she needed to see a psychiatrist and maybe even be hospitalized. He recommended the Meier Clinics, because I (Dr. Meier) had been one of his professors in seminary.

Thanks to the open and honest and empathetic communication between Erin and Tom, Erin's postpartum depression was caught in the nick of time. In the day program, I found that her fear of going psychotic and possibly harming or even killing her baby and herself were insightful. She was nearly psychotic and was already getting somewhat paranoid. We put her on atypical antipsychotics, which worked like "ego glue" to pull her back to reality within a couple of days.

Through the combined help of that medicine, plus an antidepressant, BriteAge nutrients, and, equally importantly, insight-oriented therapy to work through a lifetime of conflicts with Mom and false guilt over unrealistic expectations, Erin recovered totally. I see her every three months now for a checkup, and we are gradually reducing her medications until she will not need anything but vitamins. She and Tom and Austin are all doing fantastically.

11

Postpartum Delight for the Whole Family

Helping Your Children with the Transition

As we've talked about, the postpartum period is a transition for the new mom and dad. And if you already have one or more children, it will be a transition for them as well.

This is not a book on child rearing, but rather a book on how to have a happy family during the times that a new addition unites with the existing family—a new miracle of birth or a new adoption. It's our desire to see whole families experiencing postpartum delight. In this chapter we hope to give you some tools to reach that outcome.

Developing Realistic Expectations
We talked earlier about expectant moms and dads needing to develop a realistic view of life with a newborn. This is important for children, too, who may have even less of an idea what a new baby will be like.

Be honest with your children. Tell them that a baby brings a lot of joy, fun, and laughter. It's an incredible miracle to add a new living, breathing human being to your family. But a baby also brings work and will change your family's schedule to some extent. Kids need to know that babies are totally helpless, sometimes cry, and need to eat frequently. You may need to explain to younger children that it will be several months before the baby will be able to play with them or even respond much.

Kids also need to have some idea of how you will be affected. They need to know that Mom may need to nap more and play less for a while, and that she'll be holding the baby a lot. Older children need to know if they'll be expected to take on extra responsibilities around the house.

We encourage you to include the existing children in the entire pregnancy, letting them feel the baby kicking in Mommy's tummy and asking them if they look forward to having a little brother or sister.

Talk about what your children were like as newborns. Help them understand that this early period passes relatively quickly. The baby will grow up just as they did, and before they know it, he or she will be smiling, laughing, and rolling over!

Once the baby is here, involve your older children as much as possible in what you're doing. Even small children can help fetch a clean diaper or a burp cloth, or entertain the baby for short periods.

Remember to praise your children for giving the baby a hug or helping Mom pick up the baby's clothes. Try to avoid praising your children with such general things as "You are beautiful" or "You are good." It is much better, and more believable to the children, if you praise them for specific good deeds they do, or specific aspects of their physical appearance.

But most of all, as you go through the postpartum period, reassure your children that the good will outweigh the bad. No matter how difficult the transition, you will weather it as a family. Nothing will change the love you have for each other.

Grandparent support

When a couple has their first baby, they especially need the support and advice of their experienced parents. Wise King Solomon said in Proverbs that a righteous person would leave an inheritance not only to his children, but also to his grandchildren (13:22). This may include a financial inheritance, but we are sure it goes beyond that. Grandparents also leave behind a spiritual and emotional legacy.

Grandparents play a vital role in child rearing. No parents are perfect, and even if they were, a growing child will have many needs that even perfect parents don't have the time or resources to fulfill. Grandparents can fill in the gaps. They set an example of love to their children and their grandchildren, and they can be wise advisers. They may also offer financial support if they're in a position to do so.

Grandparents can provide essential respite for exhausted new parents. They usually love to spend time with their grandchildren (within reason!) and will be willing to give you the occasional break you need.

Good grandparents will allow you to be in charge of your new baby and future children. They should respect your parenting style, be it stricter or more lenient than their own, as long as it is not abusive. You are the head of your nuclear family, and your parents need to respect that position. They need to give you the opportunity to learn from good choices as well as from mistakes, again within the boundary of safety for the newborn.

So embrace your parents as they embrace their new role as grandparents. Let them be an encouragement to you as you transition into a new phase of life. Respect the special role they will play in your child's life and know that when approached with love and respect, the grandparent-child relationship will be enriching for everyone involved.

A number of excellent books are available on the subject of bringing a new baby into the family. Ask your library or bookstore to recommend books that are appropriate for your children.

How Mom's or Dad's Postpartum Depression Affects the Family

The stresses of having a baby can result in postpartum depression not only in mothers, but also in dads and other children already in the home. Depression is almost infectious. It can spread to the whole family—Mom, Dad, kids, and even sometimes pets. No kidding!

I (Dr. Meier) know of a case of postpartum depression in a dog that had been potty trained for several years. But when the baby came home and he saw the stress in the eyes of Mom and Dad, and also realized he would get less attention with the baby here to compete with him, he deposited a rather large "token" of his appreciation under the crib daily for several days in a row until his owners put a stop to it. (They also showed Fido more attention so he would not feel left out.) Depression in pets may strike us as somewhat humorous and easy to cure. But the reality is that depression in moms or dads can affect others in the house and can even influence a child's emotional and behavioral development.

In fact, if a father suffers any prolonged depression, postpartum or not, the children are twice as likely to have multiple behavioral problems in the preschool years. Girls tend to handle the depression of their parents better than boys do for some reason, perhaps because they are more open and likely to express their feelings. Girls tend to be more influenced by a mom's postpartum depression, and boys by a dad's postpartum depression.[1]

Research has indicated that depressive episodes of the mother during the postpartum period were linked to poor cognitive test scores in their children.[2] This may improve as the family situation improves, but it can also have lasting effects on some children. Family problems can have a negative effect on social, behavioral, cognitive, and, to some extent, even physical development.

Depression compromises the ability of fathers and mothers to respond to their children and their needs, so emotional attachment of children to parents may be more difficult to achieve.

In a happy family, every member tends to find healthy roles within the family that are beneficial to each other. But in depressed families, these roles become more blurred. Often the child of a depressed mother or father is unwittingly robbed of childhood and has to assume a role as parent to the depressed parent, or even become the unofficial family counselor. Other times, when one parent is depressed, the other parent leans too heavily on a child of the opposite sex. This can result in life-long relational problems, although of course, people can overcome almost anything with the right kind of insight-oriented therapy and some hard work.

Postpartum depression is associated with special risk to the newborn baby as well, because it can disrupt the establishment of a secure bond between mother and infant. And this bond is, of course, the cocoon in which infant development takes place.

Children benefit from interaction with Mom, even if she is depressed. So if the depression is not as severe, or if suicidal thoughts are fleeting but not plans, and the mom promises not to act on them, then we prefer day program treatment or intensive outpatient treatment. Then the mom gets to go home and be with her children every night. Interactions with Dad are also comforting.

We encourage any mother with suicidal thoughts to consider this: A child whose parent committed suicide is more likely to also commit suicide when he or she goes through a tough time in the future. One percent of all teenagers in America lose a parent to suicide each year. Many of these deaths are from postpartum depression in moms and dads, and it's our aim to prevent some of these.

Why do we tell you all of this? If you're struggling with postpartum depression, it's certainly not our intention to make you feel worse by highlighting all of the potential effects on your children. It's not your fault, and it's nothing to be ashamed of! However, we want you to be informed. And we again want to emphasize the importance of getting prompt and thorough treatment so the depression is less severe and of shorter duration, because that will lessen the effects on your kids. Also, make your best effort to maintain connection and attachment with your children, even if you're struggling. That will reap benefits.

Never feel guilty about getting treatment, even if it means you're away from your family. The result of a healthy, happy mom is always worth the stress of some separation for treatment.

Children with Postpartum Depression

Our society, psychiatrists, and therapists have all tended to focus on the new mothers having postpartum depression, and appropriately so. Moms do have postpartum depression more than dads or kids because of all the hormone shifts, physical stress, lack of sleep, responsibilities, and fears of faulty mothering. But we are now looking out more for the children, too.

We are trying to focus on the effects of postpartum depression on the entire family system, sometimes even the extended family. We often do family therapy in our day programs along with individual and group therapy sessions.

What we want to emphasize here is that we don't just treat one person. We treat the entire family system, and we want to find out if there's any significant risk that may be going on for a child. We learned in psychiatry residency that when parents bring in a child for treatment who is having emotional problems, we often have to treat the parents until the child gets better.

This can often be embarrassing to the parents. In fact, I (Dr. Meier) remember a period in my own life when one of my daughters became depressed at age fourteen. Three things determine how our children turn out—genes, environment, and choices. I assumed that since I was such a "perfect" father, and my daughter "obviously" had perfect genes and environment, her depression must be entirely from poor choices she was making.

She went to see a counselor not affiliated with my clinics, of course, so the counselor would feel free to confront us if needed. I assumed that it would not be needed. To my surprise, after a few sessions her therapist asked if her mom and I would join her for a counseling session on Saturday morning that week, because he wanted to share with me some things I was doing to contribute to my daughter's depression.

I pretended to be humble and said I would be delighted to hear what he had to say, but as soon as I hung up the phone, I was quite upset. After all, I have written books on child rearing. I went to all my kids' activities, helped with car pools, listened to their feelings since birth, and felt I had actually done a lot of things exceptionally well. I thought to myself, *What will I tell the therapist when I come? If I deny contributing to her depression he will think I am defensive, and I certainly am not defensive* (or so I thought!). *But if I go along with what he says, I will be lying. So I have a dilemma. I guess I will just listen and play it by ear.*

On Saturday morning at about 4 a.m., I woke up from an intense dream. Jesus was in the dream, and all he said, three times in a row, was "Matthew chapter seven, verses three through five." No kidding.

I didn't want to wake up my wife, so I slipped into the study and got out my Bible, just in case it really was Jesus trying to teach me something. I have had what I call "God dreams" like this every few months throughout my life, ever since I started meditating on the Bible daily at age ten.

To my surprise, the passage was about being a hypocrite and seeing the faults in others while defensively overlooking the same but even greater faults in our own lives. It dawned on me at that moment that my daughter was similar to me in disposition, and we also both have ADHD. Because we have similar faults, I had picked on her more than on the other children—without being aware of it until that moment. I realized that my criticism of her was contributing to her depression, and I wept for a long while before going back to bed.

In the morning, I did not tell a soul about my dream, but I vowed to myself and to God that I would admit what I had learned, regardless of what the therapist also shared that I was doing wrong. At 9 a.m., my wife and I joined my daughter and her therapist for the family session, and a rather miraculous thing happened.

You must remember that there are about ten thousand verses in the Bible. The therapist pulled a Bible out of his drawer and turned it to—you guessed it—Matthew seven, verses three through five: the exact passage God had showed me the night before. Call it a coincidence if you like, but that would take much more faith than calling it what it was: God reinforcing that he had spoken to me in that dream, so I had better listen. As the therapist began reading, I immediately burst into tears—good tears, I believe. He stopped and asked me why I was crying. It was then that I told him about the dream I had had five hours earlier. My daughter was even impressed, especially when I gave her a big hug, apologized, and promised to work on that bad habit of mine that I did not even know that I had.

I am sharing this embarrassing story with you in the hope that it will help you not to be ashamed to find out what you yourself may be doing accidentally to contribute to the depression of your mate or one or more of your children.

One major thing parents can do to prevent depression in their children of all ages is to ask them how they feel emotionally. Don't be afraid to ask, "Are you angry at me right now, Johnny?" Anytime a child feels free enough to express anger toward a parent, respectfully but without condemnation, whether or not the parent agrees with the reaction, it helps prevent depression. Anytime a child verbalizes anger and is listened to, the anger dissipates to some extent, and it is less likely that he or she will act out that anger.

How do you tell if your child is suffering from depression? Some of the signs include: frequent sadness, loss of interest in activities, hopelessness, decreased energy, persistent boredom, increased irritability or anger, or changes in eating or sleeping patterns.

At the Meier Clinics, children and teens who are suffering from postpartum depression see our child psychiatrist, who will use intensive outpatient counseling as much as possible, without the children missing school (unless they are suicidal). Antidepressant medications are used if necessary. Antidepressant medications in children and teens have gotten a bad rap lately, but good psychiatrists will usually only prescribe medication if they feel that it is the best choice, and they will use the ones with the most safety studies, whether prescribing for adults or teens. In thirty-three years of giving a wide variety of medications to thousands of patients, I have had a few patients who had to quit because of allergic rashes, but no serious side effects yet. We also recommend vitamins, for reasons discussed in the nutrition chapter.

If anyone in the family is depressed postpartum, the best bet is to play it safe and see a professional Christian counselor. If the problem is severe, consider an adult or child psychiatrist. If it's minor, the best way to handle it is to encourage family members to express emotions, especially pent-up anger at God, others, or themselves. A shared burden is less of a burden. Unconditional love and nonjudgmental attitudes are a must. Remember Romans 8:1, that if we are in Christ Jesus, when we sin there is no condemnation. God loves us and wants us to learn from our sins and become more loving and joyful. We should do the same when our family members make mistakes.

A Family's Postpartum Delight

Bringing a child into this world can seem like a dangerous and scary thing to do, but it's also an incredible experience. To produce a living eternal soul with thirty trillion cells, and to make an eternal friend of that human you helped create—there is not much in life that is better than that. Your family can be a place of genuine love, kindness, and teamwork as you raise your children to go out into the world. Children become self-sufficient, but the bonds that tie you together will never dissipate.

Only two things will last forever—God and people—so invest your time and energy and money in those things that will last forever.

12

When Life Gets in the Way

Emotional and Circumstantial Barriers to Postpartum Delight

As psychiatrists and a psychiatric nurse, we have seen enough to give us a very realistic view of life and human behavior. So our view of postpartum delight is also grounded in reality, not unattainable ideals.

An idealistic view would be a husband and wife who are in a rock-solid relationship and deeply love each other, have supportive families and friends, are part of a grace-oriented, loving church, have a fantastic income—enough to afford a maid twice a week and a cook every night—own a potty-trained Yorkie, live in a safe neighborhood, maintain an intimate relationship with God, have a pregnancy with no complications, go through an easy delivery, gain a healthy baby who sleeps early and often, experience easy breast-feeding, have the opportunity for the wife to be a stay-at-home mom if she chooses, and experience only insignificant stressors and hormone shifts after the delivery.

There, we got it out of the way. Now for the other 99 percent of us! Most of us have at least one if not multiple significant issues that we must address during the postpartum period. These may be circumstantial, emotional, or spiritual in nature. But dealing with real life does not mean that postpartum delight is unattainable.

In this last chapter of the book we will address some of the most common "life issues" and will give suggestions for how you can move through these difficulties to experience postpartum delight.

Good Grief

Loss. It's a simple four-letter word that is one of our constant companions throughout life. The postpartum period is not exempt. Some women may experience the terrible loss of a child through stillbirth. Others may have a child with a birth defect and may grieve the loss of the "typical" child they expected. Still others may have a sense of loss because their birth experience was traumatic or not what they expected. And many experience some sense of loss remembering the independence they had before the baby was born.

You can't avoid loss or shrug it off. Loss is not the enemy; not facing its existence is. As change takes place, you must experience the grief that accompanies it. Grief is a natural response to the loss of any significant object, person, circumstance, or ideal. Healthy grief may include intense sorrow, depression, restlessness, disorganization, irritability, loneliness, anger, denial, fantasy, pain, and more. Unhealthy grief may include acting as if the event never occurred, stuffing emotions inside, keeping the event alive (which prevents closure), exaggerating or ignoring some aspects of the event, placing the grief or blame on someone else, or not grasping the totality of grief. Symptoms of a healthy grief come and go and may last three years or longer, but they generally run a consistent course and eventually lead to restoration of mental and physical well-being. There are ten stages of healthy grief:

1. Shock. This involves being temporarily anesthetized against the overwhelming experience you're facing.
2. Emotional release. This happens about the time it begins to dawn on you how dreadful the loss is. This is the time when you must give vent to your feelings.
3. Depression, loneliness, sense of isolation. Often you feel that there is no help or hope available.
4. Physical symptoms and distress. Grief takes on a physical form such as weight loss, pain, and sleep problems.
5. Panic. You may feel that something is wrong with you, but in reality panic is the result of concentrating on nothing but the loss.
6. Guilt. You may begin to second-guess your actions, including blaming yourself or questioning if you could have done something to avoid the loss.
7. Hostility. You begin to express anger, whether at the person or thing that was lost, at God, at yourself, or at the world in general.
8. Return to normal activities. Once this happens, you may feel like you are just "going through the motions."
9. Overcoming grief. We cannot predict at what point this will happen; it may come quickly or take a long time.
10. Readjusting to reality. Although you will never be exactly your old self again after experiencing a great loss, you will be a stronger, deeper individual and better able to help those around you because of your experience.

If you are experiencing difficulty in recovering from a loss, please seek professional help from a pastor or trained counselor such as those at the Meier Clinics.

Living a Delight-Filled, Anxiety-Free Life

When terrorists struck the twin towers of New York City on September 11, 2001, I (Dr. Meier) was stunned like the rest of the world. I stayed up late watching the news and woke up the next morning with so much grief and fear that my muscles were very tense and I could barely breathe comfortably. I've never had a panic attack, but being a psychiatrist, I've seen hundreds of them and I knew I was on the brink of one.

If you struggle with anxiety or panic attacks, the postpartum period may be especially difficult. This is in part because of the normal hormone fluctuations you experience, and in part because of the new and potentially overwhelming responsibilities that come with a new baby.

How can you limit the effects of anxiety?

- Develop your relationship with God. People who have a strong faith in God's ultimate sovereignty and love fare better than those who see this life as "all there is."
- Admit your fears, anger, sadness, and other emotions.
- Develop a strong support group (close family, healthy church life, intimate friends who know all your secrets and love you anyway). James 5:16 says that if we confess our faults to one another, we will be healed. People come from around the world to attend our day programs, where they confess their faults and unresolved grief to a small group of other clients and therapists. While some individuals take longer to heal than others, this kind of openness generally brings profound healing in a short time.
- If you have a history of abuse, seek counseling to deal with it. People who grew up in open, loving, healthy families fare better than people with various kinds of emotional, physical, or sexual abuse in their childhood.

- Combat any tendency toward perfectionism. Any changes, better or worse, tend to upset extreme perfectionists who like a safe routine they can count on to have no surprises. Some are not born perfectionists but become excessively so because of childhood abuses. The more out-of-control you feel growing up (alcoholic parent, abusive parent, controlling parent, etc.), the more controlling and perfectionistic you naturally become to compensate for your fears. Perfectionists have more fear, anxiety, depression, panic, headaches, chronic fatigue syndrome, and fear of medications (and imagined and real side effects).

  Perfectionism is important to avoid in the postpartum period, since so much is outside of your control. Don't worry about being a perfect parent; that can bring lots of anxiety. Instead, aim to do your best to love this little person who is now an integral part of your life. If you don't do the first bath quite right or don't change a wet diaper right away, your baby will be fine. Your most important job is to love him or her.

- Deal with your fears head-on. Anxiety is the fear of finding out the truth about your own unconscious thoughts, feelings, and motives, such as rage, shame, fear of rejection, fear of death, or intense sadness. As a result, developing insight into your fears and dealing with them biblically is the primary cure for anxiety. One technique that helps is to carry around a three-by-five card. Whenever you start to worry about something, write down the topic on the card and promise to worry about it later, at a certain time that night. The result should be a worry-free day. At the promised time in the evening, pull out the list and pray about each of the topics. Release them to God and, with his help, think of the best solution. Now your worries become constructive and helpful as you take them all to Jesus.

- If anxiety attacks are unbearable, consider medication or therapy. Most people can overcome these with a year or two of outpatient weekly therapy from a well-trained psychologist, or several weeks of intensive therapy in a day program. Whether quickly or slowly, these pains of fear can be relieved.

- Remember that some fear is healthy. Proverbs 1:7 tells us that the fear of the Lord is the beginning of wisdom. Fear him, love him, and trust him to help you cope with your anxiety and fear.

Postpartum Delight in spite of an Abusive Spouse

Abuse in marriage sounds like a tough problem to address, and it is. The only way to have postpartum delight when you're married to an abusive spouse is to love and be loved by family and friends who know you with all your secrets and love you unconditionally just the way you are. (This obviously does not include your abusive spouse. If he loved you unconditionally, he would never be abusive.)

Secondly, you must be totally protected from any abuse. You are God's daughter, and he would never want his daughter to be abused. He is a healer; in fact, Psalm 147:3 says, "He heals the brokenhearted and bandages their wounds." If your church or anyone else tells you it is your spiritual duty to stay with an abusive husband, they are absolutely wrong and contradicting many passages of Scripture. Get out of the situation immediately and separate. Perhaps try marital counseling for a period of time—at least six months—while remaining separate. He should not move back in until the counselor is convinced he is genuinely repentant and will be kind to you now.

An abusive male who is genuinely repentant will feel horrible about the pain he has put you through. He will seek out not only individual counseling, but group therapy, a prayer partner, pastoral counseling, a Celebrate Recovery group at his church or a large church nearby, or whatever else it takes to be sure he never hurts you again. A phony will cry and act repentant. He may go a few times to counseling and then find excuses to quit. He will still have a condescending attitude toward you, even blaming you for his abuse. That guy is not going to change. Give up on it.

Be your own best friend, and be intimate with God, talking to him many times a day for support. Keep a support group around you. Protect yourself financially, even if there is a court battle, with a good lawyer helping you. If you do all these things, you can still have postpartum delight.

But we encourage you to get therapy to see why your "people-picker" was broken the first time around. Was your own father abusive? Did you marry someone like Dad to fix your family of origin or to win the approval of a father substitute? Do you feel like you deserve abuse even though that is biblically absurd? These are all areas of codependency, which means being dependent on other people in a sick way to meet needs that would be better met in other ways. Work to break the cycle of codependency or abuse in your life—if for no other reason than that you certainly don't want your children to carry it on.

Adopting a Baby

Postpartum delight can certainly include delight after adopting a child—whether a newborn or an older child. The most incredible example of an adoptive parent is God himself. The apostle Paul wrote in Ephesians, "God decided in advance to adopt us into his own family by bringing us to himself through

Jesus Christ. This is what he wanted to do, and it gave him great pleasure" (1:5).

But there is such a thing as "post-adoption depression." It is rarely hormonally based, of course, but it can be triggered by circumstances, sleep deprivation, poor nutrition, and so forth. Adoption processes are often uncertain right up until the child is placed, which can be supremely stressful and leave new parents with little time to prepare. And adoptive parents who have suffered from infertility and have fought for years to be parents may have unrealistic expectations about the transition to parenting and bonding with their new child.

Also, sometimes adopting a child, no matter how wonderful it is, requires the couple to accept their infertility in a permanent, tangible way they haven't before. If you are bitter because you were unable to have genetic offspring of your own, then get therapy to grieve that legitimate loss and move on. As your baby grows up, let him or her know that he or she was adopted and handpicked by you and your husband. Your child was chosen, just like God chose you.

During the adoption process, get advice from others who have gone through the experience. Those who have experience with the particular program you have chosen—whether domestic or international, private or through an agency—may be especially helpful. The best way to be sure you have post-adoption delight is to expect hassles along the way so you will not be disappointed. Then love the child, love your husband, maintain good sleep and nutrition, and stay close to a couple of good friends for support. Stay close to God as well.

With Insufficient Funds

The postpartum period can be tough when money is tight or nonexistent. If you are a perfectionist, you probably love helping others but hate to ask for help yourself. But when you have a new baby, any help you accept is for the both of you. Get financial assistance from your church, your family, and even willing friends if needed. You would do the same for them. Some government programs may be available as well. Pray for God to supply your needs in unique ways and watch him surprise you.

Many women prefer to stay home with their new babies, but if you can't for financial reasons, you can't. So preserve postpartum delight by seeking out safe, loving child-care arrangements for your child.

Finding Postpartum Delight

Having a baby involves many adjustments, as you know from reading this book. You will face physical, hormonal, biochemical, emotional, spiritual, and social adjustments, and often financial adjustments as well. Raising a child in today's society will add up to well over a hundred thousand dollars in a lifetime! But if you have love for each other, for yourselves, for your new baby, and for God, and toss in your families as a bonus, then you have everything important that this world has to offer.

Some of the information in this book has probably surprised you. We hope that you now understand how complex postpartum delight truly is. It does not automatically follow a new birth. Attaining it takes wisdom, preparation, protection, fellowship, margin, proper nutrition, sleep, a spiritual walk with God, and emotional intimacy with others.

We encourage you to remember that just as humans are three-dimensional—with body, emotions, and spirit—so is postpartum depression. If you're struggling, consider all three potential components. If there are medical problems, see the best doctors you can find. If your postpartum depression is genetic, and sufficiently severe, you will need proper medications. The good news is that on these new, modern meds, you are totally safe and can take them the rest of your life if needed. If you're struggling with emotional wounds from your past, please see a loving counselor who can help you unravel those components. And always seek a deeper relationship with God, even as you come to a greater understanding of his vast and unconditional love for you.

The postpartum delight you build into your life now can prepare you and your children after you for a lifetime of love and joy. Today is the first day of the rest of your life, so prepare for and enjoy your journey.

APPENDIX I

Symptoms of Postpartum Thyroiditis

Early symptoms:
- Weakness
- Fatigue
- Depression
- Constipation
- Joint or muscle pain
- Weight gain
- Change in cold tolerance
- Thin and brittle hair

Late symptoms:
- Slow speech
- Hoarseness
- Abnormal menstrual periods
- Dry, flaky skin
- Decreased taste and smell

Additional symptoms that may be associated with this disease:
- Muscle spasms
- Uncoordinated movement
- Dry hair
- Hair loss
- Joint stiffness
- Absent menstruation
- Drowsiness

APPENDIX 2

*Symptoms of Hyperthyroidism
(overactive thyroid)*
- Feeling warm
- Muscle weakness
- Tremors
- Nervousness
- Weight loss
- Excessive sweating
- Heart palpitations
- Trouble concentrating

*Symptoms of Hypothyroidism
(underactive thyroid)*
- Fatigue
- Constipation
- Loss of memory
- Intolerance for cold weather
- Weight gain
- Muscle stiffness
- Dry skin or hair
- Thinning hair

NOTES

Introduction
1. Mental Health America, "Factsheet: Postpartum Disorders," November 8, 2006, http://www.nmha.org/go/information/get-info/depression/postpartum-disorders/.
2. "Two-Thirds of Pregnant Women with Depression Not Getting Treatment for It," *Doctor's Guide*, August 14, 2006, http://www.pslgroup.com/dg/25f832.htm.

Chapter One
1. See Job 33:15.
2. See verses 5 and 6.

Chapter Three
1. "New Treatment Strategy for the Prevention of Recurrent Depression," *ScienceDaily*, November 15, 2006, http://www.sciencedaily.com/releases/2006/11/061106144928.htm.
2. Daniel DeNoon, "Pregnancy Antidepressants: Baby Risk," *WebMD Health News*, February 8, 2006, http://www.medscape.com/viewarticle/523299.

Chapter Four
1. Heather A. Bennett et al., "Depression during Pregnancy: Overview of Clinical Factors," *Clinical Drug Investigation* 24, no. 3, (2004): 157–179.
2. Brenda L. Lundy et al., "Prenatal Depression Effects on Neonates," *Infant Behavior and Development* 22, no. 1, (1999): 119–129.
3. Dwenda K. Gjerdingen and Barbara P. Yawn, "Postpartum Depression Screening: Importance, Methods, Barriers, and Recommendations for Practice," *Journal of the American Board of Family Medicine* 20, no. 33 (2007): 280–288.
4. Katherine J. Gold, Sheila M. Marcus, "Effect of Maternal Mental Illness on Pregnancy Outcomes," *Expert Review of Obstetrics and Gynecology* 3, no. 3, (May 2008): 391–401, http://www.medscape.com/viewarticle/573947.
5. Marlene Buska and Charles Vega, "New Guidelines Shed Light on Use of Psychiatric Medications During Pregnancy," *Medscape Medical News*, April 10, 2008, http://www.medscape.com/viewarticle/572803.
6. Paul Meier, "Brain Chemicals Linked to Physical & Emotional Health," Meier Clinics, http://www.meierclinics.org/xm_client/client_documents/RadioHandouts/Brain_Chemicals_Linked_to_Phy__Emot_Health.pdf.

Chapter Five
1. American Society for Reproductive Medicine, "Frequently Asked Questions about Infertility," http://www.asrm.org/Patients/faqs.html#Q1.

2. "The Adoption Photolisting," Adoption.com, http://photolisting
.adoption.com/.

3. A.D.A.M. Medical Encyclopedia, s.v. "Placenta abruptio," http://www
.nlm.nih.gov/medlineplus/ency/article/000901.htm (accessed October 28, 2008).

4. Richard C. Urbano and Robert M. Hodapp, "Divorce in Families of Children
with Down Syndrome: A Population-Based Study," *American Journal on Mental
Retardation* 112, no. 4, (July 2007): 268, www.aaidd.org/Reading_Room/pdf/
AJMRDivorceandDownSyndrome.pdf.

5. "Birth Defects," Centers for Disease Control and Prevention, http://www.cdc.gov/
ncbddd/bd/default.htm.

6. National Vital Statistics System, "Method of Delivery 2005," Centers for Disease
Control and Prevention, http://205.207.175.93/VitalStats/TableViewer/tableView.
aspx?ReportId=3846.

7. Jennifer Warner, "Study Shows Gestational Diabetes Raises Risk for Type 2 Diabetes
by 19%," MedicineNet.com, July 28, 2008, http://www.medicinenet.com/script/main/
art.asp?articlekey=91409

8. Laura Cramer, "Postpartum Thyroid Information: Are You an Exhausted New Mother,
or Do You Have a Postpartum Thyroid Problem?" Postpartum Support International,
http://postpartum.net/resources/women-mothers/thyroid/.

Chapter Seven

1. Kathy Fray, *Oh Baby . . . Birth, Babies & Motherhood Uncensored* (New Zealand:
Random House, 2005), 364–381.

Chapter Eleven

1. Anne D. Walling, "Postnatal Depression in Fathers: Effects on Children," *American
Family Physician*, January 1, 2006, http://findarticles.com/p/articles/mi_m3225/
is_1_73/ai_n26773756.

2. Kathryn A. Leopold and Lauren B. Zoschnick, "Postpartum Depression," OBGYN.net,
http://www.obgyn.net/femalepatient/femalepatient.asp?page=Leopold.

3. U.S. Department of Health and Human Services Office of Women's Health,
"Frequently Asked Questions: Depression During and After Pregnancy," October 1,
2008, WomensHealth.gov, http://www.womenshealth.gov/faq/depression
-pregnancy.cfm.

ABOUT THE AUTHORS

Paul Meier, M.D.

Paul Meier is an M.D., psychiatrist, and ordained minister, and the founder of the Meier Clinics, a national chain of nonprofit Christian psychiatry clinics. He has authored 81 books, including Christian self-help books such as *Love Is a Choice* and *Happiness Is a Choice*, and a series of Bible prophecy novels beginning with *The Third Millennium*. He has been on many Christian and secular TV and radio shows, including those hosted by Oprah Winfrey, Tom Snyder, Norman Vincent Peale, Joyce Meyer, and many others. He has also traveled to countries all over the world to train both professional and lay counselors, as well as missionaries and pastors, in the field of Christian counseling. He taught full-time for twelve years at Dallas Theological Seminary, where he discipled Tony Evans, John Trent, John Townsend, Henry Cloud, and many other students. He has also lectured at seminaries around the world, including Southwestern Seminary in Ft. Worth, the Baptist Seminary in Cuba, and the Greek Bible Institute in Athens. Dr. Meier was the team physician for a mountain-climbing expedition in 1985 with American astronaut Jim Irwin, attempting to find Noah's Ark on Mt. Ararat.

Dr. Meier's clinics have launched many ministries, including Women of Faith, which he and Steve Arterburn started after low attendance at their own seminars prompted them to hire women speakers to address women listeners. The Meier Clinics employ 144 Christian psychiatrists, psychologists, and therapists in over 30 cities, see over 3,000 clients each week, and give over $2 million of charitable care each year. About 2 million people have trusted Christ through various Meier Clinics counseling sessions and ministries.

Dr. Meier is also the only psychiatrist invited for the past five years to the private strategy meetings of the nation's top conservative governors, senators, congressmen, presidential appointees, generals, CIA personnel, and think tank experts from around the world. He lectures to them and sits in on their sessions. He has been tentatively invited to participate in the launching of a similar movement of European conservative politicians.

Dr. Meier's daily prayer partner is Dr. Jean-Luc Bertrand, of Paris, who helped the president of France get elected in 2007 and has been asked to run for the office himself in the coming years. Dr. Meier's previous daily prayer partner, Dr. David Larson, died of a heart attack in March 2002, and a permanent Chair (scholarship) in the Library of Congress was named after him, to honor his work in designing courses on spirituality that are now offered in over half of the medical schools in the United States. The only other permanent Chair in the Library of Congress belongs to Henry Kissinger.

In 2003 the Association of Christian Counselors honored Dr. Meier as a father of the Christian psychology movement. *Christianity Today* magazine called Dr. Meier a "modern-day reformer" for moving Christians toward an openness to admitting faults, getting counseling, being less legalistic, and even being willing to take psychiatric medications if necessary.

The Meier Clinics can be contacted toll-free at 1-888-7-CLINIC. Visit their Web site at www.meierclinics.org.

Todd Clements, M.D.

Dr. Clements served as a youth pastor and motivational speaker during college. Upon graduation he pursued a master's degree in divinity from Southwestern Baptist Theological Seminary in Fort Worth, Texas. The Lord had different plans for Dr. Clements, though, leading him to pursue a career in medicine.

Dr. Clements obtained his medical degree from the University of Arkansas. He served as president of his class all four years of medical school. He then completed his residency training in psychiatry at the University of Oklahoma–Tulsa, where he served as chief resident of the program. Dr. Clements began his career in psychiatry with the Meier Clinics in Dallas, Texas. While there he founded Breakaway, an intensive counseling program designed specifically for teenagers. Dr. Clements also coauthored the book *Blue Genes* with Paul Meier, M.D.

Dr. Clements spent two and a half years with the Amen Clinics in Newport Beach, California, where he specialized in SPECT brain imaging.

Dr. Clements is now the medical director of the Clements Clinic in Plano, Texas. The Clements Clinic is a full-service psychiatric outpatient clinic offering SPECT brain imaging along with a wide variety of counseling therapies. The clinic is on the cutting edge of psychiatry in an effort to better diagnose and treat mental health issues.

Dr. Clements serves on the marriage commission for the Christian Medical and Dental Association, where he and his wife, Lynda, lead conferences aimed at helping physicians and their spouses improve their marriages. Dr. Clements has been married to Lynda for twelve years. They make their home in Frisco, Texas. Visit Dr. Clements's Web site at drtoddclements.com.

Lynne Johnson, R.N.

Lynne Johnson received her BSN degree from Montana State University and spent the majority of her nursing career in Billings, Montana. Her experience includes working as a hospital staff nurse on an inpatient psychiatric unit, as a Montana State University clinical psychiatric nursing instructor, and as a hospice nurse. Eleven years ago, after moving to Texas with her family, she returned to her first love in nursing (psychiatric), and began working with Dr. Paul Meier at the Meier Clinics day program. She and her husband, Jud, have been married thirty-two years and are the proud parents of married daughters Kora and Kelsey and are blessed by grandsons Alex and twins Samuel and Joshua.

"How can I reduce sibling bickering?"

"Can I plan a memorable birthday party without breaking the bank?"

"How do I display my faith in God to my children?"

WHEN BUSY
MOMS HAVE
QUESTIONS
LIKE THESE,
THEY NEED
ANSWERS
...FAST!

Kathy Peel, America's Family Manager, offers quick solutions and practical advice in *The Busy Mom's Guide to a Happy, Organized Home*, an easy-access reference guide that covers all of the key questions asked by women who want to be the best moms possible. Containing a comprehensive index, helpful checklists and charts, and an extensive list of online resources, *The Busy Mom's Guide to a Happy, Organized Home* is the number one resource to guide moms from bewilderment and confusion to confidence and maturity as they perform the important job God has called them to do.

the things your teachers never told you could be the most important things of all . . .

We may think we know it all, but even the best of us occasionally still need a few real-life lessons. In *What I've Learned Since I Knew It All*, psychiatrist and best-selling author Dr. Paul Meier teams up with Dr. Todd Clements to share what they have learned from their own mistakes and life experiences, as well as from decades of counseling patients who also thought they knew it all. This book lays out twelve crucial secrets to a satisfied life . . . and will teach you how to gain real success and happiness.